Canada:
The State of the
Federation 1998/99

How Canadians Connect

Edited by
Harvey Lazar and
Tom McIntosh

Published for the School of Policy Studies, Queen's University
by McGill-Queen's University Press
Montreal & Kingston • London • Ithaca

Canadian Cataloguing in Publication Data

The National Library of Canada has catalogued this publication as follows:

Main entry under title:

Canada, the state of the federation

Annual
1985-
Vols. for 1998/99-   have also a distinctive title.
ISSN 0827-0708
ISBN 0-88911-779-9 (bound : 1998/99) ISBN 0-88911-781-0 (pbk. : 1998/99)

1. Federal-provincial relations – Canada – Periodicals. 2. Federal government –
Canada – Periodicals. I. Queen's University (Kingston, Ont.). Institute of
Intergovernmental Relations.

JL27.F42   332.02'3'0971   C86-030713-1

The Institute of Intergovernmental Relations

The Institute is the only organization in Canada whose mandate is solely to promote
research and communication on the challenges facing the federal system.

Current research interests include fiscal federalism, constitutional reform, the reform of federal political institutions and the machinery of federal-provincial relations,
Canadian federalism and the global economy, and comparative federalism.

The Institute pursues these objectives through research conducted by its own staff
and other scholars through its publication program, seminars and conferences.

The Institute links academics and practitioners of federalism in federal and provincial governments and the private sector.

L'Institut des relations intergouvernementales

L'Institut est le seul organisme canadien à se consacrer exclusivement à la recherche
et aux échanges sur les questions du fédéralisme.

Les priorités de recherche de l'Institut portent présentement sur le fédéralisme fiscal,
la réforme constitutionnelle, la modification éventuelle des institutions politiques
fédérales, les nouveaux mécanismes de relations fédérales-provinciales, le fédéralisme
canadien au regard de l'économie mondiale et le fédéralisme comparatif.

L'Institut réalise ses objectifs par le biais de recherches effectuées par son personnel et par des universitaires de l'Université Queen's et d'ailleurs, de même que par
des conférences et des colloques.

L'Institut sert de lien entre les universitaires, les fonctionnaires fédéraux et
provinciaux et le secteur privé.

CONTENTS

V   Identity, Citizenship and Culture

VI   Chronology

FOREWORD

This year's *Canada: The State of the Federation* provides an overview of the political health of the Canadian federation. It is concerned with whether Canadians are becoming more or less attached to their country. In an age characterized both by global and continental integration and renewed nationalism, this is an issue that merits systematic analysis.

The issues raised here are not unique to Canada. All over the world, nominally sovereign countries are attempting to cope with challenges from within and without. In the Canadian case, the domestic pressures include the ongoing failure to effect a reconciliation between Quebec and the rest of Canada and the seemingly growing alienation of many aboriginal groups from the mainstream of Canadian society. The pressures from without reflect the increasing integration of the Canadian economy into the world and especially the United States economy. But environmental, cultural and social integration is also occurring, and seemingly at an accelerating pace.

Our purpose here is to shed some new light on how these change pressures are affecting the bonds that have made Canada such a successful political nation. Have our east-west economic links been shattered in the face of the growth of north-south trade and investment? Are our distinctive cultures being eliminated by a global cultural juggernaut? What about our social ties and trends in civil society? And is the fragmentation of our national party structure the harbinger of a regionalization of political loyalties? Is the Canadian state still up to the task of nurturing an ongoing loyalty to Canada?

These are some of the questions that we tackle in this volume. The volume is different from more recent ones in that it is not focused on the conduct of intergovernmental relations in Canada. Rather, it deals with the state of the federation in a more overarching way; and it does so by examining what is happening to linkages within Canada that have been created through the economy, culture, civil society, the state, citizenship, and political institutions. The authors of the different chapters are from a variety of disciplines. They thus bring different skills and perspectives to the task, contributing to the richness of the volume.

As in other years, a chronology of major events in the federation is provided. It covers the period from July 1997 to June 1998.

The production of this volume was made possible by the contributions of several people. Patti Candido and Mary Kennedy of the Institute of Intergovernmental Relations provided assistance and organizational expertise both in the conference that preceded this volume and in the preparation of the manuscript. Alan Kary and Charles-Henri Warren contributed research and translation assistance. The conference participants, the discussants and anonymous reviewers furnished the authors with valuable feedback on their work at important junctures in the process. Valerie Jarus, Mark Howes and Marilyn Banting managed the desk-top publishing, design and copy-editing assistance that helped turn a collection of pages into a book. Finally, we would like to thank the Canadian Heritage Department for their sponsorship of the initial conference. Its financial support and the participation of officials from the department in the conference proceedings are greatly appreciated.

Harvey Lazar and Tom McIntosh
April 1999

CONTRIBUTORS

Patrick Beauchamp is Director of Qualitative Research at EKOS Research Associates Inc., a public opinion polling firm in Ottawa.

Kathleen M. Day is an Assistant Professor of Economics at the University of Ottawa.

Tim Dugas is Senior Vice-President of EKOS Research in Ottawa, Ontario.

Avigail Eisenberg is an Associate Professor of Political Science at the University of British Columbia.

R. Quentin Grafton is an Associate Professor of Economics at the University of Ottawa.

Frank L. Graves is President of EKOS Research Associates Inc., Ottawa.

John F. Helliwell is a Professor of Economics at the University of British Columbia.

Matt James is a Doctoral Candidate in Political Science at the University of British Columbia.

Melissa Kluger earned a BA (Hons) from Queen's University and is now studying law at the University of Toronto.

Harvey Lazar is Director of the Institute of Intergovernmental Relations at Queen's University.

Tom McIntosh is a Research Associate at the Institute of Intergovernmental Relations and a Lecturer in Political Studies at Queen's University.

David Pritchard is Chair of the Department of Mass Communication at the University of Wisconsin-Milwaukee.

Florian Sauvageau is Director of the Journalism Programme and Director of the Centre d'études sur les médias at Université Laval.

A. Brian Tanguay is an Associate Professor of Political Science and Department Chair at Wilfred Laurier University.

Claire Turenne Sjolander is an Associate Professor of Political Science at the University of Ottawa.

Marc Vachon, at the time of writing, was a graduate student in Economics at the Université de Montréal and now works for the federal government.

François Vaillancourt is a Fellow, C.R.D.E. and Professor of Economics at the Université de Montréal.

Reg Whitaker is a Professor of Political Science at York University.

I

Overview

1

How Canadians Connect: State, Economy, Citizenship and Society

Harvey Lazar and Tom McIntosh

Ce chapitre offre une analyse de la nature mouvante des liens unissant la fédération canadienne. Il est clair que l'État canadien est aujourd'hui plus petit que lors des décennies précédantes, à tous le moins sur le plan des programmes de dépenses et de la propriété publique. Alors que certains de ces changements sont le résultat des pressions de l'intégration continentale et mondiale, d'autres sont le reflet des leçons tirées des erreurs passées des gouvernements canadiens. Il reste qu'un État de taille réduite n'est pas nécessairement condamné à être moins efficace en matière de nation-building. *Bien que l'État canadien soit moins efficace aujourd'hui que dans les années 1950 et 1960, il l'est peut-être plus qu'il y a cinq ou dix ans en raison de l'amélioration des finances publiques et de la décentralisation. Malgré la croissance des échanges commerciaux nord-sud, les liens économiques demeurent forts. Malgré certains doutes quant à la capacité de l'État à la promouvoir et à la protéger, la culture canadienne est vibrante. Quant à l'union sociale, elle pourrait raffermir les liens sociaux. De l'autre côté de la médaille, le système national de partis politiques s'est effondré et les divisions ancestrales entre les groupes linguistiques n'ont pas été réduites. En bref, certains des liens ayant toujours unis les Canadiens demeurent solides et de nouveaux liens émergent entre eux (ce qui donne évidemment naissance à de nouveaux défis). Cependant, certaines divisions depuis longtemps au coeur de la politique canadienne sont toujours aussi présentes.*

This volume is motivated by a series of related questions concerning the current state of the ties that have traditionally linked Canadians into a shared political community. Are these ties weakening? Strengthening? Have they been changing in more complex ways that do not fit nicely on a simple "strengthening-weakening" continuum? The volume's contributors attempt to wrestle with these questions in several ways. The essays that follow examine the changing role and nature of the Canadian state, transformations in both the domestic and international economies, new conceptions of citizenship, and changes within civil society.

The chapters focus, to varying degrees, on the importance of traditional connections between Canadians, how those connections have changed, and what new connections are developing. What emerges is a complex picture that involves both continuity and change. We see a country that is being redefined in important respects as a result of domestic and international forces. We also observe much stability notwithstanding the pressures for change.

Our initial premise was not an especially optimistic one. We were more than aware that Canadian trade and investment were becoming increasingly north-south, which perhaps suggests that economic ties among Canadians were weakening. Many of Canada's largest public cultural institutions were being scaled back even while modern technology was making foreign cultural output increasingly available to Canadians, often at very low prices. The national political party system was fragmenting. The Canadian state appeared to be under assault from many quarters, including an agenda of deficit reduction and "marketization." The future of the Canadian polity was being challenged by Quebec secessionists, while important voices from mainly English-speaking regions of Canada were demanding a major transfer of effective authority from the federal government to the provincial level.

In a country where the state has played such a large role in creating the political nation,[1] these developments demanded a more systematic analysis. What were the forces of change? Did they mean inevitable long-term erosion of the Canadian state? If the state were to erode, what would this mean for the future of Canada as an independent polity? Although the state was fundamental in the building of the Canadian political nation, might the political nation now be strong enough to remain healthy and intact with a smaller state apparatus to nurture it? Are the bonds in civil society firm and the market economy robust enough to counteract a diminished role for the federal government?

We approached these questions with some trepidation, fearing that the answers would lead us to the conclusion that Canada was indeed more fractured than it had ever been in the past. Indeed, there is a long history of pessimism amongst academics about the ability of Canada to survive, let alone overcome, such challenges. Canada has been described as an "unequal union" and an "unfulfilled union." Academics have probed the nation's "divided loyalties," asked "must Canada fail?" and lamented its "silent surrender" to international economic forces. This volume covers both old and new concerns in an attempt to understand the contemporary state of these connections. The chapters cover a wide, but not exhaustive, range of questions and provide some contradictory answers. Some authors are pessimistic. Others are not. When taken together, they provide a picture of a nation that is wrestling with its understanding of itself. Some traditional connections remain strong, while some traditional disconnections just remain. Some new connections may be emerging and some new disconnections will provide serious challenges to the governance of the federation in the coming years. Although we draw on the different contributions to this volume, this introductory chapter conveys our sense of the state of the Canadian federation, not a summary of what the other authors have written.

THE CHANGING ROLE OF THE NATION-STATE

Our starting point is the global context within which all states, federal and unitary, find themselves. The backdrop to our inquiry was one of growing global and continental integration, both economic and non-economic, propelled by, among other things, the rapid advances in communications and information technologies and government policies aimed at liberalizing trade and investment flows. There is an extensive literature that suggests that the modern nation-state has passed its peak as a way of organizing, integrating and exercising power.[2] In particular, the overarching nation-state that emerged in the early post-World War II decades, with its vast powers of coercion, taxation, and regulation has begun to unravel. What were seen as state powers during those decades are being progressively moved out from under central governments. Authority is seen to be shifting upward to supra-national and international authorities, downward to regional and local governments and, perhaps most importantly, outward to the private sector and marketplace.

Those who write about these matters have differing opinions regarding the necessity and impacts of these shifts. For Kenichi Ohmae, the nation-state is "an unnatural and even dysfunctional unit"[3] for managing the modern economy. He asserts that there is "only one strategic degree of freedom" available to central governments. This is "to cede meaningful operational autonomy to the wealth-generating region states that lie within or across their borders, to catalyze the efforts of those regions to seek out global solutions, and to harness their distinctive ability to put global logic first and to function as ports of entry to the global economy."[4] Peter Drucker believes that the "mega-state in which this century indulged has ... not delivered on a single one of its promises."[5] The policy of any country "will have to give primacy to the country's competitive position in an increasingly competitive world economy."[6] Neither Ohmae nor Drucker completely dismisses the role of government. What they do discard, however, is the idea of the overarching nation-state as a functional approach to the issues of governance in the world that lies ahead.

Susan Strange sees a disconnection between what the state attempts to do and its accomplishments. In the opening passage of her *Retreat of the State,* she declares:

> Today it seems that the heads of government may be the last to recognize that they and their ministers have lost their authority over national societies that they used to have. Their command over outcomes is not what it used to be. Politicians everywhere talk as though they have the answers to economic and social problems, as if they really are in charge of their country's destiny. People no longer believe them.[7]

Richard Barnet and John Cavanagh use similar language: "Leaders of nation-states are losing much of the control over their own territory they once had."[8] They too observe that as "the world economy becomes more and more integrated, the processes of political disintegration are accelerating."[9] Wolfgang Reinicke refers to the growing misalignment between economic geography and political geography.[10]

Not all of these observers applaud what they see. And indeed some offer an agenda to right the balance. In his *Work of Nations*, Robert Reich makes the case that the challenge to government is to help reconnect the four-fifths of the American people who are being left behind by the global information economy. He argues for a more activist state that encourages "new learning within the nation, to smooth the transition of the labor force from the older industries, to educate and train the nation's workers, to improve the nation's infrastructure, and to create international rules of fair play for accomplishing all these things."[11] Reich's agenda includes a broad view of how the state would nurture learning, including programs for pre- and postnatal care, child care, and preschool preparation. Dani Rodrik worries that social disintegration will be the price of economic integration. Global integration not only produces many "losers," but the mobile "winners" may have little interest in the political compromises required to find solutions to the uneven impact of economic integration on the citizenry. He emphasizes the need to strike a balance between openness and domestic needs, including the necessity of preserving social insurance as a social buffer as well as a larger role for international institutions.[12]

In Canada, there is also an influential literature that sees a smaller nation-state as a normal and natural consequence of changing technology and the economic restructuring that accompanies such developments. Gilles Paquet regards centralized and hierarchical organizations, including governments, as dysfunctional "because of their poor capacity to respond quickly and effectively to fast changing circumstances." He writes of "a more distributed governance that deprives the leader of his or her monopoly on the governing of the organization."[13] And he suggests "decoupling of the nation from the state ... as one of the central features of the recent evolution."[14] Sylvia Ostry declares that "many of the arguments about the natural forces of (technological and economic) integration are intellectually persuasive and suggest that globalization may well be a positive force in sustaining liberalization and that business will play an increasing role in the evolution of the global market."[15] Tom Courchene aligns himself with "Daniel Bell who ... asserted that nation states had become too large to tackle the small things and too small to address the large things."[16]

As in the foreign literature, there is also a range of views in the Canadian literature regarding the desired role of the state. Mark Zacher observes that it is "absolutely crucial for TNCs [transnational corporations] that there are political authorities throughout the many regions of the world that can enforce international regimes on commercial actors."[17] But he also argues that the state has a parallel obligation to its citizens with regard to social matters and that states collectively, at least the advanced industrial democracies, will eventually grope toward an international social covenant. He anticipates NGOs initially playing an important role in this process, but in the end it will have to be "states that have legitimacy and power to make it effective."[18] For his part, Charles Taylor observes that the state is essential because it is the only existing instrument of democratic control — the only way people can hope to have some control over their destiny. Even decisions that have to be made at the international level can only come close to being democratic, he argues, because they are made between democratically elected governments and then must be implemented by them.[19]

While these Canadians come from different ideological perspectives and varying disciplines, many would probably agree with Ostry that the fundamental question for the future is whether "there is the political will and skill to re-invent government and global governance."[20]

Although much of the literature relating to global and regional integration is focused on economic issues, these developments are much more than an economic phenomenon. The information and communications technologies have also opened up the world to "real-time" coverage of global events and have facilitated the emergence of popular culture with worldwide audiences. For some, this is an unparalleled opportunity to spread knowledge and sell "cultural products" at good prices in a free market. For others, such cultural competition offends the idea of the nation-state as protector of cultural space as a "defence of shared values and identity against alienation and anonymity, of the sacred against the profane, and of citizenship against consumerism."[21] Barnet and Cavanagh remark that "television is the most powerful force for mass education in most poor countries"[22] and that American television and film products dominate the airways in many of these countries. This is also the case in Canada.

International rates of migration are still substantial, although not as high as they have been at some points in the past. As the sources of immigration have become more diversified, many nation-states are becoming more divided ethnically and religiously. This is particularly true in the Canadian case. The change in immigration patterns in Canada over the last few decades has made Canada a much more diverse — especially a more visibly diverse — nation than it was during its first century. Canada's old multiculturalism reflected the diversity of Europe, whereas its new multiculturalism reflects a wider ethnic and religious spectrum. As a result, what Kymlicka has called the "fair terms of integration," or the contract between immigrant and adopted country, has also changed. Both Eisenberg and James argue in this volume that Canadian notions of citizenship are undergoing important changes that, while they may have positive effects, require Canadians to confront traditional understandings of what it means to be a Canadian. The process is essentially dialectical, an ongoing transformitory process.

These developments require policy responses that cross borders. In *non-economic* areas like disease control and the fight against international crime, international cooperation is growing, but with national governments retaining substantial *de facto* sovereignty. More often than not, in the *economic* sphere, the responses entail a process under which nation-states accommodate to the demands of the market.[23] This is seen in the prominent role played by the international economic institutions, especially the International Monetary Fund and World Bank, in promoting market solutions as the condition of their support for poor countries, for transition economies, and for economies undergoing temporary difficulties. The rules of the World Trade Organization and major regional trade agreements like the North American Free Trade Agreement not only limit the freedom of participating governments to restrict trade flows. Increasingly, they aim at "deep integration," seeking to persuade governments to harmonize domestic policies (as with various types of standards, national treatment for foreign investment, common approaches to rules on intellectual property).

There are also parallel developments in civil society, often prompted by a need to respond to economic integration pressures, whether they be economic, cultural or social. Zacher claims, for example, that there are approximately 5,000 international non-governmental organizations today and that many of them participate in the rule-making activities of intergovernmental institutions.[24]

As already noted, ideologies divide commentators regarding what can and should be done about the pressures transforming the nation-state, including the Canadian state. For critics, the events of the last two decades have begun to raise questions about the legitimacy of both the outcomes and the processes through which they are reached. In his chapter in this volume, Reg Whitaker describes a diminished domestic state that serves the interests of the marketplace and the security needs of the economy, but with a declining role in economic redistribution or in serving social ends. Claire Sjolander's chapter presents a picture of the Canadian state that increasingly sees its role as an economic cheerleader for Canadian capital in the international marketplace or for attracting international capital to Canada. It is less and less a (relatively) autonomous actor in its own right pursuing its own political economic agenda. In a sense, Whitaker and Sjolander's understanding of the state constitute the two sides of a single coin — a different kind of state for a different international and domestic political economy. Whether this rather pessimistic outlook for the Canadian state is widely shared in Canadian society is a different issue, one to which we shall return.

Against this background, it is normal for individuals, even while embracing, or perhaps just tolerating these changes, to feel some loss of power. They perceive their capacity to influence international institutions to be non-existent, if only because they play no direct role in electing their executives or legislative bodies. Even national governments can appear captives of the "globalization" ideology ("we have no choice"), and thus, either distant or ineffective in providing to individuals traditional safeguards and services. In a Canadian context, Sjolander argues that these "representations of globalization as a necessary and inevitable reality of the late twentieth century have exacerbated the existing tendency to de-politicize foreign economic policy (and economic policy more generally)." She postulates that while "Canadian ... economic policy in an era of globalization attempts to present a homogeneous view of the world 'out there' and of the way Canadians need to adjust to it, there is a consequent fragmentary impact on the way Canadians 'connect'." Those who do not or cannot accept this world view are marginalized from the political process, while those who accept it are "driven" to act according to its dictates.

This loss of domestic control may help to explain the urge to bring any issues that do not absolutely demand international or national attention to the local or regional level. The popularity of "subsidiarity" as an operating principle reflects less an empirical analysis of the merits of local decision making than it does a political response to the anonymity of seemingly distant authorities. It also provides a convenient rationale for distinct peoples or nations in binational and multinational states to argue for a shift in power toward the constituent units where they are in the majority. More than one observer has noted that the left-right politics of earlier decades are being replaced by a "politics of identity." This is a central argument in Reg Whitaker's chapter. He declares:

> Canada has been particularly exposed because the Canadian state as a political space has been under severe pressure, from both within and without, for an extended period of time. Global market forces have eroded the capacity of the Canadian national state to act effectively as an economic manager, while the rise of the Quebec sovereignty movement has brought the political legitimacy of the state and constitution into question.

Jane Jenson has conveyed a somewhat different perspective. She has argued that all politics are essentially about the promotion of identities and that it is just the identities that have changed, not the politics.[25] However, the extent to which more traditional left-right politics, rooted in a materialist conception of society, are in fact being replaced by an "identity politics" more rooted in a non-materialist understanding of the socio-political order, is not a debate we propose to resolve here. Whatever the extent of this transformation, it is certainly true that much of the content of political discourse has altered over the past few decades. Thus, as Whitaker rightly asserts, the role of the state in the promotion of pan-national connections — be they economic, cultural or societal — has similarly changed.

Within the Canadian political arena, these trends have been noted by the Bloc Québécois. In recent months the party has launched a process of reflection and reexamination of its sovereignty project. The intention is to examine the role of the nation-state in the context of globalization, and how this relates to its conception of an independent Quebec. As global and continental forces narrow the scope for the exercise of *de facto* sovereignty, it becomes progressively more important for the Bloc to ensure that such powers as remain domestic are reserved for Quebecers.[26]

The argument to this point is that the Canadian federation is being buffeted by two kinds of forces. One set reflects global trends and would be present regardless of domestic developments. To be sure, Canada may be experiencing these global pressures somewhat differently than other countries. For example, a higher proportion of Canadians are born outside Canada than is true of almost any other country. The prevalence of divided loyalties may therefore be more widespread here than in many other countries. Also, given that Canada shares a very long border with the world's most powerful state, and imports much of what globalization has to offer via the United States, Canada's room to manoeuvre is considerably different than that of similarly sized countries in Europe or indeed even smaller ones. Moreover, among industrialized democratic federations, Canada is close to being unique. Like the United States and Australia, Canada is continent-sized. Like Belgium and Switzerland, it is home to more than one major language group. For both reasons, it has become quite decentralized.[27] Yet it would be unwise to see the magnitude of the challenges facing the Canadian state as unusual, even if in some respects they are unique. As Vincent Cable observes, in writing about broad global trends in relation to the future of the modern state, "nation-states are under pressure from within and without."[28]

WHAT HAS BEEN HAPPENING TO THE CANADIAN STATE?

The remainder of this chapter examines more closely what has been happening to the Canadian state and to the linkages among Canadians. We explore economic, social, cultural, and political connections, as well as those that reflect trends in citizenship and civil society. In some cases, it is the actions of the state that are directly responsible for changes in connectedness. In other situations, the state is not the originator of the change pressures, although questions do arise about whether the state can or should become more involved in responding to those pressures.

Several questions kept arising as we considered the changes to the Canadian state in recent decades. One question was whether what has been happening is better understood as diminishing the state or redefining it or what the balance has been between these two types of change. A second had to do with whether these changes are part of a long-term continuous process or whether they will be seen, with the benefit of hindsight, as a large one-time adjustment. Whether a diminished and redefined state would matter for the connections that bind Canadians together was yet another question. Having successfully built linkages in the past, a weakened state today may not necessarily signal a weakened political nation. As John Helliwell points out in his chapter, borders still matter. Concepts of loyalty and citizenship are also evolving, as the chapters by Avigail Eisenberg and Matt James observe. And Frank Graves documents that, by many standards, Canadians have remarkably high levels of attachment to Canada. These issues suggest that there is not necessarily a one-to-one correlation between a changed state and the connections that bind Canada.

At the same time, few would dispute the notion that what the state does has some effect on the well-being of the nation and the sense of shared purpose among its citizens. In this section, we try to shine some light on what has been happening to the Canadian state — both its effect on desired outcomes (public goals) as well as the instrument regime it uses for that purpose. We consider what the transformation that has occurred may imply for connectedness among Canadians.

The desired outcomes from state activity involve some combination of peace and security, law and public safety, protection and advancement of freedoms and rights, sustainable economic growth, and some sense of fairness about how the fruits of this growth are to be shared. Similarly, there is (or at least was) a consensus that the state had an important role to play in the protection, promotion, and inculcation of a civil society that was both "civil" and "social." The state is, to some extent, the final guarantor of that public space in which the organizations and relationships that constitute many of Canadians' connections grow.

The instrument regime employed by the state has entailed taxation, spending, regulation (both economic and cultural), diplomacy (both internal and external), information sharing and the "bully pulpit" as well as the means to enforce law and protect order (through the police and the armed forces). In recent years, this instrument regime has been modified through a more intensive use of market-related and softer instruments.

By and large, the desired outcomes of state activity themselves have changed little over the last 50 years. Indeed it is remarkable how stable those objectives have been. Despite a history of self-doubt about the nation's survival, Canada has displayed a remarkable level of political stability over the last 132 years. In more recent years, civil, political, and social rights have been expanded and constitutionally entrenched. The rule of law and democratic practices, even for those who wish to break up the country, are the norm for Canada's political discourse. Whatever the public's perception, violent crime is on a consistent downward trend and, at least in comparison to the United

States, Canada remains a relatively safe country even in its largest urban centres. In short, Canadian civil society is, for the most part and in relation to many other parts of the world, remarkably civil. And while the choice of instruments will always matter, in this context what matters most is the state's effectiveness in achieving the desired outcomes.

This, of course, does not suggest that the state's effectiveness in relation to the above goals has been achieved or distributed in a way that satisfies all interests or viewpoints. For example, there are few that would argue that the poor are as well treated by the justice system as are the rich. The socioeconomic conditions endured by many of Canada's Aboriginal peoples are horrifying. There remains great controversy about the state's performance over the last 20 to 25 years in promoting and redistributing economic prosperity. Its relative lack of success here is symbolized by a quarter-century of weak productivity growth, unstable public finances, high and rising levels of taxation and of unemployment, and widening economic disparities.

Whatever the combination of market influences and government performance that led to this undesired set of outcomes, it has contributed to a sense that the Canadian state has been falling well short of the mark. It has detracted from the sense of shared pride in a noble common purpose. Part of this failure may be linked to the forces of global integration discussed above and the sense that Canadian governments were finding it increasingly difficult to protect and advance Canadian interests in ways that had worked in the decades following World War II. But mistakes and mismanagement by successive Canadian governments over more than two decades beginning in the mid-1970s have contributed even more heavily to these outcomes.

By the early 1990s, in at least some respects, the Canadian state had become enfeebled. The Canadian government was delivering less and taxing more. Average living standards had not improved for a long time and many Canadians were worse off than they had been 20 years earlier. A sense was emerging that the children of the working age population would have lower living standards than their parents.

What about the Canadian state today? By several important criteria we know it is smaller. Public ownership has been reduced. Program spending has been cut sharply. Federal spending as a share of Gross Domestic Product is in the process of falling by about one-third from over 18 percent to perhaps 12 percent. Federal outlays are now at levels that have not been seen since the early 1950s. While taxation remains high, in large measure because of heavy interest charges on the public debt, the political momentum for tax cuts is rising. It is true that the regulatory role of the federal state remains huge, but deregulation has removed some safeguards, notably in labour markets where "flexibility" has been eroding traditional social protections. This smaller state, with its changing instrument mix, has not yet found the winning formula for enhancing productivity growth or controlling the growth in disparities.[29] The

Canadian state today is a less effective state than was the case from the 1950s through to the early 1970s.

Compared to five or ten years ago, however, the Canadian state is in some respects more effective. For example, in the run-up to the 1999 federal budget, there was a lively public debate about whether to enhance health spending, cut taxes or reduce public debt. It has been many years since this kind of choice was a part of the public discourse. Restoring public finances has been painful. The outcome, however, contributes to a stronger Canadian state, not a weaker one, at least in relation to budgetary matters.

It is also important to recognize that, on the basis of expenditure, the smaller Canadian state — as we approach the millennium — bears little resemblance to the state of 50 years ago. From a program-spending perspective, the federal state has become a *social* state. In the early 1950s, defence spending constituted more than one-quarter of federal program outlays. Spending for social purposes was smaller. Today, even after federal cutbacks, social spending makes up more than three-fifths of federal program expenditures, whereas defence represents less than one-tenth. This transformation is not at the expense of the provincial governments. At that level, social spending has also risen and now constitutes around three-quarters of all program spending.

ECONOMIC CONNECTIONS

One of the central features of federal government policy since World War II has been its support for an open and liberal international system of trade and payments. The result contributed to Canada's economic prosperity, at least until the 1970s. It also implied a limitation on Ottawa's freedom to intervene in matters of international trade and payments; and it, of course, increased economic ties between Canada and the rest of the world.

Over the last 15 years, Canada and other advanced industrial countries have placed increasing emphasis on market-based policies in the expectation that they would result in strong economic growth and that the benefits of this growth would more than offset any additional disparities that the market generated.[30] This policy paradigm not only requires the continuing elimination of border measures by national governments. It also entails "deep integration"; that is, a growing harmonization of domestic policies, including microeconomic policies, across these countries in an effort to level the competitiveness playing field. This agenda does not detract from the *de jure* sovereignty of the Canadian state. Indeed, it can be argued that negotiating and signing international agreements is as much about the exercise of sovereignty as it is about self-imposed restrictions on the way that sovereignty is used. But in the world of *realpolitik*, the great powers and important non-state corporate actors play a very large role in dictating the terms of the harmonization policies, with the result that *de facto* operational sovereignty is squeezed.

. In the context of this volume, what matters is how these policy trends, and their results, impact on economic linkages among Canadians and whether, and to what extent, they constrain the Canadian state from acting to protect and promote these connections. In this regard, the chapter by John Helliwell is of particular interest.

Helliwell's analysis indicates that the closed economies of the developing world stand to benefit hugely from the flow of technology, ideas, and capital, if and when they open up. But once an economy is substantively open and effectively able to draw on the best of what the world has to offer, as is the case for Canada, the incremental gains to productivity from further openness may be very small. Indeed, he suggests that the gains may be more than offset by the losses in policy autonomy that accompany such additional openness. This view is supported by Dani Rodrik, who argues that "as policy makers sort economic and social objectives, free trade policies are not automatically entitled to first priority."[31]

Within the Canadian intellectual community, economist Thomas Courchene is the most prominent in drawing attention to the rapid increase in bilateral trade with the United States and the fact that international trade has grown much more rapidly in recent years than has interprovincial trade. Whether Courchene applauds this development, or simply sees it as inevitable, his writings make clear his belief that this process has profound implications for how Canadians govern themselves, the relative role of the two orders of government and what he has called the "social policy railway" that connects Canadians.[32]

The facts that underlie Courchene's analysis are not in doubt. Nor is the seriousness of the issues that he has brought forward. Yet there is more than one way to interpret the trade and investment data. It may be a case of someone seeing the glass as half-empty while another sees it as half-full; but drawing heavily on John Helliwell's chapter, and his related research reported elsewhere, we find good evidence that borders continue to matter.[33] Path dependency is real. What has happened in the past in the northern half of North America profoundly affects who and what we are today. Without denying the vast growth in Canada's trade, investment, and other linkages with the United States, and the smaller increase with the rest of the world, the data presented by Helliwell indicate that our historical experience has created a rich network of domestic connections that is remarkably durable.

Building on work first started by John McCallum,[34] Helliwell has found that merchandise trade among Canadian provinces is 12 times greater than trade between Canadian provinces and US states, when taking account of differences in population size and distance. For trade in services, the density of Canadian transactions is 30 to 40 times greater among Canadian provinces than with their American neighbours. The multiple for merchandise trade has fallen relative to where it was prior to the Canada-US Free Trade Agreement. With regard to services, the data do not show the same evidence of a sharp reduction following on the free trade agreement. Helliwell observes that the large post-FTA increase in merchandise trade between Canada and the United States was "to some extent linked to decreases in interprovincial trade" but even after this displacement effect, the density of Canadian connections remains much denser than continental density. He reinforces his argument by noting that there is no evidence of cross-border price arbitrage for city pairs of any distance. In other words, the impact of the border remains very large. Helliwell suggests that the existence of separate national institutions, cultures, and information networks lowers the uncertainty of operations within the national economy. Given differences in national tastes, the result is to reduce transaction costs within national economies relative to costs among economies.

The chapter by Vachon and Vaillancourt shows that the rate of internal migration has declined significantly since the early 1980s, falling by almost one-third. While this may have something to do with aging, they indicate that this drop-off is true within various age, gender, and education groupings. This might suggest that the border effect is of declining importance. But even with the results that Vaillancourt and Vachon report, Helliwell finds it is 100 times more likely that an American will move to another US state than to Canada, once again taking account of population, distance, and the economic incentives for migration. The border effect on Canadian migrants is considerably smaller but nonetheless still very significant.

It is important to put Helliwell's findings into context. What they emphasize is the density of the economic ties within Canada, ties which doubtless spill over into the social, cultural, and political dimensions of Canadian life. This finding is not inconsistent, however, with Canada's growing economic linkages internationally and especially the United States. For one thing, Helliwell's results take account of differences in levels of population. And since the United States has roughly ten times the population of Canada, even with Canadian internal trade densities being high, the actual volume of Canadian trade with the United States now substantially exceeds the volume of interprovincial trade. Whether Canada's dependence on access to the US market stabilizes at roughly current levels, or whether it continues to grow, it will remain in Canada's interest to maintain good commercial and political relations with our southern neighbour. This has had implications for the state's room to manoeuvre on the policy front, an issue we return to below. Our main observation here, however, is that notwithstanding the growth of north-south ties, the economic bonds among Canadians remain far tighter than is commonly assumed.

SOCIAL CONNECTIONS

The post-World War II decades saw a vast expansion in the Canadian welfare state, as reflected in the spending data noted above. With this came the idea of the social rights of citizenship. Canadians, wherever they lived in the country, would have broadly similar social benefits. Over time, the myth emerged that there were national standards for social benefits in Canada.[35] In conjunction with mobility rights, these national standards became a part of the idea that Canadians were connected by a shared sense of social purpose, by the bonds of reciprocal obligations that are entailed in a social contract.

The size of the social state, and the extensive network of intergovernmental and personal transfers, reinforced this sense of social connectedness. Thus, it was not surprising that the large cuts in federal government transfers to the provinces, which accompanied the Canada Health and Social Transfer (CHST) legislation announced in the 1995 budget, were widely interpreted as threatening to weaken the social connections among Canadians in relation to health, education, and welfare.

By 1999, however, some of the damage to this social connectedness was in the process of being repaired. In early 1999, Ottawa and nine provinces, all but Quebec, signed a framework agreement on the social union. Among other things, this may help over time to clarify the role of each order of government in the design, delivery and financing of existing and new social programs. It may also facilitate a more collaborative approach among governments in setting social-policy priorities and improving accountability for program outcomes. Simultaneously, in its 1999 budget, Ottawa agreed to restore some of the cuts made to the CHST in exchange for unanimous provincial agreement to spend those "new" dollars on health-care programs. Ottawa's current tentative shift in emphasis from fewer intergovernmental transfer programs to more direct transfers to individuals held the prospect of enhancing the sense of social connectedness among Canadians.

These developments suggest that the social dimension of Canadian citizenship has sunk deep political roots within Canada. The view that Canadians appear to hold about themselves as constituting a "kinder, gentler" society, and as a country of national standards in social policy, may be more myth than reality. But this view helped to mobilize Canadians politically during the years of severe fiscal restraint earlier in the 1990s. Political leaders read the poll results telling them the public wants both orders of government to work together on social issues. Political leaders read polls about the weight Canadians attached to national social programs, especially health care. In responding as they have in early 1999, governments have acted on the public's wishes. Equally important, in formalizing the social union, they have also created an instrument that could further encourage a stronger sense of shared social rights among Canadians. Myth may have begot reality. But the result could be growing social connections among Canadians.

There is also a risk in the formalizing of the social union. They could potentially enhance social bonds among Canadians outside Quebec but at the price of creating a new and large irritant between the Government of Quebec and other Canadian governments. How the framework agreement on the social union plays itself out will be crucial. Will Quebec effectively abide by the rules even though it has not signed? Alternatively, will the signatories behave in a way that makes it easy for Quebec to accommodate to what occurs within the social union framework? More generally, how signatory governments behave will go a long way toward answering these questions and others relating to social connectedness.

CULTURAL CONNECTIONS

With respect to cultural matters, the Canadian Broadcasting Corporation (CBC) was the only large federal government commitment 50 years ago. This has clearly changed. The original CBC/Radio Canada radio networks have expanded to include English and French television. The National Film Board was created during World War II and has since transformed itself from a wartime propaganda instrument into a purveyor of high-quality short and feature-length documentaries chronicling all aspects of the Canadian identity(s).[36] The Canadian Film Development Fund and its successor, Telefilm Canada, continue to finance and nurture a domestic feature film industry and finance much of Canada's independent television production.[37] At present the Canadian government is moving to a major restructuring of its financial commitments in this area which, if successful, would increase the amount of monies available for domestic producers. Yet, in recent years the cut-backs to the already limited funds available for cultural production have made Canada not only more vulnerable to the importation of cultural products but increasingly unable to present Canada to Canadians in a consistent and meaningful manner.

Direct government spending in the cultural sector is but one element of the state's cultural policy and it seems unlikely that spending on the arts will ever meet the demand that exists for funding within the arts communities. As well, this spending will always be controversial insofar as it necessitates choosing particular kinds of cultural product over others. Thus, the Canadian state has chosen to integrate its direct funding of some cultural industries within a broader regulatory framework covering both public and private cultural enterprises. Indeed, it has been the Canadian state's regulatory role that has been the most visible, and arguably the most successful, element of its cultural policy. This can be seen in the role of the Canadian Radio and Telecommunications Commission (CRTC) and its enforcement of "Canadian content" regulations in the area of radio and television broadcasting. In terms of the current processes of trade liberalization, the challenge faced by the Canadian state is embodied in a number of political disputes in which issues of cultural policy, and specifically regulation of cultural industries, have become issues of trade and economic policy.

It is also shown by the current efforts of the federal government to protect the domestic magazine industry against split-run editions of American magazines that are aimed at the Canadian market; and in the efforts to remove the practical restrictions on the distribution of Canadian feature films within Canada, which has involved the federal government in disputes with the powerful Motion Picture Association of America (MPAA), the lobbying arm of the Hollywood film industry. The CRTC is struggling with how to preserve the relevance of Canadian-content regulations in broadcasting in the coming 500-channel television world. In these and many other examples, it is almost certainly the case that the techniques that the state uses, or would like to use, in these and related areas will need modifying in the face of technological change and the challenges from trading partners.

These challenges to the state's regulatory role vis-à-vis cultural policy, come, ironically, at a time when Canadian culture appears to be flourishing. Canadian writers such as Michael Ondaatje, Rohinton Mistry and Neil Bissoondath, have created a "new Can-Lit" *oeuvre* with unprecedented domestic and international sales and critical appreciation. Performers as different as k.d. lang, Bryan Adams, and Ben Heppner have achieved widespread international and domestic success. Film and television production is, on balance, improving, though much of the economic benefits of this come from foreign productions made in Canada or through international co-productions. At the same time, film-makers such as Atom Egoyan, David Cronenberg, and Denys Arcand live and work in Canada which is something that few before them could easily do.

Thus, whatever position one takes on the Canadian state's regulatory role, it seems that there is more "Canada" in both pop and high culture, both domestically and internationally, than ever before. At the same time, it is increasingly easy for Canadians to consume cultural products from elsewhere. And the very act of that consumption changes the cultural output of Canadian artists. Unlike in the past, domestic popular culture is increasingly mediated through a global popular culture that, in some instances, blurs specific national identities, but which can also create space for smaller, regional cultural outputs. Ultimately, as Canadian culture permeates other domestic cultures, it becomes more permeable. The result is not the development of a "Canadian pop culture" but, as Pevere and Dymond argue in *Mondo Canuck*, the integration of Canadians, in a variety of ways, into that global pop culture.[38]

This mediation can, thus, change the manner in which culture serves as a form of connection between Canadians. Canadian artists reach Canadians increasingly through non-Canadian, and especially American, vehicles, particularly in the areas of film, television, and music. This mediation may be less important, or less apparent, with regard to Canadian authors. Insofar as popular artists aim their art at that global audience, this may increase the distance between the Canadian artist and Canadians. Yet insofar as Canadians see Canadian artists within that global popular culture, we appear much more willing to embrace them as our own and to proclaim their "Canadian-ness." To some extent this may assuage Canada's cultural insecurity which traditionally manifested itself as being both fiercely defensive of Canada's cultural products and yet convinced that those products never quite measured up on the international stage.

Canadians are now more able to sample a much wider array of cultural products from around the world. At the same time, Canadian cultural products, whether mainstream or not, are both more available to the world and to other Canadians than ever before. If the political and economic processes of globalization produce both integration and fragmentation, then the globalization of culture surely has the same effects. The technological and economic changes that have produced a global popular culture, rooted in but not merely the equivalent of American popular culture, have also created the vehicles for more local cultural expressions to find their voice and their audience — an audience that may be thousands of miles away or may be next door.

These changes have at least as much to do with developments in the artistic community and the marketplace as they do with government interventions. But some also have to do with opportunities and inducements that reflect past and current government interventions. As for the future, given the raw power that the United States government has in crafting the rules of international trade, and the power of the American entertainment and cultural industries, it will be increasingly difficult for the Canadian government to preserve even its current limited room to manoeuvre. The more that "cultural products" are perceived as any other set of goods in the marketplace, and cultural industries as any other industry, then the harder it will be for other states to resist the process of commodifying cultural production. Every time Canada raises the issue of the lack of screen space available for Canadian feature film, the government can be assured a phone call from the MPAA threatening the withdrawal or restriction of the American product from Canadian theatres.[39] The most viable option, perhaps, will be for Canada to build alliances with the governments of other countries that also wish to see special international trade rules on culture to enable governments to meet domestic cultural goals.

Whatever one makes of Canada's place in the international cultural marketplace, on the domestic front the greatest failure has been in bridging the language divide among Canadians. The cultural output of English-speaking Canada remains largely unknown in Quebec and vice versa. At all levels, but especially in the realm of popular culture, there appear to be few common points of reference. Pevere and Dymond's tongue-in-cheek history of Canadian popular culture is, the authors admit, a history of English-Canadian popular culture. French-speaking music, television and film (and to a lesser degree books) are simply horses of different colours. The chapter by Sauvageau and Pritchard in this volume is but another reflection of this continuing chasm. The irony in their study is that French- and English-speaking journalists practise the same kind of journalism, but do so in what appears to be complete isolation from each other. The irony turns to concern in the context of the ongoing political tension between Quebec and the rest of Canada. This inability to bridge the language barrier can only bode ill for our future ability to overcome this particular disconnection.

CIVIL SOCIETY AND CITIZENSHIP

A possible qualification to earlier observations about the ongoing economic linkages within Canada emerges from the literature, which suggests that the "new economy" is creating a divide between well-educated and technologically adept people and the semi-skilled, unskilled, and those with skills that are out-of-date.[40] The first group is in short supply and becoming relatively more prosperous, whereas the second group is falling behind economically. More important, the first group is seen to have many connections outside national borders and to be highly mobile internationally, whereas the second group has few linkages of this kind. The self-interest of the first group is to further liberalize the national and world economies as it improves their opportunities economically. They are also easily able to absorb the adjustments that such changes impose. The less skilled and less mobile group is the loser.

This qualification in turn leads to questions about the extent of ties among Canadians in civil society. This volume has several chapters that touch on these connections. Tom McIntosh assesses the situation and prospects of the Canadian "house of labour." On the one hand, he acknowledges its difficulties and setbacks. These include the retrenchment of the state. This has had two effects. It has damaged public sector unions directly, as a result of government downsizing and extended freezes on public sector wages. It has also reduced the bargaining power of the private sector as a result of "flexible" labour market policies. The labour movement has also experienced difficulties in maintaining effective coalitions with other groups on the political left (including environmentalists and feminists) and has been hurt by the strains between the private and public sector unions.

On the other hand, unions continue to represent a large share of Canadian workers, and the size of the Canadian unionized workforce has remained relatively constant. Furthermore, one of the consistent characteristics of the labour movement's history, both in Canada and elsewhere in the western world, has been that it grows during periods of increasing prosperity. The length (if not the intensity) of the current economic expansion and the improvements in public finance have provided some new opportunities for organized labour to again make itself a voice for Canadian workers as seen in increased strike activity and activism, especially on the part of white-collar unionists.

Maintaining this momentum requires, however, that it deal with a membership whose interests and expectations are more diverse than was the case in earlier parts of this century.

McIntosh's cautiously optimistic observations in this regard do not, however, extend to the relationship between the Canadian Labour Congress and the Quebec unions. Here, as in the area of culture discussed above, the labour movement has "never managed to bridge the gap except in the most formal manner." The arrangement is one of sovereignty-association and his analysis does not suggest the likelihood of closer ties in the future.

The opportunity and desire of postsecondary students to pursue their education outside their home province is another avenue for building pan-Canadian consciousness. Over the last quarter-century, the proportion of full-time undergraduates studying outside their home province has been relatively constant, at between 7 and 9 percent. In their chapter, Kathleen Day and Quentin Grafton indicate that over this period 150,000 Canadian undergraduates have studied outside their home province. This typically entails four years away from home at a formative time in their lives. And since the leaders of the private and public sectors come almost exclusively from the university educated, they suggest that the impact of this experience can have a disproportionate effect on Canadian connectedness over time. Their point in this regard is no doubt one channel for forming the information networks that Helliwell points to and which help maintain the density of economic linkages among Canadians. Day and Grafton also show that student mobility is affected by differential costs between provinces, including accommodation and tuition costs, so that recent provincial and federal policies that affect access to postsecondary institutions will have an effect over time.[41]

Interprovincial family connections also help to build a sense of shared consciousness among Canadians. In this regard, we saw above that Vachon and Vaillancourt have noted the decline in mobility within Canada. Their chapter also shows, however, the cumulative effects of internal Canadian mobility over many years; that is, the proportion of residents living in any one province who were born in another province. In the economically more prosperous provinces of British Columbia, Alberta, and Ontario in the early 1990s, the percentage of residents who had been born elsewhere in Canada were approximately 33, 33, and 11 respectively. From the opposite side of the coin, about 27 percent of those born in Atlantic Canada had migrated to other regions of Canada. Across the mainly English-speaking areas of the country, therefore, thanks to internal migration, family ties are considerable. The same is not true, however, about family ties between francophone Quebecers and other Canadians.

Taken together, these contributions demonstrate the ebb and flow of the connections within civil society, especially with regard to English Canada. Yet the very nature and make-up of that civil society has itself changed profoundly in recent decades. The ethnic, racial, and religious profile of the Canadian citizenry has been significantly altered as immigration patterns have shifted. The adoption of the *Charter of Rights and Freedoms* gave Canadians, new and old, a different way of viewing the citizen-state relationship, one articulated in a language of rights. Postmaterialist and social movement politics shifted the political discourse away from its traditional concerns with federal-provincial, east-west, and metropolis-hinterland debates rooted as they are in territorial notions of citizenship. All of this has resulted in the articulation of different conceptions of citizenship rooted in non-territorial identities such as ethnicity, sexuality, rights-holder, etc.

Avigail Eisenberg's chapter in this volume points to the challenges of balancing territorial and non-territorial identities. The territorial pluralism that is inherent in a federal state must make room for a different kind of pluralism, one that is often centred around claims to rights and the enhancement of cultural identities. This need not be a zero-sum equation, though the politics of such confrontations may often present the choice in this manner. Like so many of the authors collected here, Eisenberg's analysis does not fall easily into a simple categorization around the effects that such developments have had on the connections that bind the country. Non-territorial identities, based in common rights, common ethnicity or sexuality, may create new bonds between Canadians previously disconnected from each other. At the same time, such connections may sever bonds based on territoriality or between those who are members of a particular group and those who are not.

Eisenberg leaves the reader with something of a dilemma. Territorial pluralism was designed as a means to limit state power through the division of state sovereignty as reflected by two orders of sovereign governments. Non-territorial pluralism, in its efforts to enhance the political and social cohesion of cultural groups, often requires increased state intervention to effect its aims. The tensions between these different pluralist approaches necessitate political trade-offs between proponents of each view. What Eisenberg suggests is that proponents of each type of pluralism have overlooked the advantages that both views offer to what she calls a "resuscitation" of a serious discussion of both "group life and local participatory politics."

In his chapter, Matt James presents a case study of how a particular group's conception of themselves as Canadians underwent profound change as a result of a process of reconciliation with a Canadian state that had, in the past, treated them as decidedly un-Canadian. James argues that the apology and compensation offered Japanese Canadians for their treatment during the Second World War can be understood as a bid on the part of a marginalized group to garner civic respect. Although what James calls redress politics has been criticized as a threat to a common Canadian citizenship, it is argued here that such processes of reconciliation have important integrative effects and that they result in a more robust and inclusive understanding of citizenship. In short, seeking redress should be understood as an attempt to build a social identity that facilitates participation in the civic arena and, ultimately, strengthens civic solidarity.

This model of reconciliation has important implications not only for redefining a common citizenship in a multicultural society, but may also point to a means of reconciling Canada's "other solitude" — namely that which exists between aboriginal and non-aboriginal Canadians. The recent steps taken by both government and non-governmental actors in the recognition of the harm done to aboriginal nations (the apologies from those who ran residential schools and the creation of a "healing fund" for those who suffered under such systems) may be the beginning of a process that could ultimately integrate aboriginals and other Canadians into a common understanding of a shared citizenship. Of course, the damage done to aboriginal cultures goes far beyond that done to those the government interned during World War II and, thus, the reconciliation process will be decidedly more complex. The healing fund and the limited apologies from both religious and state officials are a beginning, not an end. Yet, as James argues, the result could be a more robust, more comprehensive understanding of citizenship and not only stronger, but deeper, connections between citizens.

POLITICAL CONNECTIONS

We have acknowledged that the ties that have bound Canada together have been under challenge from without and within. From outside our borders the impacts of forces that are integrating Canada more and more into the wider world are both economic and non-economic. One result is that policy challenges increasingly require transnational responses. *De facto* authority therefore increasingly resides in supranational and international organizations. For this reason, and perhaps even more because of domestic mismanagement, the Canadian state has been redefining its role and instrument regime. We also suggested, however, that the Canadian state has made at least the beginnings of a recovery with its improved finances; and its efforts to re-tool in a way that reflects the impact of changes in technology may be a step to becoming a more strategic and nimble actor. The state may be a less effective nation-builder than it was in the 1950s and 1960s but it is not only premature but also wrong to write it off as an important actor in creating ties among Canadians.

We also saw that while the cultural outputs of the world have never been more available to Canadians, Canadian culture is itself flourishing. The social rights of citizenship have been adversely affected by expenditure reductions. But the reductions in turn have created something of a backlash, suggesting that there is indeed a widely shared social contract, or at least the mythology of such a contract, among Canadians and that this myth can be a potent force for reinforcing these connections. Economic bonds with the rest of the world and especially the United States have grown, but the economic linkages within Canada are dense. The border that defines the Canadian political space is wider that the thin line on the map. Ties within civil society, including a distinctive set of institutions, culture and interpersonal connections both reflect and nurture the border effect.

Yet it is all too obvious that such an optimistic note does not reflect the Canadian reality. Throughout this chapter, we have observed that the two language solitudes remain intact. Much of our discussion above was on the changing role of the state. We did not discuss, however, the expansive role the Quebec government took in both leading and responding to the Quiet Revolution within that province. One result has been that many people who might have once been described as French-Canadians now view themselves as Quebecers. If opinion polls are to be believed, a significant majority of French-speaking Quebecers have attachments to Quebec and to Canada, but the stronger emotional tie is to Quebec. Quebec is homeland (*patrie*); Canada is country (*pays*).

Moreover, many Canadians living in the four western provinces have long been voicing their sense that Canadian governments too often leave them on the outside. Over a decade and half ago, historian Doug Owram referred to the west as a "reluctant hinterland."[42] Though hinterland may no longer be an apt description of the west, the sense of frustration with the political institutions of the nation remain. The west has consistently felt that its political power, especially in federal institutions, did not equal its economic or social importance in the federation. The west has regularly sought either significant intrastate restructuring (e.g., a Triple-E Senate) or the devolution of federal powers to the provinces. It should be made clear that this is a desire to either restructure or restrain the federal government and federal institutions, which should not be seen as a lack of attachment to the Canadian nation. At the same time, the current sympathy that many Quebecers have for a decentralized federation comes not so much from a sense of being excluded from the exercise of power on the federal scene, but from a desire to limit federal powers over provincial areas of concern. Thus, many Quebecers are searching for an accommodation with the rest of Canada that would leave them with ample room to do much of their nation-building within Quebec while retaining a more limited attachment to the Canadian family.

These cleavages are reflected in the growing fragmentation of the Canadian political party system. The 1993 election saw regionally-based parties from Quebec and western Canada emerge as the second and third largest parties in the House of Commons. By 1997, the splintering of parties along regional lines had advanced even further. The Liberals were strong only in Ontario, the New Democratic Party in Atlantic Canada, while the Reform Party gained official opposition status without winning a seat east of the Manitoba border and the Bloc Québécois won a sizeable majority of Quebec constituencies. Whereas national parties had once served as brokers and mediators between regional, linguistic, and economic interests, by the 1990s, they were no longer trusted in this role.

In Brian Tanguay's chapter, he argues that this transformation has several explanations. In part, it has to do with the globalization phenomenon. He maintains that the room for manoeuvre that remains for political parties has been seriously compromised by the structural changes under way. The result is convergence among parties. He quotes Stephen Harper and Tom Flanagan to the effect that the "Conservative voters are getting better results as outsiders influencing a Liberal government than they did as an inside influence within a Progressive Conservative government." He notes also a decline in deference among voters associated with this gap between party electoral promises and performance, which has helped to fuel .voter cynicism that anti-parties like Reform have been quick to exploit. Tanguay also argues that the explicitly pan-Canadian political vision embodied in Trudeau government policies alienated governments in both western Canada and Quebec, which served as a catalyst to the regional responses reflected in the Reform Party and the Bloc Québécois. In addition, the first-past-the-post electoral system often deprives parties of any representation in the House of Commons even when they garner a significant minority share of the regional popular vote. The result is the erosion of national parties.

FINAL THOUGHTS

Our analysis leads to both positive and negative conclusions about the connections that link Canadians. On a positive note, the Canadian state has been taking some of the steps that are necessary to once again become a more effective force for strengthening the bonds among Canadians. Its fiscal outlook has improved markedly and it has been modernizing the delivery systems for its programs. Within much of civil society there is evidence of new connections being forged, without a noticeable deterioration in old ties. Economic connections are denser than many have appreciated. With important qualifications relating to Quebec, social connections appear strong. Canadian cultural output remains a source of pride and, in some respects, is flourishing.

On a more troubling note, some older sources of tension, namely between French- and English-speaking Canadians and between aboriginal and non-aboriginal Canadians have not lessened and may have become more entrenched in some respects. Globalization and technology has perhaps made some cultural industries and pursuits more vulnerable. The political party structure is fragmented badly and with few signs of imminent healing. But for all this, the picture painted above is not one of a Canada fast eroding in the face of a global juggernaut.

How then does one explain the marketization trend of the last 15 years? To some extent, the conventional answer is correct. It is the belief among many governments around the world, including Canada's, that they do have to focus on competitiveness. In an age of footloose factor inputs, this necessitates creating an attractive environment for the capital, know-how, skills, and technology which is mobile. But we also believe that the historical ebb and flow in the relative roles of the market and the state, which has characterized much of this century, constitutes a good part of the answer. The politics of the 1920s, 1950s and 1980s/90s were dominated by a strong orientation to the market. The 1930s and 1960s were periods when the state was given primacy. In democratic societies, where citizens may periodically be disappointed by what both the market and the state have to offer, there are shifts back and forth, at least in relative emphasis, as reality falls short of the political promises made by both the political right and left. Whether the early part of the next century will again be marked by such a reaction remains to be seen. But the election of numerous social democratic governments in Europe, the content of President Clinton's 1999 State of the Union address in the United States and the 1999 Canadian federal budget all suggest this as a possibility.

If this turns out to be the case, we would not expect the Canadian state to return to the instruments and methods of the 1960s and 1970s. Lessons have been learned as a result of the experience of the last several decades. The tool kit has been revamped. For one thing, there is considerable support for the idea that the state must be suppler and faster acting in a world of frequent surprises and rapid change. Very large organizations do not easily acquire and retain such qualities. This suggests that even with improvements in the federal government's fiscal status, there may be reason to control the sheer size and complexity of the federal state. In this modified approach, the federal focus might be more on framework policies and the establishment of more transparent accountability frameworks for measuring achievements. And as will be discussed more below, we anticipate a much larger role for the federal government in the international arena. This would leave provinces, other governments, the third sector, and other partners with more scope to design and deliver programs.

Turning to the connections between Quebec and the rest of Canada, it is our sense that the political chasm is as wide as ever. Economic connections remain thick, but there is little cross-pollination in culture. Connections within civic society are uneven. In labour they are formal but not strong. French-speaking Quebecers generally do not move to other regions of Canada. Business ties between English- and French-speaking Canadians are substantial but many of the pan-Canadian social movements are poorly represented or not represented at all in Quebec, where Quebec-based groups may have entirely separate organizations.

The chapter by Frank Graves, drawing heavily on his ongoing research into Canadian attitudes and opinions and related comparative research, lends support to both of the elements in our analysis. Graves finds that, among Canadians overall, levels of attachments to Canada are high. They have been strengthening over the last 30 years while more local attachments have been weakening. In fact, levels of national attachment in Canada are the highest among the countries tested in the World Values Survey. Graves reports further Canadians' belief that there is a distinctive national identity that is a source of pride and belonging. His analysis also suggests that government in general and the federal government in particular is a key player in creating this sense of national attachment.

Graves also finds, however, that patterns of attachment in Quebec are different. The people of that province reveal significantly lower levels of attachment to Canada than do Canadians in other provinces. According to his survey instruments, the attachment of Quebecers to Canada has also fallen a little in recent years. At the same time, Quebecers' attachment to Canada remains substantial compared to reported levels of national attachment in other countries. Perhaps surprisingly, attachment to province has also declined among people in Quebec. These observations are consistent with the argument by David Cameron that Quebecers are less intense about politics and political commitments today than they were in the 1970s and 1980s. Cameron sees in this transformation within Quebec the seeds of an opportunity for all Canadians to make progress toward national reconciliation.[43]

While the intensity of Quebecers' politics may have cooled somewhat, it seems equally clear that the intensity of aboriginal politics is much higher now than a few decades ago. The promises of the 1980s that were linked to the constitutional reform package of 1982 have gone unfulfilled. The recommendations of the Royal Commission on Aboriginal Peoples in the mid-1990s have yielded only minor policy innovations. The country is well aware of the devastating social and economic conditions of its First Nations' people. For them the healing fund noted above is only the first step that Canadians need to take in a process of reconciliation. The controversy over the treaty concluded between the governments of British Columbia, Canada and the Nisga'a is but the most recent manifestation of the depth of this divide.

Recent trends in the federation indicate a new pattern may be emerging in intergovernmental relations. There is evidence of, at one and the same time, enhanced collaboration among governments and growing disentanglement. The enhanced collaboration is reflected in several formal federal-provincial agreements reached over the last several years. These include, but are by no means limited to, the Agreement on Internal Trade, the National Child Benefit, the Canada-Wide Accord on Environmental Harmonization and, most recently, the Framework to Improve the Social Union for Canadians. They signify a more collaborative federalism in that they entail governments working together to identify national objectives. These arrangements, none of which involve constitutional amendment, are also the beginning of a renewed cooperative effort over the last decade to clarify the roles and responsibilities of both orders of government in relation to these objectives. Within these broad agreements, individual governments have the responsibility to design and deliver their own programs. And it is in that sense that they also signify a disentangled or classical federalism. There is also a growing commitment at both levels to better and more transparent accountability frameworks.

To be sure, much remains to be done, especially around the development of mature processes for establishing national objectives, clarifying roles and responsibilities and enhancing public accountability. But this approach has much to be said for it. It combines the attractive aspects of classical and collaborative federalism by recognizing the sovereignty of both orders of government as well as the growing interdependence between them in a world of increasing independence. It could also give rise to a more democratic process to the extent that the more open approach to accountability enables citizens to be informed about the relative value of different programs. And with the expanding need for more international governance, the requirement for national mechanisms to establish and re-establish a sense of national purpose and, with it, the respective roles of both federal and provincial governments can only rise. This process will require continual ongoing adjustments as the world unfolds.

Given the necessity of enhanced international governance, representing Canadian interests at that level may well be one of the largest roles of the federal government in the twenty-first century, although not necessarily on its own. In this regard, the broad scope of provincial powers within Canada suggests that it will become more important than ever that Ottawa develop new techniques of working with the provinces so that Canadian interests can be more effectively served.

This may alter the nature and scope of the debate between Quebec nationalism (in both its federalist and secessionist guises) on the one hand and Canadian nationalism on the other. As the roles and responsibilities of both orders of government are clarified, Ottawa's role may increasingly be to protect and advance Canadian interests in the international arena. The federal government will have to be in continuous dialogue with provincial governments and other Canadian actors concerning Canadian negotiating positions. And it will need to be in ongoing negotiation with representatives of other governments. Negotiation will not be a one-time event. Implementation tasks associated with international arrangements may often be as important as the negotiation themselves, as the example of the follow-up to the Kyoto Agreement on Climate Change illustrates.

In such an environment — one where the lines between domestic and for-eign have effectively disappeared and where the linkages between federal and provincial jurisdiction have inevitably grown — it will be essential to the effective functioning of the Canadian political system that there be a more mature set of working relations between federal and provincial governments than the relations of recent decades. To be sure, pontificating that the govern-ments must work out a more trusting and effective set of understandings will not make it happen. In this scenario, however, what could make it happen is simply a new set of international conditions that effectively impose a need on all governments within Canada for a more smoothly functioning federation. We are not yet at the point where sheer necessity creates the political will for such action, although we are moving incrementally toward it. The pace of change being set by new technologies and market forces may well help us reach that point in the first decade of the next century. When it is reached, the price of failure will help to bring about such an outcome. (As an addendum here, we do not remotely imagine that such a scenario means the end of politi-cal disputes among governments within Canada, but it does anticipate negotiated mechanisms and channels for resolving them.)

It is implicit in this approach that Ottawa will find it necessary to make a significant shift in the way it deploys its political energy relative to the way it does today. It will have less time for the details of domestic programs that are not at the centre of its constitutional legislative authority simply because, in addition to its areas of legislative competence, it will have a huge task in building and maintaining the bridges between domestic and international governance. In order to play this role, institutional mechanisms and processes will be needed that enable governments to help Canadians seize the opportu-nities that a smaller world offers even while protecting overriding Canadian interests, be they economic, cultural, social, or political. These institutions will have to be robust enough, and flexible enough, to withstand the differ-ences in ideology or interests among governments in Canada as well as periodic personal clashes among political leaders.

With this kind of change in the institutions and processes of the federation, the political tensions that envelope federal-provincial relations, and especially federal-Quebec relations are more likely to focus on the effectiveness and symbolism of Ottawa managing a growing international agenda, much of which involves areas of provincial legislative competence. For this to be accepted, the new institutions of the federation will not only have to possess the effec-tiveness noted above, they will also have to be trusted by the provinces — Quebec included. This means that provinces will need to be equal partners in their construction and maintenance.

In short, current tensions regarding the federal spending power could re-cede as sources of irritation between Canadian and Quebec nationalism. The more sensitive area will likely be in relation to the conduct of international relations that impinge directly on provincial interests, including health, education, and social policy. Anticipating these shifts, and constructing the required machinery to deal with it, will be a big challenge for federal and provincial governments in the decades ahead. It is also a task where governments can perhaps establish a few guiding and overarching principles. But the nuts and bolts are best left to line departments, in consultation with the interests they represent. If handled mainly through "low politics," rather than the more rarified "high" politics of first ministers, finance ministers, and intergovernmental ministries, trust among governments may be easier to establish. In any case, the agenda for federal-provincial relations is likely to be determined increasingly by events that originate outside our borders. This will create the opportunity to redefine how governments relate to one another, and how Canadians inside and outside Quebec relate to one another. The seeds of current tensions between English- and French-speaking Canadians were planted many decades ago, when grievances were ignored and myths created. A new set of circumstances will create new opportunities. It remains to be seen whether Canadians from both groups will learn from past mistakes.

NOTES

1.   Donald V. Smiley, *The Federal Condition in Canada* (Toronto: McGraw-Hill Ryerson, 1987).

2.   See, for example, Vincent Cable, "The Diminished Nation-State: A Study in the Loss of Economic Power," *Daedelus* 124 (1995); Kenichi Ohmae, *Borderless World: Power and Strategy in the Interlinked Economy* (New York: HarperPerennial, 1990); Kenichi Ohmae, *The End of the Nation State: The Rise of Regional Economies* (New York: The Free Press, 1995); Matthew Horsman and Andrew Marshall, *After the Nation-State: Citizens, Tribalism and the New World Order* (London: Harper Collins, 1994); Robert B. Reich, *The Work of Nations* (New York: Vintage Books, 1991); Wolfgang Reinicke, *Global Public Policy: Governing Without Government?* (Washington, DC: The Brookings Institution, 1998); Dani Rodrik, *Has Globalization Gone too Far?* (Washington, DC: Institute for International Economics, 1997); Susan Strange, *The Retreat of the State: The Diffusion of Power in the World Economy* (Cambridge: Cambridge University Press, 1996).

3.   Ohmae, *The End of the Nation State*, p. 42.

4.   Ibid, p. 142.

5.   Peter Drucker, "The Age of Social Transformation," *Atlantic Monthly*, November 1994, p. 80.

6.   Ibid.

7. Susan Strange, *The Retreat of the State: The Diffusion of Power in the World Economy*, p.3.

8. Richard J. Barnet and John Cavanagh, *Global Dreams: Imperial Corporations and the New World Order* (New York: Simon and Schuster, 1994), p. 19.

9. Ibid., p. 423.

10. Reinicke, *Global Public Policy.*

11. Reich, *The Work of Nations,* p. 312.

12. Rodrik, *Has Globalization Gone too Far?*, pp. 77-85.

13. Gilles Paquet, "States, Communities and Markets: The Distributed Governance Scenario," in *The Nation State in a Global/Information Era: Policy Challenges,* The Bell Canada Papers on Economic and Public Policy, ed. T.J. Courchene (Kingston: John Deutsch Institute for the Study of Economic Policy, Queen's University, 1997), p. 34.

14. Ibid., p. 36.

15. Sylvia Ostry, "Globalization and the Nation State," in *The Nation State in a Global/Information Era: Policy Challenges,* ed. T.J. Courchene, p. 62.

16. Thomas J. Courchene, with Colin Telmer *From Heartland to North American Region State: The Social, Fiscal and Federal Evaluation of Ontario* (Toronto: University of Toronto Press, 1998), p. 271.

17. Mark W. Zacher, "The Global Economy and the International Political Order: Some Diverse and Paradoxical Relationships," in *The Nation State in a Global/Information Era: Policy Challenges*, ed. T. J. Courchene, pp. 76-77.

18. Ibid., p. 80.

19. Charles Taylor, "Globalization and the Future of Canada," *Queen's Quarterly* (Fall 1998): 331.

20. Ostry, "Globalization and the Nation State," p. 64.

21. John Kincaid, "Peoples, Persons and Places in Flux," in *Integration and Fragmentation*, ed. Guy Laforest and Douglas Brown (Kingston: Institute of Intergovernmental Relations, Queen's University, 1994), p. 77.

22. Barnet and Cavanagh, *Global Dreams*, p. 159.

23. Claire Turenne Sjolander, "The Rhetoric of Globalization: What's in a Wor(l)d," *International Journal* (Autumn 1996): 603-16.

24. Zacher, "The Global Economy," p. 72.

25. Jane Jenson, "Understanding Politics," in *Canadian Politics,* 2d ed., ed. Alain Gagnon and James Bickerton (Toronto: Broadview, 1997). See also, Jane Jenson and Fuat Keyman, "Must We All Be 'Post-Modern'?" *Studies in Political Economy* 31 (1990): 141-58.

26. *The Globe and Mail*, 29 January 1999, p. A4.

27. Ronald L. Watts, *Comparing Federal Systems in the 1990s*, (Kingston: Institute of Intergovernmental Relations, Queen's University, 1997).

28. Cable, "The Diminished Nation-State," p. 46.

29. The Canadian state continues to tax heavily. Even though social expenditures have been cut, its social spending also remains substantial. The result is that the Canadian state continues to influence heavily the distribution of disposable incomes. The growth in disparities is due to the growth of inequality in market incomes which has overwhelmed what the state has done to redistribute incomes.

30. The result has been widening disparities, but without the productivity growth that had been anticipated. Harvey Lazar and Peter Stoyko, "The Future of the Welfare State," in *International Social Security Review* 51 (March 1998): 3-36.

31. Rodrik, *Has Globalization Gone too Far?* p. 77.

32. Of particular interest are *Assessing ACCESS: Towards a New Social Union,* Proceedings of a Symposium on the Courchene Proposal (Kingston: Institute of Intergovernmental Relations, Queen's University, 1997); and Courchene with Telmer, *From Heartland to North American Region State.*

33. John Helliwell, *How Much Do National Borders Matter?* (Washington DC: The Brookings Institution Press, 1998).

34. John McCallum, "National Borders Matter: Canada-US Regional Trade Patterns," *American Economic Review* 85 (June 1995): 615-23.

35. National standards, in a meaningful sense, have never existed in the areas of health, postsecondary education, and welfare. For example, under the Canada Assistance Plan at its heyday, there were wide differences in provincial social assistance regimes. Every province has had different rules about its insured health services.

36. C. Rodney James, *Film as a National Art: The NFB of Canada and the Film Board Idea* (New York: Arno, 1977).

37. David A. Cook, *A History of Narrative Film,* 3d ed. (New York: WW Norton, 1996).

38. Geoff Pevere and Greig Dymond, *Mondo Canuck: A Canadian Pop Culture Odyssey* (Toronto: Prentice-Hall, 1996), pp. viii-x.

39. Though the MPAA would be unlikely to deny the Hollywood studios the revenue generated in the Canadian market, a "trade war" over film distribution would be nearly impossible for Canada to win. The MPAA, the Screen Actors Guild (SAG) and a number of the craft unions have expressed concern about the increased use of Canada as a production site. From their perspective this is costing American workers jobs and American communities the economic spin-offs associated with location shooting. The Canadian film industry has been built, in recent years, on its ability to provide cheaper yet equally skilled labour of all kinds to American productions using Canadian locations. A concerted effort by the American film industry to "punish" Canadian content regulations vis-à-vis film distribution (scaling back production in Canada, visa restrictions for Canadian artists in the US, etc.) could likely have a devastating effect on the Canadian industry in a relatively short time.

40. Reich, *The Work of Nations*, pp. 171-315; Rodrik, *Has Globalization Gone too Far?* pp. 4-7 and 69-71.

41. The recent framework agreement on the Social Union, agreed to by the federal government and nine provinces, explicitly calls for the removal of "residency based policies" (section 2: Mobility within Canada) that constrain access to education. At present, only the province of Quebec, which did not sign the framework document, charges out-of-province tuition fees for postsecondary students. It seems unlikely that Quebec will withdraw this provision any time soon, which could lead to other provinces charging higher tuition fees to students coming from Quebec, though not to other out-of-province students.

42. Doug Owram, "Reluctant Hinterland," in *Western Separatism*, ed. Larry Pratt and Garth Stevenson (Edmonton: Hurtig, 1981), pp. 45-64.

43. David Cameron, "National Unity and Paradigm Shifts," in *Drift, Strategy and Happenstance: Towards Political Reconciliation in Canada?* ed. T. McIntosh (Kingston: Institute of Intergovernmental Relations, Queen's University, 1998), pp. 11-16.

II

The Role of the State

2

The Changing Canadian State

Reg Whitaker

Le «retrait de l'État» semble être un phénomène généralisé à l'ère de la mondialisation. L'État canadien y a été particulièrement vulnérable en raison de la faiblesse et des divisions de son assise nationale. L'évaluation des perspectives d'avenir de l'État canadien est confrontée à une difficulté d'ordre conceptuel : les frontières entre l'État et la société sont changeantes et, partant, la représentation de la politique le long d'un continuum gauche-droite s'en trouve bouleversée. Les anciennes explications politiques ont été remplacées par une nouvelle dialectique entre populisme et revendications identitaires à l'intérieur de laquelle la contraction et l'expansion simultanées de l'État est contestée de manière imprévisible. L'État est secoué par des pressions contradictoires, tant internes qu'externes, qui réduisent son autonomie. Pourtant et paradoxalement, l'État, même décentré et faiblement intégré à la société, demeure au centre de la politique. Sur le plan international, face à l'insécurité inhérente à une économie sans règle l'État apparaît comme le seul ancrage possible d'un ordre mondial fondé sur la coopération multilatérale. Le désordre global contient la possibilité d'une alliance néo-keynésienne entre les puissances moyennes, comme le Canada, les ONG et les mouvements sociaux afin de gérer les dysfonctions de la mondialisation. Un tel rôle sur le plan international pourrait même renforcer l'unité de la communauté nationale canadienne.

As the end of the twentieth century draws near, the idea of Canada as a viable national project is increasingly in question. Beset from the outside by the challenges of globalization, and from the inside by the imminent threat of Quebec secession, the future of Canada as a political community appears more fragile than ever. Other western societies have also experienced political and communitarian turbulence, and some have grown introspective and doubtful about long-held beliefs about their national identities.[1] The pressures and strains experienced by traditional nation-states, however, are less acute than those of a political project like Canada where "nation" and "state" have always been categories in uneasy, even arm's-length, relationship with one another.

There is no doubt that the state is under very considerable duress today. Some would say it is in retreat, others that it is being profoundly restructured. Virtually no observers any longer would argue that the state in the twenty-first century will closely resemble its predecessor. Where state and nation have in this century been locked closely together, the retreat/transformation of the state may very well have an explosive impact on the structure of civil society. In the case of Canada, a crucial question must be: To what extent is the very existence of a Canadian civil society bound up with the fragile linkages of the national state? If, as George Etienne Cartier liked to say, Canada was always a "political nationality,"[2] can that nationality survive severe strains to the political institutional structures? If the state is weakening as the agent of the nation/community, is Canadian civil society tied together strongly enough to avoid internal disintegration and/or external absorption? These are complex questions to which various authors in this volume address themselves. But to even begin to answer these questions, it is necessary to first address the prior question of the specific role of the state in Canada. What did it do in the past that it may not do in the future?

In 1977 I published an article on "Images of the State in Canada," in which I examined successive images through which Canadians had understood the Canadian state system.[3] I traced the linkages from the dominant nineteenth-century "Tory" image of the state through the dominant twentieth-century "liberal" image. Both these images were dependent upon the smooth inter-locking of the Canadian state with capitalism, but I noted a "fatal continuity ... founded on capitalism without a viable national basis." I also noted the persistent weakness of any alternative, socialist or social democratic, image of the state. The major challenges to the viability of the Canadian state system which I discerned in the late 1970s were both economic and political: the first in the threat of US economic domination, and the second in the emergence of a serious secessionist movement in Quebec. I predicted the continued decline of the power of the national state and continued decentralization or peripheralization and/or "Balkanization" of the Canadian state system in the face of these challenges.

Looking back two decades later, I am struck by my earlier insistence on the continuity of Canadian development. At the end of the twentieth century, radical *discontinuity* is now the rule, and is reflected in a sense of postmodern anxiety pervasive throughout Canadian society. The traditional set of ideological images or narratives (liberalism, Toryism, and social democracy) that explained the political world to Canadians, for example, have come unstuck. They seem increasingly empty and irrelevant, but have yet to be replaced by rival narratives that address with any real authority the political community as a whole, as opposed to particular parts of it.[4] The challenges have deepened, but become more complex. Quebec sovereignty is far closer to achievement than it was in the 1970s, but the responses to it in the rest of Canada are more complicated and ambiguous. Canada has entered into two successive regional trading pacts in the 1980s and 1990s (first the Canada-US Free Trade Agreement and then the North American Free Trade Agreement or NAFTA) but the challenges of what is now called "globalization" are far more complex and multifaceted than the simpler threat of "US economic domination" that was perceived in the 1970s.

I am also struck by the conceptual transformation of how we understand politics and the state since my 1977 article. There was first of all a sense then that politics was played out on an ideological map or grid that ran from "right" to "left," and that players and spectators alike could be situated in relation to that map. Second, institutional boundaries seemed much clearer. The "state" stood out in sharp relief from the "civil society," or the public sector from the private sector. The federal government was apparently locked into a kind of zero-sum struggle with the provincial governments, so that variants of federalism could be characterized in a series of sharp oppositions, along an axis of centralization-decentralization, unity-disunity. And the "Canadian state" was seen in dramatic relief against the backdrop of other national states. The Canadian state was expected to claim as its own a fixed quantum of national sovereignty, and was assessed on its performance in maintaining or losing amounts of that sovereignty.

None of these conceptualizations appear to make as much sense as they once did. Somewhere over the past 20 years, the right-left ideological map has been lost, or at least obscured. As for boundaries, whether national or institutional, they are disappearing or reforming rapidly. It is becoming more and more difficult to draw precise lines between the state and the private sector, when governments are privatizing and deregulating and corporations are assuming functions that were once considered strictly "public." Of course, this is in one sense a very old story in Canadian economic development; in 1977, I referred to a Canadian tradition of "private enterprise at public expense." But the collapse of boundaries between what were once two sectors is now proceeding so rapidly that the proliferation of "partnerships" and "cosponsorships" call into question the very definition of a distinct state. Federalism in its competitive 1970s guise continues at the political level. Federal and provincial governments debate jurisdictional issues as of old, and projects are launched for "disentanglement," or "rebalancing" federalism or for reasserting the federal "presence." But these appear as increasingly empty charades, unconnected to real issues of political economy and public policy. In a survey of "non-constitutional renewal" from 1993 to 1997, Harvey Lazar writes about a trend away from a hierarchical model of intergovernmental relations toward "governments working together on a *non-hierarchical* basis in a way that reflects their *interdependence*."[5] Polar opposition of centralization versus decentralization is an increasingly irrelevant axis of federalist controversy in a world in which globalization and regional blocs coexist with the "subsidiarity" principle. Or in which political jurisdictions are largely irrelevant to the pattern of international investment flows.

Just a few years ago, the "deficit problem" became, by near-universal consent, the number one priority for public policy in Canada. Canadians were warned of the "debt wall" the country was about to run into. The *Wall Street Journal* shrilly proclaimed that Canada was falling out of the premier league of nations and facing relegation to Third World status. Globalization and international competition, speaking through the oracular voice of "The Market," had laid down the law. Eliminating the deficit became a new fiscal orthodoxy which only the most marginal elements tried, ineffectually, to challenge. Business, politics, and the media preached — and public opinion appeared to accept — that governments would have to downsize and to eliminate from their repertoire much that they had previously practised. The tacit postwar Social Contract was to be torn up. Programs that people had mistakenly taken to be their social entitlements were to be withdrawn.

A new political party was successfully launched that placed fiscal conservatism at the centre of its populist program, while attacking the then ruling Conservative Party for failing to reduce the federal deficit. Even the social democrats joined the bandwagon, to the extent that a New Democratic (NDP) government in Ontario found itself drawn inexorably into a suicidal confrontation with its own core political supporters over a "Social Contract" imposed on its public sector workers. The Mulroney Conservatives, who had failed to practise the fiscal restraint they preached, were virtually destroyed by an angry electorate. The Liberals, restored to their place as the Government Party after a nine-year interregnum, effortlessly shed the free-spending social-Liberal skin of the Trudeau-Pearson years and transformed themselves into a late-1990s version of the old frugal, pro-business, managerial Louis St. Laurent-C.D. Howe regime of the 1950s.

The 1980s was dominated by Reaganism in the United States and Thatcherism in the United Kingdom. These currents, which appeared for a time to have heralded a "turn to the right," proved in the end to be no more than ideological fashions, superceded by Bill Clinton's New Democrats and Tony Blair's New Labour. In retrospect, what the Reaganite-Thatcherite moment actually heralded was not a turn to the right so much as a transformation of the ideological landscape itself, rendering the traditional orientational categories of "right" and "left" irrelevant, if not downright misleading. Nor need we give too much credit to Reagan and Thatcher as transformative agents. As political leaders, they shrewdly and energetically capitalized on trends in the political economy, and resolutely stuck to their guns when under fire. Brian Mulroney, modelling himself on Reagan and Thatcher, proved irresolute and ineffectual in practice — yet the ultimate result in Canada has not been that much different from the US and the UK. Something deeper has been at work than political leadership styles.

The same observation could be made about the relative ease with which the successors of the parties of the right have been able to fulfill the ideological agendas set by their predecessors. Reagonomics ran up stratospheric deficits; it is the Democrat Clinton who is balancing the books. The Tories in Britain sniped at the social welfare state, but it is the Blair Labourites who are actually transforming the underlying principles of the welfare system, along lines not at all uncongenial to Tories.

The smooth transition is just as striking in Canada. Deficit reduction was quickly adopted as a priority by all parties at all levels of government. A Liberal government in New Brunswick and an NDP government in Saskatchewan demonstrated that relative economic underdevelopment was no impediment to balancing the provincial books — even when, as in the Saskatchewan case, the incoming government inherited a treasury virtually bankrupted by the profligacy, not to say corruption, of its Conservative predecessor. And the federal Liberals, inheriting a Mulroney deficit as high as that bequeathed Mulroney by Pierre Trudeau, within less than five years were able to become the first national government in a major western industrial state to declare their books in balance. So much for the threatened debt wall and Canada's Third World relegation! This achievement, it should be noted, was based on principles pioneered by Reagan and Thatcher, namely: download fiscal responsibilities to lower levels of government which then have to make the actual program cuts and justify them to the voters. The Liberals, it seems, have actually performed this trick more efficiently and to greater fiscal effect than their teachers.

One answer to the scenario I have just been sketching is to blame the left, or the centre-left, for having sold out or betrayed its principles. This may be true, up to a point. But the indictment rarely comes to terms with why these parties have felt compelled to change their programs. Nor is it good enough to assert that mere political opportunism is the problem, if the critics are unwilling or unable to explain why it is this kind of platform and this kind of performance that facilitates electoral success. Moreover, both Reaganism and Thatcherism manifested themselves in the first instance as challenges to a traditional notion of what a right-wing party was supposed to stand for. Before dispatching the Democrats, Ronald Reagan had first to dispatch the old Eastern Seaboard/Eisenhower hegemony in the Republican party. Before consigning Labour to opposition, Margaret Thatcher had first to crush the Macmillan-Heath "One Nation" tradition in the Tory party. Brian Mulroney reduced the influence of the Diefenbaker-Stanfield-Clark moderate or "red Tory" wing of the PC party, but his own immolation left two antagonistic parties in his wake. It is not that one side in a contest has capitulated to the other. It is rather that the rules of the contest have been changed, and thus the behaviour of all the contestants has changed as a consequence.

Another objection to this line of argument is that with the end of deficits, politics will return to more traditional lines. Liberals will be able to be Liberals again, brokering the conflicting demands for spending more and taxing less, while opponents to their right wax moralistic about fiscal laxity and those to their left publicly display their bleeding hearts. Liberals will undoubtedly spend more than in their first term. I strongly doubt, however, that the ideological and partisan framework within which public policy will be made will much resemble the familiar patterns of the past. Too much has changed.

One way of understanding the ideological reconfiguration of the past few decades is to see a gradual shift away from a centred and relatively consensual public philosophy to a decentred and more contested public terrain. The 1960s is the watershed in this shift. North American conservatives certainly point to the 1960s as Paradise Lost, when time-tested values were demeaned and undermined by a cultural revolution that lost its way in pursuit of egocentric self-gratification. Out of this turmoil, the argument goes, came the feminist and multicultural movements and "political correctness "— and the debilitating drain on the public treasury from the incessant demands of special interest groups. Hence the counter-revolution of the 1980s, when fiscal sanity was restored and patriotic and family values put back in their proper place at the centre of society. From the other side of the ideological divide, contemporary history is described differently. The 1960s are seen as a turning point in which elitism and oppression were challenged by resistance from below, these challenges being sharpened and deepened in the 1970s. The1980s are presented in this view as a brutal reaction or backlash by the privileged, a reassertion of traditional hegemony that is being consummated in the vicious neo-liberal globalization agenda of the 1990s, and further consolidated by the centre-left's abject and deplorable acceptance of this neo-liberal agenda.

Both sides at least agree on the broad historical lines: cultural revolution in the 1960s and 1970s, followed by cultural counter-revolution in the 1980s and 1990s. Both sides also seem to be in tacit agreement that contemporary history began *de nouveau* in the 1960s. The cultural revolution of that decade arose as a kind of autonomous force, miraculously for the left, demonically for the right, but not situated, unconnected to what had come before. The emphasis in the 1960s on *generational* conflict highlighted apparent discontinuity. The children were rejecting their parents' values. The counter-revolution, like all reactions, did not and could not, whatever some of its accompanying rhetoric might indicate, simply restore the old order before the fall. Counter-revolutions are also revolutions, of a kind. It was a common theme in the 1980s that Thatcherism and Reaganism were being installed by a "new generation" that rejected the 1960s counterculture, and, as already indicated, these political projects were explicitly based on a rejection of the older traditions of the very parties that served as their vehicles. The 1990s neo-liberal globalization rhetoric is determinedly anti-traditional, demanding dedication to unrelenting change and remorseless discarding of old ways and inherited allegiances. The "progressive" thrust of neo-liberal rhetoric helps explain the relative ease with which centre-left governments have slipped into the same broad policy lines as their more conservative predecessors. New Labour professes a commitment to "modernization" that differs only in some details from the Thatcherite renovation of antiquated British institutions that came before Blair.

Perhaps there is more in common between the 1960s and 1980s [counter]revolutions than meets the eye. This was amusingly illustrated by the furore set off in Canada when the Bank of Montreal capped an advertising campaign that featured ordinary people holding up hand-lettered protest signs with a notorious appropriation of 1960s' icon Bob Dylan's song, *The Times They Are a' Changin'*. Aging sixties veterans expressed indignation at the conscription of this hallowed protest song in the service of corporate capitalism. Perhaps Dylan himself, who licensed the bank to use his music, understood something that his fans could not, or would not, admit: the words of sixties protest fit seamlessly into nineties corporate rhetoric. Dylan sang of "change" without content, as a "happening" (to use another sixties catch phrase, as in Dylan's sneering "Something is happenin', but you don't know what it is, do you, Mr. Jones?"). The answer was "blowin' in the wind." What wind? The wind of change, presumably. In *The Times* ..., Dylan is brutally direct: "You'd better start swimmin', Or you'll sink like a stone, For the times they are a'changin'."

One of the MBanx ads features a young boy blandly declaring, with apparent wisdom beyond his years: "Change is good." Once, change may have meant social justice and personal liberation, racial and gender equality. This time change is global competition, restructuring, and innovation — not to forget, of course, mega bank mergers. In both instances, the normative message is the same: swim with the tide (whatever it is) or you will "sink like a stone." This is amoral prescription. Then and now, it has the same effect. It is precisely what George Grant long ago identified as a primary error of modernity, the confusion of necessity with goodness.[6] That it is now self-proclaimed "conservatives" who are stridently asserting that what must happen is what ought to happen gives ironic substance to Grant's dictum concerning the impossibility of conservatism in our era.

If the old right and old left have both been bypassed by "history," we might examine the ground of "necessity" on which most of the current political contenders stand. What has shifted so decisively under our feet? The answers to this question are many, and some have even become so familiar as to become clichés. But leaving aside pseudo-explanations like "globalization" that substitute labels for causes, I would like to consider the conjuncture of two sets of factors, one political and the other broadly technological, that may cast light on where we are going. The first set relates to the transformation of the terms of domestic political discourse in relation to the changing political economy of the state. The second has to do with the impact of new information technologies. In putting forward these factors, I am not claiming definitiveness, by any means, merely relevance. Both sets of factors impact on the state, and have had the effect of hastening the decentring of the state, and of encouraging the diffusion and dispersal of power.

The expansion of the liberal social welfare state in the 1960s and 1970s and the reaction and cutbacks of the 1980s and 1990s have been well-documented and subject to much polemical interpretation. What I find more interesting is the way in which the rise and decline of the liberal welfare state has transformed the terms of political discourse, and the ways in which the state is perceived. Prior to the 1960s, there had been a certain acceptance, across a broad range of Canadian society, that the "community" and the "state" had some shared identity. The state, or the Crown in specifically Canadian usage, could stand in for the community when actions were needed to be taken in the community's name. Two world wars and a Cold War focused and strengthened this association of the state as agent for the community. Although there was a competitive political system, partisan competition usually stopped short of questioning the foundations of the community itself and the legitimacy of the state as the community's agent. This is well illustrated by the key role that social democracy played in legitimating a Cold-War consensus in Canadian society in the 1940s and 1950s, and in approving Canadian membership in NATO and NORAD.[7] Even though social democrats were themselves being marginalized as a result of an aggressively anti-communist and anti-left ideological consensus, they shared enough in the sense of community to defer to the state's leading role in defining Canada's position in the world and in drawing the boundaries around the politically acceptable and unacceptable. Generally, the three leading political narratives that interpreted politics to Canadians — liberalism, conservatism, and social democracy — arranged themselves in a competitive-complementary configuration that reproduced the legitimacy of the state as agent of the community.

The decay of political narratives has been a widely noted phenomenon throughout western societies. The relative decline of the power and influence of the great institutions of civil society, be it established churches, trade unions, or political parties shadow or reflect the weakening of traditional intellectual and moral certitudes that have been described as constituting a crisis of authority or a crisis of legitimacy. The state in democratic societies, with its inbuilt expectations of public accountability, has suffered a particular loss of public esteem and a rise of distrust toward its role. Nor have corporations escaped the generalized suspicion of large institutions and their self-justifying rationales. The impact on previously dominant political narratives has been devastating: the great "isms" of western political life have fallen into discredit and disarray. The effects have been most dramatic on the left, where greater weight had always been placed on ideology, but political narratives of the centre and right have not been immune to a decay that is no less ruinous for being less visible.

If there has been a generalized legitimacy crisis in western democracies, Canada has found itself on the cutting edge, with the effects already more apparent than in most other western countries. Canada has been particularly exposed because the Canadian state as a political space has been under severe pressure, from both within and without, for an extended period of time. Global market forces have eroded the capacity of the Canadian national state to act effectively as an economic manager, while the rise of the Quebec sovereignty movement has brought the political legitimacy of the state and the constitution into question. The implicit social contract that underlay postwar relations between government, business, and labour has broken down with the assault on the welfare state and the triumph of an anti-statist neo-liberal model of fiscal and monetary policy; while this has happened elsewhere, it has coincided in Canada with a persistent questioning of the fundamental political basis of the state, embodied in two Quebec secession referenda in 15 years, with another on the horizon. A populist and egalitarian attack on the older elite-driven structures of governance (in which the older political narratives were deeply implicated) has eroded the trust and deference that underpinned the political process. The legitimacy crisis in Canada is thus compounded, with the different elements playing against one another in unpredictable ways.

With the decline and crisis of the older political narratives, what has taken their place? The discourse of neo-liberalism seems triumphant throughout the western world, but it is not really a replacement for a *political* narrative, being mainly an economic model that fails to address deep needs for political expression and communitarian identity. At best, it must be dressed up in borrowed clothes which lend a popular legitimacy that hardly arises from the technocratic discourse itself. In Canada two new narrative streams have begun to reshape political space. One is the *politics of identity*, a phenomenon dialectically related to the crisis and decline of the national state. Identity politics is, in Manuel Castells' words, "the process of construction of meaning on the basis of a cultural attribute, or related set of cultural attributes, that is/are given priority over other sources of meaning."[8] Identities are subnational and refocus attention and loyalties away from the national state toward attributes that emphasize differences,[9] rather than universality, among the constituent elements of the political order. The most salient attributes of identity politics have been culture, language, ethnicity, gender, and sexual orientation — with the first two being especially powerful in Canada. The most spectacular case of identity politics is the Quebec sovereignty movement, which seeks fulfilment in secession from the Canadian political community altogether. Sovereignist parties have rewritten the scripts of Quebec-Canada politics, first at the provincial level beginning in the 1970s, and then at the federal level in the 1990s. Although generally stopping short of secession, aboriginal demands for self-government and recognition as a "third order" of government (after the federal and provincial levels) are founded firmly on the idea of cultural self-determination. Gender and race/ethnicity have also come to play leading roles in defining the political agenda. The constitutional politics that has come to such prominence in the past two decades (itself an indication of drastically changing parameters of political space) has not only focused on questions of accommodation/separation of Quebec, but on aboriginal claims, and on equity and recognition demands around gender, ethnicity, and culture: adversarial litigation around the equality sections of the Charter of Rights has paralleled debates over the constitutional extension of these rights. First bilingualism, then multiculturalism, and (multi-ethnic) immigration have generated deep and often very divisive political controversy.

The second new political narrative generated by contemporary crisis has been what I call the "new populism." While some have spoken of a neo-conservative discourse that emerged in the 1980s, combining so-called moral majoritarianism, the Christian Right and "family values," along with anti-statism and economic *laissez-faire*, this American-style description misses much of the Canadian reality. Here, the impact of the Quebec sovereignty movement on the rest of the country, through two Quebec referenda and three rounds of attempted constitutional reform within a decade and a half, cannot be discounted. An English-Canadian reaction to "special treatment" of Quebec and a demand for recognition of the equality of the provinces has developed in tandem with a strong populist reaction to the elite accommodation model of federalism which had previously dominated. This combined with a reaction to the liberal welfare state, its mushrooming deficits and rising tax burden, and its redistributionist politics, especially as it appeared to favour "special treatment for special interests." The new populism integrates neo-liberal economic policies with anti-welfare state social conservatism (the market will provide a "fairer" system of redistribution than the politically-biassed welfare state); it also seeks to democratize the political system to allow the majority to take control back from the minorities and special interests. This new political narrative has made some inroads across the political spectrum, but it has found its most focused image in the Reform Party, which in a very short period of time has displaced the older conservative narrative, and its increasingly incoherent political expression in the Conservative Party. In the latter, traditional Tory themes stressing the organic nature of society, historical continuity through the monarchy and the British connection, and slow, evolutionary change, gave way during the Mulroney years to the replacement of politics by markets on both the national and international stages, reductions in public services, and tax cuts. "Red" Tories like Joe Clark and Hugh Segal[10] seem occasionally unhappy contemplating the results of this shift, but the continued domination of the remnants of the Conservative Party by their wing simply results in a continued division with the Reform Party that benefits the Liberals, while hardly posing a coherent national conservative alternative to either Reform or the Liberals.

The new populism is indeed new, even though it incorporates older elements in its discourse. Above all, it is in a dialectical relationship with identity politics, being in some measure a reaction to gains (modest though they may be) made by groups seeking recognition and benefits via the liberal welfare state. Similarly, identity politics sharpens group consciousness and feeds politicization as these gains (seen as rights and entitlements) are rolled back in the downsizing of the state. Just as the older, now eclipsed, narratives played together systematically, so too identity politics and the new populism operate together in an antagonistic/complementary way, competing with one another, yet at the same time drawing both energy and self-definition from the very existence and threat of their antagonist. This process was highlighted dramatically in the 1997 federal election when the Reform Party targeted "Quebec politicians" as the enemies of national unity, while the Bloc Québécois pointed to Reform's anti-Quebec stance to rally Quebecers back to the sovereignist cause.

There is one dramatic difference between the old and new dialectic of political narratives. The old narrative system presupposed, as I have suggested, a consensual notion of community that transcended politics. The state had a double identity, both as *government*, which was under partisan control, and the *state as embodiment of community*, which was beyond partisanship. The new narrative system tends to weaken consensual identification with the community, as it is the very boundaries of the community itself, the terms of citizenship, that are part of the problematic of political controversy. The state loses yet more obviously: generalized distrust of the state comes from all sides. The populists see the state as a blockage to private sector economic growth, and as the mechanism for redistributing resources away from the taxpaying majority and into the hands of the special interests. Identity politics advocates on the other hand increasingly see the state as attacking their rights and their social programs as a direct result of neo-liberal restructuring and majoritarian backlash against groups seeking equity.

It is important to realize that in the new dialectic of Canadian politics, the contested nature of the state — decentred, battered, and in retreat as it may be, is still an influential presence. Indeed, its very displacement from the centre defines the political agenda, even if only negatively. Alan Cairn's article on the "embedded state" remains crucial, even when the state is under attack.[11] Political agendas on all sides are set in relation to the state as either a positive or negative presence. This leads to what is, by traditional standards, an unprecedented degree of ideological incoherence. Is the Parti Québécois/Bloc Québécois a "left" or "right" party, a "progressive" or "reactionary" force? How is that Reform, a party of the "right," with a neo-liberal economic agenda, is the leading advocate of expanded grassroots democratic reform? Why are the social democrats the most "conservative" political force, in terms of defending existing institutions against pervasive changes, which are in turn directed enthusiastically by parties of the centre-right? Is this muddle, or is it a new political dialectic?

For an example of the philosophical discontinuity in Canadian politics, we might look at the hepatitis C controversy in the spring of 1998. A group of Canadians, the precise numbers being in doubt but probably somewhere in the five figure range, have contracted a debilitating liver disease from unsafe blood transfusions (a larger number have contracted the disease from unsanitary needle use, etc.). The federal government, after intensive consultation and negotiation with the provinces, had agreed to provide compensation to victims who had contracted the disease from tainted blood from 1986 to 1990, a period during which tests for blood supplies had been available, but were not used. Those who had contracted the disease prior to 1986 were not to be covered by the compensation package, on the principle that neither the government nor the Red Cross had been negligent during that period, in the absence of firm medical knowledge about the dangers of untested blood. The federal health minister, Allan Rock, although personally in favour of compensating all victims, agreed to present the common front of all Canadian health ministers. Not surprisingly, the various advocacy groups representing the victims shouted foul, and sections of the media reported their objections sympathetically. Rock reiterated that a deal was a deal, and that opening up the door to compensation for all victims, even in the absence of malpractice or negligence on the part of the government, could, by extension to other potential health areas, bankrupt the medicare system.

Once the issue reached Parliament, relative ideological coherence fell apart totally. The Reform Opposition, sensing a popular issue, abandoned fiscal probity for a newly found sense of "compassion" for victims. Allan Rock, hated by Reform for his left-liberal actions such as the gun control legislation in the previous Parliament, was now depicted as "hard-hearted" and lacking in compassion; his resignation was demanded daily. The Quebec National Assembly, on a motion drafted by the leader of the opposition, unanimously moved that all hepatitis C victims should be fully compensated — by Ottawa. The premier of Ontario, Mike Harris, leader of a "Common Sense Revolution" that was bitterly dividing Ontario society by wholesale assaults on the entire fabric of social programs in the province, announced that Ontario would "do the right thing" and come up with more of its own money to spur greater federal spending. The Ontario health minister then walked angrily out of a hastily reconvened federal-provincial meeting that failed to alter the earlier consensus. A poll found that no less than 87 percent of Ontarians agreed with their provincial government on the issue.

Apart from brazen displays of sheer hypocrisy and political opportunism — hardly new elements in our public life — this bizarre controversy, which completely dominated the media for weeks on end, is notable for exposing the ineradicable embeddedness of the state. Having assumed overall responsibility for the health-care system through medicare, the state had also assumed ultimate responsibility for the safety of the blood system administered by a non-governmental monopoly, the Canadian Red Cross Society. When things went badly wrong, as they had with HIV infection through tainted blood, a royal commission recommended compensation for all victims. In the case of hepatitis C, governments at both levels had tried to draw a line on the principle of fault/no fault. That at least was a coherent principle, balancing the rights of victims with fiscal responsibility for tax dollars. The capacity of the advocacy groups to present hepatitis C sufferers as victims through "no fault of their own" quickly established in public opinion a putative entitlement to compensation from the state that undermined the authority of consensual federal-provincial public policy. Parties like Reform and the Ontario Tories, who normally are extremely leery of groups claiming victim status and who regularly denounce the idea of entitlements for special interest groups, apparently found no difficulty in wearing "compassion" on their sleeves for this particular group of victims. The leader of the opposition, Preston Manning, solved the question of the fiscal implications, to his satisfaction at least, by insisting that compensation should come out of the health-care spending envelope. In other words, other Canadians dependent upon health programs would have to accept less so that hepatitis C sufferers should get more. New populism tries to construct an undifferentiated image of the "people" in theory, but in practice, new populists opt for this or that particular segment as standing in for the people and deserving of special treatment. New populism meets old social welfarism.

It would be easy to denounce the arbitrary and incoherent nature of Manning-Harris "compassion" as a public policy prescription. But it would be less than honest not to admit that some of the same arbitrary and incoherent reasoning went into the growth of the liberal welfare state. There has never been a consistent public standard governing the extension of state services and programs — or their retraction. In a pluralist democracy with a competitive party system, the old dictum that "the squeaky wheel gets the grease" has some descriptive merit, but it has never been very compelling as public policy, then or now. As the state is downsized, it appears at one level as more decentred. Yet at other levels, the state remains embedded throughout the society. No political party or political narrative can escape persistent engagement with the state. Nor can any participant in politics escape the requirement for constantly renegotiating the relationship between the state and different groups and segments of the society. Both positive and negative redistribution involve redefinition of the interface between state and society, and in the current era of long-term fiscal restraint, redistribution tends to be both positive and negative at the same time. To Mike Harris, hepatitis C victims are deserving, but single mothers on welfare are not. To federal Liberals, students are worth a multibillion dollar federal investment in scholarships to offset Ottawa's cutback of transfers to the provinces for postsecondary education, but health-care users whose hospitals have been closed and medical services restricted as a partial result of federal cutbacks in health transfers, are apparently to look to their provincial governments for relief. One would search in vain for any consistency in the current ideological maps, but there is one common factor: everything in politics continues to relate primarily to the state, to its simultaneous expansion/contraction.

The incoherence runs deeper yet, when redistribution is set within the context of the rights culture and the mechanisms that have been created to arbitrate rights claims. This is illustrated by the decision of the Canadian Human Rights Tribunal in 1998 to award somewhere between two and four billion dollars (the precise amount is in dispute) to some 200,000 female federal public servants whose union had complained they had not received "equal pay for work of equal value" according to a formula recognized by the tribunal but not written in the original statute, and not enshrined in the language of the collective agreement signed by the union before appealing. Armed with a conflicting judgement of the federal court in another pay equity case, the federal government chose to appeal this ruling, its own offer of a smaller settlement having been rejected by the union. The decision to appeal brought down a firestorm of criticism on the Liberals for allegedly holding the human rights of women public servants in contempt. If they had not appealed, they would have faced at least as fierce criticism from the opposite direction for squandering taxpayers' money on "special interests." The point here is not the justice of the case, but rather the implications for government and public policy. As *Globe and Mail* columnist Jeffrey Simpson not unreasonably asked, if the government had decided to spend a few billion dollars to assist low-paid women in Canada, would it have directed it at this relatively small, and not disproportionately disadvantaged, group of women?[12] What rational public policy criterion privileged federal public servants over, say, single mothers on welfare, as worthy recipients of two to four billion dollars in compensation? The less than rational criterion was apparently the leverage exercised by a union armed with a statute and the Charter of Rights, the interpretation of which would be determined by a tribunal setting its own formula, quite independently of either the will of Parliament or the policy priorities of the government.

Both the hepatitis C and the pay equity controversies can be taken as emblematic of a deep dilemma surrounding the rules governing the simultaneous expansion/contraction of the state. Public policy in the allocation of the fiscal dividend between debt retirement, tax reductions, and increased social expenditure is held hostage to forces that are outside parliamentary or even more broadly democratic control. Just as anthropomorphized global "market forces" demand deficit elimination, debt retirement, and downsizing of the welfare state, so too the relatively small margin for new or increased social expenditure freed up by a balanced budget is constricted by rights claims of particular groups that, if accepted at face value, have the effect of trumping the claims of other groups. In both cases, the state and its policy "makers" are immobilized, buffeted this way and that by forces that elude their grasp. Yet paradoxically the state remains the focal point for all these intersecting pressures.

To this point, I have been looking mainly at issues about social programs. But many of the same observations could be made about the state's role in the economy. Public ownership has become passé; the public sector in the provision of goods and services has shrunk considerably, and will continue to shrink in the immediate future. Deregulation has become as fashionable as government intervention has become unfashionable. Yet deregulation regimes are still state-directed regimes that require extensive deregulatory regulations, and in which delegation to the private sector does not eliminate state responsibility when things go wrong (as in issues around air traffic and airport safety). Governments at both levels continue to manipulate the tax system to encourage the private sector, and to offer inducements of various kinds for new investment. Governments express deep concern about fostering global competitiveness and to this end strive for partnerships with the private sector. All this is symbolized in the federal-provincial-corporate trade missions abroad. "Team Canada" is a public-private partnership for mutual benefit, and it is also a federal-provincial partnership. Even the sovereignist premier of Quebec puts on the metaphorical team sweater and joins the lineup. The prime minister is the "captain" of Team Canada, but the other players, both premiers and business people, are equally important. And Canadian exporters and investors know full well that it is the presence of the federal and provincial government leaders that gives them additional credibility in swinging deals and signing contracts. Team Canada is a kind of metaphor for a decentred but diffusely embedded state.

There is convincing evidence of the diffusion and multiplicity of power and authority in the global economy, and of the "retreat of the state" from the centre of global governance.[13] While there are a number of forces contributing to this, the revolution in communications brought about by the new information technologies is particularly striking.[14] The new technologies, by abolishing the barriers of space, leap effortlessly across borders, and undermine the old, centralized hierarchies of power. The "network society"[15] spawns new organizational forms: corporations, with their capacity for flexibility and market-responsive behaviour, are better adapted than states for taking advantage of the new opportunities. Capital flows around the globe in cyberspace, while governments remain fixed within antiquated national boundaries. Some have gone so far as to predict a new era of "virtual feudalism" in which private economic forces more or less displace states altogether.[16] The Canadian state is widely viewed as particularly susceptible to the corrosive pressures of globalization, weakened as it is by internal divisions, and deeply penetrated by foreign ownership and direct investment.

This picture is persuasive, but the extrapolation of the state's retreat into terminal decline is highly exaggerated. Leo Panitch has argued that globalization is to a considerable degree the result of conscious state design.[17] But the effects of globalization have also created a Hobbesian problem of disorder and insecurity that will require cooperative state regulation. In 1998, the Asian financial crisis and the Russian economic meltdown, and the threat of further instability in world markets, have called into serious question the capacity of the existing institutions of neo-liberal global regulation, mainly the International Monetary Fund (IMF) and the World Bank, to control the downward spiral. Leading capitalists like George Soros have raised the need for renewed state regulation and control. To be effective, such a regulatory regime would have to be cooperative on a global scale, but might include various forms of controls over capital flows that would be exercised by individual states. It is of interest that the Canadian government, through federal Finance Minister Paul Martin, have been especially vocal about the need to explore new forms of cooperative regulation.[18]

Environmental degradation is a particularly pressing example of the diseconomies of globalization that will require bringing the state back in. Even the networked, informational economy is engaged in production that is not abstract, but material. Material production and the consumption of resources have environmental consequences, as most of us are only too well aware; and these consequences are often cumulative and very, very costly indeed, and may perhaps even be fatal. A future globe in which all political and regulatory power is effectively dispersed to an evanescent multitude of profit-seeking private parties with short organizational life spans and limited institutional identities, each pursuing the micro-rationality of immediate economic self-interest, is surely a prescription for global environmental degradation on a life-threatening scale: a macro-irrationality of staggering proportions. I suggest that this very gap is already being recognized in the contemporary global political economy, and is actually pushing states, otherwise in retreat, to assert a serious presence in global authority and decision making. Environmental degradation is in no one's interest in the larger sense, even if in the narrow microeconomic sense, profit-seeking activity that produces environmental devastation is "rational." So long as regulation of self-destructive behaviour is universal, so that no one party loses competitive advantage by accepting limitations on its activity in relation to other, unregulated competitors, there is no real loss, only general betterment. This means global regulation.

There exists, however, only one site for effective enforcement of environmental rules, the nation-state; global regulation requires binding agreements among governments — with teeth, which is to say, individual states with the strength and will to compel private actors within their jurisdictions to comply. Hence, the tentative steps in the 1990s toward state-to-state cooperation to control damage to the ozone layer and greenhouse gas emissions. How well these specific agreements will work in practice is debatable, but the enactment in principle of cooperation among (relatively strong) states in enforcing global environmental rules is likely only the beginning for more such agreements in other areas of common concern and common danger. Contemporary capitalism has the capacity to threaten the global ecological balance — and thus its own security.

There are other forms of global insecurity. Transnational corporations are threatened in their global business dealings by "illegitimate" actors whose operations are themselves global in scope: terrorists, some political, some non-political, who attack corporate executives or hold them to ransom, or threaten the security of corporate investments; transnational organized crime that may be in drug traffic, illegal arms trade, gambling, prostitution, or even in legitimate "front" activities; money laundering as a global financing mechanism for all types of illegal activities; and systematic corruption of vulnerable governments. There are eerie parallels between criminal activities and the global economy. Mafias are organized along networked lines that ignore borders and national jurisdictions, just as transnational corporations tend to operate. They not only utilize the new information technologies to do business, they have restructured their own organizational forms to take advantage of the opportunities of the new technologies: flexibility in seeking out and seizing opportunities, an ability to strike strategic alliances and partnerships and an ability to dissolve these briskly when they no longer serve a purpose. Finally, they have shown considerable capacity to exploit the new technologies for their own purposes through inventive forms of "cyber crime."

The "global criminal economy," embodied in money laundering, has, in Manuel Castells' words, become a "significant and troubling component of global financial flows and stock markets," but "the impact of crime on state institutions and politics is even greater. State sovereignty, already battered by the processes of globalization ... is directly threatened by flexible networks of crime that bypass controls, and assume a level of risk that no other organizations are capable of absorbing."[19] But even if directly threatened, states are made even more necessary than ever, precisely because of the threat. In the face of pervasive transborder threats, which we might call the dark side of globalization, "legitimate" private interests are relatively helpless without the assistance of states and their extensive policing, security and intelligence apparatuses, expertise, and enforcement powers.

As Hobbes lucidly and convincingly argued in the seventeenth century, at the birth of the market, unregulated markets alone could not guarantee fulfilment of contractual obligations, or even security of property. Left to its own devices in the "state of nature" without government, the market is a war of all against all, where life is "solitary, poor, nasty, brutish, and short."[20] The way out of this dilemma is the social contract, whereby everyone agrees to transfer their power to the sovereign: a common power over all who can impartially enforce contractual obligations and make the market work. Thus the historical conjuncture between the rise of capitalism and the relatively strong nation-state. Today's global economy has freed capitalism from the constraints of the nation-state, and transnational capitalism is making the most of its freedom. But as Hobbes understood, the state not only constrains but protects and enables. Contemporary global economic competition threatens to reproduce some of the conditions of Hobbes' state of nature. Clearly there cannot and will not be any global Leviathan reproducing the terms and conditions of a universalized Hobbesian social contract. The structural conditions for centralized, absolute sovereign authority have slipped away, even at the level of the nation-state, let alone on a global scale. The conditions of global competition will require, if not a global Leviathan, as such, then at least a functional equivalent thereof.

Why should transnational corporations undertake the huge investments in human and material resources required to equip themselves with a capacity that replicates what large states already possess — and at the same time gird themselves for the intimate, perpetual and immensely difficult cooperation with their competitors that would be necessary to run an effective global security operation? Why not instead urge their respective states to cooperate closely on their behalf in policing the emergent global economy, so that they can get on with their primary business, making money? That is precisely what transnational corporations are doing at the end of the twentieth century, and in the process are encouraging a level of strong state activity and strong state cooperation.

This is not to say that states will continue to look like states have looked in the past. Already states are recreating themselves along less overarching and more flexible lines. States, which of course are not all equal, with many weak and a few relatively strong, may become more specialized entities, retaining functions for which they possess a comparative advantage over the private sector, while dropping others altogether or assigning them to the private sector. Nor will states be in any sense stand-alone entities. Rather they, too, will constantly be forming and reforming transnational networks and alliances with other states, with corporations and other private sector actors, and with non-governmental groups and movements.

One area in which states do have a comparative advantage over corporations is in the exercise of coercion. The technologies of surveillance and repression may be developed in the private sector for profit, but they will be deployed and exercised more by states, and by state networks. Whether confronting the perceived security threat of immigrants and refugees to the prosperous West with transnational police cooperation, shared databases and sophisticated technologies of political control,[21] or with the awesome panoply of surveillance powers from spy satellites to communications intercepts deployed against terrorists or suspected terrorists, cross-border networks of cooperation in coercion are sophisticated and well-developed. These are the kinds of things states and state agencies do rather well, and that they will concentrate upon and specialize in. But they will not do them as ends in themselves, or as means to the pure self-aggrandizement of the state. Rather, the exercise of coercion will be a functional specialization within a complex, networked world. In this context, the Canadian state has a global future, although certainly not as a stand-alone entity.

Another blindspot in the neo-liberal globalization agenda is the idea that market forces will proceed to their ultimate logical conclusion without any effective resistance, on a global scale, of those marginalized and excluded from the benefits. This is quite absurd, and flies in the face of history. Nor is there any reason to imagine, along with the bland theorists of corporate hegemony, that only the capitalist enterprise will be able to grasp and successfully exploit the new organizational forms that the new informational technologies encourage and reward. Networking for resistance is part of a new dialectic of power and ideology that cuts across national boundaries. The *Zapatista* movement in Chiapas province, Mexico is the best known example of an "informational revolutionary" movement, where the Internet has been a weapon of struggle. There are examples closer to home, including the spectacular victory achieved by the Cree of northern Quebec over the Quebec government and Hydro-Québec in the cancellation of the "Great Whale" or James Bay 2 hydroelectric megaproject. The Cree skilfully networked to mobilize international opinion against the project.

Another recent example of networking for resistance is the successful campaign against the Multilateral Agreement on Investment (MAI). This proposed agreement, hammered out in secret by governments under the aegis of the Organization for Economic Cooperation and Development (OECD), would have instituted binding rules on treatment of foreign investors.[22] Everything was proceeding smoothly behind closed doors, until a Canadian public interest advocacy group got its hands on a draft of the agreement. As *The Globe and Mail* describes subsequent events:

> High-powered politicians had reams of statistics and analysis on why a set of international investing rules would make the world a better place. They were no match, however, for a global band of grassroots organizations, which, with little more than computers and access to the Internet, helped derail a deal. Indeed, international negotiations have been transformed after [the] successful rout of the Multilateral Agreement on Investment (MAI) by opposition groups, which — alarmed by the trend toward economic globalization — used some globalization of their own to fight back.[23]

The Canadians, many of whom like Maude Barlow and Tony Clarke, had previously been involved in unsuccessful campaigns against the implementation of the Canada-US Free Trade Agreement of 1989 and the subsequent NAFTA treaty, had learned from the shortcomings of their earlier pre-cyberspace campaigns. This time they linked with online groups in other countries, such as the Malaysian-based Third World Network. Every bit of new information about the secret draft agreement was instantly made available, and critical analysis of the MAI's implications for national governments sped quickly around the globe. Information gathered in one country that might prove embarrassing to a government in another was quickly publicized. Caught in their own secrecy, national governments were crippled in their capacity to respond. Indeed, non-governmental groups became better informed about the details and implications of the MAI than many of the government ministers they were confronting. A global wave of protest engulfed the OECD negotiators, who admitted defeat in early 1998. "'This is the first successful Internet campaign by non-governmental organizations,' said one diplomat involved in the negotiations. 'It's been very effective.'" Having blocked the draft agreement, the same groups are anxious to play a more positive role in the future, to make constructive proposals for what ought to be in trade agreements, for example, rather than simply opposing what government negotiators propose. As Tony Clarke puts it: "We're against this model of economic globalization. But the global village, the idea of coming together and working together, is a great dream."[24]

If the domestic ideological map has become blurred and confused, there are new ideological maps that are being drawn that are transnational. They may be mainly negative in their impact as yet, but even in this form they present the challenge of "negarchy" — the power to negate, limit, or constrain arbitrary power.[25] Less obviously, the growing importance of NGOs and global advocacy networks presents middle-power states like Canada with interesting opportunities for strategic partnerships and alliances. Take, for instance, the case of the worldwide campaign against landmines. A cross-border alliance of non-governmental organizations, utilizing such high-profile media personalities as the late Princess Diana, mobilized world opinion and a group of states of middle-power status, led by Canada, that succeeded in establishing a global treaty against landmines, despite the reluctance, if not the opposition of the United States. It is interesting that Canadian initiatives like this tend to command a high level of domestic support that cuts across both ideological and community divides.

The return of the state onto the global stage is unmistakable, but the political meaning of that return is less clear. Some of the role I have described for states is hardly progressive in an economic or social sense. States, including Canada, will tighten cooperative policing and security on behalf of transnational corporations, just as the coercive power of the national state was exercised in the past to protect private domestic corporations. Yet this is only part of the story. Dreams of a new global progressive bloc of the Third World and the underprivileged in the West are no doubt unrealistic, or at worst delirious. Yet the diffuse but growing power of "negarchies" does offer some counter-pressures to the demands of capital. When we consider the problems of instability, insecurity, and diseconomies inherent in the global state of nature, we might discern the faint outlines of a kind of potential global Keynesianism.[26] Like the Keynesianism of the postwar era, this will not be a socialist or even social-democratic vision. Rather it will seek to stabilize and sustain the dominant economic and social order. Unlike neo-liberalism, however, it will seek to do so by strategic compromises and concessions to oppositional forces, as the price of order. The alternative may be very dark and threatening indeed: militaristic, authoritarian states employing racism and xenophobia as regime-supports and a slide into war and genocide — in other words, a globalized replay of the experience of interwar Europe. This alternative is so ugly that neo-Keynesianism has much to commend it, both to governments and transnational capital and to oppositional forces. There is a distinct role here for Canada to play as a broker and as a middle-power voice for rational compromise. And it is one that should garner considerable domestic support, strengthening the bonds of national community.

In conclusion, this essay has been highly speculative. When the ground is shifting under our feet, it is often difficult to get our bearings. I hope to have suggested at least some of the directions in which things are moving. Among these is the strong implication that while the Canadian state is changing, change does not mean decline or disappearance.

NOTES

1. The challenges of European union have raised questions of national identity and national sovereignty, nowhere more acutely than in the United Kingdom where widespread "Euroscepticism" is matched by the internal strains of Scottish and Welsh nationalism and the persistent problem of Ulster. Devolution of powers to Scottish and Welsh parliaments, and the intriguing framework in the proposed Northern Irish peace process for Protestant-Catholic cooperative self-government within the context of overlapping Anglo-Irish sovereignties, raise a series of issues in British governance that create eerie parallels to the Canadian experience. This time it is the former colonial state that can offer the lessons of history and experience to the old mother country.

2. Donald V. Smiley, *The Canadian Political Nationality* (Toronto: Methuen, 1967).

3. Reg Whitaker, "Images of the State in Canada," in *The Canadian State: Political Economy and Political Power,* ed. Leo Panitch (Toronto: University of Toronto Press, 1977), pp. 28-70; also, in Reg Whitaker, *A Sovereign Idea: Essays on*

Canada as a Democratic Community (Montreal and Kingston: McGill-Queen's University Press, 1992), pp. 3-45.

4.   Reg Whitaker, "Canadian Politics at the End of the Millennium: Old Dreams, New Nightmares," in *A Passion for Identity*, ed. David Taras and Beverly Rasporich, 3d ed. (Toronto: ITP Nelson, 1997), pp. 119-38.

5.   Harvey Lazar, "Non-Constitutional Renewal: Toward a New Equilibrium in the Federation," in *Canada: the State of the Federation 1997: Non-Constitutional Renewal,* ed. Harvey Lazar (Kingston: Institute of Intergovernmental Relations, Queen's University, 1998), p. 21.

6.   George Grant, *Lament For a Nation: the Defeat of Canadian Nationalism* (Toronto: McClelland & Stewart, 1964).

7.   Reg Whitaker and Gary Marcuse, *Cold War Canada: The Making of a National Insecurity State, 1945-1957* (Toronto: University of Toronto Press, 1994).

8.   Manuel Castells, *The Information Age: Economy, Society and Culture*, vol. 2, *The Power of Identity* (Oxford: Blackwell, 1997), p. 6.

9.   By speaking of difference in opposition to universality, I am not supporting the controversial insistence of some liberal analysts that there is an *intention to divide* implicit in identity politics. Indeed, the politics of difference may often reflect a desire for equity, and thus a fuller sharing in the wider community, rather than for separatism, but it is premised upon the *recognition of difference*. See Charles Taylor, *Multiculturalism and the Politics of Recognition* (Princeton, NJ: Princeton University Press, 1992).

10. See Hugh Segal, *Beyond Greed: A Traditional Conservative Confronts Neoconservative Excess* (Toronto: Stoddard, 1997). The increasing incoherence of the Conservative Party is further illustrated by the support of another old "Red" Tory, Dalton Camp, for the bizarre campaign of anti-free trade zealot David Orchard for the party leadership in 1998.

11. Alan Cairns, "The Embedded State: State-Society Relations in Canada," in *State and Society in Canada: Comparative Perspectives,* ed. Keith Banting, Research Studies of the Royal Commission on the Economic Union and Development Prospects for Canada, vol. 31 (Toronto: University of Toronto Press, 1986), pp. 53-86.

12. Jeffrey Simpson, "C'mon, folks, a little common sense," *The Globe and Mail,* 12 August 1998.

13. Susan Strange, *The Retreat of the State: The Diffusion of Power in the World Economy* (Cambridge: Cambridge University Press, 1996).

14. Ronald J. Diebert, *Parchment, Printing, and Hypermedia: Communications in World Order Transformation* (New York: Columbia University Press, 1997).

15. Manuel Castells, *The Information Age: Economy, Society and Culture*, vol. 1, *The Rise of the Network Society* (Oxford: Blackwell, 1996).

16. Abbe Mowshowitz, "Virtual Feudalism," in *Beyond Calculation: The Next Fifty Years of Computing,* ed. Peter J. Denning and Robert M. Metcalfe (New York: Springer-Verlag, 1997), pp. 213-31. I have challenged this concept at some length

in Reg Whitaker, *The End of Privacy: How Total Surveillance is Becoming a Reality* (New York: The New Press, 1999), ch. 7.

17. Leo Panitch, "Globalization and the State," *Socialist Register 1994* (London: Merlin Press, 1994).

18. See, for instance, Shawn McCarthy, "Martin Maps Out Plan to Deal with Global Economic Crises," *The Globe and Mail,* 30 September 1998, p. B6.

19. Manuel Castells, *The Information Age*, vol. 3, *End of Millennium* (Oxford: Blackwell, 1998), pp. 201-02.

20. Hobbes, *Leviathan* I:13.

21. This is certainly the case in "Fortress Europe": Michael Spencer, *States of Injustice: A Guide to Human Rights and Civil Liberties in the European Union* (London: Pluto Press, 1995); Tony Bunyan (ed.), *Statewatching the New Europe* (Nottingham: Russell Press, 1993); Steve Wright, *An Appraisal of Technologies for Political Control* (Luxembourg: European Parliament, Directorate General for Research, 1998).

22. Tony Clarke and Maude Barlow, *MAI: The Multilateral Agreement on Investment and the Threat to Canadian Sovereignty* (Toronto: Stoddart, 1997).

23. Madelaine Drohan, "How the Net Killed the MAI: Grassroots Groups Used their own Globalization to Derail Deal," *The Globe and Mail*, 29 April 1998.

24. Ibid.

25. Daniel Deudney, "Binding Powers, Bound States: The Logic and Geopolitics of Negarchy," paper presented at the International Studies Association, Washington, DC, 1994.

26. I am using "Keynesianism" in a generic sense to refer to the idea of a broad cross-class political compromise, not in relation to specific Keynesian fiscal policies, which are now quite outmoded.

3

Two Types of Pluralism in Canada

Avigail Eisenberg

Le fédéralisme et le multiculturalisme représentent deux types de politiques pluralistes dans la mesure où ils visent à distribuer des ressources entre des groupes. Néanmoins, chaque type de pluralisme vise un objet différent. Je soutiens que la distinction entre ces objets a été mal comprise par certains analystes politiques et sociaux. En conséquence, l'interaction entre le fédéralisme et le multiculturalisme a elle aussi été mal comprise. Historiquement, le fédéralisme a été conçu selon une théorie pluraliste visant à limiter la souveraineté de l'État de manière à favoriser la «vie de groupe» à l'intérieur des communautés provinciales. Pour ces premiers pluralistes, c'est dans le contexte du groupe que les individus développaient leur personnalité et que la liberté individuelle était protégée. Au contraire du fédéralisme, le multiculturalisme requiert une intervention étatique plus poussée dans la vie du groupe. Le multiculturalisme vise à améliorer l'égalité sociale en protégeant l'identité du groupe de même que les caractéristiques qui l'informent. La reconnaissance publique des identités est un moyen d'assurer un accès plus équitable aux ressources pour les groupes. L'objectif est donc l'équité entre les groupes et non pas l'autonomie de ceux-ci.

In political analysis, pluralist theories are often employed in discussions about the different ways in which resources can or ought to be distributed to groups. Federalism and multiculturalism[1] are both pluralist policy in the sense that they distribute resources amongst particular groups. Moreover, both types of policies have been historically shaped by pluralist theory. Beyond these features, they have little in common. In fact, their aims are contradictory in some senses. By this, I do not mean to suggest that they are inherently incompatible policies or that they cannot be pursued simultaneously within the same state. However, they have different purposes and, in some cases, impose opposite expectations on the state. In Canada, federalism was historically instituted to limit the authority of the central state, and in so doing, to sustain what pluralists have called "group life," in this case, of provincial communities.[2] In contrast, multiculturalism is meant to advance the social equality of cultural groups and, to this end, it has required that the state become more rather than less involved in the affairs of ethnic minorities.

The two policies seem to clash when their aims are confused — when federalism is viewed as a means to social equality, or when multiculturalism is interpreted as heightening the autonomy of ethnic minorities — as they often are in Canadian political debates. Moreover, the relation between these policies is apt to be misunderstood as creating a competitive relation between ethnic minorities and national groups unless their aims are accurately understood as distinct from each other. The purpose here is to show that distinguishing between federalism and multiculturalism as different pluralist strategies for preserving group life clarifies the tensions that arise between them and why these tensions arise.

I distinguish between the aims of federalism and multiculturalism by discussing both policies in terms of the pluralist strategies they express. Two types of pluralist strategies are particularly relevant to this discussion. The first type is labeled "pluralism to limit state sovereignty" and is associated with the late-nineteenth- and early twentieth-century ideas of Harold Laski and other British pluralists. It divides resources between groups, first, in order to limit the power that any one group can exert over other groups or individuals and second, to sustain group life. The historical and thematic connections between Laski's pluralist ideas and the ideas that inform Canadian federalism are discussed in the first section.

The second section discusses "pluralism to enhance cultural equality" which includes pluralist theories that aim at distributing resources to cultural groups so that individuals can enjoy similar resources regardless of which cultural group they belong to. This second type is informed by ideas that are well-expressed in the writings of Iris Marion Young and Will Kymlicka. The third section shows that, according to the aims of these theories, the more successful a federal system is at limiting the authority of the central state, the less it is able to enhance the social equality of individuals in that state. Conversely, the more successful multiculturalism is at enhancing social equality, the more it expands state power and thus diminishes the autonomy of the groups that are its direct beneficiaries.

PLURALISM TO LIMIT STATE SOVEREIGNTY

Historically, "pluralism to limit state sovereignty" was developed by British pluralists such as Harold Laski, J.N. Figgis, and G.D.H. Cole who sought to discredit the traditional notions of state sovereignty.[3] The mistake of theorists such as Hobbes, Bodin and Austin, according to Laski, was to believe that the central state was the locus of sovereign power. He proposed instead a more sociallygrounded theory of sovereignty which would better capture where sovereignty actually lay and could be reconciled with the limitations that the state imposed upon itself or, as Laski put it, the "conditions it dare not attempt to transgress."[4] Laski highlighted the idea that despite how sovereign power is distributed *de jure* in constitutions, *de facto* the state shared, at times competed for, power with various groups. For example, he argued that Catholic dissent had shaped the British state's authority just as defiant trade unions had led the state to reconsider its position on picketing and strikes.[5] Sovereignty had to be viewed as based in the groups through which individuals lived their lives because only this understanding granted individuals the freedom to decide where their loyalties lie and to be true to their complex natures as "bundles of hyphens" with ties to many different groups.[6]

Federalism was the best system to give expression to the nature of individuals and to the liberty needed to preserve it because, in dividing sovereign power between different groups to which the individual simultaneously belongs, federalism allows individuals to partake in meaningful group life in more local communities while minimizing the risk that these local communities will become powerful enough to oppress and dominate the individual in the way that powerful, closely knit communities sometimes do. Laski stated:

> [f]or where the creative impulses of men are given full play, there is bound to be diversity, and diversity provokes, in its presence, a decentralized organization to support it. That is why the secret of liberty is the division of power. But that political system in which a division of power is most securely maintained is a federal system; and, indeed, there is a close connection between the idea of federalism and the idea of liberty.[7]

So close is this connection, that Laski argued that societies were inherently federal in the sense that, whether the state recognized it or not, power, that is, individual loyalty, is in fact distributed amongst various groups. Constitutions such as Canada's, upon which Laski commented and enthused,[8] merely gave legal expression and capacity to this social reality.[9]

Laski's pluralist arguments, which incidentally changed dramatically in the course of his life, were part of "the federalist feeling" that was widespread in Britain in the early part of the century and which helped to shape understandings of Canadian federalism.[10] Pluralists, such as Laski, saw federalism as the means to protect individual liberty in two senses: (i) by dividing state sovereignty so that no one group was powerful enough to dominate any other group or any individual; and (ii) by enhancing the life of groups in which individuals were directly involved, and which expressed, in some ways, their personality and loyalties. The requirement that sovereign power be situated in many diverse groups was bound to the idea that sovereign power was held by individuals. Groups gave expression to the aggregation of individual power and will.[11] At the same time, groups were the context in which individuals developed their personalities. So, federalism's division of power created local communities that expressed local individual loyalties and in which individuals could meaningfully participate. At the same time, it ensured that no province could entirely dominate an individual's life. Individual loyalty, like individual personality, belonged simultaneously to more than one community: namely, national and provincial communities.

The sort of pluralism for which Laski argued is relevant to Canada in at least two ways. First, as David Schneiderman argues, Laski's arguments may have indirectly shaped the character and history of Canadian federalism through the influence he had over the ideas of his good friend Lord Haldane. Haldane was Lord Chancellor of the Judicial Committee of the Privy Council and is credited in Canada for writing the committee's decisions from 1912 to 1928. These decisions are famous in Canadian federal history for having "shielded provincial authority from the threat of federal domination" by restricting the federal trade and commerce power, narrowing the interpretation of Peace, Order and Good Government, and denying the federal government power to regulate labour relations.[12]

Second, and more generally, Laski's pluralism captures the spirit of federalism in Canada as it was defended by many advocates of provincial rights. Federal-provincial relations from Confederation until approximately World War I are often understood as struggles between rival executives engaged in a zero-sum relation to enhance their own power. This struggle hardly invokes the ideals of group life and individual liberty extolled by Laski's pluralism. However, the principles invoked by those engaged in the debates over provincial rights, in particular the federal use of reservation and disallowance, are similar in two ways to the pluralist ideals that Laski proposed.[13]

First, as in Laski's theory, enhancing provincial rights was understood in the nineteenth and early twentieth centuries primarily as a means to limit the potentially despotic power of the state as wielded in this case by the Dominion executive and the courts. In other words, rather than being struggles between federal and provincial governments, they were often debates about whether to rely on executive or legislative power. According to Richard Risk and Robert Vipond, the provincial rights debates reveal that one of the main distinctions in the nineteenth century between American and Canadian legal culture was that "[f]or Canadian lawyers, the principal threat to individual liberty seemed to come not from tyrannical legislatures but from the arbitrary actions of unaccountable executive authority. In the United States, protecting liberty required placing limits on the power of legislatures. In Canada, protecting liberty meant fostering robust legislatures that would be able to constrain executive power."[14]

Second, decentralized and coordinated federalism was thought by its supporters to express more completely individual personality because it gave more legal standing to the provincial communities to which individuals were loyal and because it ensured that public policy was shaped by the governments of these more local communities, in which members of that community had some control. Provincial rights advocates argued that individual liberty was best protected by recognizing the sovereign power of the legislature over which individuals had some control. In other words, because the "life" of provincial communities was expressed through responsible government, individual liberty was expressed there as well. Anything that limited the supremacy of provincial governments within their areas of jurisdiction — such as disallowance and reservation — threatened the group life of provincial communities and thereby threatened the individual liberty that responsible government had historically protected.

Risk and Vipond point to these characteristics of the provincial rights advocates in a number of debates and legal cases centred around reservation, disallowance, and individual rights. One case which demonstrates in several ways the point being made here involved the *Rivers and Streams Act*. The Act, passed by the Ontario legislature in 1880, regulated property rights by allowing individuals who had improved the waterways to charge tolls to other users. It was introduced four times in the Ontario legislature and disallowed by the federal government three times, which makes it a clear candidate for the zero-sum explanation of Canadian federal-provincial struggles. However, the debates over this Act reveal the pluralist nuance of the provincialist position. The federal government argued that its use of disallowance was justified because the Act violated the constitutional requirement that government protect individual property rights. The provincial government countered that individual rights belong to the local legislature: "the provincial community assembled in the legislature should determine its own needs. The recourse for a minority was not to invoke some external power, but to involve itself in politics."[15] In other words, by defending local self-government, provincialists viewed themselves as defending individual liberty.

In commenting on this and other cases of a similar sort, Risk and Vipond argue that a deep ambiguity lay in the conflation of questions about individual liberty and jurisdictional autonomy. Local self-government is not an adequate "surrogate for the protection of individual rights,"[16] a fact that Canada eventually accepted with the adoption of the *Charter of Rights and Freedoms*. But this surrogacy was precisely what British pluralists like Laski advocated. The trick for Laski, as for provincial rights advocates, was to find a way of sustaining group life while limiting group power. Individualism and individual rights were widely criticized in idealist and pluralist intellectual circles at the turn of the century for undermining group life and community.[17] Without rights, the only way to limit group power would be, first, to divide sovereignty amongst groups and, second, to adhere to the principle of responsible government that sovereignty ultimately rests in the hands of individual voters. Canadian federalism was designed precisely along these lines. And for this reason it invited

Laski's accolades in 1923, when he described it as "a magnificent piece of decentralization."[18]

In sum, Canada's federal system and Laski's pluralism were motivated by some of the same principles. Both expressed a desire to limit state sovereignty and to locate sovereign power in the groups to which individuals were loyal. Both were committed to sustaining group life. And both viewed the division and fragmentation of sovereign power as a means to protect individual liberty.

As optimistic as Laski was about what federalism could accomplish politically, he also recognized its limitations, particularly in the case of Canada. The Canadian federal system, Laski lamented in the early 1920s, only gave power to *territorial* group life whereas the pluralist principle is meant to give expression to *functional* as well as territorial groups.[19] Power, particularly economic power, is distributed and exerted on a non-territorial basis. Individual loyalty is also distributed to territorial and non-territorial groups. In order to attain economic equality, federalist solutions had to become more creative than the territorial, organized federalism of Canada.[20]

By the 1930s, Laski was probably well aware of the ways in which Canada's territorial federalism imposed formidable obstacles to social equality and specifically to the efforts of federal states to develop social welfare programs. In 1925, Lord Haldane, speaking for the Privy Council, struck down the federal *Industrial Disputes Investigation Act,* the effect of which was to remove from the federal government jurisdiction over labour relations.[21] Over 30 years later, F.R. Scott characterized Haldane's judgement as having created a "legal morass in labour matters from which the country has never recovered."[22]

For Scott, the case revealed a more general problem of federalism, namely its potential as a strategy for government inaction:

> If the subject-matter of legislation is too vast for a province to control ... then an interpretation of the constitution which leaves it to the provinces simply means that no government control of any kind is possible. Private interest, whether of capital or labour, or even of both in collusion, dominates the society, and the public interest tends to get lost in the power struggle.[23]

Scott's assessment nicely captures the first and most obvious of two reasons why pluralism to limit state sovereignty is so ill-suited to enhancing social equality: limiting the sovereignty of the central state in order to allow other groups such as provinces, to enjoy a greater share of the power means fragmenting the financial and administrative resources that might be required to institute redistributive programs. This fact is well-known in Canada as federalism is often cited as an obstacle that the welfare state has had to overcome. For example, given the costs involved, Canada would probably not have socialized health care or social welfare assistance if the development of these policies was left entirely to the provinces, as was intended in 1867. This is not to say that provinces are generally less interested in instituting social welfare policies. To the contrary, the local particularities and "group life" of Saskatchewan are largely responsible for generating and implementing socialized health care in the first place. As Laski noted, creativity often accompanies diversity. But creativity is only one of many resources needed to develop social welfare programs. Even without Saskatchewan's Cooperative Commonwealth Federation (CCF) government, Canadians might now be enjoying socialized health care; but it is highly unlikely that the level of health care available to Canadians today would be as widely accessible had the federal government stayed out of this area of provincial jurisdiction.

Another illustration of Scott's point — that protecting the "group life" of provincial communities is sometimes a means to government inaction, or in this case, of diminished government involvement in social welfare programs — is a recent proposal to devolve power over employment insurance (EI) to the provinces. In defending one such restructuring proposal, Gordon Gibson argues that "if the provinces ran the EI program, they could have never afforded the economic distortions that [it] eventually brought us to today."[24] Yet, according to this logic, if the provinces had jurisdiction over EI, they could never have afforded a generous and broad program regardless of whether such a program led to economic distortions or not. Here, the tail wags the dog. A central attraction of Gibson's proposal from a provincialist point of view is that it shrinks considerably the resources required to govern employment, but unsurprisingly, it does this by circumscribing the aims of the program. In doing so, it is clearly better suited to the capabilities of provinces, such as British Columbia, to fund and administer it, as Gibson points out. Yet, surely the more important question is whether it is better suited to the needs of Canada's labour force. My point here is not to dispute the wisdom of decentralizing EI. In fact, decentralizing EI might be a better way of responding to regionally diverse labour forces in Canada.[25] The proposal to decentralize ought to be examined in terms that emphasize what best suits the labour force rather than what best fits a decentralist's agenda.

The second obstacle that pluralism to limit state sovereignty erects against the pursuit of social equality is that it may fragment the social cohesiveness of the broader community by enhancing group life and empowering group loyalties at a subnational, provincial level. This may undermine the success of redistributive programs because such programs work best when individuals are motivated to share their wealth. Individuals are more likely to be thus motivated if they feel part of the same community. One virtue of nationalism is that, when combined with the state's political framework, national solidarity is highly effective at motivating and directing collective action, including collective action of the sort required to redistribute wealth. According to David Miller, "[t]rust requires solidarity not merely within groups but across them, and this in turn depends upon a common identification of the kind that nationality alone can provide."[26] Concerted and cohesive national power, which is needed in order to advance social justice, is precisely the target of a federal system whose purpose is to limit the sovereignty of the central state in order to enhance the group life of provincial communities. Although national redistributive programs are not unworkable within such states, they are often considered either less efficient or less comprehensive than programs in nationally cohesive states.[27]

Canada's solution to this potential lack of motivation and inefficiency is to entrench in the constitution a system of equalization. In other words, in place of a communally-based motivation to share, Canada's success relies on interprovincial agreements and carefully worked-out constitutional trade-offs that display, for each provincial community, how such programs are fair to them. The need to entrench constitutionally the principle of equalization is some indication of the fragility of a motivation to redistribute wealth nationwide. Moreover, despite constitutional guarantees, this fragility reemerges every time a province views itself as more of a donor to, than a recipient of, the benefits of social programs. In this regard, Gérald Bernier and David Irwin observe that "[t]he citizens of rich provinces, suffering from the effects of the crisis in public finances, will believe they have contributed too much to the welfare of other provinces."[28] Jennifer Smith succinctly offers the same observation: "it is hard ... to square autonomy with dependency on equalization payments."[29] The more that provincial "group life" engages individual loyalties, the more the need arises to institutionalize the obligation to share across the country.

In sum, as a pluralist strategy to limit state sovereignty, federalism in Canada has had two aims: to protect individuals and groups from one all-powerful state; and to sustain the group life of provincial communities to which individuals are loyal and in which individual personality is partly developed. Provincial rights advocates viewed federalism similarly as a means to check the potentially despotic power of the state by empowering provincial legislatures and, through an increased reliance on responsible government, to protect individual liberty. But as a strategy to secure liberty in these ways, federalism is evidently a poor way to enhance social equality. Notwithstanding Laski's arguments for a federalism of functional as well as territorial groups, insofar as pluralism to limit state sovereignty aims at preserving group life by engaging individual loyalties to subnational groups and by dividing up administrative and financial resources amongst different groups, it establishes serious obstacles to large-scale redistributive programs. This observation motivated Laski to find pluralist means to social equality that were more effective than territorial federalism. It is further borne out by the noted effects of Haldane's judgements on social equality and by the implicit aims of some current proposals to decentralize social welfare programs.

PLURALISM FOR CULTURAL EQUALITY

The aim of the second type of pluralism is to enhance the equality of cultural groups. This type of pluralism and the multicultural policies by which it is expressed are unlike pluralism to limit state sovereignty largely because the groups upon which it focuses are cultural rather than territorial ones and because it does not confer autonomy on the groups to which it applies. One claim made here is that multiculturalism distributes resources to cultural groups for reasons entirely different from those of federalism and that critics of multiculturalism often fail to realize this difference. A second claim made here is that multiculturalism appears to conflict with federalism not because it introduces still more groups that desire autonomy from the central (or provincial) state, but because federal and provincial governments have an incentive to compete for jurisdiction over the sort of programs that comprise multiculturalism in order to direct the integration of cultural groups into provincial societies. This competition only makes sense, I argue, because multiculturalism confers power on governments — not on cultural groups.

The origins of pluralism to enhance cultural equality are difficult to place partly because in the past pluralist theories have been more apt to show that when societies distinguish between social or cultural groups in law or public policy they reinforce social inequality rather than alleviate it. In distinguishing between plural societies such as Indonesia and societies with "plural features" such as Canada, J.S. Furnivall observed that plural societies often contain a division of labour along cultural lines with some cultures dominating others.[30] Furnivall and M.G. Smith,[31] who wrote 30 years later, both concluded not only that cultural membership helped to determine one's economic and social status in plural societies but, more disturbingly, that the cultural domination of one group was essential in order to hold plural societies together.[32]

Differentiating people on the basis of culture is certainly no indication of an intention to enhance social equality. Apartheid in South Africa, Indian reservations in Canada and the United States, and segregation in the American South are all ways in which majorities have protected their advantages by distinguishing between people on the basis of culture or race. In the postwar period, these and other similar examples served to strengthen the civil rights approach to equality which required laws and institutions to be blind to differences in race, culture, and gender.

The origins of pluralism to enhance cultural equality, which is sometimes called the "new pluralism,"[33] are found in the critique of the postwar interpretation of equality. This critique, which began to develop in the 1960s and 1970s, targeted the inadequacies of interpretations of equality that required all individuals to be treated identically. Contemporary interpretations of social

equality and specifically of cultural equality, rest largely on this critique. Therefore, understanding this critique is required in order to understand the sort of
aims and strategies that have been employed to enhance cultural equality
through pluralism. Three components of the critique are outlined below. This
is followed by an explanation of how multiculturalism expresses these
components.

THE CRITIQUE'S COMPONENTS:

THE SIGNIFICANCE OF DIFFERENCE

Advocates of the so-called "politics of difference"[34] argue that equality has
been interpreted in a way that speaks to interests which are more often those
of men than women and are usually the interests of cultural majorities rather
than minorities. Iris Marion Young argues that the welfare state fails to address pervasive inequalities between men and women and between different
cultural and racial groups because it views power in terms of possessions to
redistribute rather than relations to restructure. She claims, for instance, that
by focusing on the distribution of money, the welfare state avoids asking questions about which groups have decision-making power and which do not, about
how labour is divided between men and women and stratified according to
cultural groups, and about the ways in which institutions favour the values,
lifestyles, and choices typical of one cultural group, of heterosexuals and of
men.[35] The chief engine for achieving social justice in western nation-states,
namely social welfare programs, fails to address all sorts of injustice that,
when left unchecked, contributes to the oppression, exploitation, and
marginalization of various groups in society.

The neglect of group difference can have profound implications for ensuring equity through social programs. A good illustration of this is found in
health-care policy where cutbacks have different impacts, particularly on men
and women. For instance, using home care to take pressure off hospital services has a disproportionately greater effect on women than on men because
women are typically the caregivers in most homes in Canada.[36] Despite the
fact that health-care systems such as Canada's, aim at ensuring equal access
to health-care facilities for all individuals, they fail to address, and indeed
might obscure, the reasons why better facilities are available for some types
of illnesses than for others or why certain groups, particularly the poor, experience more illness than others. Although an equal number of "health-care
dollars" might be allocated to each citizen, the maldistribution of burdens and
benefits resulting from cutbacks and broader health-related policies distinguish
women from men and certain cultural minorities from the majority. According to Young, these issues arise because of sexism and racism that is structural

to the social system and that reinforces the fact that women and certain cultural minorities are more likely to be powerless, marginalized, exploited, and poor. Universal access to health care does not address these divisions.

If institutions, structures, attitudes, and values contain biases that privilege characteristics typical of some cultures but not others, then applying the norms of society to all people in the same way will merely perpetuate the disadvantages they face — and to make matters worse, will do so in the name of advancing equal treatment. Those who advocate a politics of difference argue that public policies must abandon the idea that equality always requires identical treatment and instead address the ways in which the social needs of groups differ. A central means to eliminate disadvantage born out of difference is through affirmative action which Young argues is a primary means to eliminate gender and cultural stratification in all decision-making institutions, including elected legislatures.[37]

THE IMPORTANCE OF CULTURAL CONTEXT

Will Kymlicka also argues that the postwar conception of what is to count as a resource might leave untouched a cultural imbalance of power that violates the individual's right to equality. Kymlicka argues that a secure cultural context must be treated as a resource that plays a crucial role in facilitating individual well-being. To understand our culture, its history, traditions and conventions "is a precondition of making intelligent judgements about how to lead our lives."[38] Cultural minorities, especially those that speak a different language from the majority, may be disadvantaged because, as a minority group, their cultural narrative does not define public life, is not taught in the schools and does not inform the practices, conventions, and traditions of public institutions. They may have an impoverished or insecure cultural context of choice with which to deliberate about their lives. The cultural cues written into literature, institutions, social practices, public holidays, etc. are cues for some other culture with a different history. As it stands, if we were to count the ready availability of a rich and secure cultural context amongst the sort of resources that ought to be equalized in a liberal society, individuals who are members of minorities have access to fewer of such resources than do members of the majority. According to Kymlicka, the principle of individual equality requires that individuals have equal access to a secure cultural context on which they can draw in making decisions about their lives and making sense of their world.

Two different methods ensure access to a rich cultural context. The first method is group rights that legally protect a group or an aspect of a group's culture from the majoritarian influences that would otherwise prevail over public life. For example, the constitutional protections for the French language in Canada are designed to shield French speakers from at least some of the pressures exerted by a North American, English-language majority. Similarly, rights for the anglophone minority in Quebec are a means of protecting anglophones from the pressure to communicate in French that other minorities in the province experience. These rights are part of a broader commitment to protect both English and French cultural contexts in Canada so that individuals from either cultural tradition are not disadvantaged in the sense of having a less secure cultural context on which to draw.

A second method by which the commitment to equality can be met is by providing minority cultural groups with access to the mainstream cultural context(s). According to Kymlicka, the state's commitment to ensure equality need not entail a commitment to provide access to each individual's *indigenous* cultural context. Individuals who voluntarily immigrate from one country to another incur the obligation of familiarizing themselves with a new cultural context.[39] The state that receives immigrants is obligated to institute policies that allow integration to occur fairly and expeditiously. Integration is made possible by policies that lower the barriers experienced by cultural minorities to participate fully in public life, that actively include minority groups in public life, and that provide cultural minorities with the means, usually the education and language training, required to understand the cultural cues of the majority. In helping to provide each individual with access to a secure cultural context, these policies enhance equality.

THE NEED FOR RECOGNITION

Finally, the need for recognition follows from the observation that the cultural values of majority groups may have to be altered because they are inhospitable and sometimes demeaning to other cultural groups. Edward Said's arguments about culture, imperialism and literature illustrate this problem well.[40] Said argues that because culture develops in relational terms, literary works that explore the cultural character of one group do so by juxtaposing it to the character of another. Western culture is built upon the construction of other cultures with whom westerners have had contact. Historically, the self-image of westerners as colonizers and civilizers of the "unexplored" and "savage" world, relied upon the construction of non-western cultures — "Orientals," Africans, Asians and Aboriginal peoples — as "the other": savage and childlike, in need of "our" governing hand and civilization.[41] These constructions, though part of the cultural context from which westerners draw cues in making sense of and deliberating about their lives, are racist and exclusive. Asian, African, and Middle Eastern students who read the "great works" of the West without a critical eye toward these cultural constructions, find reflected, at least in the western canon, distorting and disempowering images of their cultural group as the conquered, the childlike, and the savage.

In order to ensure that cultural resources are accessible equally to all individuals, liberal states must assess the substance of their culture, including the nature of their literary canon, educational curricula, public traditions, and practices. According to Charles Taylor, societies that are committed to treating minorities equally ought to recognize formally their membership and contribution and ought to promote a commitment to diversity.[42] By doing so, liberal states help to counteract those historic aspects of their culture which are exclusive and preclude diversity.

In sum, the theoretical basis for cultural pluralism to enhance equality rests on three arguments for realizing equality. First, equality requires that the biases, which are built into institutions and structures of societies, be eliminated. Identical treatment cannot eliminate these biases. Therefore, equality requires the accommodation of differences. Second, because cultural context is a resource that plays a crucial role in facilitating individual well-being, individuals ought to have equal access to a secure cultural context. This may require policies that teach cultural minorities to understand the cultural context of the majority. And third, equality requires a critical re-reading of cultural self-understandings in order to eliminate the ways in which we have understood ourselves by demeaning others. This requires changing the majority culture as well as counterbalancing its biases by explicitly recognizing the identities and contributions of the communities outside the mainstream.

EQUALITY AND CANADA'S MULTICULTURALISM

Each of these arguments for cultural equality is reflected in Canada's multicultural policies. The approaches adopted in Canada to enhancing the equality of cultural groups (other than the founding cultures) are based on four types of policies: (i) anti-discrimination legislation; (ii) official multiculturalism; (iii) employment equity; and (iv) language training and cultural education. With the possible exception of anti-discrimination legislation, each policy distributes resources to cultural minorities as a means to enhance their equality. And all of them, again with the possible exception of the first one, implement the central ideas of the arguments for difference, cultural context, and recognition.

Anti-Discrimination Legislation. Anti-discrimination legislation is an exception here because, until the 1980s it promoted the notion of equality as identical treatment. From World War II until the 1970s, anti-discrimination legislation was the primary means to protect cultural equality. In 1944, Ontario was the first province to pass anti-discrimination legislation.[43] By the 1970s, all provinces and the federal government had passed human rights acts. One purpose of this legislation was to eliminate discrimination in order to help integrate cultural minorities.[44] In this way, even though human rights legislation was not designed to distribute resources *to* cultural minorities, it aided integration, for example, by removing the majority's power to run businesses in ways that discriminated against minorities. In this sense, it redistributed resources.

Official Multiculturalism. The significance of cultural difference and the importance of recognition became central parts of government policy in the 1970s through the policy of official multiculturalism. The policy statement introduced by the Trudeau government in 1971, which became the *Multiculturalism Act*, and the entrenchment of section 27 in the *Charter of Rights and Freedoms* intentionally raised the exposure of Canadian ethnic diversity and attempted to redesign Canadian culture to suit its culturally pluralistic reality. The *Multiculturalism Act* was explicit about this goal. One of the four pledges made by the federal government in 1971 was to "promote creative encounters and interchange among all Canadian cultural groups in the interests of national unity."[45] The government carried out this pledge by incorporating multiculturalism into the federal policy-making process: establishing a minister of state responsible for multiculturalism in 1972, a Multicultural Council to advise the minister in 1973, a Multiculturalism Directorate within the Department of the Secretary of State which, in turn, funded research, activities, and projects by and about ethnic minorities in Canada and which engaged in liaison activities with minority ethnic communities.[46] Throughout the 1970s, numerous programs were funded, advisory boards established, and conferences held to further multiculturalism. In addition, federal agencies responsible for film, museums, libraries and archives, radio, and television promoted cultural diversity.[47] The 1988 Act explicitly employed the language of recognition and difference: the government was committed to "foster the recognition and appreciation of the diverse cultures of Canadian society…" and to ensure "that all individuals receive equal treatment and equal protection under the law, while respecting and valuing their diversity."

Employment Equity. The third type of policy, affirmative action, distributes resources to cultural minorities by increasing the employment and advancement opportunities of individuals who belong to visible minorities. The principle of affirmative action, "to ameliorate disadvantage," was incorporated into the constitutional guarantees for equality entrenched in the Charter and have since been interpreted by the Supreme Court of Canada as informing the protection of equality found in all provincial human rights legislation, regardless of whether or not the provincial codes explicitly acknowledge this.[48] In 1986 the federal government instituted the *Employment Equity Act*[49] and the Contractors Program. The Act requires that employers compile evidence of their reasonable efforts to hire women, visible minorities, individuals with disabilities, and Aboriginal peoples. The Contractors Program gives preference in awarding federal contracts to companies that meet the federal standards of gender and cultural diversity.

Language Training and Cultural Education. Finally, Canada's multiculturalism has been devoted to improving the access of cultural minorities to the main-stream cultures through language training, educational programs, settlement services, and counseling centres. English/French as a Second Language (ESL/FSL) training has been a central component of multiculturalism from the start to which a large percentage of program-funding is devoted. However, pro-grams were also funded to help cultural minorities preserve their own languages and traditions. In other words, the strategy of multiculturalism was not sim-ply to open the door for cultural minorities to French and English culture. Rather, the goal was to integrate cultural minorities by allowing them to feel comfortable with their own cultural backgrounds in Canadian public life.[50] As Will Kymlicka puts it, multiculturalism "has made the possession of an ethnic identity an acceptable, even normal, part of life in the mainstream society."[51] By doing so, it has equalized the access individuals have to a secure cultural context.

In sum, the general aim of multiculturalism in Canada, as guided by the four types of policy discussed above, is to enhance the equality of cultural minorities primarily by lowering the barriers to integration. This is done through anti-discrimination legislation, by changing Canadian culture through the official recognition of the culturally pluralistic dimension of Canadian life, by accelerating the inclusion of cultural minorities into public life through employment equity programs, and by providing cultural minorities with the language training and education they need to have access to the mainstream culture.

The key accomplishment of this second type of pluralism is that it enhances equality by improving the access of cultural minorities to the resources that majorities have access to and it does so by integrating cultural minorities and majorities. According to evidence compiled by Kymlicka, Reitz and Breton,[52] and Harles,[53] the overall effect of multiculturalism has been to improve the rate of the integration of immigrants from cultural minorities into Canadian society. Compared to other countries Canada experiences relatively low levels of segregation in housing and education, only moderate ethnic inequality in income and earnings, and similar cultural participation rates across the labour market and in unions.[54] Kymlicka shows that, with respect to naturalization, political participation, and official language acquisition, immigrants are more integrated today than they were before multiculturalism was instituted.[55] Poll-ing of the majority cultures has generally shown that cultural "acceptance, tolerance, and mutual understanding has ... increased over time."[56] Survey studies also confirm that multiculturalism eases the transition of immigrants, who then become devoted to Canada and eager to identify with the political community and the government of that community.[57]

As with the first type of pluralism examined, one of the questions consid-ered here is how the goals of this type of pluralism limit what it is able to accomplish. The most significant limitation is that enhancing cultural equality involves the state extensively in the affairs of cultural groups. Distributing resources is, after all, a large part of what it means to be a self-directed community. When the state manages this function through socialized health care, education, and social assistance, as well as through the four types of policies associated with Canadian multiculturalism, it performs functions traditionally fulfilled by families, neighbours, churches, and other associations indigenous to cultural communities. The second type of pluralism enlarges the scope of the state's power over cultural groups through, for example, language and acculturation programs, human rights education, employment opportunities, and state-funded and organized cultural events. In doing so, it interferes significantly with the autonomous development of group life for which Laski treasured pluralism.

Whereas enhancing group life, in the way Laski imagined, requires that state power over groups is minimal, most means of redistributing resources will have the effect of increasing the power of the state over groups. Groups that are not self-sufficient, as most groups are not, are unlikely to be entirely self-directed. In this way, the welfare state loosens the bonds between cultural and religious groups and their members.[58] A similar process occurs with respect to redistributing resources to cultural groups in order to enhance social equality. The incorporation of difference into public institutions, for instance, through employment equity means that differences will shape the public as well as be shaped by the public.

A good example of this is the official recognition of minority groups through the constitution. During the Charlottetown negotiations, the federal government proposed to include a "Canada Clause" which would recognize the significant features and groups of Canada. The clause made explicit mention of the parliamentary tradition, individual and collective rights, Aboriginal peoples, French and British Canadians, men, women, and the multicultural character of the country. It failed to mention people with disabilities. When asked to justify this omission, the minister of constitutional affairs, Joe Clark, explained that they had forgotten to include disabled people because people with disabilities were not at the negotiating table.

The problem with Clark's explanation is not simply a matter of "out of sight, out of mind." The Canada Clause was primarily a symbolic means of recognition offered to groups by the Canadian state. Groups expended their resources vying for this form of recognition even though being named in the clause was only remotely tied to improving the well-being of group members. The politics surrounding who was in the clause and who was not illustrates that the more the state becomes involved in the recognition and regulation of ethnic minorities, the more groups craft their interests and even their identities in terms of categories to which the state is likely to respond. Cultural recognition places power in the hands of those who do the "recognizing," which, in the case of multiculturalism, means in the hands of the mainstream and the Canadian state.

My intention in pointing to this drawback is not to argue that, on balance, enhancing equality of cultural groups is not worthwhile for those groups or that it ought not to be pursued. Rather, my point is that, like the first sort of pluralism, in which group life was secured at the cost of raising obstacles to social equality, the second type involves a trade-off. In this case, social equality is exchanged for group autonomy. This trade-off is rarely acknowledged either by advocates or critics of multiculturalism to the detriment of our understanding of multiculturalism.

A common assumption about multiculturalism is that it increases rather than decreases the autonomy of groups. For example, Kymlicka begins his book by quoting from Richard Gwyn who argued in 1995 that "official multiculturalism encourages apartheid, or to be a bit less harsh, ghettoism."[59] The analogy of a ghetto or cultural separateness has also been used by Neil Bissoondath, R.W. Bibby, and Arthur Schlesinger. It implies that resources are distributed to cultural groups to use as they please, and furthermore, that they have chosen to live their lives separately from the mainstream rather than integrating into it; that multiculturalism gives to minority groups cultural autonomy within Canada. The concern raised by critics is that, because multiculturalism distributes resources to cultural minorities, it enhances the group life of minorities (at the taxpayers' expense) and prevents them from integrating into Canadian society. Advocates of multiculturalism have inadvertently contributed to this line of criticism by defending the strategy, as did the formal federal secretary for multiculturalism, Sheila Finestone, by emphasizing that in Canada "[o]ne can choose how one wants to live."[60]

This line of argument is entirely inconsistent with the aims and outcomes of the pluralism that has shaped Canada's multiculturalism and the critique of equality that has shaped this second type of pluralism. Multiculturalism, and the pluralism that it reflects, distributes to cultural minorities certain types of resources to be used in specific state-directed ways. As a policy by which the state manages cultural diversity, its terms are largely controlled by the state. Consequently, the groups that hope to benefit from the policy are also partly controlled by the state.

A consequence of misinterpreting multiculturalism as a means to enhance the autonomy of cultural groups is that doing so implies that a conflict between federalism and multiculturalism is owing to a potential competition between these two systems as strategies to enhance the autonomy of groups. The only difference between them appears to be the type of groups that advocates of each system favour; advocates of a stronger and more decentralized federalism favour provincial communities whereas advocates of multiculturalism favour cultural minorities regardless of whether they are territorial or not. If both systems are viewed as a means to group autonomy, then their conflict must be owing to differing views about which type of groups ought to enjoy autonomy in Canadian society.

But this is not what the conflict is about. Federalism and multiculturalism clash for two reasons. First, there may be a struggle between the federal and provincial governments over which level of jurisdiction ought to make the policies that manage the cultural pluralism to which multiculturalism responds. The desire by provinces to have jurisdiction over shaping multicultural policies only makes sense because of the power multiculturalism gives the province to direct the integration of cultural minorities. In other words, the concern is not that strongly autonomous cultural groups will compete with the provinces for the loyalty of individual Canadians. Rather, provinces, particularly Quebec, are concerned that multiculturalism is a means whereby cultural groups become integrated into federal not provincial society. For this reason they are inclined to be just as generous as the federal government in developing and funding multiculturalism — an inclination they would not have if multiculturalism empowered cultural groups to compete with provinces for individual loyalty.

Second, the mistake of viewing both multiculturalism and federalism as means to group autonomy is that this leads one to misunderstand the complex trade-offs involved when a group wants the benefits of both types of pluralism. A group that wants both autonomy from the central state and cultural equality, such as Aboriginal people and the Québécois, may be caught in a crossfire created by the drawbacks of each type of pluralism. Strategies that enhance equality, like multiculturalism, impinge on self-sufficiency and group autonomy. Strategies that enhance group autonomy, such as self-government or secession, impede access to the financial, administrative, and motivational resources of the central state that might be needed to establish or enjoy large-scale social programs.

In sum, multiculturalism, I have argued, is a means to integrate cultural minorities and majorities. The policies that contribute to this goal include anti-discrimination legislation, official multiculturalism, employment equity, and language and cultural education. The notion of equality upon which these policies are based is informed by the significance of difference, the importance of cultural context, and the need for recognition. Multiculturalism is not a means to group autonomy despite the fact that it accords to cultural groups certain types of resources. Its primary purpose, and the purpose of the pluralist idea that has helped to shape it, is to enhance the equality of cultural groups by improving their access to the resources that majorities have access to. It does this by integrating cultural minorities and majorities. This fact is often misunderstood by critics and advocates of multiculturalism alike. Moreover, one consequence of misunderstanding multiculturalism is that it leads to misunderstanding the relation between multiculturalism and federalism as a competition between provincial and cultural communities and a misperception of the trade-offs involved and the choices that must be made by groups that seek both autonomous "group life" and cultural equality.

CONCLUSION

Canadians may "connect" best through the policies and programs that appear to divide and distinguish them, such as federalism and multiculturalism. One purpose of this chapter is to explain why this might be the case. Historically, "pluralism to limit state sovereignty," which informs federalism, was viewed as a means to enhance the group life of provincial communities. The development of individual personality required a social context, such as a provincial community, in which individuals could have some measure of control over governments that were more closely accountable to them. Individual liberty was developed and expressed through the development of these local communities. Federalism facilitated the "group life" of these communities while, at the same time, dividing sovereign power between federal and provincial states and thus ensuring that different levels of the government would check each other's tendencies to dominate and oppress individuals or communities. Federalism was a means of striking the balance between empowering communities and checking their tyrannical tendencies. Thus, according to Laski, individual liberty is secured by federalism.

The second type of pluralism, "pluralism to enhance cultural equality," is not directed as sustaining the group life of cultural groups by granting them autonomy. Rather, its key purpose is to redistribute resources in a way that ensures that cultural minorities have equal access to the resources that majorities have access to. In this sense, it is also a powerful means to connect Canadians.

The aim here has been to show how these connections are inevitably accompanied by drawbacks. I have argued that the more federalism succeeds at enhancing the group life of provincial communities, for instance, through policies that decentralize powers to provincial governments, the more it erects obstacles to social equality. Notwithstanding the fact that provincial governments are better informed about the sort of programs that are needed in their communities, the establishment of large-scale social programs is impeded by the fragmentation of administrative and financial resources and by the fragmentation of individual loyalties and their attachment to provincial rather than national communities. This fragmentation helps to define the purposes of pluralism to limit state sovereignty.

In the case of multiculturalism, its success at ensuring that cultural minorities have access to the same resources as the majority undermines the ability of these groups to enjoy the autonomous group life extolled by the first type of pluralism. Multiculturalism is about integration, not about autonomous group life. This fact is largely misunderstood in political and social analysis and as a result so is the complex interaction between federalism and multiculturalism.

NOTES

My thanks to Claire Hunter, David Schneiderman and the anonymous reviewers for helping to clarify the arguments in this chapter. Imperfections remain despite their good advice.

1. Here, I use the term multiculturalism in a manner consistent with how it is used in many philosophical and sociological analyses, as a strategy for managing cultural pluralism. The term includes reference to multicultural programs and policies aimed at protecting the identity-related interests of ethnic minorities. Moreover, it is consistent with policies such as the *Multiculturalism Acts*, 1971 and 1988 in that it is not intended to apply to indigenous peoples or to groups that are considered founding nations, such as French and British Canadians. In order to avoid confusion, the term "cultural pluralism" will be used to refer to the sociological reality that many cultures (indigenous, non-indigenous, founding, non-founding) co-exist in the same state. For a similar use of the term multiculturalism, see Augie Fleras and Jean Leonard Elliot, *Multiculturalism in Canada* (Toronto: Nelson, 1992); and Will Kymlicka, *Finding Our Way: Rethinking Ethnocultural Relations in Canada* (Toronto: Oxford University Press, 1998).

2. The term "group life" refers to the shared experiences of individuals within a group. Individuals share experiences within many sorts of groups, of which communities (e.g., nations, provinces, municipalities and neighbourhoods) are amongst the most important today. But pluralists such as Harold Laski and Arthur Bentley were interested in all sorts of groups, including territorial communities, guilds, unions, and interest groups. They recognized that not all groups were communities, but, as I explain below, considered all sorts of group life to be crucial to individual liberty and development. For a discussion of the pluralist theories of Laski and Bentley, see Avigail Eisenberg, *Reconstructing Political Pluralism* (Albany, NY: State University of New York Press, 1995), ch. 3 and 4.

3. See Ernest Barker, "The Discredited State," *The Political Quarterly* 5 (1915): 101-21.

4. Harold Laski, *Foundations of Sovereignty and Other Essays* (New York: Harcourt Brace and Co., 1921), p. 22.

5. Harold Laski, *Studies in the Problem of Sovereignty* (New Haven: Yale University Press, 1917), pp. 136-37.

6. Laski, *Foundations of Sovereignty*, p. 170.

7. Ibid., pp. 86-87. Also see H.J. Laski, *Authority in the Modern State* (New Haven: Yale University Press, 1919), p. 90.

8. H.J. Laski, "Canada's Constitution," *The New Republic* 35 (4 July 1923). This reference is drawn from David Schneiderman's interesting analysis of Laski's

views on federalism and their connection to Canada in "Harold Laski, Viscount Haldane, and the Law of the Canadian Constitution in the Early Twentieth Century," *University of Toronto Law Journal* 48, 4 (Fall 1998): 76, fn 74.

9. See Laski, *Authority in the Modern State*, p. 74; H.J. Laski, *A Grammar of Politics*, 5th ed. (London: George Allen & Unwin, 1948), pp. 59 and 471.

10. Schneiderman, "Harold Laski, Viscount Haldane, and the Law of the Canadian Constitution in the Early Twentieth Century," p. 71.

11. For a short time in his career, Laski adopted the notion that groups had personalities separate from those of their members and worthy of distinct legal protection. Other pluralists, in particular G.D.H. Cole, were adamantly opposed to this aspect of pluralist theory. Laski's interest in the notion seemed to dissipate quickly: having endorsed the notion of group personality in 1916, he is unwilling to defend it in 1925. See Eisenberg, *Reconstructing Political Pluralism,* pp. 75-76, including fn 64.

12. Schneiderman, "Harold Laski, Viscount Haldane, and the Law of the Canadian Constitution in the Early Twentieth Century," p. 64.

13. Notwithstanding any similarities, Laski's arguments for pluralism, which he wrote in the 1910s and 1920s, and the arguments of late nineteenth-century provincial rights advocates were made in two significantly different historical periods. The connection between these ideas is based on the fact that some of the issues about sovereignty and group life, which I mention here, were common to both periods.

14. Richard Risk and Robert C. Vipond, "Rights Talk in Canada in the Late Nineteenth Century: 'The Good Sense and Right Feeling of the People'," *Law and History Review* 14, 1 (Spring 1996): 15.

15. Ibid., p. 9.

16. Ibid., p. 20.

17. Eisenberg, *Reconstructing Political Pluralism,* pp. 63-68.

18. As quoted in Schneiderman, "Harold Laski, Viscount Haldane, and the Law of the Canadian Constitution in the Early Twentieth Century," p. 91.

19. Ibid., pp. 76-78.

20. See ibid., p. 76, fn 74.

21. *Toronto Electric Commissioners v. Snider* (1925 A.C. 396).

22. F.R. Scott (ed.), "Federal Jurisdiction over Labour Relations: A New Look" (1959) in *Essays on the Constitution: Aspects of Canadian Law and Politics* (Toronto and Buffalo: University of Toronto Press, 1977), p. 336.

23. Ibid., p. 345.

24. Gordon Gibson, "Renewing the Federation: Section 4," http://www.pdalliance.bc.ca/index2.html.

25. On this question, see John Richards, *Retooling the Welfare State* (Toronto: C.D. Howe Institute, 1997), p. 247.

26. David Miller, *On Nationality* (Oxford: Clarendon, 1995), p. 140.

27. See Keith Banting, *The Welfare State and Canadian Federalism*, 2d ed. (Montreal and Kingston: McGill-Queen's University Press, 1987); S. Gould and J. Palmer, "Outcomes, Interpretations, and Policy," in *The Vulnerable,* ed. J. Palmer, T. Smeeding and B. Torrey (Washington, DC: The Urban Institute Press, 1988), pp. 426-27; David Miller, *Market, State and Community* (Oxford: Oxford University Press, 1989), p. 284; Richards, *Retooling the Welfare State,* p. 278.

28. Gérald Bernier and David Irwin, "Fiscal Federalism: The Politics of Intergovernmental Transfers," in *New Trends in Canadian Federalism,* ed. François Rocher and Miriam Smith (Peterborough, Ont.: Broadview Press, 1995), p. 272.

29. Jennifer Smith, "The Meaning of Provincial Equality in Canadian Federalism," *Working Paper* 1998 (1) (Kingston: Institute of Intergovernmental Relations, Queen's University, 1998), p. 17.

30. J.S. Furnivall, *Colonial Policy and Practice* (New York: New York University Press, 1948), p. 305.

31. M.G. Smith, *A Plural Society in the British West Indies* (Berkeley and Los Angeles: University of California Press, 1975).

32. Leo Kuper, "Plural Societies: Perspectives and Problems," in *Pluralism in Africa,* ed. L. Kuper and M.G. Smith (Berkeley and Los Angeles: University of California Press, 1969), p. 13.

33. See, for example, Harry Goulbourne, "Varieties of Pluralism: The Notion of a Pluralist Post-Imperial Britain," *New Community* 17, 2 (1991): 211-27; Kirstie McClure, "On the Subject of Rights: Pluralism, Plurality and Political Identity," in *Dimensions of Radical Democracy: Pluralism, Citizenship, Community,* ed. Chantal Mouffe (London: Verso, 1992), pp. 108-27; and Sheldon Wolin, "Democracy, Difference, and Re-Cognition," *Political Theory* 21, 3 (1993): 464-83.

34. See, for example, Iris Marion Young, *Justice and the Politics of Difference* (Princeton, NJ: Princeton University Press, 1990).

35. Ibid., p. 75.

36. See Joan Anderson and Sheryl Remier Kirkham, "The Gendering and Racializing of the Canadian Health Care System," in *Painting the Maple: Race, Gender and the Construction of Canada,* ed. Veronica Strong-Boag *et al.* (Vancouver: UBC Press, forthcoming 1999).

37. Young defends a legislative system based on group representation. See Young, *Justice and the Politics of Difference,* pp. 183-91. For a useful critique of group representation, see Will Kymlicka, *Multicultural Citizenship* (Oxford: Oxford University Press, 1995), pp. 138-49.

38. Kymlicka, *Multicultural Citizenship,* p. 83.

39. Ibid., p. 63.

40. Edward Said, *Culture and Imperialism* (New York: Vintage, 1994).

41. Ibid., p. xi.

42. Charles Taylor, "The Politics of Recognition," in *Multiculturalism: Examining the Politics of Recognition,* ed. Amy Gutmann (Princeton, NJ: Princeton University Press, 1994), pp. 25-74.

43. *Racial Discrimination Act*, S.O. 1944, c. 51.

44. For an interesting account of this see Les A. Pal, "Identity, Citizenship and Mobilization: The Nationalities Branch and World War Two," *Canadian Public Administration* 32, 3 (Fall 1989), especially p. 421.

45. *House of Commons Debates*, Statement of P.E. Trudeau, 8 October 1971.

46. Jean Burnet, "Multiculturalism in Canada," in *Ethnic Canada*, ed. Leo Driedger (Toronto: Copp Clark Pitman, Ltd., 1987), p. 69.

47. Ibid., p. 69.

48. *Ontario Human Rights Commission v. Simpson-Sears Ltd.*, (Ont 1985), 23 *DLR* (4th) SCC.

49. *Employment Equity Act*, RSC, 1985, c. 23.

50. The funding of non-official language training might seem to be an exception to the equality aims of multicultural policies as they have been discussed here. However, Kymlicka argues to the contrary that given the evidence which suggests that ESL/FSL is ineffective for individuals who are not literate in their mother tongues, language training in their mother tongues may be the first step toward enabling them to become literate in English or French. See Will Kymlicka, *Finding Our Way*, pp. 49-53.

51. Ibid., p. 44.

52. J. Reitz and R. Breton (eds.), *The Illusion of Difference* (Toronto: C.D. Howe Institute, 1994).

53. John C. Harles, "Integration before Assimilation: Immigration, Multiculturalism and the Canadian Polity," *Canadian Journal of Political Science* 30, 4 (December 1997): 711-36.

54. Hermann Kurthen, "The Canadian Experience with Multiculturalism and Employment Equity: Lessons for Europe," *New Community* 23, 2 (April 1997): 261. Also see Kymlicka, *Finding Our Way*, pp. 21-22; and Reitz and Breton, *The Illusion of Difference*.

55. Kymlicka, *Finding Our Way*, p. 18.

56. Kurthen, "The Canadian Experience with Multiculturalism and Employment Equity: Lessons for Europe," p. 260.

57. Harles, "Integration before Assimilation," pp. 734-35.

58. See Koogila Moodley, "Canadian Multiculturalism as Ideology," *Ethnic and Racial Studies* 6, 3 (July 1983): 321-25.

59. Richard Gwyn, *Nationalism Without Walls: The Unbearable Lightness of Being Canadian* (Toronto: McClelland &Stewart, 1995) quoted in Kymlicka, *Finding Our Way*, p. 17.

60. Sheila Finestone, "I Don't Enjoy Neil Bissoondath," *The Globe and Mail* (Toronto) 7 February 1995; quoted in Harles, "Integration before Assimilation," p. 713.

III

The Economic Context

4

Canada's National Economy:
There's More to It Than You Thought

John F. Helliwell

Les résultats présentés ici suggèrent que le tissu économique canadien est tricoté beaucoup plus serré qu'on ne le croyait auparavant et que l'annonce de la mort de l'économie nationale apparaît prématurée. Bien que l'ouverture économique ait un impact positif sur la croissance économique, il arrive un moment où une ouverture sans cesse croissante ne se traduit plus par une augmentation proportionnelle de la croissance économique. En même temps, les frontières nationales permettent de diviser de très grands marchés en unités plus faciles à gérer en termes de préférences, d'histoire, de valeurs et d'institutions communes, ce qui n'est pas sans conséquence pour la gestion des enjeux politiques canadiens. Par exemple, le coût de la séparation du Québec pourrait s'avérer plus lourd que prévu en raison de la solidité du tissu économique canadien. De même, la force de ce tissu assure aux gouvernements une plus grande indépendance économique dans une économie mondialisée.

INTRODUCTION

Do national political boundaries still mark important boundaries in economic space? If so, is this because political boundaries are still blocking economic transactions? Or do markets segment naturally where there are differences in tastes, history, values, and institutions? Many commentators have argued that the economic importance of national boundaries has largely disappeared, swamped from the one side by economic globalization and supplanted at the more local level by cities and regions. Thus Tom Courchene writes of Ontario having evolved from a national heartland to a North American region state, and Kenichi Ohmae treats regional economies and multinational firms as the chief building blocks of the modern global economy.[1] If this is true, then we would expect to find that national borders no longer mark separations in economic space. This chapter assesses the facts of the matter, searches for their implications for Canada, and contrasts the facts with the widespread perception that the economic nation state is a relic of the past.

To start with the impressions first, I can report from a series of surveys among students, professional economists, and Canadians from all walks of life, that there has been a widespread impression that the trade linkages between Canadian provinces are less tight that those between Canadian provinces and US states, after making due allowance for the differences in distance and economic size. To be more specific, when asked how much merchandise trade there was, in 1988, between two typical Canadian provinces, in comparison to that between a province and a US state of the same size, and at the same distance, the median response, in mid-1995, was that interprovincial flows were 20 percent less intense than those between provinces and states.[2] Yet, based on research published about that time by John McCallum, the best evidence was that in 1988 the interprovincial flows were not one-fifth less but 20 times more intense than those between provinces and states.[3]

This vast gulf between perceptions and evidence was very striking, and demanded further research. Was the evidence wrong? If not, why does it come as such a surprise? How could Canadians so widely think that globalization, in at least a North American version, was not just already in place, but had actually overshot the mark, with trade ties to the United States being even tighter than those within the country? A full answer to the latter question will require detailed studies of economic psychology, while a search for answers to the first question has occupied much of my research for the past four years. The main results of that research will be summarized in the next section, followed by an attempt to assess the consequences for Canada at the dawn of the twenty-first century.

But first it may be useful to speculate about why there is such a widespread Canadian perception that economic ties with the United States are so strong relative to those among the Canadian provinces. It is useful to divide this into two parts: Why do people think that linkages with the United States are so strong? And what do they know and think about interprovincial linkages? For the widespread impression of tight linkages with the United States, there are many reasons. The Canada-US trade linkage has long been known by Canadians, if not by Americans, as the largest bilateral trading relation in the world. Brand names from US firms are everywhere, Canadian television screens are full of US channels, Canadians travel south in search of sunshine or cheap gasoline, and everyone knows that the oranges and grapefruit come from the same country as Hollywood films. It is also widely known that Canada has a high degree of foreign direct investment, and that US firms are the largest players in the Canadian market. When quizzed about the reason for trade ties being stronger north-south than east-west, Canadians with knowledge of trade matters refer to comparative advantage, thinking of Canadian raw materials being exchanged for US manufactures, services, and fruits and vegetables from the same states they go to in search of their own winter sunshine. Car drivers are not exactly sure where their cars come from, but suspect that their vehicles have been across the Canada-US border several times, in one form or another, before they reached their local dealership.

With respect to the strength of internal trade linkages, Canadians have frequently heard complaints from someone or other about how hard it is to get beer, or bricks, or construction workers, or lawyers, or something else from one province to another. They know about provincial marketing boards designed to support local farmers. They probably have also read or heard that interprovincial trade barriers have become such a concern as to lead to the negotiation and signing of an internal trade agreement, but that the agreement is thus far a toothless paper tiger.

What Canadians have probably never seen, however, are data that are actually designed to measure the relative strength of internal and international trade linkages.[4] Indeed, until recently there was not even any data widely available to make such comparisons. Only since the middle 1980s have there been systematic data for interprovincial merchandise trade flows, and the 1988 data for trade between Canadian provinces and US states, collected to help monitor the consequences of the Canada-US Free trade Agreement (FTA) signed in 1988, did not become available until the early 1990s. The data are even less well developed in other countries, as only federal states have much interest and need for subnational accounts, and among such countries only Canada has statistics of the quality and consistency of those provided by Statistics Canada.

Thus Canadians see lots of available evidence attesting to large and growing trade linkages between Canada and the United States, hear much talk of globalization, are aware of much concern about interprovincial trade barriers, and have no data at hand to permit the international and intranational trade densities to be compared. Perhaps it is after all not so surprising that Canadians think as they do. But now that the data are available, it is important to inspect them carefully, because false impressions, however understandable, can have important consequences. These consequences will be examined more thoroughly after the facts are inspected.

EVIDENCE

As already noted, John McCallum fitted a gravity model to 1988 merchandise trade flows among Canadian provinces and between Canadian provinces and US states, and found that the interprovincial flows were 20 times greater than those between provinces and US states of comparable size and distance.[5]

The gravity model explains the strength of economic and other interactions between two geographically distinct bodies in terms of their mass and distance.

In the simplest Newtonian version, the strength of the interaction increases proportionately with the product of the two masses and falls proportionately as distance increases. The model has been used to explain trade flows, migration and many other forms of economic and social interaction. Over recent decades, the gravity model, always a great empirical success, has gone from being a theoretical orphan to being the favoured child of all main theories of international trade.[6] This makes it a solid tool for the evaluation of border effects.

How can the gravity model be used to estimate the possible effects of national boundaries? The key requirement is to have comparable measures of intranational and international trade, so that the strength of the two linkages can be compared in the context of the gravity model. During the 1990s, data have become available for trade among Canadian provinces and between Canadian provinces and US states. It is thus now possible to explain all these pair-wise trading relations in terms of the economic sizes of the states and provinces, and of the distances between them. The data set is not fully symmetric, since there are no data available for trade among US states. Thus the estimation of border effects is based on a comparison of the density of trade flows between provinces in comparison with trade flows between provinces and states of equivalent size and distance. In statistical terms, this is done by adding a variable that takes the value of 1.0 for each observation relating to a trade flow from one province to another, and zero otherwise. If this variable takes zero coefficient, the implication is that trade linkages are equally dense among provinces and between provinces and states, after taking account of differences in distance and economic size. If the coefficient is negative, it would indicate that north-south trade linkages were tighter than those east-west. A significant positive coefficient would show that interprovincial trade flows were greater than those between provinces and states, after allowing for differences in economic size and distance. Given the multiplicative form of the gravity model, and its estimation as an equation linear in logarithms, the antilog of the estimated coefficient on the dummy variable shows typical province-to-province flows as a fraction (or multiple) of typical province-state flows, where the provinces and states are of the same size and are separated by the same distance.

As noted in the introduction, and reported in "Do National Boundaries Matter for Quebec Trade?" a survey of Canadian economists and political scientists showed that the median respondent expected that province-province trade would be 0.8 times as large as province-state trade, implying a negative value for the coefficient on the border variable. John McCallum found a significant positive coefficient on the special variable marking interprovincial trade flows, and calculated the implied border effect to be 20 for 1988.[7] Thus the density of interprovincial trade flows was 20 times greater than that of trade flows between provinces and states, and more than 20 times larger than people thought.

To ensure that this startling finding is not some mysterious result generated by some feature of the model used for estimation, it is useful to see if it matches the data for specific pairs of provinces and states. For example, Ontario is almost equidistant from British Columbia, Washington State, and California. In 1990 the Californian economy was almost 12 times larger than that of British Columbia, and thus should have provided, without border effects, a market almost 12 times as large. Ontario merchandise shipments to British Columbia were actually almost twice as large as to California, for a total border effect of 21. Washington State GDP was more than one-third larger than that of British Columbia, but Ontario's exports to British Columbia were more than 12 times larger than to Washington, for a total border effect of 21.

In the earlier paper, I extended the sample to include data for 1989 and 1990, found an increase of the border effect from 1988 to 1990, and showed that the preference for Canadian over US markets applied as much to Quebec as to the other provinces. Since that time, there has been additional work by Statistics Canada to improve the province-state data to make them match more closely the concepts used in the construction of the interprovincial trade data, and to refine the assignment of trade to its province of origin or destination. In addition, the data have now been extended through 1996, permitting the consequences of the FTA to be assessed.

Results for 1988 through 1996, including disaggregation by province, by industry, and by direction of trade, are all reported elsewhere.[8] The industry results show that border effects are pervasive, and not just concentrated in industries subject to many border restrictions. Border effects are indeed very large in food, beverages and textiles, industries marked by substantial tariff and non-tariff barriers to international trade. However, they are large and significant in all industries, averaging over 20 across 26 industry groupings. It was initially surprising to find a border effect for cars and parts that was as high as that for all other industries, despite the fact that there had long been US ownership of the major North American car producers, and free trade in autos and parts, at least for producers, since 1965. The answer to the puzzle turned out to be that there is no border effect evident in the flows among the three main producing provinces and states — Ontario, Quebec, and Michigan — while there are above-average effects covering the flows along all the other province-province and province-state pathways. The fact that there is no border effect for cars and parts between Ontario and Michigan shows that a unified industrial structure under common ownership, coupled with complete free trade, can produce international trade densities as great as domestic ones. However, the vast gap between this result and those for trade along other pathways, and in other industries, shows how different the car industry is from all the rest.

Some readers of an earlier version of this chapter have asked if the pattern of regional and industry results can be used to cast light on the extent to which the greater tightness of the national economy has been due to specific nation-building policies, such as the construction of national railways and pipelines. Estimates of the distance effect show it to be the same for interprovincial as for international trade, suggesting that transportation costs rise with distance in a similar way for both domestic and cross-border trade flows. Many of the interprovincial trade flows follow US transportation pathways, from central Canada both east and west. This is true for railways, roads, and pipelines. Although having a national railway no doubt sped and shaped the distribution of population in Canada, it is less easy to see any more contemporary effect on trade patterns. Since the pattern of border effects is so pervasive across industries, and characteristic of all the provinces, it is not likely to be primarily due to the level and structure of tariffs, or to the existence of specific transportation facilities.

The best summary measure of the results is for total merchandise trade, along with some more approximate calculations for trade in services. The estimated border effects, shown separately for merchandise and for services, for each year from 1988 through 1996, are pictured in Figure 1. The improvements in the classification of province-state trade flows for 1990 have lowered the estimated border effect for merchandise trade for that year from a previously estimated 21 to about 17. The subsequent sharp drop in the border effect from 1990 to 1993, coupled with its rough constancy since, at a level of about 12, suggests that the major adjustments of trade patterns following the FTA may have been completed.

The estimated border effects for services are in every year much larger than those for merchandise trade, and do not show the same evidence of sharp reduction in the wake of the FTA. The high values of border effects for services are not simply caused by the fact that services are generally less traded than goods, since the border effects being estimated relate only to those services that do enter trade, whether interprovincial or between provinces and states. Intraprovincial consumption of goods and services does not enter these calculations, although it is perhaps worth noting, in light of all the discussion about interprovincial trade barriers, that attempts to estimate interprovincial border effects show them to be small and insignificant.

Thus Figure 1 is consistent both with the large increase in north-south trade flows in the 1990s, and with continuing national border effects of about 12 for goods and almost three times that for services. Two features of the post-FTA changes in border effects are worth further discussion here. First, the post-1990 increases in north-south trade are more than twice as large as those that were predicted in various studies before the FTA came into effect.[9] Second, the forecast productivity gains have not materialized to any significant degree. This combination poses a puzzle for future research, but in the meantime

Figure 1: Canada-US Border Effects 1988-1996

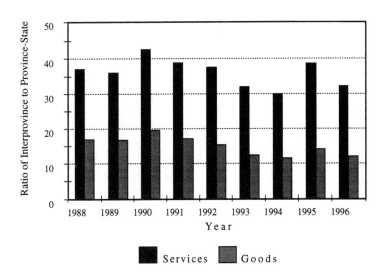

Source: John F. Helliwell, *How Much Do National Borders Matter?* (Washington, DC: The Brookings Institution, 1998), ch. 2.

provides some evidence to support the tentative conclusion of the next section — that the continuing high levels of national economic densities, relative to international ones, may not suggest that there are large productivity gains thereby lost.

A third feature of the post-FTA results is also worth flagging here. There is some evidence that the large post-FTA increases in merchandise trade between Canada and the United States were to some extent linked to decreases in interprovincial trade. Relative to the levels of GDP, 1996 interprovincial trade was almost 15 percent less than expected. Cross-industry estimation results reported in Helliwell, Lee and Messinger[10] suggest that about half of this reduction was due to the FTA-induced increases in north-south trade. Thus there is some evidence that some part of the increases in north-south trade was diverted from interprovincial trade. Nonetheless, even after the surprisingly large FTA effects are factored into north-south and east-west trade linkages, merchandise trade flows remain about 12 times denser east-west than north-south.

The finding of large border effects for Canadian merchandise trade led to attempts to develop data that could lead to replication, or not, of these results in an international setting. Unfortunately, domestic interregional trade data are not available for other countries, so that it is necessary to estimate total domestic sales (using data from input-output tables, not available even for all of the OECD countries) and then to use some plausible procedure for guessing what might be the typical internal trade distances. This is no mean feat, since the estimate hinges a great deal on how much internal trade goes on within rather than between the large cities and industrial areas. Wei assumed that internal trade distances were generally one-quarter those between the capitals of a country and its nearest neighbour.[11] On this basis, the latest estimate of the 1992 border effect for merchandise trade within and among the OECD countries is about 10 for countries not sharing a common language or membership in the European Union. Sharing a common language increases trade densities by more than 60 percent, while EU membership increases trade between member countries by about 40 percent. This 40 percent is a significant effect, but it emphasizes once again the surprisingly large size, almost equivalent to the cumulative EU effect, of the trade-increasing effects of the relatively small changes in tariffs that were embodied in the FTA.

Comparable estimates of border effects for developing countries show them to be up to 100 or more, with a strikingly tight relation between GDP per capita and the size of the border effect. If the gravity model is fitted to the data for the OECD countries plus a sample of other countries for which suitable data are available, the wide variety of border effects is successfully explained by the hypothesis that international differences in border effects are entirely due to international differences in real GDP per capita.[12] The link between GDP per capita and the size of border effects probably shows that countries become more open as their levels of income and education increase. It also interesting to consider the linkage the other way around, with countries having smaller border effects being more productive as a result. For developing countries, there is some evidence that this is the case, as Sachs and Warner have found higher growth rates among the more open developing countries.[13] However, for the richer economies the evidence is much weaker.[14] As will be noted below, if there were large productivity gains likely to flow from increasing international trade densities to the much higher levels of internal trade densities, we would expect to find that GDP per capita is much higher in larger than in smaller economies, since they have a much larger trade network within their national boundaries. There is no such effect apparent in the data. The possible implications of this will be discuss further in the next section.

Engel and Rogers reasoned that if trade densities are greater within than between national economies, then it should also be true that inter-city price differentials are larger and more enduring internationally than within the same country, for city pairs of the same distance from one another.[15] Using data for the inter-city co-variability of components of the consumer price index, for a sample of Canadian and US cities, they found that this was indeed the case, and calculated that the implied width of the US-Canada border was more than 2,000 miles. Subsequent research using their data[16] has shown the result to be even starker, since there is no evidence of cross-border price arbitrage for city pairs of any distance, making the border of infinite width in terms of their calculations. Of course, there is no doubt a lot of cross-border price competition, but it does not show up in month-to-month changes in the components of the consumer price index. National economies are so much tighter than the international economy that arbitrage of these prices among city pairs does show up even using the short-term data for components of the consumer price index, but not across national borders.

Turning to capital markets, there was an important finding by Feldstein and Horioka that domestic savings and national investment rates are correlated across countries, leading them to conclude that capital markets are separated rather than integrated.[17] To avoid such correlation entirely would require that markets for goods and capital both be tightly integrated. If provincial markets are tightly integrated, but national ones are not, then the Feldstein-Horioka result should be less evident, or disappear entirely, using interprovincial data. Helliwell and McKitrick pooled OECD and provincial data, and confirmed the Feldstein-Horioka result among the OECD countries, with the effect being completely reversed for the provincial data.[18] This is a strong confirmation of the Feldstein-Horioka interpretation, and shows that the interprovincial markets for goods and capital are tightly knitted together, while the international ones are not.

Border effects for migration, at least that from states to provinces, are even greater than for goods and services. Interprovincial migration is about 100 times more likely than is migration from a US state to a Canadian province, after taking due account, using the gravity model, of population, distance, and the economic incentives for migration.[19] The border effect is much smaller for migration from Canada to the United States, reflecting the greater southbound flows of migrants and the high interprovincial migration flows.

Finally, even though Coe and Helpman have provided convincing evidence that research and development spending has important productivity-enhancing effects both at home and abroad, the implied border effects are even larger than those for goods, services and population.[20]

IMPLICATIONS

If the evidence presented above is to be believed, the economic fabric of Canada, and of other nation states, has a much tighter weave than previously thought. Is this good or bad, and what does it suggest for current and future national policies?

Many studies have shown that among developing countries, and to a lesser extent among OECD countries, those that are more internationally open have had higher rates of growth of productivity and of incomes per capita. The basic intuition behind this result is that developing countries gain most by learning from the successes and failures of other countries, and tailoring the best of foreign ideas to suit domestic conditions. This is also consistent with studies of R&D spillovers, which find them to be larger for countries that have higher degrees of openness. If some degree of openness is a good thing for economic development, is much more openness even better? If so, then the fact that economic densities are much higher within than among national economies means that there is more to be gained from further increases in international linkages. On the other hand, if some degree of openness is sufficient to achieve the major gains from international exchange, specialization, and the acquisition of fresh ideas, then there may be diminishing returns to openness. If so, and if there are some efficiency effects offered by the partial segmentation of global markets into national pools, then there may be some right amount of openness that may not differ much from the levels already achieved by the industrial countries.

What is the available evidence on these issues? First, as already noted, there is evidence than some degree of openness is good for growth. However, if further increases in openness, beyond those already achieved by the richer OECD countries, promised great efficiency gains, then we would expect to find that bigger countries (in terms of GDP, not hectares) would have substantially higher levels of real GDP per capita, since they already have much larger trading networks, given the fact that trade is much denser within than among nation-states. However, there is no systematic evidence that larger countries have higher levels or rates of growth of productivity.

If income levels are not significantly higher in larger countries, and yet economic relations are much denser within than between countries, there are two broad types of explanation possible. One possible explanation is that while there are initially large gains from trade, both to exploit comparative advantage and to achieve efficient levels of scale in production, these gains have been largely reaped by the time international linkages have become as tight as they now are among the industrial countries. There may be more scope for increased openness to lead to temporarily higher growth rates in the developing countries, since there is still much for them to learn from elsewhere, but even here it is clear, as is evident from the recent experiences of cascading loan defaults across Asia, that interdependence may have costs as well as benefits.

The second possible reason why the insular nature of national economies may not be costly is that national boundaries may provide fairly efficient means of segmenting impossibly large markets into manageable chunks. It is well known that in a fully informed and frictionless world of a seamless global market place there would be no need for borders, for firms, or for most of the other institutions of the old and new worlds. But the real world has frictions; knowledge is tough to acquire and becomes obsolete; people cannot always be trusted; contracts are not always what they seem to be; one bad apple can spoil the whole bushel; and Murphy's Law may the only one that applies without an expensive legal process. In such a world, which is the only one on offer, not everyone is equally informed, and people are best informed about the events, institutions, and people they know best.

To deal with those you know and trust, under shared and well-understood rules and institutions, can mean lower costs and lower risks for all participants. Those who understand a market better are better able to guess its moods and changes, and to adapt flexibly to new patterns of demand and new and better ways of doing things. To the extent that national boundaries separate communities that have common institutions and shared views, local businesses are likely to be able to meet local market needs at lower cost than are their foreign or global competitors. There are limits to this, of course, set on the one hand by economies of scale and on the other by the possibility of exporting tastes and preferences, thus building a global market from scratch. Even the most successful global products, however, often have national systems of production and distribution, and characteristics specially put in to suit national tastes. What is surprising, in the latest evidence about the strength of national economies, is that the global market is very much the exception, and the national market the rule.

How does this view of tightly woven national economies tie in with the rediscovery of local economies as poles of growth? There is one strong link between the two. The benefits of close interaction, and the bonds of trust that are built up among those who have many repeated dealings underlie the logic of local economies and the strength of the national economy. Distance is costly, and tends to cause economies to cluster. The regional literature focuses on the effects of distance and also on whatever historical events may have led to a city to get started in the first place. The national borders results, on the other hand, show that distance has many more dimensions than simply kilometres or miles. To whatever extent history, politics and geography have spread people around in groups with different institutions, values and networks, their economic relations will follow similar patterns. This may be partly because patterns, once started, are costly to change, but it also reflects the cost advantages possessed by those who are nearby, well-informed, and well-trusted. Physical distance is indeed an important separating device, but national boundaries are also important. One of the findings from recent research is that for different markets the effects of national borders can be interpreted in terms of distance, and the implied numbers are strikingly large, often in the order of thousands of miles.

Currently, the Canadian economy operates as a fairly seamless web of intersecting regional markets for goods, services, capital, and migration. Although there is some slight evidence of segmentation by province of some markets for goods, but not for capital, the degree of segmentation is tiny compared to that between nations, even in post-FTA North America. Further research will no doubt help to show places where national borders, and other elements of distance, have stopped good ideas travelling to where they could have been of use. The same will be true for bad ideas. In the meantime, the evidence suggests that there is still a strong fabric underlying the Canadian national economy, and that this structure may have continuing economic advantages relative to the more homogenized global economy than many think has already arrived.

What are the political implications of these results? One important Canadian implication of the economic integrity of Canada, already noted[21] relates to the economic implications of political separation. If Canadians in Quebec and other provinces think that trading linkages between Quebec and the United States are as tight as those between Quebec and the rest of Canada, they are likely to be seriously wrong in their estimates of the economic consequences of separation, since the reality is that the economic fabric of Canada is much tighter than they thought. A second implication of the relatively tight fabric of national economies is that national economic policies have greater national impact, and more international independence, than they would in a more globalized economy. Despite the increasing scope of international movements of goods and capital, and the fast and often synchronous operation of international capital markets, nation-states tend to comprise individuals and businesses sharing much by way of tastes, familial and social ties, institutions, and economic structure. To some extent, which will be tested by the introduction of the Euro, this is due to political borders also defining currency areas, but there is no doubt much else in play. How enduring these special linkages will be remains to be seen. They are currently so large that they are likely to remain important for a long time even in the face of substantial changes.

NOTES

I am very grateful for helpful comments by the editors and two anonymous referees.

1. Thomas J. Courchene, *From Heartland to North American Region State: The Social, Fiscal and Federal Evolution of Ontario* (Toronto: University of Toronto Faculty of Management, 1998); Kenichi Ohmae, *The End of the Nation State: The Rise of Region Economies* (New York: The Free Press, 1995).

2. John F. Helliwell, "Do National Boundaries Matter For Quebec's Trade?" *Canadian Journal of Economics* 29 (1996): 507-22.

3. John C.P. McCallum, "National Borders Matter: Canada-U.S. Regional Trade Patterns," *American Economic Review* 85 (1995): 615-23.

4. For example, in John N.H. Britton, *Canada and the Global Economy: The Geography of Structural and Technological Change* (Montreal and Kingston: McGill-Queen's University Press, 1995), there are no data presented on the rela-

tive strengths of interprovincial and international economic linkages, and no reference is made to Ross Mackay's "The Interactance Hypothesis and Boundaries in Canada: A Preliminary Study," *The Canadian Geographer* 11 (1958): 1-8, a review of long-distance telephone calls from Ontario and Quebec cities, showing national border effects much larger than those between cities differing greatly in the relative use of French and English.

5. The derivation and details of the gravity model are presented more fully in John F. Helliwell, *How Much Do National Borders Matter?* (Washington, DC: The Brookings Institution, 1998), ch. 2. Here I shall try to give a less technical explanation.

6. Despite its use in many early studies of international trade, the equation was considered suspect in that it could not easily be shown to be consistent with the dominant Heckscher-Ohlin model explaining net trade flows in terms of differential factor endowments. In "A Theoretical Foundation for the Gravity Equation," *American Economic Review* 69 (1979): 106-16, James E. Anderson showed that the gravity model could be derived from expenditure share equations assuming commodities to be distinguished by place of production. Anderson also showed that the model, to be fully consistent with the generalized expenditure share model, should include remoteness measures in bilateral share equations, as we do here. E. Helpman, "Increasing Returns, Imperfect Markets, and Trade Theory," in *Handbook of International Trade*, ed. R. Jones and P. Kenen (Amsterdam: North-Holland, 1984), vol. 1, pp. 325-65; and Jeffrey H. Bergstrand, "The Gravity Equation in International Trade: Some Microeconomic Foundations and Empirical Evidence," *Review of Economics and Statistics* 67 (1985): 474-81 showed that the gravity model can also be derived from models of trade in differentiated products. Such trade must lie at the core of much of manufacturing trade, given the very large two-way flows of trade in even the most finely disaggregated industry data. Finally, Alan Deardorff showed in "Does Gravity Work in a Frictionless World?" in *The Regionalization of the World Economy*, ed. Jeffrey A. Frankel (Chicago: University of Chicago Press, 1997), p. 728, that a suitable modelling of transport costs produces the gravity equation as an estimation form even for the Heckscher-Ohlin model.

7. McCallum, "National Borders Matter."

8. Helliwell, *How Much Do National Borders Matter?* ch. 2.

9. John F. Helliwell, Frank C. Lee and Hans Messinger, "Effects of the Canada-US FTA on Interprovincial Trade" (Ottawa: Industry Canada draft working paper, 1998), Tables 5 and 6, show the forecast and actual post-FTA changes in Canada-US trade for each of 25 major sectors. Averaging across the sectors, Canadian exports were forecast, by the trade model used to support the official forecasts, to increase by 33 percent, relative to GDP, but actually increased by more than 90 percent. Imports were forecast to increase by 12 percent, while actual growth, relative to GDP, from 1989 to 1996 was 46 percent. These are simple averages of the sectoral results, which are larger than the figures for total trade because some of the smallest sectors, such as knitted products, have had the fastest post-FTA growth in two-way trade.

10. Helliwell *et al.*, "Effects of the Canada-US FTA on Interprovincial Trade."

11. Shang-Jin Wei, *Intra-national Versus International Trade: How Stubborn Are Nations in Global Integration?* NBER Working Paper 5531 (Cambridge: National Bureau of Economic Research, 1996).

12. These international results, along with further discussion of their trends and implications, are reported in Helliwell, *How Much Do National Borders Matter?* ch. 3.

13. Jeffrey D. Sachs and Andrew Warner, "Economic Reform and the Process of Global Integration," *Brookings Papers on Economic Activity* 1 (1995): 1-118.

14. John F. Helliwell, "Trade and Technical Progress," in *Economic Growth and the Structure of Long-Term Development*, ed. Luigi L. Pasinette and Robert M. Solow (London: Macmillan, 1993), pp. 253-71.

15. Charles Engel and J.H. Rogers, "How Wide is the Border?" *American Economic Review* 86 (1996): 1112-25.

16. Reported in Helliwell, *How Much Do National Borders Matter?* ch. 4.

17. M. Feldstein and C. Horioka, "Domestic Saving and International Capital Flows," *Economic Journal* 90 (1980): 314-29.

18. John F. Helliwell and Ross McKitrick, *Comparing Capital Mobility Across Provincial and National Borders*, NBER Working Paper (Cambridge: National Bureau of Economic Research, 1998).

19. Helliwell, *How Much Do National Borders Matter?* ch. 5.

20. D.T. Coe and E. Helpman, "International R&D Spillovers," *European Economic Review* 39 (1995): 859-87; see also Helliwell, *How Much Do National Borders Matter?* ch. 6.

21. Helliwell, "Do National Boundaries Matter For Quebec's Trade?"

5

Interprovincial Mobility in Canada, 1961-1996: Importance and Destination

Marc Vachon and François Vaillancourt

Ce chapitre démontre que le taux de migration interne a subi une baisse importante depuis le début des années 1980 chutant de près du tiers. Bien que le vieillissement de la population y soit sans doute pour quelque chose, cette baisse est visible dans différentes catégories d'âge, de sexe et de niveau de scolarité. Les liens familiaux interprovinciaux favorisent la création d'une conscience partagée par les Canadiens. Ce chapitre souligne également l'effet à long terme des migrations interprovinciales, nommément la proportion de résidants vivant dans une province autre que leur province d'origine. Au début des années 1990, la proportion de résidants nés ailleurs au Canada dans les provinces riches — Colombie-Britannique, Alberta et Ontario — était respectivement de 33, 33 et 11 pour cent. En revanche, environ 27 pour cent des natifs des provinces de l'Atlantiques ont migré dans une autre région du Canada. Conséquemment, les liens familiaux interprovinciaux au Canada anglais sont fort importants.

INTRODUCTION

The purpose of this chapter is to present evidence on the importance and determinants of interprovincial migration. This is of interest for two reasons. First, the importance of migration. Since 1962, at least 300,000 Canadians move each year between provinces. From 1961 to 1982, gross migration grew, peaking at 435,000 in 1982. Since 1982, yearly internal migration has remained between 300,000 and 380,000, a flow more important than international migration to Canada. Gross flows between provinces matter because this explains the extent to which individuals in any one region may have ties to another region based on previous residence. This is appropriate in a volume whose purpose is to shed light on linkages among Canadians. Interprovincial migration affects each province in different ways. Ontario, Alberta, and British Columbia are net gainers, while others such as Newfoundland, Quebec, Manitoba, and Saskatchewan are the main losers.

Second, interprovincial migration has economic and political implications. Migration helps real wages and unemployment converge between Canadian regions by allowing a better match between employment opportunities and place of residence. Migration also affects provincial public finances since some intergovernmental grants, such as Established Programs Financing/Canada Health and Social Transfer (EPF/CHST) and equalization grants, are calculated using population. Finally, it has an impact on the political weight of each province in the Canadian federal Parliament given that the number of constituencies by province depends, in part, on provincial population.

The chapter is divided into two sections. The first uses population flow data to describe the levels of interprovincial migration and population stock data to examine the changes in the age and schooling of interprovincial migrants. The second presents the origin and destinations of migrants and the impact of migration on the composition of the resident population, using respectively flow and stock data.

LEVELS OF INTERPROVINCIAL MIGRATION, 1961-1996

This section first presents net-migration rates for the 1971-96 period for Canada as a whole and for each province individually. That done, it examines graphically migration flows for each province for the 1961-96 period. We use data from Statistics Canada's family allowance files, found in Table A-1 in the Appendix, on out- and in-migration flows to prepare the figures used in this section. We also use these data and population figures to calculate the net-migration rates reported in Table 1.

Statistics Canada uses administrative data to estimate annual interprovincial mobility. Data from two sources are used: family allowances/child tax benefit recipients and income tax filers. Estimates calculated using family allowances/child tax benefits data are affected by the coverage of this program. Three phases can be distinguished: (i) 1961-73, when children aged 0-15 years, of citizens or landed immigrants, were eligible; (ii) 1974-92, when children aged up to 18 were eligible; (iii) 1993-96, family allowances were replaced by the Child Tax Benefit, which is income-based. Income tax data have been used since 1976. Such data cover only tax filers whose number may be affected by changes in both tax laws and social programs using family income for calculating benefits. We are using family allowance migration estimates for the whole period to improve intertemporal comparability at the provincial level. As a result, numbers reported here, while obtained from Statistics Canada, differ from published final estimates (such as those found in the annual *Report on the Demographic Situation in Canada*).

The first key finding of Table 1 is the reduction in the Canadian gross-migration rate. From 1971 to 1996, this rate decreased by one-third — from

Table 1: Interprovincial Migration: Net-Migration Rates by Province and Gross Migration Rates, Canada, 1971-1996 (in percent)

	Nfd.	PEI	NS	NB	Que.	Ont.	Man.	Sask.	Alta.	BC	Canada
1971	-0.694	0.204	-0.456	-0.075	-0.614	0.601	-0.712	-2.511	0.445	0.942	1.790
1972	0.156	0.321	-0.057	0.060	-0.350	0.189	-0.876	-2.001	0.281	1.209	1.724
1973	-0.112	0.604	0.606	0.320	-0.316	0.013	-0.514	-1.756	0.335	1.133	1.701
1974	-0.490	0.714	0.121	0.340	-0.198	-0.120	-0.157	-1.142	0.140	1.243	1.861
1975	0.133	1.149	0.304	0.891	-0.164	-0.334	-0.583	0.059	1.275	0.394	1.718
1976	0.026	0.376	0.436	0.846	-0.208	-0.225	-0.443	0.572	1.389	-0.180	1.545
1977	-0.269	0.979	-0.015	0.358	-0.386	-0.078	-0.336	0.718	1.223	0.090	1.615
1978	-0.424	0.704	0.092	0.285	-0.711	0.110	-0.699	0.133	1.248	0.609	1.634
1979	-0.311	0.026	0.139	0.178	-0.486	-0.103	-1.097	0.185	1.414	0.736	1.590
1980	-0.154	0.221	-0.084	0.051	-0.473	-0.246	-1.537	-0.064	1.413	1.413	1.668
1981	-0.293	-0.806	-0.099	-0.383	-0.351	-0.355	-1.017	-0.117	1.569	1.278	1.734
1982	-0.923	-0.629	-0.202	-0.349	-0.338	-0.121	-0.196	0.044	1.677	0.180	1.730
1983	0.247	0.288	0.183	0.357	-0.330	0.183	0.067	0.271	-0.310	0.115	1.416
1984	-0.448	0.295	0.484	0.147	-0.283	0.468	-0.096	0.440	-1.777	0.399	1.475
1985	-0.564	0.508	0.257	-0.058	-0.140	0.418	0.379	-0.431	-1.077	-0.086	1.447
1986	-0.910	-0.197	-0.176	-0.392	-0.035	0.345	-0.257	-0.761	-0.121	-0.226	1.395
1987	-0.838	-0.233	-0.052	-0.356	-0.062	0.460	-0.298	-0.708	-1.220	0.272	1.385
1988	-0.767	0.430	-0.093	-0.290	-0.130	0.265	-0.534	-1.283	-0.634	0.780	1.355
1989	-0.290	0.284	-0.072	-0.097	-0.140	0.076	-0.983	-1.586	-0.113	1.076	1.328
1990	-0.380	-0.391	-0.059	0.105	-0.082	-0.076	-0.696	-1.658	0.143	1.118	1.280
1991	-0.584	-0.832	0.019	-0.067	-0.198	-0.093	-0.699	-1.168	0.358	1.148	1.338
1992	-0.350	-1.022	-0.043	-0.287	-0.192	-0.025	-0.725	-0.927	0.102	1.067	1.213
1993	-0.588	0.447	-0.209	-0.181	-0.207	-0.039	-0.540	-0.838	-0.050	1.154	1.179
1994	-0.756	0.462	-0.074	0.044	-0.171	-0.097	-0.413	-0.309	-0.205	1.105	1.260
1995	-1.392	0.646	-0.390	-0.115	-0.208	0.041	-0.193	-0.399	-0.160	0.849	1.212
1996	-1.262	0.622	-0.084	-0.030	-0.178	-0.051	-0.174	-0.093	0.199	0.612	1.163

Source: Calculations by the authors using data from Table A-1 and population data from Statistics Canada.

1.8 to 1.2 percent. This reduction is not a gradual one, but rather is character-ized by a sharp break between 1981-82 and 1982-83, from 1.7 to 1.4 percent. Between 1971-1981, the rate never went below 1.5 percent, while any time after that, it never went above that figure. From 1971 to 1982, it fluctuated, while after that, it trends downwards. Such a reduction in internal migration can reduce the capability of labour markets to adjust to outside shocks, par-ticularly if the composition of migrants changes. We examine this using census data in Tables 2 and 3.

Table 2: Migration Rates, Percentage by Age Group and Level of Education, Men, 1976-1981 and 1986-1991 Changes in Rates between the Two Periods

Age Group	Less than High School	High School Diploma	Community College (Cegep) Diploma	University	Total
			1976-1981		
15-19	4.25	4.40	3.03	4.79	4.19
20-24	8.13	7.37	9.03	9.13	8.40
25-34	6.24	6.05	8.48	12.57	8.61
35-44	4.02	4.39	5.17	8.50	5.46
45-54	2.10	2.75	4.14	5.93	3.18
55-64	1.33	1.52	2.82	5.09	2.06
65 +	1.43	1.74	3.27	3.37	1.80
Total	3.66	4.64	6.35	9.09	5.32
			1986-1991		
15-19	3.27	2.25	1.63	4.87	3.03
20-24	4.75	4.36	5.00	6.35	5.18
25-34	4.95	4.68	6.41	10.26	6.72
35-44	3.13	3.29	4.44	5.92	4.34
45-54	1.82	2.52	3.20	3.86	2.75
55-64	1.41	1.59	2.68	2.80	1.87
65 +	1.21	1.85	2.17	2.81	1.61
Total	2.69	3.23	4.55	6.33	4.00
			Changes in Migration Rates		
15-19	-23.1	-48.9	-46.2	+1.7	-27.7
20-24	-41.6	-40.8	-44.6	-30.4	-38.3
25-34	-20.7	-22.6	-24.4	-18.4	-22.0
35-44	-22.1	-25.1	-14.1	-30.4	-20.5
45-54	-13.3	-8.4	-22.7	-34.9	-13.5
55-64	-6.0	+4.6	-5.0	-45.0	-9.2
65 +	-15.4	+6.3	-33.6	-16.6	-10.6
Total	-26.5	-30.4	-28.3	-30.4	-24.8

Changes: $1- \dfrac{1986-1991\%}{1976-1981\%}$

Note: Selected Education Levels.

Source: Public microdata files, 1981 (2 percent sample) and 1991 (3 percent sample).

Table 3: Migration Rates, Percentage by Age Group and Level of Education, Women, 1976-1981 and 1986-1991 Changes in Rates between the Two Periods

Age Group	Less than High School	High School Diploma	Community College (Cegep) Diploma	University	Total
		1976-1981			
15-19	4.67	3.91	3.19	5.77	4.40
20-24	7.32	6.87	8.85	10.11	8.19
25-34	6.32	5.57	8.95	12.18	8.19
35-44	3.31	3.62	6.55	6.84	4.72
45-54	2.03	2.09	4.06	4.15	2.65
55-64	1.73	2.12	3.29	3.53	2.16
65 +	1.46	2.30	2.73	3.07	1.79
Total	3.41	4.43	6.50	8.63	4.93
		1986-1991			
15-19	3.56	2.93	2.59	4.27	3.38
20-24	5.67	4.85	5.74	6.64	5.85
25-34	4.65	4.22	6.24	9.16	6.25
35-44	2.87	3.16	4.22	5.10	3.88
45-54	1.81	1.91	2.98	3.18	2.36
55-64	1.34	1.55	2.71	2.74	1.76
65 +	1.23	1.70	2.20	2.14	1.48
Total	2.47	3.07	4.49	5.95	3.73
		Changes in Migration Rates			
15-19	-23.8	-25.1	-18.8	-26.0	-23.2
20-24	-22.5	-29.4	-35.1	-34.3	-28.6
25-34	-26.4	-24.2	-30.3	-24.8	-23.7
35-44	-13.3	-12.7	-35.6	-25.4	-17.8
45-54	-10.8	-8.6	-26.6	-23.4	-10.9
55-64	-22.5	-26.9	-17.6	-22.4	-18.5
65 +	-15.8	-26.1	-15.4	-30.3	-17.3
Total	-27.6	-30.7	-30.9	-31.1	-24.3

Changes: $1 - \dfrac{1986 - 1991\%}{1976 - 1981\%}$

Note: Selected Education Levels.

Source: Public microdata files, 1981 (2 percent sample) and 1991 (3 percent sample).

Tables 2 and 3 present some evidence about migration rates per age group and level of education, obtained from the microdata files of the 1981 and 1991 Canadian censuses.[1] We find, as usual, that the more mobile groups are found amongst the youngest group (the 20-24 age group for the less educated and the 25-34 age group for the more educated), that migration rates decrease with age and that individuals with more education have a higher propensity to migrate.

From 1976-81 to 1986-91, the reduction in mobility rates is greatest for those with a university degree and for those aged 20-24, indicating that young bachelors move less in the second period than in the first. This may reflect a leveling of the growth rates between the Canadian provinces with the disappearance of the oil boom in the 1986-91 period. There is no evidence of increased institutional impediments to mobility over the period.

Let us now turn to an examination of provincial migration flows since, as we will show, the Canadian numbers hide a diversity of provincial patterns.

ATLANTIC CANADA

We first examine Newfoundland. During the 1961-96 period, this province had a negative net out-migration 31 of the 35 years, losing 101,000 migrants in total, or 18 percent of its 1996 population. One notes the recent increase of gross out-migration in 1995 and 1996 to about 18,000, the highest for the entire period, as shown in Figure 1. This is probably linked to recent fishing restrictions. Another point of interest is that positive net-migration flows were observed mainly when unemployment insurance was the most generous since its inception, that is, in the 1971-79 period.[2]

Figure 1: Newfoundland, In-, Out- and Net-Migration, 1961-1996

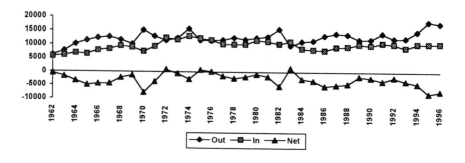

Source: Table A-1 in Appendix.

Turning to the Maritimes, we note, as shown in Figures 2, 3, and 4, that out-migration decreased and then in-migration increased after 1970, leading to positive net-migration between 1972 and 1976, which is probably explained by the increase in the generosity of unemployment insurance in 1970. Second, the recession of 1981-82 reduced out-migration from these provinces. Out-migration from Prince Edward Island fell over the 1992-96 period, perhaps because of the economic activity generated by the building of the fixed link.

Figure 2: *Prince Edward Island, In-, Out- and Net-Migration, 1961-1996*

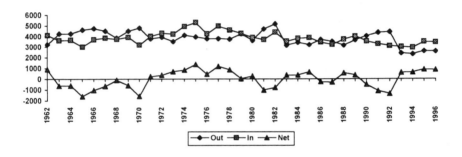

Source: Table A-1 in Appendix.

Figure 3: *Nova Scotia, In-, Out- and Net-Migration, 1961-1996*

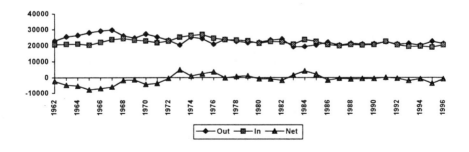

Source: Table A-1 in Appendix.

Figure 4: New Brunswick, In-, Out- and Net-Migration, 1961-1996

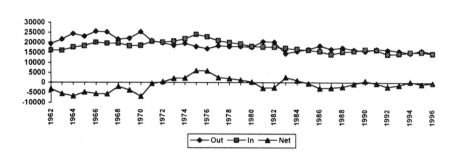

Source: Table A-1 in Appendix.

In total, Prince Edward Island, Nova Scotia, and New Brunswick had a negative net-migration of 73,000 individuals from 1961 to 1996 or about 4 percent of their 1996 population.

QUEBEC

Quebec is a different (distinct, unique) labour market, given the use of the French language and the lack of knowledge of English by the majority of the population. It is also the only province where an (active) independence movement exists. A knowledge of the evolution of nationalism over the 1961-96 period is necessary for a better understanding of migration flows. The election of the liberals in 1960 initiated the "révolution tranquille," aimed at increasing the control by francophones of Quebec's economy.[3] The visit of the French president Charles de Gaulle in 1967 and his famous "Vive le Québec libre" gave a boost to nationalist groups.

From a migration perspective, the first important event was the combination of the first language law (Bill 63) in 1969 and the October crisis in 1970. As shown in Figure 5, it generated an important increase in out-migration, with the number of out-migrants rising from 55,000-60,000 to 70,000+ in 1969-71. Most of these migrants went to Ontario, as shown by the in-migration data for that province. The second shock was the election of the Parti Québécois in 1976. Out-migration again reached 70,000 in 1977-78 for a third year since 1962. The election of the Liberal Party in 1985 reduced out-migration (1985-86) to its lowest level since 1962 (35,000-40,000). The third shock was the failure of the Meech Lake Accord in 1990, which gave momentum to nationalists, with surveys showing that 60-70 percent of the population favoured sovereignty at that time. Out-migration rose in 1990-91 to 45,000, the highest level in the 1984-96 period. Overall, Quebec suffered a net out-migration of 563,000 individuals between 1961 and 1996. This represents nearly 8 percent of the 1996 population of Quebec.

Figure 5: Quebec, In-, Out- and Net-Migration, 1961-1996

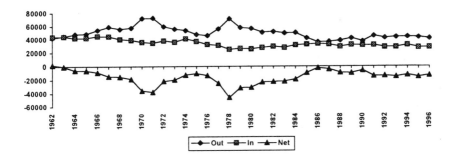

Source: Table A-1 in Appendix.

ONTARIO

In- and out-migration for Ontario (the largest province) is related to both economic and political events. As shown in Figure 6, in-migration reached a peak of approximately 130,000 individuals in 1969-71, mainly as a result of Quebec out-migration.

Figure 6: Ontario, In-, Out- and Net-Migration, 1961-1996

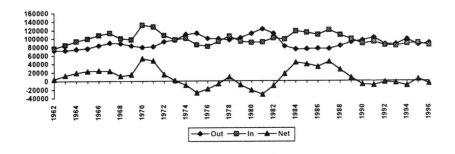

Source: Table A-1 in Appendix.

Migration in and out of Ontario is also linked to the economy of Alberta between 1974 and 1988. Following the increases in petroleum prices of 1973 and 1979, almost 100,000 Ontarians left each year from 1973 to 1982. After the recession in the early 1980s, in-migration increased to 100,000 per year from 1981 to 1988, while out-migration dropped. This increased in-migration is linked to out-migration from Alberta.

Over the 1961-96 period, Ontario gained 297,000 migrants, which is less than 3 percent of its 1996 population.

PRAIRIES

Manitoba and Saskatchewan, referred to as the Prairies in this text, lost 448,000 migrants to other provinces between 1961 and 1996, almost as much as Quebec, but at 21 percent, a much larger share of their 1996 population (21 percent). They are net gainers in only 4 of the 35 years, as shown in Figures 7 and 8. Manitoba appears to be more sensitive to oil prices than Saskatchewan where, the price of grain may matter more.

Figure 7: Manitoba, In-, Out- and Net-Migration, 1961-1996

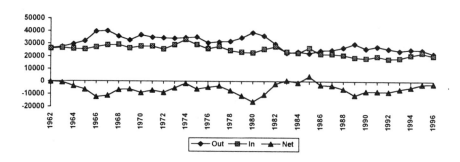

Source: Table A-1 in Appendix.

Figure 8: Saskatchewan, In-, Out- and Net-Migration, 1961-1996

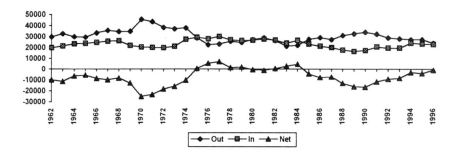

Source: Table A-1 in Appendix.

ALBERTA

If Quebec is unique in terms of its culture, Alberta is unique in terms of its economy. As shown in Figure 9, migration to Alberta is strongly related to the price of oil. After the increase in the price of oil, in-migration doubled from 61,000 in 1972-73 to 124,000 in 1981-82. Out-migration began to climb with the recession of the early 1980s and reached a high in 1984 when 105,000 individuals left the province.

Figure 9: Alberta, In-, Out- and Net-Migration, 1961-1996

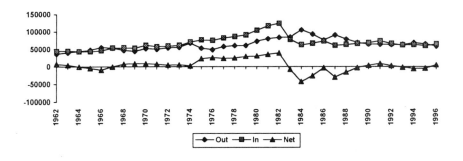

Source: Table A-1 in Appendix.

Overall, Alberta is a gainer from in-migration. Between 1961 and 1996, this province gained 161,000 migrants or 6 percent of its 1996 population.

BRITISH COLUMBIA

For British Columbia, both interprovincial and international migration represent important factors of population growth. Over the 1961-96 period interprovincial, net-migration yielded a gain of 725,000 migrants, the highest gain by a province in Canada and equal to 19 percent of its 1996 population. British Columbia has had positive in-migration 33 of 36 years. It gained more than 30,000 individuals every year between 1988 and 1996, with a peak of 41,000 in 1993, as shown in Figure 10.

Figure 10: British Columbia, In-, Out- and Net-Migration, 1961-1996

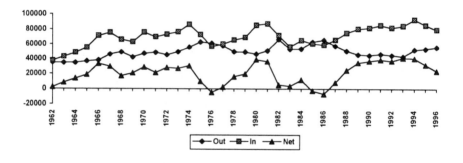

Source: Table A-1 in Appendix.

ORIGIN – DESTINATION OF MIGRANTS

This section describes where migrants originate from and go to for selected years (1971, 1981, 1991, and 1996) for six regions of Canada.

ATLANTIC CANADA

As shown in Table 4, Ontario is the main migration partner of Atlantic Canada, sending and receiving about 55 percent of the relevant migration flow, with its share slowly decreasing over time. This may reflect the fact that Ontario is

Table 4: Atlantic Canada, In- and Out-Migration Flows and Shares, 1970-71, 1980-81, 1990-91 and 1995-96

	Quebec		Ontario		Prairies		Alberta		BC		Total
	N	%	N	%	N	%	N	%	N	%	N
In 1971	8,805	21.6	24,483	60.1	2,596	6.4	2,138	5.2	2,738	6.7	40,760
In 1981	5,812	14.5	21,769	54.5	2,721	6.8	6,230	15.6	3,433	8.6	39,965
In 1991	4,964	13.3	23,300	62.3	1,898	5.1	4,042	10.8	3,172	8.5	37,376
In 1996	4,116	12.0	19,512	56.9	1,550	4.5	4,667	13.6	4,446	13.0	34,291
Total	23,697	15.6	89,064	57.1	8,765	5.8	17,077	11.2	13,789	9.0	152,392
Out 1971	6,416	13.1	32,583	66.6	2,890	5.9	2,962	6.1	4,090	8.4	48,941
Out 1981	4,757	10.3	20,533	44.4	3,369	7.3	12,502	27.1	5,053	10.9	46,214
Out 1991	4,747	11.3	24,976	59.2	2,267	5.4	4,889	11.6	5,305	12.6	42,184
Out 1996	3,784	9.1	21,513	51.6	2,081	5.0	7,193	17.3	7,103	17.0	41,674
Total	19,704	11.0	99,605	55.6	10,607	5.9	27,546	15.4	21,551	12.0	179,013

Note: *Total:* This is the sum of the four flows and the average in percentage.

Source: Table A-1. Calculations by the authors using annual migration data from Statistics Canada.

the closest English-speaking province to Atlantic Canada. From 1971 to 1996, Quebec became less and Alberta and British Columbia more of a migrating partner. Ties between Atlantic Canada and Alberta may strengthen as the former's oil and gas production becomes more significant.

QUEBEC

Quebec and Ontario are important migration partners, sending and receiving 60 percent of the relevant flow, as shown in Table 5. This may reflect, in part, the exchanges between field operations and head offices in both provinces. Out-migrants to Alberta peaked in 1981, while one notes an increase in the share of out-migrants to British Columbia over time.

ONTARIO

While Quebec is the most important in-migrant source for Ontario, over time Atlantic Canada has been replaced by British Columbia, as shown in Table 6, as the most important destination for out-migrants. Neither, however, plays as important a role for Ontario as Ontario plays for them. Put differently, Ontario

Table 5: Quebec, In- and Out-Migration Flows and Shares,
1970-71, 1980-81, 1990-91 and 1995-96

	Atlantic Canada		Ontario		Prairies		Alberta		BC		Total
	N	%	N	%	N	%	N	%	N	%	N
In 1971	6,414	18.6	21,222	61.6	2,526	7.3	1,743	5.1	2,565	7.4	34,470
In 1981	4,757	17.3	16,135	58.6	1,430	5.2	2,921	10.6	2,286	8.3	27,529
In 1991	4,747	15.2	20,848	66.9	1,268	4.1	1,864	6.0	2,419	7.8	31,146
In 1996	3,784	13.6	19,153	68.7	915	3.3	1,564	5.6	2,482	8.9	27,898
Total	19,702	16.3	77,358	63.9	6,139	5.1	8,092	6.7	9,752	8.1	121,043
Out 1971	8,805	12.2	51,091	70.7	2,447	3.4	3,448	4.8	6,467	8.9	72,257
Out 1981	5,812	11.5	29,254	57.9	1,582	3.1	9,004	17.8	4,910	9.7	50,562
Out 1991	4,747	10.6	30,072	66.9	1,499	3.3	3,213	7.2	5,391	12.0	44,922
Out 1996	4,116	10.0	27,522	67.0	1,146	2.8	2,131	5.2	6,157	15.0	41,072
Total	23,480	11.2	137,939	66.1	6,674	3.2	17,796	8.5	22,925	11.0	208,813

Note: *Total:* This is the sum of the four flows and the average in percentage.

Source: Table A-1. Calculations by the authors using annual migration data from Statistics Canada.

Table 6: Ontario, In- and Out-Migration Flows and Shares,
1970-71, 1980-81, 1990-91 and 1995-96

	Atlantic Canada		Ontario		Prairies		Alberta		BC		Total
	N	%	N	%	N	%	N	%	N	%	N
In 1971	32,583	25.4	51,091	39.9	17,812	13.9	11,293	8.8	15,256	11.9	128,035
In 1981	20,533	22.6	29,254	32.2	10,976	12.1	17,450	19.2	12,744	14.0	90,957
In 1991	24,976	27.2	30,072	32.7	11,719	12.7	12,919	14.1	12,249	13.3	91,935
In 1996	21,513	25.7	27,522	32.9	8,844	10.6	10,368	12.4	15,418	18.4	83,665
Average (%)	99,605	25.2	137,939	35.0	49,351	12.5	52,030	13.2	55,667	14.1	394,592
Out 1971	24,483	30.3	21,222	26.3	9,456	11.7	8,763	10.9	16,788	20.8	80,712
Out 1981	21,769	17.8	16,135	13.2	13,938	11.4	45,833	37.5	24,684	20.2	122,359
Out 1991	23,300	22.9	20,848	20.5	10,415	10.2	20,768	20.4	26,365	25.9	101,696
Out 1996	19,512	21.8	19,153	21.4	8,929	10.0	13,668	15.3	28,093	31.4	89,355
Average (%)	89,064	22.6	77,358	19.6	42,738	10.8	89,032	22.6	95,930	24.3	394,122

Source: Table A-1. Calculations by the authors using annual migration data from Statistics Canada.

is a more diversified region than Quebec or Atlantic Canada on the migration market. Overall, the importance of British Columbia has increased from 1971 to 1996 in Ontario's migrating flows.

PRAIRIES

Table 7 shows that migration to and from the Prairies mainly involves the following three provinces: Ontario, Alberta, and British Columbia, with Alberta increasing its role over time. The second destination is British Columbia, followed by Ontario. Migration between the Prairies, on the one hand and Quebec and Atlantic Canada on the other, is small and decreasing over time.

ALBERTA

The share of Atlantic Canadians and Ontarians in Alberta in-migration increases over the period, as indicated in Table 8. This reduces the share of the Prairies and British Columbia. Out-migrants go mainly to British Columbia; Atlantic Canada and Quebec are unpopular destinations.

Table 7: Prairies, In- and Out-Migration Flows and Shares, 1970-71, 1980-81, 1990-91 and 1995-96

	Atlantic Canada		Ontario		Prairies		Alberta		BC		Total
	N	%	N	%	N	%	N	%	N	%	N
In 1971	2,596	7.4	2,447	7.0	9,456	27.1	11,673	33.5	8,722	25.0	34,894
In 1981	3,369	7.6	1,582	3.6	13,938	31.0	16,490	37.4	8,691	19.7	44,070
In 1991	2,267	6.7	1,499	4.4	10,415	30.6	12,484	36.7	7,363	21.6	34,028
In 1996	2,081	5.7	1,146	3.1	8,929	24.5	15,098	41.4	9,230	25.3	36,484
Average (%)	10,313	6.9	6,674	4.5	42,738	28.6	55,745	37.3	34,006	22.8	149,476
Out 1971	2,890	4.4	2,526	3.9	17,812	27.2	23,494	35.9	18,764	28.7	65,486
Out 1981	2,721	4.9	1,430	2.6	10,976	19.7	25,006	44.8	15,648	28.1	55,781
Out 1991	1,898	3.5	1,268	2.4	11,719	21.9	23,480	43.8	15,198	28.4	53,563
Out 1996	1,550	3.9	915	2.3	8,844	22.4	17,261	43.8	10,845	27.5	39,415
Average (%)	9,059	4.2	6,139	2.9	49,351	23.0	89,241	41.7	60,455	28.2	214,245

Source: Table A-1. Calculations by the authors using annual migration data from Statistics Canada.

116   Marc Vachon and François Vaillancourt

**Table 8: Alberta, In- and Out-Migration Flows and Shares,
1970-71, 1980-81, 1990-91 and 1995-96**

	Atlantic Canada		Ontario		Prairies		Alberta		BC		Total
	N	%	N	%	N	%	N	%	N	%	N
In 1971	2,962	5.1	3,448	6.0	8,763	15.1	23,494	40.6	19,259	33.2	57,926
In 1981	12,502	10.7	9,004	7.7	45,833	39.4	25,006	21.5	23,993	20.6	116,338
In 1991	4,889	6.6	3,213	4.4	20,768	28.2	23,480	31.9	21,320	28.9	73,670
In 1996	7,193	11.1	2,131	3.3	13,668	21.2	17,261	26.7	24,326	37.7	64,579
Average (%)	27,546	8.8	17,796	5.7	89,032	28.5	89,241	28.6	88,898	28.4	312,513
Out 1971	2,138	4.2	1,743	3.5	11,293	22.4	11,673	23.1	23,634	46.8	50,481
Out 1981	6,230	7.8	2,921	3.6	17,450	21.8	16,490	20.6	37,101	46.3	80,192
Out 1991	4,042	6.3	1,864	2.9	12,919	20.1	12,484	19.4	33,055	51.4	64,364
Out 1996	4,667	7.9	1,564	2.6	10,368	17.6	15,098	25.6	27,322	46.3	59,019
Average (%)	17,077	6.7	8,092	3.2	52,030	20.5	55,745	21.9	121,112	47.7	254,056

Source: Table A-1. Calculations by the authors using annual migration data from Statistics Canada.

BRITISH COLUMBIA

Table 9 shows that British Columbia's two major migration partners are Alberta, its neighbour, and Ontario. The importance of migrants from the Prairies has fallen since 1971. Migration between British Columbia and Atlantic Canada and Quebec is small.

In summary, Canadians migrate from east to west, with Atlantic Canadians and Quebec residents going to Ontario, that province and Quebec swapping some residents, and Ontario and residents from the Prairies going to Alberta and British Columbia.

Since more than 300,000 Canadians move between provinces every year, this has an impact on the composition of the provincial population by place of birth and of residence. Table 10, constructed using the 1991 census microdata files, presents information on the pattern of population retention in each province. The first six columns are for Canadian-born individuals, while the seventh is for foreign-born individuals.

The retention rates of Canadian-born individuals are highest for Quebec, Ontario, and British Columbia, and lowest for Saskatchewan and Manitoba. Notwithstanding the considerable out-migration caused by both the independence movement and language policies, Quebec has the highest retention rate

Table 9: British Columbia, In- and Out-Migration Flows and Shares, 1970-71, 1980-81, 1990-91 and 1995-96

	Atlantic Canada		Ontario		Prairies		Alberta		BC		Total
	N	%	N	%	N	%	N	%	N	%	N
In 1971	4,090	5.9	6,467	9.3	16,788	24.1	18,764	26.9	23,634	33.9	69,743
In 1981	5,053	5.8	4,910	5.6	24,684	28.2	15,648	17.9	37,101	42.5	87,396
In 1991	5,305	6.2	5,391	6.3	26,365	30.9	15,198	17.8	33,055	38.7	85,314
In 1996	7,103	8.9	6,157	7.7	28,093	35.3	10,845	13.6	27,322	34.4	79,520
Average (%)	21,551	6.7	22,925	7.1	95,930	29.8	60,455	18.8	121,112	37.6	321,973
Out 1971	2,738	5.6	2,565	5.3	15,256	31.4	8,722	18.0	19,259	39.7	48,540
Out 1981	3,433	6.7	2,286	4.5	12,744	24.9	8,691	17.0	23,993	46.9	51,147
Out 1991	3,172	6.8	2,419	5.2	12,249	26.3	7,363	15.8	21,320	45.8	46,523
Out 1996	4,446	8.0	2,482	4.4	15,418	27.6	9,230	16.5	24,326	43.5	55,902
Average (%)	13,789	6.8	9,752	4.8	55,667	27.5	34,006	16.8	88,898	44.0	202,112

Source: Table A-1. Calculations by the authors using annual migration data from Statistics Canada.

Table 10: Composition of Regional Population, Canada 1991 Region of Residence by Region of Birth, Percentage of Regional Population Born Abroad and Percentage Born in Region of Residence

	Region of Birth							
	Canada							
Region of Residence	Atlantic (1)	Quebec (2)	Ontario (3)	Prairies (4)	Alberta (5)	British Columbia (6)	Born Abroad (7)	% Born in Region of Residence (8)
Atlantic	74	1	1	0	0	1	3	90
Quebec	4	91	2	1	0	0	9	87
Ontario	15	6	90	8	4	4	27	61
Prairies	1	0	1	62	3	2	11	74
Alberta	3	1	3	13	76	7	18	50
British Columbia	3	1	3	16	17	86	25	41

Note: Columns (1) to (6) sum vertically to 100 percent.

Source: Calculations by the authors using the 1991 Census Public microdata files (3 percent sample), rounded.

of all the provinces. This means that, given the mother-tongue composition of Quebec's population, anglophones have disproportionately left the province, something also found by Vaillancourt.[4]

The lowest retention rate is observed in the Prairies: it loses almost one in every three sons or daughters (close to one to two in Saskatchewan). Intriguingly enough, retention rates are higher in Atlantic Canada than in the Prairies, where economic conditions are usually better. Is it because the Prairies' residents are better educated than Atlantic Canadians and thus better suited for employment in the other provinces? Or is it because transfer payments are skewed toward fishermen and not farmers? Or is it because privately owned natural resources (farms) in the Prairies better transmit information about employment prospects than common property resources (fisheries) in Atlantic Canada? We do not know.

This stock information on the choice of the province of residence by migrants is in agreement with the flow information of Tables 4 to 9. Ontario is the most popular choice of Atlantic Canada- and Quebec-born migrants. We also observe that British Columbia is the first choice of Ontarian, Prairies, and Atlantic Canada migrants. Atlantic Canada, Quebec, and the Prairies are not popular destinations.

The share of non-native-born individuals varies greatly between provinces. They behave like Canadian-born individuals in their choice of residence, that is, residing mainly in Ontario and British Columbia. Finally, the last column of Table 10 shows that in Alberta and British Columbia, province-born residents are not a majority. This may have important implications for government policies and politics.

CONCLUSION

Our main findings are that:

- internal mobility has diminished by one-third from 1971 to 1996. This reduction was not smooth, but is marked by a break in the years 1982-83. The exact source of this break is unknown, but perhaps the higher mobility in 1971 to 1983 was a temporary phenomenon due to the oil boom and the Quebec political scene that masked a longer term declining trend due to aging and federal transfer programs;

- national mobility patterns mask marked differences in provincial ones which are linked to local issues such as the collapse of the cod fisheries (Newfoundland), the victory in 1976 of the PQ (Quebec), the prices of wheat (Saskatchewan) and oil (Alberta). One common factor in the Atlantic provinces is the generosity of the Unemployment Insurance system;

- Atlantic Canada, Quebec, and the Prairies do not attract migration on a net basis. Atlantic residents migrate to Quebec and Ontario, Quebec residents to Ontario and Prairies residents to Alberta and British Columbia. Overall, there is a westward drift ending at the Pacific;

- the reduction in overall mobility is particularly marked for the university-educated group, but is observed across all age and education groups;

- internal migration has a marked impact on the composition of the population of provinces. Eastern provinces are populated overwhelmingly by those born there while only a minority of British Columbia residents were born there.

Overall, migration appears to be a less binding tie over time and one that binds various regions more or less strongly.

NOTES

1. At the time of writing, the 1996 microdata file was not yet available.

2. Z. Lin, "Employment Insurance in Canada: Recent Trends and Policy Changes," *Canadian Tax Journal* 46, 1 (1998):58-76.

3. F. Vaillancourt, "Le français dans un contexte économique," in *De la polyphonie à la symphonie,* ed. J. Erfurt (Leipzig: Presses de l'Université, 1996), pp. 119-36.

4. F. Vaillancourt, "English and Anglophones in Québec: An Economic Perspective," in *Survival: Official Language Rights in Canada* (Toronto: C.D. Howe Institute, 1992), pp. 63-94.

APPENDIX

Table A-1: Interprovincial Migration in Canada: In-Migrants and Out-Migrants, 1961-1996

					In-Migrants						
End Year	Nfd.	PEI	NS	NB	Que.	Ont.	Man.	Sask.	Alta.	BC	Canada
1962	5,618	4,121	20,519	16,160	44,051	76,758	26,079	19,789	44,148	37,487	29,4730
1963	6,008	3,624	20,738	16,035	44,103	84,793	26,507	21,341	45,282	42,985	31,1412
1964	6,770	3,660	20,999	17,624	42,002	93,902	25,918	23,299	43,736	48,429	32,6344
1965	6,451	3,010	20,160	18,317	42,255	99,828	25,547	23,697	43,684	55,416	33,8365
1966	7,839	3,715	21,991	20,018	45,076	108,139	27,250	24,545	46,270	71,211	37,6055
1967	8.297	3,856	23,640	19,513	44,564	113,222	28,850	25,589	53,994	75,527	39,7052
1968	9,426	3,748	24,287	19,579	40,307	100,096	29,145	26,105	54,906	66,121	37,3720
1969	8,929	3,924	23,251	18,343	38,892	97,758	26,506	21,657	53,527	62,917	35,5704
1970	7,441	3,201	22,876	18,482	36,063	131,865	27,885	20,298	61,588	75,853	40,5552
1971	9,281	4,018	21,653	20,413	34,472	128,035	27,919	19,904	57,926	69,743	39,3364
1972	12,338	4,304	22,711	20,149	37,777	107,750	25,757	19,670	59,374	73,279	38,3109
1973	11,752	4,217	25,213	20,658	35,997	97,042	29,039	20,870	61,443	76,474	38,2705
1974	13,042	4,947	26,150	21,793	41,024	100,044	33,125	27,312	70,593	86,399	42,4429
1975	12,262	5,315	26,698	24,027	37,067	84,588	29,271	29,162	76,532	72,800	39,7722
1976	11,604	4,231	24,371	22,812	32,383	80,926	26,116	27,803	75,302	56,793	36,2341
1977	10,151	4,976	23,535	20,897	30,965	92,670	27,905	29,865	82,035	60,230	38,3229
1978	10,073	4,607	23,315	19,995	25,012	105,399	24,609	26,826	85,997	65,671	39,1504
1979	10,061	4,286	22,841	19,330	26,127	92,796	23,374	26,196	90,724	69,119	38,4854
1980	11,579	3,905	21,187	18,077	25,451	90,060	22,904	26,518	103,922	85,527	40,9130
1981	11,161	3,706	22,448	17,791	27,529	90,957	25,768	27,536	116,338	87,396	43,0630
1982	10,278	4,406	22,173	17,751	29,135	100,845	27,726	26,600	123,785	71,892	43,4591
1983	11,102	3,531	20,718	17,153	27,497	97,987	23,552	23,845	77,457	56,519	35,9361
1984	8,559	3,814	23,504	16,691	31,227	117,291	22,758	26,377	62,574	65,286	37,8081
1985	8,165	3,869	22,444	16,204	32,411	113,808	26,711	22,980	66,981	60,578	37,4151
1986	7,947	3,451	20,374	15,523	33,394	108,637	21,931	21,083	73,207	58,820	36,4367
1987	9,164	3,228	19,626	14,117	32,173	119,785	21,954	19,742	60,931	65,817	36,6537
1988	9,290	3,724	20,365	15,310	29,075	108,328	21,133	17,591	63,274	75,144	36,3234
1989	10,193	4,035	20,098	15,662	31,738	98,784	19,118	16,237	66,244	80,394	36,2503
1990	9,735	3,543	20,373	16,446	31,072	87,573	18,549	17,108	68,462	81,793	35,4654
1991	10,614	3,296	22,341	16,224	31,146	91,935	20,026	20,410	73,670	85,314	37,4976
1992	10,212	3,099	20,267	14,100	28,317	83,553	18,022	19,357	66,148	82,069	34,5144
1993	8,935	3,003	19,201	14,386	28,162	82,268	18,501	19,357	61,933	84,449	34,0195
1994	10,302	2,946	19,297	15,067	31,201	87,632	20,914	23,984	63,192	92,982	36,7517
1995	10,297	3,494	18,784	15,187	27,565	89,485	22,873	23,225	60,473	85,465	35,7934
1996	10,453	3,444	20,175	14,475	27,898	83,665	20,321	22,901	64,579	79,520	34,7431
Total	335,329	134,254	768,323	624,309	1,183,128	3,448,204	863,563	808,779	2,380,231	2,465,419	

Table A-1 (continued)

End Year	Nfd.	PEI	NS	NB	Que.	Ont.	Man.	Sask.	Alta.	BC	Canada
					Out-Migrants						
1962	6,139	3,235	22,793	19,346	42,296	72,675	26,440	29,742	36,876	35,188	294,730
1963	7,699	4,251	25,491	21,597	44,642	72,124	27,428	32,679	40,747	34,754	311,412
1964	10,193	4,266	26,365	24,356	47,976	74,845	29,636	29,754	44,201	34,752	326,344
1965	11,427	4,612	27,971	23,079	48,462	76,598	32,023	29,389	48,067	36,737	338,365
1966	12,369	4,742	29,040	25,577	53,976	83,571	39,619	33,316	55,810	38,035	376,055
1967	12,726	4,510	29,635	25,236	59,018	89,769	40,120	35,568	54,314	46,156	397,052
1968	11,645	3,857	25,996	21,574	55,544	88,448	35,810	34,488	47,158	49,200	373,720
1969	10,193	4,511	24,637	22,105	57,436	82,731	32,728	34,667	44,530	42,166	355,704
1970	15,176	4,793	27,158	25,326	71,876	79,188	36,880	45,484	52,509	47,162	405,552
1971	12,979	3,788	25,296	20,895	72,258	80,712	35,046	43,369	50,481	48,540	393,364
1972	11,491	3,939	23,169	19,756	59,477	92,670	34,545	38,142	54,597	45,323	383,109
1973	12,368	3,524	20,276	18,552	55,694	95,969	34,230	36,923	55,642	49,527	382,705
1974	15,743	4,118	25,155	19,526	53,504	109,905	34,724	37,716	68,125	55,913	424,429
1975	11,522	3,961	24,182	17,977	47,456	112,445	35,255	28,615	53,403	62,906	397,722
1976	11,456	3,785	20,724	16,963	45,737	99,870	30,695	22,458	49,277	61,376	362,341
1977	11,678	3,800	23,659	18,398	55,852	99,341	31,399	23,066	58,134	57,902	383,229
1978	12,482	3,749	22,539	17,997	70,960	95,965	31,900	25,560	60,676	49,676	391,504
1979	11,834	4,254	21,660	18,073	57,682	101,762	34,780	24,418	60,953	49,438	384,854
1980	12,463	3,631	21,907	17,716	56,359	111,660	38,841	27,143	72,819	46,591	409,130
1981	12,850	4,706	23,294	20,505	50,562	122,359	36,330	28,685	80,192	51,147	430,630
1982	15,599	5,187	23,912	20,230	51,468	111,640	29,787	26,164	83,917	66,687	434,591
1983	9,665	3,169	19,127	14,590	49,388	81,402	22,835	21,127	84,904	53,154	359,361
1984	11,165	3,440	19,251	15,627	50,045	74,197	23,791	21,899	105,194	53,472	378,081
1985	11,441	3,219	20,165	16,623	41,801	74,796	22,598	27,411	92,949	63,148	374,151
1986	13,210	3,705	21,941	18,374	35,730	75,920	24,738	28,946	76,152	65,651	364,367
1987	13,998	3,529	20,094	16,719	36,388	75,261	25,238	27,078	90,744	57,488	366,537
1988	13,711	3,166	21,201	17,437	38,025	82,178	27,037	30,827	78,898	50,754	363,234
1989	11,865	3,664	20,754	16,378	41,434	91,042	29,989	32,462	69,068	45,847	362,503
1990	11,937	4,056	20,910	15,664	36,840	95,393	26,263	33,871	64,816	44,904	354,654
1991	14,002	4,385	22,169	16,727	45,139	101,696	27,805	32,166	64,364	46,523	374,976
1992	12,254	4,443	20,668	16,265	42,065	86,193	26,121	28,695	63,455	44,985	345,144
1993	12,370	2,409	21,143	15,754	43,177	86,467	24,570	27,820	63,284	43,201	340,195
1994	14,699	2,325	19,990	14,735	43,638	98,266	25,574	27,106	68,775	52,409	367,517
1995	18,336	2,619	22,447	16,058	42,839	84,909	25,063	27,277	64,879	53,507	357,934
1996	17,665	2,593	20,969	14,703	41,072	89,355	22,307	23,846	59,019	55,902	347,431
Total	436,350	133,941	805,688	660,438	1,745,816	3,151,322	1,062,145	1,057,877	2,218,929	1,740,121	

Table A-1 *(continued)*

					Net-Migrants					
End Year	Nfd.	PEI	NS	NB	Que.	Ont.	Man.	Sask.	Alta.	BC
1962	-521	886	-2,274	-3,186	1,755	4,083	-361	-9,953	7,272	2,299
1963	-1,691	-627	-4,753	-5,562	-539	12,669	-921	-11,338	4,535	8,231
1964	-3,423	-606	-5,366	-6,732	-5,974	19,057	-3,718	-6,455	-465	13,677
1965	-4,976	-1,602	-7,811	-4,762	-6,207	23,230	-6,476	-5,692	-4,383	18,679
1966	-4,530	-1,027	-7,049	-5,556	-8,900	24,568	-12,369	-8,771	-9,540	33,176
1967	-4,429	-654	-5,995	-5,723	-14,454	23,453	-11,270	-9,979	-320	29,371
1968	-2,219	-109	-1,709	-1,995	-15,237	11,648	-6,665	-8,383	7,748	16,921
1969	-1,264	-587	-1,386	-3,762	-18,544	15,027	-6,222	-13,010	8,997	20,751
1970	-7,735	-1,592	-4,282	-6,844	-35,813	52,677	-8,995	-25,186	9,079	28,691
1971	-3,698	230	-3,643	-482	-37,786	47,323	-7,127	-23,465	7,445	21,203
1972	847	365	-458	393	-21,700	15,080	-8,788	-18,472	4,777	27,956
1973	-616	693	4,937	2,106	-19,697	1,073	-5,191	-16,053	5,801	26,947
1974	-2,701	829	995	2,267	-12,480	-9,861	-1,599	-10,404	2,468	30,486
1975	740	1,354	2,516	6,050	-10,389	-27,857	-5,984	547	23,129	9,894
1976	148	446	3,647	5,849	-13,354	-18,944	-4,579	5,345	26,025	-4,583
1977	-1,527	1,176	-124	2,499	-24,887	-6,671	-3,494	6,799	23,901	2,328
1978	-2,409	858	776	1,998	-45,948	9,434	-7,291	1,266	25,321	15,995
1979	-1,773	32	1,181	1,257	-31,555	-8,966	-11,406	1,778	29,771	19,681
1980	-884	274	-720	361	-30,908	-21,600	-15,937	-625	31,103	38,936
1981	-1,689	-1,000	-846	-2,714	-23,033	-31,402	-10,562	-1,149	36,146	36,249
1982	-5,321	-781	-1,739	-2,479	-22,333	-10,795	-2,061	436	39,868	5,205
1983	1,437	362	1,591	2,563	-21,891	16,585	717	2,718	-7,447	3,365
1984	-2,606	374	4,253	1,064	-18,818	43,094	-1,033	4,478	-42,620	11,814
1985	-3,276	650	2,279	-419	-9,390	39,012	4,113	-4,431	-25,968	-2,570
1986	-5,263	-254	-1,567	-2,851	-2,336	32,717	-2,807	-7,863	-2,945	-6,831
1987	-4,834	-301	-468	-2,602	-4,215	44,524	-3,284	-7,336	-29,813	8,329
1988	-4,421	558	-836	-2,127	-8,950	26,150	-5,904	-13,236	-15,624	24,390
1989	-1,672	371	-656	-716	-9,696	7,742	-10,871	-16,225	-2,824	34,547
1990	-2,202	-513	-537	782	-5,768	-7,820	-7,714	-16,763	3,646	36,889
1991	-3,388	-1,089	172	-503	-13,993	-9,761	-7,779	-11,756	9,306	38,791
1992	-2,042	-1,344	-401	-2,165	-13,748	-2,640	-8,099	-9,338	2,693	37,084
1993	-3,445	594	-1,942	-1,368	-15,015	-4,199	-6,069	-8,463	-1,351	41,248
1994	-4,397	621	-693	332	-12,437	-10,634	-4,660	-3,122	-5,583	40,573
1995	-8,039	875	-3,663	-871	-15,274	4,576	-2,190	-4,052	-4,406	31,958
1996	-7,212	851	-794	-228	-13,174	-5,690	-1,986	-945	5,560	23,618
Total	-101,021	313	-37,365	-36,126	-562,688	296,882	-198,582	-249,098	161,302	725,298

Notes: - The year indicated is the end-year of a 12-month period beginning 1 July of the preceding calendar year.
   - Numbers are net of migration flows to the Northwest Territories and Yukon.

Source: 1961-1971: Statistics Canada, Catalogue no. 91-208.
   1972-1996: Cansim, series C122742-C122849.

6

How Canadians (Dis)connect: Foreign Economic Policy in an Era of Globalization

Claire Turenne Sjolander

La mondialisation ne fait pas que redéfinir les règles de l'économie internationale et établir de nouveaux paramètres guidant la politique économique étrangère, elle modifie aussi la manière qu'ont les Canadiens d'entrer en relation. On soutient dans ce chapitre que la mondialisation définit un nouveau mode de relation entre les Canadiens à mesure que ceux-ci acceptent la «réalité» de l'économie mondialisée et les limites ainsi imposées à la formulation des politiques économiques. Il est important de souligner que ce nouveau mode de relation n'est pas décrit en termes politiques, mais plutôt comme l'acceptation d'un donné. Ce mode de relation est manifeste dans deux piliers de la politique économique étrangère du Canada : la recherche de nouveaux partenaires commerciaux et la promotion du commerce international. Paradoxalement, ce mode de relation est aussi une source d'isolement. La mondialisation marginalise certains Canadiens alors que d'autres sont confrontés à la concurrence dans un marché international plus compétitif. Il est difficile de contrer ces formes d'isolement à l'ère de la mondialisation car l'établissement d'un véritable mode de relation n'est possible qu'à l'intérieur d'un espace d'abord conçu en termes politiques. Il est toutefois possible d'établir un nouveau mode de relation en concevant la mondialisation comme un processus politique plutôt qu'un phénomène économique inévitable.

The new confidence at home has allowed us to reassert ourselves on the international stage and take a leadership role in fighting for what is right. All Canadians feel pride in the signing of an International Treaty banning Landmines last December in Ottawa, as well as the prominent role taken by our peacekeepers in places like Bosnia.

Our challenge as a people is to harness this new spirit and work together to ensure that our country continues to be recognized as the best place in the world to live.[1]

Celebrating Canada's accomplishments over another year on the eve of Canada Day 1998, Prime Minister Jean Chrétien underscored Canada's international contribution. While applauding the fact that "many of the economic challenges which plagued our nation for far too long" have been overcome, Chrétien went to some length to point out that one of the measures of Canada is to be found in the deeds it accomplishes abroad, and in the leadership it shows within the international community of states. Intergovernmental Affairs Minister Stéphane Dion recently suggested that "Canadians can take pride that they have never had an empire and have never sent troops abroad in the 20th century for reasons other than defending democracy and peace." In keeping with this spirit, Canadians "proposed the United Nations peacekeeping force ... and drafted the initial version of the Universal Declaration of Human Rights," continuing this tradition when it "fulfilled its role as a good global citizen by undertaking a vast worldwide initiative to ban antipersonnel mines."[2] What Canada can do, or achieve, internationally, becomes a prism through which Canadians define themselves, and a reflection of national pride.

The question of how Canadians define themselves in relation to the international community of states, and how this "definition" shapes Canada, has been a central focus of Canadian foreign policy studies. Maureen Molot has argued, for example, that scholars of foreign policy have been almost obsessive in their concern with Canada's place, role, or power on the international stage.[3] This obsession notwithstanding (and perhaps as a result of it), Canadian lore is replete with references to the special talents and skills of Canadians acting abroad. Andrew Cooper once recounted, "John Kennedy praised the Canadian foreign service as 'probably unequaled by any other nation'," while Henry Kissinger "extolled the high quality of Canada's diplomatic contribution: 'Canadian leaders had a narrow margin of manoeuvre that they utilized with extraordinary skills'."[4] Canadians have taken pride in their accomplishments in the international arena,[5] in part because the more high-profile of these activities are perceived to reflect fundamental Canadian values. Martin and Fortmann have argued with respect to peacekeeping, for example, that "Canadians like to think of their country as a mosaic of cultures, cemented by tolerance, good will, and respect for individual and collective rights. Peacekeeping, with its emphasis on conflict prevention and peaceful settlement of disputes, clearly embodies this ideal of human relations."[6] It should come as no surprise that the Chrétien government uses images of Canadian peacekeepers, or references to the United Nations' ranking of Canada as the best place in the world in which to live, to argue the case for national unity. The activities of Canadians abroad and the view of Canada held by others are in important respects a mirror of the image Canadians have of themselves at home, and indeed, a mirror to Canadians of what they think they can be. One non-governmental organization (NGO) representative claimed that with Canada's place in the international arena,

[s]uch prestige, voice, influence and clout as we have on the world stage — and we have a lot of it, far out of proportion to our relative strength as an economic power — is there because we have a history of altruism, compassion, fairness, and of doing things irrespective of our own national self-interest.... We have been respected and we have a voice in the world not because the world perceives us to be powerful but because the world perceives us to be good.[7]

If foreign policy is one of the ways by which Canadians define themselves, thereby contributing to the creation of a sense of "national" identity or purpose (Canadians as "good"), the role of foreign economic policy in interpreting Canadians to themselves is somewhat more ambiguous. There are, of course, important echoes of the general foreign policy orientation to be found in foreign economic policy; Canadians have been "team players" and active members in — at times, architects of — a wide variety of multilateral economic fora, including the GATT (now the World Trade Organization), the International Monetary Fund, the World Bank, and the G7 (now the S8). Canadians' commitment to the construction of a multilateral post-World War II economic order is unquestionable. As pioneers in the creation of this multilateral order, Canada's international activities promoted an image of a country committed to an open, rules-based, liberal trading regime. Further, and significantly, this commitment was a matter of political *choice*, based on the belief that stronger international organizations and trade liberalization "served the world community as a whole, and were not just a means of promoting Canada's national interests."[8] As Macdonald has argued, the events of the Second World War "convinced the Canadian foreign policy elite as well as the general public that isolationism was no longer a viable option." A postwar order needed to be self-consciously fashioned, "based on principles of economic liberalism and multilateralism, with the establishment of political and economic institutions designed to promote international peace and the opening of markets,"[9] and Canada would choose to participate actively in the fashioning of that order.

Foreign economic policy today is, in important respects, less a self-conscious political choice — or at least, it is rarely represented as such. Globalization appears to have, and indeed, has, altered the lay of the policy landscape. To begin, foreign economic policy has come to represent such a significant part of Canadian foreign policy activity that it is increasingly defined *as* foreign policy. Indeed, if foreign economic policy is not conceptualized as foreign policy,[10] there is relatively little foreign policy — high profile initiatives notwithstanding — about which to speak. Roy MacLaren, Jean Chrétien's first minister for international trade, stated it most bluntly when he argued that, for Canada, "foreign policy *is* trade policy."[11] This portrayal of the confluence of traditional "foreign" policy (traditional diplomacy) with foreign economic policy suggests the extent to which economic considerations have come to dominate the foreign policy agenda, in Canada as elsewhere. The place that foreign economic policy has assumed in the shaping of Canadian foreign policy is in part defined by new, more narrowly economic, criteria motivating much of foreign policy activity. No longer is foreign economic policy about "serving the world community as a whole," rather, the Chrétien government "has announced that the first objective in foreign policy decisions must be the extent to which they promote prosperity and employment within Canada."[12] Foreign policy is but another element on the continuum of domestic economic policy; globalization, in fact, can be said to blur the distinctions between the two. If foreign policy is a mirror reflecting Canadians back to themselves, then that mirror increasingly defines Canada in terms of the hackneyed campaign slogan "jobs, jobs, jobs."

On the other hand, while more self-consciously economic in its orientation, foreign policy is less about conscious policy choices than ever before. In many respects, politics have been suppressed in the formulation of foreign economic policy, and the space for debate and discussion is concomitantly constrained. In this international dimension of the shaping of Canadian identity, choices are limited if they exist at all, masked under the rubric of globalization. Of course, the logic of this is simple. Robert Cox has pointed to the transformation of the state — a change in state form — under globalization, as the welfare state is superceded by a hyper-liberal, "transmission-belt" state, with new responsibilities to the international economic system. No longer is the primary goal of the state to act as a buffer between the domestic and international economy, in order to defend the interests of domestic constituencies against the upheavals born of a turbulent international economy. Rather, the state's role has become one of facilitating the integration of the domestic economy into the global one, of promoting the restructuring of the domestic economy in order to better respond to international economic exigencies, rather than of mediating between the national and international economic spheres.[13] In this respect, the place of politics is ambiguous at best; global economic conditions appear to "impose" norms and standards (either implicitly, or, as in the case of International Monetary Fund pronouncements or the activities of currency speculators, explicitly) to which states must be responsive, or dire consequences await. Choices, which at least indirectly characterized an earlier era of foreign economic policy, are now absent and replaced with a need to embrace the world the way as it "is."

This chapter, then, seeks to explore the extent to which globalization and the current economic restructuring affects the expression, and thereby the implicit definition, of a Canadian "identity" on the international stage. In so doing, the chapter argues that we need to take globalization seriously, not simply as something "out there" that may or may not have changed the opportunities and constraints under which policy is formulated or framed, but as a set of meanings which fundamentally alters our ability to conceive of foreign economic policy in the first instance, whether as analysts or as practitioners. More specifically, the chapter suggests that we need to understand the discursive construction of globalization; how it represents itself and shapes the terrain upon which policy is framed, in order to understand the vision of Canada which is reflected back to it in the mirror of foreign economic policy. Such an exercise is not merely a game of semantics; the way we understand globalization and what it might be profoundly affects our conception of the space for political action. The way we understand globalization conditions the perception of foreign economic policy as a relatively non-political activity of government — "non-political" in the sense that it forecloses the counterposing of vastly different visions of Canada's place in the global economy, and limits itself to the negotiation over differences in the technical details of particular policy initiatives. Of course, the political project of globalization is not about opening up political space to debate fundamentally different conceptions of social organization and integration. To that end, the way in which the discourse of globalization is articulated informs and constrains our conception of what is legitimately political in the first place, that is, it sets the boundaries or the terrain of policy making by identifying what constitutes the "legitimate" subject matter of politics and thus, of foreign economic policy.

With respect to the manner in which Canadian foreign economic policy contributes to a sense of national identity, definition, or purpose, therefore, what is most instructive is the way in which representations of globalization as a necessary and inevitable reality of the late twentieth century have exacerbated the existing tendency to de-politicize foreign economic policy (and economic policy more generally). Where it has always been useful for capitalists to claim an empirical distinction between the political and the economic,[14] at no time has that distinction lived so much in practice and meaning as it does now. At the same time, however, the more the discourse surrounding globalization insists on its apolitical nature, the greater the likelihood of political reaction by those "outside" the "legitimate" political terrain. The discourse surrounding globalization delimits what is legitimate in politics (for example, it is increasingly difficult to suggest that the state's role should be to intervene in the market), and makes alternative conceptualizations difficult to articulate, and even more difficult to understand. Yet, these are the stresses that confront the national project which is Canada in an era of globalization; stresses born of increased social and political consensus around the implications of globalization on the one hand, and growing social fissures on the other. While Canadian foreign — and domestic — economic policy in an era of globalization attempts to present a homogeneous view of the world "out there" and of the way Canadians need to adjust to it, there is a consequent fragmentary impact on the way Canadians "connect." Those who do not accept the representation of the world "out there" are inevitably marginalized from a political process which takes consensus about the nature of globalization and its impact as its starting point, while those who accept the interpretation and consequences of globalization are driven to act according to its dictates; dictates that preach efficiency, liberalization, and competitiveness as foundations of the global economic order. In the pursuit of greater competitiveness, however, Canadians often find themselves "connecting" as competitors, despite — and in fact, because of — their common interpretation of globalization. Globalization thus becomes a double-edged sword more likely to promote fragmentation than the homogeneity it claims to represent. In essence, globalization becomes the mechanism by which Canadians "disconnect" from each other, even as they "connect" in their view of Canada's place in a globalizing economy.

DEFINING GLOBALIZATION

Globalization is evocative of universal and universalizing practices, intensifying "global" interdependence, compressing space, accelerating time, and increasing the "consciousness of the global whole in the twentieth century."[15] However defined, all peoples and all states are said to be equally subject to its logics, which are on the whole beneficial and, in any event, inevitable, and states and societies have no choice but to adapt to this new international conjuncture. Globalization is inherently multifaceted. While its economic dimensions are key, it is possible, and indeed necessary, to speak of globalization in terms of human security, human rights and identity, democratization, the world environment, and global culture (including sport) — all pointing to a growing list of elements of human activity which have "gone global." Advances in transportation and communication technologies, together with the competitive spread of standardized systems and technologies of production, have hastened and facilitated the transformation of a segmented world into a more "global" one.

The technological underpinnings of globalization point to the phenomenon as a series of processes.[16] These processes are not necessarily self-conscious; that is, the activities of any one firm or group are not necessarily chosen in order to enhance the prospects of globalization, although this may be their combined or cumulative result. At the outset, globalization manifested itself in fundamental global economic restructuring, and it is these economic processes which are key to situating Canadian identity construction in terms of foreign economic policy. Globalization implies, in the first instance, a fundamental reorientation in the international investment strategies of transnational firms. Responding to the economic downturn and the crisis of profitability of the 1970s, and facilitated in large part by technological advances making possible the fragmentation of the production process, significant numbers of large companies began to conceive of primarily *national* lines of production in *international* terms. Transnational firms were able to establish different *parts* of their production lines in different jurisdictions around the world, taking advantage of favourable local conditions, whether these included cheap labour or energy sources, lax anti-pollution standards, a highly educated workforce with high technology skills, and so forth. Under such a "delocalized" model of production, new transnational spaces for production are defined, though these increasingly are unlikely to coincide with national borders. These delocalization strategies have been coupled with a host of new strategic innovations with regard to the organization of the activities of the firm, also developed in response to the upheavals of the international economy over the past three decades. Michael Hart has described how global firms now "rely on a much more fragmented and decentralized approach," not only to production, but also "to design, engineering, ... marketing and service." These firms "use strategic alliances in such forms as joint production, R&D and other ventures, licensing arrangements, contracting out and brokering among global corporations and networks" in order to organize their activities in a globalizing world. These new strategies have meant that "there has been a tremendous growth in intra-corporate and intra-sectoral trade in parts and other components, as well as an increasing reliance on activities taking place far from corporate headquarters or ultimate markets."[17] As Hart suggests, pressures on national borders created by the reorganization of production have been heightened by a similar, although at the outset less rapid, "delocalization" of service industries.

It is significant, and in fact, crucial, to appreciate that the processes involved in the restructuring of global production emerged within a definite political context. The global multilateral financial and trade institutions (the multilateral postwar economic order which Canada helped to construct, governed by the Bretton Woods institutions) put into place a regulatory regime facilitating the ease and security with which goods and capital could flow across international borders. The political ground work of post-World War II economic liberalization made it possible for firms to envisage a delocalization strategy once technological changes made it feasible, and the economic crisis of the 1970s made it attractive in order to enhance stagnating or declining profitability. In this sense, and without this political groundwork, economic globalization would certainly not have taken the form that it has — globalization as it manifests itself today depends upon an international regulatory regime encouraging the loosening of national regulation and the lowering of barriers (both tariff and non-tariff) to trade and investment. In this respect, globalization is not only a set of ad hoc processes which, when taken together, constitute a profound restructuring of the postwar world, but also a political project. This is not to argue that Canada, or indeed, other countries participating in the construction of the postwar economic order envisaged globalization as its outcome, far from it.[18] Rather, in the construction of the Bretton Woods institutional structures, political conditions were created which enabled the emergence of particular kinds of restructuring processes, and these processes in turn, have fuelled a political push to reinforce them.

If, as I have suggested, global economic restructuring was born of a particular political context, such economic restructuring also has profound political implications. On the one hand, the economic liberalization of the post-World War II era continues apace, witnessed in the negotiation of the World Trade Organization (WTO) as well as in the continuing work to broaden the scope of its regulatory structure, in the conclusion of an increasing number of regional trade blocs, including the North American Free Trade Agreement (NAFTA), as well as in the stalled, although not yet completely aborted, negotiations over the Multilateral Agreement on Investment (MAI). This economic liberalization goes far beyond that originally envisaged by the Bretton Woods institutions, and increasingly circumscribes the capacity of national states to intervene in their markets in ways that might be perceived as prejudicial to the interests of "foreign" firms.[19] To the extent that delocalization has become a significant calculation in the investment strategies of transnational firms, such strategies have limited the capacity of individual states to regulate the activities of these firms. If firms can delocalize all or part of their production in the search for a "better deal," states need to be conscious of how they compare with others in the international investment bazaar. Further, such delocalization strategies also limit the capacity of any individual country to satisfy the investment requirements of transnational firms, and thus place a premium on defining the "attractiveness" of potential investment locations in the race to attract investment dollars. As a corollary to this, pressures are thereby created for the broadening of national markets, and for their more complete integration into larger (whether regional or international) trading blocs.[20] Canada has been an active participant in, and promoter of, the extension of this political project of economic liberalization, a political project which structures the context in which economic restructuring (and thereby globalization) takes place.

Whether or not firms are in fact as footloose as this portrayal suggests is not particularly important; what is important is that states behave *as if* they are. As argued earlier, globalization has to be understood as a discourse which has real implications for political action. If firms are perceived to be footloose, to have an open menu of investment choices (and locations) before them, then certain political choices affecting the economic environment are seemingly necessarily foreclosed. In responding to the opportunities created by the post-World War II political project of economic liberalization, globalization has pushed that agenda forward onto the terrain of the inevitable. In bringing with it, as its necessary backdrop, the (globalized) diffusion of a neo-liberal ideology, political parties of both the right and the left are increasingly constrained to adopt similar political agenda, although their rhetoric may differ. States appear to be relegated to playing a facilitator role, assisting in the adaptation of the national economy to the new realities of emerging international economic structures,[21] that is, to creating the policy environment both nationally and internationally favouring the globalization of production and service industries. Political speeches focus on the lack of alternatives; if globalization cannot be ignored (or ignored at dire peril), than its opportunities must not be missed. Like the economic changes which set the stage, the political and ideological consequences of globalization are seen to be homogeneous and totalizing, as likely to constrain states in the richest industrialized countries as in the developing world. "Competitiveness, efficiency, liberalization, and the minimalist state" have become the mantra of this new political climate.

Seen in this way, globalization can be compared to a three-headed hydra; a series of material practices or processes (relating, in the specific case of this chapter, to the restructuring of the global economy, although such universalizing practices are not limited to the economic sphere), a political project adopted by key economic actors and some states,[22] and an ideology that proposes globalization as the only, and necessary, alternative, however much the "global reality" portrayed may not be experienced on the ground. Together, these three elements make up the discourse surrounding globalization; they become our constructed "reality," our view of what globalization *is*. The very real understanding of globalization as a series of (technologically driven) economic processes, supported by powerful political actors, and defended by a pervasive ideological framework, defines a terrain upon which political action can, and cannot, take place. More particularly, because globalization sets itself up discursively as a process for which there are no alternatives and from which there is no escape, there can be no political choice but to conform to its exigencies.

In essence, what is at its roots a profoundly political process (for the restructuring and extension of the market cannot take place in the absence of a regulatory framework, both domestic and international) becomes an apolitical "reality." We are either part of globalization, on the global bandwagon so to speak, or we are nowhere. We either become more competitive, efficient, leaner and meaner, or we are left to face some void or chasm of unknown dimensions and perils. Globalization sets itself up as a "my way or the highway" reality; where "my way" (globalization and all that this implies about the capacity of states to intervene in national or international economies) promises some prosperity after the pain, and the "highway" looks long and bleak, leading to an even more desolate future. In this sense, globalization is not represented or understood as a political project, for the only "sensible" choice is to follow an uncontestable reality. Once globalization is represented and accepted in such a way, it becomes at once more persuasive (because alternatives truly are impossible to conceive), and depoliticized, because politics (or the expression of fundamentally different options for Canada) are removed from the globalizing process. Globalization simply "is."

CANADIAN FOREIGN ECONOMIC POLICY IN THE CONTEXT OF GLOBALIZATION

Policy efforts to better situate Canada in the global economy have focused on two broad parallel initiatives, each articulated within the context of globalization as an either/or proposition. In some respects, these initiatives — situated at the level of multilateral fora, regional trade blocs or bilateral trade deals, as well as defined in terms of national trade promotion strategies — are consistent with previous efforts by the Canadian state to "stake out" a piece of the global economic pie. Since the 1970s, however, there has been a significant reorientation of the fundamental assumptions guiding Canadian foreign economic policy. Where the lessons of the immediate postwar period were that Canada was *de facto* an attractive place in which to do business and the Canadian economy thus needed very little salesmanship to attract economic interest or partners, Canadians now have to compete for business with thousands of other jurisdictions in the international marketplace. The exigencies of such competition, defined within a context of globalization, appear to limit the economic options available to Canadian policymakers, and to attribute to those selected an air of inevitability.

Canadian policy initiatives, in the first instance, have been focused on broadening and strengthening international trade and investment rules, in preference through the expansion of multilateral fora. "[M]ultilateralism is part of the Canadian DNA,"[23] Sergio Marchi claimed in a speech to the Centre for Trade Policy and Law, and indeed, the continued commitment to multilateral institutions and processes does not belie such an assertion.[24] While the (at least) rhetorical argument continues to be made that such fora act to benefit the international community as a whole, what is more transparent in this era of globalization is the contrast between such options and the abyss. Lloyd Axworthy put it most starkly in stating that "[i]n this day and age, no government — especially Canada's — can ignore the consequences of globalization." In effect, Canada must be actively engaged in the construction of a multilateral order because "Canada has no choice — in view of its inherent nature, its qualities and its history — but to make a commitment, because it is on this commitment that its very survival will depend."[25] Putting a somewhat less fatalistic spin on the issue, Michael Hart has argued that "[h]aving weathered the adjustment to a more open economy, the federal government has become a more activist participant in the making of global trade policy."[26] Clearly, the continued endorsement of rules-based international economic regimes remains a central feature of Canadian foreign economic policy, whether or not Canadians are perceived to have a choice in this regard.

It is important not to understate the extent to which Canadian diplomats and policymakers have been active in structuring the multilateral international economic order. Most visible in increased diplomatic representation to the Geneva-based World Trade Organization, the support given by Canadian political leadership to the reinforcement and expansion of the WTO system is unwavering. Several months before the first WTO conference of ministers, held in Singapore in December 1996, then Trade Minister Art Eggleton was emphasizing the importance of the WTO to global — and Canadian — economic growth. "We must maintain the momentum of world trade liberalization.... It is key to economic growth and job creation in Canada and the world. The WTO is playing a central role in this process as the linchpin in the global trading system."[27] At the first WTO Ministerial Conference, Canadian representatives pushed for concrete steps to be taken toward freer trade in information technology, agriculture, and basic telecommunications and financial services. Further, Canada pushed for discussions on the link between investment and trade, as well as a study on how to increase openness in government procurement.[28] The conclusion of a financial services agreement within the context of the WTO was heralded a year later by Finance Minister Paul Martin. "This is an important agreement for Canada. It will provide Canadian financial services suppliers with greater certainty with respect to their investments. As well, Canadian companies will benefit from enhanced access to markets abroad, creating new export and job creation opportunities."[29] Two things seem particularly apparent in this support for the WTO regime: first, a multilateral rules-based system is to be supported and second, support of such a system will bring jobs and economic growth to the Canadian economy; in essence, a multilateral rules-based international economic order will respond to the exigencies of national economic adjustment. What is perhaps more crucial to underscore, however, is that Canada has hardly been a wallflower in the construction and consolidation of such a multilateral system, and that the construction of such a system is in itself a political choice, however it might be portrayed.

If political choices are defined in a particular context — in this case, the globalization which leads Axworthy to argue that Canadians in fact have no choice in making the commitment of engagement — they also are framed with respect to that context. Where the extension of a global trading regime is itself a political act, that regime at the same time becomes part of the world "out there" through which globalization is imposed or made inevitable. The WTO ruling against Canada in the now infamous *Sports Illustrated* split-run edition case was telling in that regard. While Heritage Minister Sheila Copps pledged to find a new set of policy instruments which would protect some market share for Canadian magazine publishers, lamenting the fact that "[t]rade watchdogs such as the WTO ... fail to recognize the 'uniqueness' of national cultures,"[30] Trade Minister Art Eggleton made it clear that such instruments might best be set aside in favour of greater (international) market liberalization. "Are the instruments designed to promote Canadian culture at home in fact hindering its success abroad? ... The question is not whether we ought to support Canadian culture, but how best to support it ... the coming of age of Canadian culture may not depend on our ability to protect it at home, but to project it on the world's stage."[31] What Copps' lament does not acknowledge, and Eggleton's assessment only implies, is the degree to which Canada is supportive of WTO processes, and actively participates in fashioning them. The WTO is not a disembodied trade watchdog "out there," but rather a concrete manifestation of political choices — including those of the Canadian government.

The same rhetorical posture is evident in the ardent defences of the now stalemated, and potentially moribund, MAI. Considered by some a potential Charter of Rights for transnational firms, the MAI, negotiations for which have taken place to date within the ambit of the Organization for Economic Cooperation and Development (OECD), seeks to enshrine national treatment (non-discrimination) and assured protection for investors and their investments in an international agreement. Protesting the MAI negotiations is portrayed as akin to "trying to hide from globalization," with the concomitant "decline in our standard of living"[32] that such a posture would entail. Voices against the MAI have to be listened to, but they must be weighed "against the Canadian reality ... The MAI debate must focus on the facts."[33] The "fact" is globalization, inescapable, omnipresent, and negotiations such as those seeking to create the MAI are the best technical responses to the "reality" of globalization out there. While there are technical choices to be made and positions to be argued within the context of the negotiations, fundamentally different views of the political possibilities within a context of globalization are discounted as ignoring reality. As Marchi argued colloquially, "You know, anyone who played hockey as a kid or who has children playing hockey now will remember what every good coach drills into young players: "You can't score if you don't shoot." The same is true of international trade negotiations: You can't score a good deal if you don't take your best shot at negotiating it."[34] Good sense, perhaps — as far as it goes. But in this representation of the world, the only game in town is hockey, and the kids who would rather play baseball simply don't get to play at all.

The same representations of globalization and the inevitabilities which it occasions (however politically structured these "inevitabilities" in fact are) are to be found in the enthusiasm greeting the myriad bilateral and regional trade agreements in which Canada participates. While the 1988 Canada-US "free trade election" was fought over fundamentally different visions of Canada, subsequent trade agreements have garnered much less emotion, and in many cases, little attention. Beyond the North American Free Trade Agreement, a fairly minor and much less volatile issue in the 1993 election than Canada-US free trade had been five years earlier, free trade agreements have been signed with Chile and Israel, and prospects for a Free Trade Area of the Americas (FTAA), together with a partnership in the Asia-Pacific Economic Cooperation (APEC) round out the trade agenda. Chilean free trade is to be heralded not only for the "potential that it holds," but also as "an important contribution to the cause of freer trade around the globe — an example for others to follow."[35] This example of freer trade is lent some of its urgency, however, by the fact that "[b]oth Chile and Canada have recognized that freer trade is an idea whose time has come, that the way to future prosperity does not lie in hiding behind protectionist barriers."[36] Again, a reality has become clear, although the policy implications are not without their critics, even amongst dedicated free-traders. As Michael Hart has described, "Canada seemed to be bent on majoring in the minors, prepared to negotiate free trade agreements with almost anyone interested, including Israel, Jordan, Chile, New Zealand, and Singapore. Two of these negotiations, with Israel and Chile, have now been concluded, even though there was little basis for them, either on commercial or foreign policy grounds."[37] Where Hart objects to trade agreements which cannot, by reason of limited trade relations and geographic distance, confer the potential for greater economic integration, the Canadian willingness to negotiate trade agreements with interested parties seems perfectly consistent. If globalization has taught the lesson that protectionism cannot work, it is difficult to elaborate the grounds upon which certain agreements should be negotiated while others are put aside, particularly if there is willingness to do so on both sides of the negotiating table. Hockey is the only game, and one cannot shoot — strategically or otherwise — if one is not playing.

The FTAA and APEC, for their part, are inherently more ambitious initiatives, seeking to bind together entire geographic regions (and in the case of APEC, an increasingly far-flung region) in trade liberalization agreements. At the close of the Santiago Summit in April 1998 which formally launched negotiations toward a hemispheric-wide free trade area by 2005, Prime Minister Chrétien heralded the role of freer trade in "helping our peoples to prepare themselves to take advantage of the new economy."[38] Despite the growing reluctance of certain Latin American countries toward the prospect of a hemispheric agreement, the prime minister insisted upon its inevitability, reflecting that "[t]he history of this century shows us the undeniable failure of isolationism and protectionism."[39] Globalization is both the new economy and the demonstration of the failure of protectionism, and regional agreements which adapt to this changing international economic reality are to be embraced as the wisest course of action. The fact is, of course, that negotiations leading toward a FTAA or in the context of the Asia-Pacific Economic Cooperation

forum promoting the initiative of Pacific Rim Free Trade by 2015 actively
contributes to shaping globalization as well as responds to it.

While there has been criticism of both the FTAA and the APEC initiatives,
in part on the ground of human rights issues, there has been no consistent
indication of the government's willingness to consider seriously foreign economic policy under any optic other than trade. Some rhetorical
acknowledgement of the lack of democracy in potential trading partners has
been made, but there does not appear to be any willingness to slow down the
free trade bandwagon. Rather, "the Canadian government continues at a re-
lentless pace to join one trade deal after another, creating an immense web of
agreements to allow Canadian business access to markets all over the world,"[40]
and this despite talk of human rights and democracy. In contrast to the free
trade election of 1988, however, political debate around these freer trade initiatives is often absent — or defined in terms of assisting those who oppose
such agreements to face "honestly the natural fear of change."[41] It is as though
the free trade fight having been lost (or won, depending on one's position),
the legitimate terrain of politics has been redefined. Trade agreements are
economic arrangements made necessary by the restructuring exigencies of
globalization, and the political and social impacts, if any, are incidental. Trade
arrangements have moved from being on highly contested political terrain to
being accepted (and often barely noticed) as an inevitable part of globalization, one other thing to be done on the road to eventual prosperity. It is simply
not conceivable to imagine the political engagement around trade policy which
was evident a decade ago — the space for politics has been profoundly
redefined.

Beyond the attempted negotiation and occasional conclusion of formal free
trade agreements, the Liberal government has also embraced trade promotion
through a series of "Team Canada" initiatives. These voyages, travelling international road shows with the prime minister at the helm, and a supporting
cast including Cabinet ministers, provincial premiers, municipal government
officials, and business leaders, have targeted quickly growing regions of the
world economy in search of trade and investment opportunities for Canadian
firms. These high-profile delegations are considered necessary to give political importance to what are essentially business trips. As one senior foreign
affairs official argued: "We open the doors, and our business people walk
through them. We can act as a catalyst and, if it comes down to competition
between Canada and another country, that's where the political overlay can
make the difference."[42] Foreign economic policy became akin to an economic
dating service, with state officials at all levels actively engaged in supporting
the pairing up of firms and market opportunities, ever hopeful that the right
"match" will be made. What is most interesting about the "Team Canada"
initiative, however, is the extent to which it also plays onto the depoliticized
terrain surrounding the discourse around globalization.

Team Canada, most visibly manifested in a series of trade promotion "pilgrimages" launched in November 1994, and held every January since, is in fact part of a larger government strategy to promote Canadian business abroad, and to encourage partnerships between Canadian firms and foreign companies. Team Canada Inc., an elaborate interdepartmental, intergovernmental network developed in partnership with the Canadian business community, provides the technical support required by Canadian firms in their search for business opportunities and partners abroad. "Exports and foreign investment create jobs in Canada,"[43] explained Art Eggleton simply as he announced the launch of a Global Opportunities Response Team (Go-Team) made up of "rapid deployment" trade commissioners who can head out quickly to posts abroad to follow-up recently concluded trade agreements or Team Canada initiatives. What is particularly striking about Team Canada is that it is not conceived in political terms at all, but rather, as a technical response to globalization.[44] This is what the Canadian state can now do for business in order to help it position itself in the international marketplace.

This chapter is not arguing that the Team Canada initiatives are an inherently bad strategy, or even an inherently doubtful one. Rather, it is the non-politicized nature of Team Canada ventures which is so telling. "Political" questions relate to whether or not particular premiers should be participating; during this past foray in January 1998, more for reasons of ice-storm-related weather than to any real questioning of the value of the exercise.[45] It is instructive that Lucien Bouchard has dismissed his predecessor's boycott of Team Canada voyages, for this underscores the extent to which Team Canada is seen as an apolitical response to the exigencies of globalization. There is, in fact, no other way for the state to play the globalization "game" once globalization becomes defined as an apolitical process. Industrial policy, for example, becomes anathema to the meaning which is attributed to globalization (competition, free market, liberalization, efficiency), and, of necessity, becomes increasingly associated with trade policy. If the state, any state, must be seen to be doing something (if only for reasons of political legitimacy), then globalization would seem to profoundly limit its options. Its choices are to be found in some combination of trade agreement development, domestic infrastructure building to attract foreign investors, and international trade cheerleading. Of course, the Canadian state is not the only one engaged in this type of activity; Canadian provincial and municipal governments are active in promoting their firms and investment attractiveness as well. The discursive framing of globalization is widely understood and shared, and involves the activities of a myriad of governments and organizations, each cheer-leading for their opportunity to "score" the economic goal.

CONCLUSIONS: CONTESTATION FROM THE MARGINS

What does the discourse surrounding globalization tell us in terms of a Canadian "image" on the world stage — an image reflected back to Canada? If, as has been argued, discourse is as much material or empirical practice as the ideas and interpretations formed to give meaning to such practice, it is not as though the state can simply "change its mind" and thus discover or create a new reality. In increasingly accepting globalization as an inevitable "given" bringing with it its own exigencies, however, the discourse surrounding globalization profoundly alters the terrain of the political. In particular, what is not highlighted by this discourse is the extent to which the Canadian state participates in the shaping of globalization. Team Canada initiatives, for example, make no sense *except* in a world of market liberalization and an increased number of trade agreements, for without the pressure to liberalize and the international frameworks facilitating liberalization, the position of Canadian business in the world economy takes on a different interpretation.

This does not mean that the limited "technical" role of the state in responding to the exigencies of globalization is wholly unquestioned. The number of non-governmental organizations assembled — and protesting — during the parallel APEC People's Summit in Vancouver in November 1997 was large by any measure. Posters dotting union halls and university campuses protesting the MAI are similarly indicative of the fact that the terrain on which the discourse surrounding globalization is articulated is not completely closed. Again, though, what is instructive here is the difficulty in achieving any profound political debate over the issues at hand; anecdotally evidenced in the prime minister's unfortunate jokes about the use of pepper spray against APEC protesters on the one hand,[46] or, as outlined earlier, Sergio Marchi's frustration over disagreements about the MAI on the other.

In terms of Canadian foreign economic policy, however, what is clear is that for most analysts, and in most analyses, globalization has become an apolitical backdrop, a conditioning variable, a "given." This is, of course, consistent with the discourse surrounding globalization. In placing globalization as part of the world out there, rather than as a discourse that defines the very meaning of what is a legitimate subject for politics and therefore of foreign policy itself, these analyses are limited to the positing of globalization as some kind of *deus ex machina*, imposing limits but not of our own making, or to the observation that despite change, nothing much has changed (because globalization is not seen within the terrain of the political). What is not perceived is the displacement of the political — to other areas, off to the side — and the fragmentary consequences that this has for Canadian society as a whole. This fragmentation occurs not only because segments of Canadian society are left behind in the forward march of globalization, but because their protests are not understood within the redefined terrain of the political. Globalization is paradoxically fragmentary in its homogenous effects; as all levels of Canadian society and government accept the mantra of the minimalist state and the competitive ethos, various levels of governments begin to compete against each other for investment dollars — all the while accepting the "non-political" and "technical" nature of their responses to the globalization itself.

The consequences of this two-fold fragmentation are problematic in terms of the Canada that is reflected back to itself. Rather than being a reflection of choices made for the international good (however self-serving those choices might in fact have been), foreign economic policy is a technical process born of global circumstances. Politics does not exist in this space. Even if foreign economic policy is to be defined rather narrowly in terms of the actors who participate, as earlier commentators have celebrated, we are still left with a paradox in the matter of foreign economic policy under globalization. Foreign policy, connoting "the actions, goals, and decisions of authoritative political actions,"[47] suggests that at some level at least, such policy is about the political, and is defined on a political terrain. A new understanding of foreign economic policy — and of Canada — in the era of globalization would necessitate such an acknowledgement.

NOTES

1.   Jean Chrétien, Prime Minster of Canada, "Message on the Occasion of Canada Day," 29 June 1998, Ottawa, Ontario. http://pm.gc.ca/cgi-win/pmo_view.exe/ENGLISH?807+0+ NORMAL.

2.   Stéphane Dion, President of the Privy Council and Minister of Intergovernmental Affairs, "Notes for an address before the Israel Association for Canadian Studies at the Hebrew University of Jerusalem, Israel," 28 June 1998. http://www.pco-bcp.gc.ca/aia/ro/doc/spchjun2898.htm. See also, Stéphane Dion, "Canada is going to make it after all!" Notes for an address to the biennial conference of the Association for Canadian Studies in the United States, Minneapolis, Minnesota, 21 November 1997.

3.   Maureen Appel Molot, "Where Do We, Should We, or Can We Sit? A Review of the Canadian Foreign Policy Literature," *International Journal of Canadian Studies* 1-2 (1990): 77-96.

4.   Andrew F. Cooper, *Canadian Foreign Policy: Old Habits and New Directions* (Scarborough, Ont.: Prentice Hall Canada Inc., 1997), p. 35.

5.   For a discussion of the way in which the discourse of Canadian foreign policy has been articulated around this perception of the uniqueness of the Canadian contribution internationally, see David Black and Claire Turenne Sjolander, "Multilateralism Re-constituted and the Discourse of Canadian Foreign Policy," *Studies in Political Economy* 49 (Spring 1996): 7-36.

6.   Pierre Martin and Michel Fortmann, "Canadian Public Opinion and Peacekeeping in a Turbulent World," *International Journal* 50, 2 (Spring 1995): 384.

7. Cited in Cooper, *Canadian Foreign Policy*, p. 20.

8. Laura Macdonald, "Canada and the 'New World Order'," in *Canadian Politics in the 1990s*, ed. Michael S. Whittington and Glen Williams (Toronto: Nelson Canada, 1995), p. 43.

9. Ibid., p. 42.

10. Foreign economic policy is often conceptualized, whether explicitly or implicitly, as industrial, rather than foreign, policy. On this question, see Claire Turenne Sjolander, "International Trade as Foreign Policy: 'Anything for a Buck'," in *How Ottawa Spends 1997-98. Seeing Red: A Liberal Report Card*, ed. Gene Swimmer (Ottawa: Carleton University Press, 1997); or G. Bruce Doern and Brian W. Tomlin, "Trade-Industrial Policy," in *Border Crossings: The Internationalization of Canadian Public Policy*, ed. G. Bruce Doern, Leslie A. Pal and Brian W. Tomlin (Toronto: Oxford University Press, 1996).

11. Cited in Kim Richard Nossal, *The Politics of Canadian Foreign Policy*, 3d ed. (Scarborough, Ont.: Prentice Hall Canada Inc., 1997), p. 30.

12. Mark Neufeld and Sandra Whitworth, "Imag(in)ing Canadian Foreign Policy," in *Understanding Canada: Building on the New Canadian Political Economy*, ed. Wallace Clement (Montreal and Kingston: McGill-Queen's University Press, 1997), p. 203. The Chrétien government's statement on Canadian foreign policy puts this most bluntly: "The promotion of prosperity and employment is at the heart of the Government's agenda," and is thus central to Canada's foreign policy objectives. Foreign Affairs and International Trade Canada, *Canada and the World: Government Statement* (Ottawa: Canada Communication Group, 1995), p. ii.

13. On this point, see Robert W. Cox, *Production, Power and World Order: Social Forces in the Making of History* (New York: Columbia University Press, 1987), pp. 254-55.

14. For a useful discussion of the theoretical and practical consequences of the separation of politics and economics, see Robert W. Cox, "Production and Hegemony: Toward a Political Economy of World Order," in *The Emerging International Economic Order: Dynamic Processes, Constraints, and Opportunities*, ed. Harold K. Jacobsen and Duncan Sidjanski (Beverly Hills: Sage Publications, 1982).

15. Roland Robertson, *Globalization: Social Theory and Global Culture* (London: Sage Publications Ltd., 1992), p. 8. See also James H. Mittleman, "The Dynamics of Globalization," in *Globalization: Critical Reflections*, ed. James H. Mittleman (Boulder, CO: Lynne Rienner Publishers, 1996).

16. I am indebted to my colleague Jeanne Kirk Laux for the processes, project, and ideology typology which is developed in this section.

17. Michael Hart, "The End of Trade Policy?" in *Canada Among Nations 1993-94: Global Jeopardy*, ed. Christopher J. Maule and Fen Osler Hampson (Ottawa: Carleton University Press, 1993), p. 89.

18. For a statement of the objectives and principles guiding postwar multilateralism, see John Gerard Ruggie, "Multilateralism: the Anatomy of an Institution," *International Organization* 46, 3 (Summer 1992): 561-98, or from a more critical

perspective, Robert W. Cox, "Multilateralism and World Order," *Review of International Studies* 18, 2 (April 1992): 161-80.

19. It is no surprise, for example, that initiatives such as the Foreign Investment Review Agency (FIRA), which had as its mandate to review investment proposals for their ability to confer benefit to the Canadian economy, could not fulfill its mandate. The emergence of new investment strategies which no longer conceived of a sovereign territory as the foundational building bloc for the organization of production made it difficult, if not impossible, to protect production defined along national lines, a point which Canadian, as well as foreign firms, made increasingly clear to the Canadian government.

20. On the emergence of an investment "triad" comprising North America, Europe, and Asia, see the United Nations Conference on Trade and Development (UNCTAD) *World Investment Report 1994: Transnational Corporations, Employment and the Workplace* (New York: United Nations, 1994).

21. This role contrasts with the earlier postwar role of the state described earlier, whose emphasis was on protecting or cushioning the national economy from disruptions emanating from international economic processes.

22. Canada here is not marginal, given its participation in the key structures of global economic governance, including the G7, the WTO, and the OECD.

23. Sergio Marchi, Minister for International Trade, "Notes for an Address to the Centre for Trade Policy and Law," Ottawa, 13 February 1998. http://www.dfait-maeci.gc.ca/english/ news/statements/98_state/98_008e.htm.

24. For an assessment of the importance of multilateralism in Canadian foreign policy, see Tom F. Keating, *Canada and World Order: The Multilateralist Tradition in Canadian Foreign Policy* (Toronto: McClelland & Stewart, 1993).

25. Lloyd Axworthy, Minister of Foreign Affairs, "Between Globalization and Multipolarity: The Case for a Global, Humane Canadian Foreign Policy." http://www.dfait-maeci.gc.ca/english/ foreign/humane.htm.

26. Michael Hart, "Canada in the Global Economy: Where Do We Stand?" in *Canada Among Nations 1997: Asia-Pacific Face-Off*, ed. Fen Osler Hampson, Maureen Appel Molot and Martin Rudner (Ottawa: Carleton University Press, 1997), p. 53.

27. Department of Foreign Affairs and International Trade, "World Trade Organization Head to Visit Canada," 23 May 1996 (No. 95). http://www.dfait-maeci.gc.ca/english/news/press_~1/96_press/96_095E.HTM.

28. Department of Foreign Affairs and International Trade, "Conference Lays Foundation for Stronger Trading System," 13 December 1996 (No. 247). http://www.dfait-maeci.gc.ca/english/news/press_~1/96_press/96_247E.HTM.

29. Department of Foreign Affairs and International Trade, "Canada Welcomes WTO Financial Services Agreement," 12 December 1997 (No. 209). http://www.dfait-maeci.gc.ca/english/news/press_~1/97_press/97_209E.HTM.

30. Cited in John Schofield, "Back to Square One: Washington Wins a Hotly Contested Trade Fight," *Maclean's*, 14 July 1997, p. 36.

31. Cited in Hart, "Canada in the Global Economy," p. 73.

32. Marchi, "Notes for an Address to the Centre for Trade Policy and Law."

33. Sergio Marchi, Minister for International Trade, "Notes for an address to the Standing Committee on Foreign Affairs and International Trade," Ottawa, 4 November 1997. http://www.dfait-maeci.gc.ca/english/news/statem~1/97_state/97_048e.htm.

34. Marchi, "Notes for an Address to the Centre for Trade Policy and Law."

35. Sergio Marchi, Minister for International Trade, "Notes for an Address at the Canada-Chile Free Trade Agreement Plenary Session," Santiago, Chile, 21 January 1998. http://www.dfait-maeci.gc.ca/english/news/statements/98_state/98_006e.htm.

36. Marchi, "Notes for an Address at the Canada-Chile Free Trade Agreement Plenary Session."

37. Hart, "Canada in the Global Economy," p. 75.

38. Heather Scoffield, "Summit Maps Path to Free Trade," *The Globe and Mail*, 20 April 1998, p. A8.

39. Mike Trickey, "Canada to Host Next Free-Trade Summit," *The Ottawa Citizen* 20 April 1998, p. A2.

40. Heather Scoffield, "Trade Talks to Touch on Rights," *The Globe and Mail*, 16 April 1998, p. A8.

41. Jean Chrétien, cited in Scoffield, "Summit Maps Path to Free Trade," p. A8.

42. Cited in Alan Freeman, "Why our Political Leaders Have Gone into Sales," *The Globe and Mail*, 4 November 1994, p. A13.

43. Art Eggleton, Minister for International Trade, "Announcement of the Creation of Global Opportunities Response Team (Go-Team)," 7 February 1997. http://www.dfait-maeci.gc.ca/english/news/press_~1/97_press/97_022E/HTM.

44. A similar argument is developed in Claire Turenne Sjolander and Miguel de Larrinaga, "Mission Impossible: Canadian Diplomatic Initiatives from Mines to Markets," in *Worthwhile Initiatives? Canadian Mission-Oriented Diplomacy*, ed. Andrew F. Cooper and Geoffrey Hayes (Toronto: Irwin Publishing, forthcoming 1998).

45. This is not to say that there are no criticisms addressed to the Team Canada initiatives. In high profile comments made in April 1998, for example, Sylvia Ostry suggested that it would be a mistake to "confuse this trade development idiocy with economic policy.... In terms of the resources allocated to these [Team Canada] missions, they don't give us much.... Nobody in their right minds, except the airlines, would defend the trade missions." (Cited in Richard Foot, "'Team Canada' Has Zero Benefits," *The Ottawa Citizen*, 26 April 1998, p. A1). Ostry's comments went on to suggest, however, that a more appropriate strategy would be to negotiate detailed trade agreements with other countries — in effect, to concentrate more attention on the first of the Canadian government's parallel trade policy initiatives.

46. During the APEC meetings in Vancouver in November 1997, the RCMP used pepper spray against student demonstrators. Prime Minister Chrétien, in response to press questions about the appropriateness of the use of pepper spray, commented that he uses pepper on his steak. CBC transcript courtesy of Terry Milewski, "Charter-Free Zone," *CBC National Magazine*, 19 December 1997.

47. Kim Nossal, *The Politics of Canadian Foreign Policy*, p. 4.

IV

The Societal Context

7

Organized Labour in a Federal Society: Solidarity, Coalition Building and Canadian Unions

Tom McIntosh

Ce chapitre étudie comment les syndicats se sont intégrés à la société civile canadienne et ont ainsi pu devenir un lien entre les Canadiens d'un bout à l'autre du pays. Plusieurs obstacles économiques, politiques et sociaux ont ralenti et continuent de ralentir la croissance du mouvement ouvrier et sa capacité à surmonter la barrière linguistique au sein du mouvement. Historiquement, le mouvement ouvrier a réussi, dans une certaine mesure, à surmonter ou, du moins, à faire face à ces obstacles en s'alliant avec d'autres mouvements et d'autres groupes au sein de la société canadienne. Ce processus a non seulement modifié la politique et la société canadiennes, il a aussi changé les revendications dominantes, tant politiques que sociales, du mouvement ouvrier. Le mouvement ouvrier fait maintenant face à de nombreux défis dans la réaffirmation de son rôle dans l'économie politique canadienne des années 1990. Les décennies 1980 et 1990 ont été particulièrement difficiles pour le mouvement ouvrier en raison des restrictions étatiques imposées aux négociations collectives, de l'hostilité croissante des employeurs et d'une série de tensions internes avec ses partenaires sociaux et politiques. Au moment où le mouvement ouvrier s'engage dans le prochain millénaire, sa légitimité est contestée à l'intérieur de la société canadienne. Bien que cette contestation soit importante, il y a lieu de croire que le mouvement ouvrier possède la volonté et la capacité de se réinventer pour y faire face.

Work, or lack of it, shapes people's identity and provides both the material and, to some extent at least, creative basis of existence.... Thus labour, the human expression of work, is the essential object of concern for the study of society. In the Canadian economy today, wracked by high unemployment, rising inequality, falling real wages, and a collapsing welfare state, it is labour that is at the centre of the political and economic storm.[1]

INTRODUCTION

This chapter explores the manner in which organized labour in Canada became and remains an integral part of civil society. The focus is specifically on the changing institutional, political and economic relationships that provided trade unions with opportunities to overcome or offset the effects of barriers to their growth and, thus, to create linkages between working people across the country. The chapter begins with a look at the specific conditions that helped to shape contemporary trade unionism in Canada and how these factors influenced the specific response of organized labour in the pursuit of its particular economic and political agendas. What becomes apparent is that the specific conditions in which unionism took root in Canada necessitated responses that both extended and constrained the labour movement's political and social agendas.

In more recent years, organized labour has suffered a number of setbacks that have, when taken in combination, served to weaken its ability to act both politically and within civil society. Numerically the labour movement remains relatively stable. However, two decades of economic restructuring, legislative restrictions on union activity, a general ideological shift to the right, internal tensions within the labour movement and a somewhat uneasy relationship with other elements of the Canadian left (the social movements, the New Democratic Party [NDP], etc.) have taken their toll.

Organized labour has long relied on two relationships that were crucial to its position in civil society. The first was the accommodation with the state and private capital in the postwar era which allowed the labour movement a measure of institutional security. The second was its participation in a number of political and social coalitions with other "progressive" elements in Canadian society. The first relationship is clearly in tatters and labour must cope with the ascendancy of a different political economy predicated on different strategies of capital accumulation. The second relationship still adheres, but is under significant stress. Labour's social democratic political allies are themselves being transformed by the harsh "new realities" of turn-of-century capitalism while both the Canadian state and the civil society in which it is embedded are being similarly transformed.[2]

Yet, as discussed in detail below, the challenges faced by the Canadian labour movement are not entirely new and, despite the seriousness of those challenges, labour is not completely unable or unwilling to meet them. This chapter examines, then, how those two relationships were built, how they have faltered and how they may look in the future. The story is necessarily non-linear and complex. At its heart, though, is the ongoing attempt by the labour movement to anchor itself securely within civil society while engaging in a series of political and economic struggles with both capital and the state. Those struggles in turn serve to alter how the labour movement fits into civil society and the nature of the coalitions it builds.

Throughout its history(s), organized labour in Canada has continually struggled to build a labour movement that was "national" in scope, linking working people across the country into a single coherent movement pursuing a single political and economic agenda. Yet, as will become apparent, a number of factors have continually undercut labour's ability to build such a movement and to speak with a single voice. Like other elements of civil society, Canadian unionism reflects not only the divisions that are inherent in a federal society but also those divisions and cleavages that have long been the stuff of Canadian politics. The regional differentiation of the Canadian economy coupled with significant variations in the political culture of those regions, the persistent linguistic divide and a host of institutional factors have all been barriers to the growth of a truly national labour movement. In addition, internal debates and divisions, such as those between skilled and unskilled workers and between immigrant and native-born labourers further hindered labour's growth.

The specific importance of particular barriers has differed throughout Canadian history, but it is important to note that the linguistic divide between French- and English-speaking labour in Canada has resisted all attempts at resolution. As will be discussed in more detail below, there currently exists a relationship between English-Canadian and Quebec labour predicated on what is best described as "sovereignty-association" within the confederally organized Canadian labour movement as represented by the Canadian Labour Congress (CLC). Insofar as this chapter is focused on the nature of the linkages between working Canadians across the country and their bonds with other elements of civil society, it needs to be stressed that only the most formal connections exist across the linguistic divide. Thus, the attempts to build both a pan-Canadian labour movement and that movement's attempt to build political and social coalitions within civil society are, in essence, the attempts of English-Canadian trade unionists.[3] To the extent that organized labour in "the rest of Canada" interacts with Quebec labour, it does so for the most part through the CLC.

The CLC's relations with the Quebec Federation of Labour (QFL) may, as discussed below, provide some important lessons in terms of how the CLC approaches a more decentralized federation in the years to come. In most policy areas the CLC has been consistently nationalist on economic issues and centralist in its approach to the federation. The exception to this, however, has been a willingness to accommodate the aspirations of both Quebec labour and Quebec nationalism more generally which has been an equally consistent theme of both the CLC and the NDP policy since the 1960s.

At the same time, organized labour in Canada has struggled, with varying degrees of success, to accommodate, if not overcome, most of these other barriers. Though stagnant for the past decade, the unionization rate in Canada continues to hover at about one-third of the non-agricultural workforce.[4] There is some evidence, albeit not overwhelming, that organized labour stands poised to again play an important political and economic role in the next century. As the fiscal crises of the federal and provincial states, which dominated much of recent political discourse, begins to fade and the process of Canada's integration into a new international political economy proceeds, though unevenly and sometimes haphazardly, opportunities exist for organized labour to reassert its role as the defender of working people's political and economic interests. Such conclusions are, of course, both tentative and contingent. The barriers that faced labour in the past continue to exist and there are important new challenges that will need to be met, but it remains the case that organized labour in Canada is by no means ready to give up the ghost.

The contingency on which labour's future rests is its ability and willingness to rearticulate a political and economic strategy reminiscent of the strategies employed in the last so-called "golden age" of labour's growth and consolidation, namely the decades following the end of World War II. Of course, the period of labour's growth and consolidation in this era, often referred to as "the years of consent"[5] or the achievement of "industrial legality,"[6] were not always as golden as a cursory examination might suggest.

What is evident is that labour's own political and social agendas underwent a significant transformation both prior to and following WWII as it grappled with its position within the Canadian political economy and Canadian civil society. For some this meant that the *raison d'être* of trade unionism was ultimately compromised beyond recognition. For others, labour's accommodation with capital, the state, and civil society was the means by which it secured its position in the Canadian socio-economic structure and which allowed it to give voice to a political and social agenda in defence of working people and other elements of Canadian society. Yet, at its core, the Canadian labour movement has remained committed to a principle of solidarity, not only within the house of labour, but more generally within Canadian society. What becomes evident though is that Canadian labour has often failed to turn its commitment to solidarity into long-term practice.

It was the extension of the notion of solidarity into political and social coalitions with non-labour elements of Canadian society that helped the Canadian labour movement integrate itself more fully and more successfully into the mainstream of Canadian society than might otherwise have been expected. As a consequence, this strategy (which characterized the labour movement's success in the postwar years) meant a fundamental reorientation of its political and social agendas from its earlier incarnations. Indeed, it meant a fundamental transformation in the way in which labour viewed Canadian society — the giving way of its historical class-based focus, with its attendant radical and even revolutionary politics, and the embracing of social-democratic reformist politics.

However, in the 1980s, the economic and social conditions that allowed Canadian labour to build the coalitions that were part of its success began to change in significant ways. As a result, therefore, the coalitions on which organized labour relied (and which it had helped to build) began to founder. Throughout the 1980s and into the 1990s, organized labour's ability to articulate a coherent political, economic, and social agenda which linked together working people, social activists, and what could be termed the "broad left" of Canadian politics also foundered. The weakening of these coalitions and their marginalization within a shifting political discourse centred on neo-conservative politics and neo-classical economics further served to highlight the institutional barriers that mitigated against labour's "national" focus.

The first section of this chapter will examine the economic, social, and political conditions that were faced by organized labour in the years prior to and after World War II, the time period in which organized labour solidified its legitimacy and began its largest period of growth and political and social influence. The second section explores how and why organized labour entered into a succession of political and social alliances and how those alliances both transformed civil society in Canada while also transforming the labour movement, its agenda, and its prospects. The third section examines how the changing political economy of the 1980s and 1990s poses new and important challenges to organized labour and how labour's position within the Canadian left is increasingly being challenged. In spite of labour's difficulties in finding a secure position within the changing political economy and the tensions that exist within its coalitions with other socio-political actors, there is some evidence that labour is again in the process of reinventing itself. Rising militancy and a recognition of its own need to adapt to a society that is changing rapidly may well mean that the Canadian labour movement is prepared to secure its position in the socio-economic order once again. That this struggle will result in a "different" labour movement is relatively certain.

LABOUR IN CONTEXT

At the time of Confederation trade unions in Canada were, simply put, illegal. The formation of unions was deemed a criminal conspiracy designed to restrain trade and violate fundamental concepts of the individual's right to enter into contracts. The *Trade Union Act, 1872* made unions legal, but offered them no protection and certainly guaranteed them no legitimacy.[7] The legal recognition of trade unions as legitimate representatives of the working class with both legal rights and obligations came first during the Second World War with *Order in Council 1003* and after the war with the so-called *Rand Formula* that created the "union shop," allowed on-site workplace organizing and the automatic check-off of union dues from employees' wage packets. These became the basis for the union security provisions that we currently find in the various labour codes across the country

Prior to and in the years immediately following the *Trade Union Act, 1872* the labour movement in Canada consisted essentially of a series of locally organized "friendship societies" and collectivities of skilled workers.[8] In the absence of widespread industrial development, these proto-unions were designed to preserve the rights and privileges of skilled workers, often but not exclusively self-employed, by controlling entry into these trades by others. Unions of the kind with which we are now familiar had to await the arrival of larger scale industrialization, which, in the Canadian case, came significantly later than it did in other western nations. At the same time, the process of industrialization in Canada occurred within a different set of historical and social circumstances than in, for example, the United States.[9] If it is the case that organized labour began its entry into the mainstream of Canadian civil society during the economic and social chaos of the Great Depression, then it did so at a time when a variety of factors continually served to undercut its progress.

The division of Canadian labour into an English-speaking and French-speaking component remains to this day as one of the biggest barriers to the attempts to create a "national" labour movement. From the very beginnings of the labour movement, the attempt to build a pan-Canadian movement representing workers from all regions and within all sectors of the economy has run up against the nationalist aspirations of both the Quebec working class and Quebec society more generally. At the same time, the Catholic church played a defining role in shaping the character of the Quebec labour movement. Originally opposed to organizations such as the Knights of Labour (which drew significant support in Quebec in the early years of the twentieth century), the Catholic church later pursued a strategy of integrating labour organizations into corporatist arrangements that sought, at least nominally, to balance the interests of capital, labour, and the Quebec state — arrangements overseen by the Catholic church.[10]

In addition to the French-English split (which was also, in this period, a Catholic-Protestant split), uneven economic development and large variations in regional industrialization, coupled with regional political cultures highly resistant to such changes,[11] meant that the Canadian working class was isolated in small pockets separated by large distances. Thus, the class structure of Canadian society was skewed in favour of rural Canadians. This further exacerbated the religious, ethnic, and linguistic cleavages, to create an environment which was openly hostile to the class politics inherent in unionism at this time. In short, organized labour was, as one historian put it, a minority within a class that was itself a minority within the Canadian social structure.[12] This was compounded by a political system that still only paid lip-service to notions of popular sovereignty through property qualifications (as well as racial and gender restrictions) on the right to vote in various jurisdictions.[13]

To further hinder the early labour movements' attempts to create a pan-Canadian working class base from which to build, the Canadian federation has a constitutional structure which forces unions to focus at the provincial rather than national political arena. The responsibility for labour-capital relations stems from the provincial responsibility for matters relating to "property and civil rights" as set out in the *Constitution Act, 1867*. Thus, working-class organization was forced to take place within political boundaries that served to undercut trade unionism's pan-Canadian objectives. As will be discussed later, organized labour, and indeed much of the Canadian left, has long had an ambivalent relationship with the Canadian federal condition — it continually saw its agenda as essentially "national" in scope which led to a consistent "centralist" thrust to its politics despite the fact that its political success was as much, if not more, on the provincial scene as it was on the national. Again, though, the exception to this was the general acceptance of Canada's "bicultural" condition that necessitated the recognition and accommodation of Quebec's special status within the labour movement.

The combined result of these factors was that in the years before the Second World War there really was no "Canadian" labour movement. Instead there was a series of independent, uncoordinated labour movements that rose and fell in response to essentially local economic and social conditions. As a result, the achievement of political gains for workers was a fragmented, piecemeal and often temporary phenomenon in which local gains were difficult to carry forward onto the national scene and even more difficult to hold onto in the face of often brutal opposition from both the state and capital.[14]

Through the interwar years it is evident that Canadian labour had a political as well as an economic agenda. Unions nominated their own candidates for Parliament and provincial legislatures, small independent labour parties were formed both in the west and in Ontario, and the Communist Party of Canada took a leading role in organizing the previously unorganized. As well, the Progressive Party became the first significant political party to link the interests of farmers and industrial labourers in the 1920s.[15] The reasons for this political and social action on the part of Canadian trade unions may well lie in the fact that capital showed no reluctance to call on the state to protect its interests, such as in the general strikes of 1919 in Winnipeg and British Columbia. This in turn forced labour to articulate its own political voice in opposition to such tactics. At the same time Canada entered a new phase of economic development in the early decades of the twentieth century whereby capital became increasingly concentrated and centralized and the application of scientific management strategies attempted to wrest control of production from skilled workers. An increasingly coherent state apparatus with a clear desire to regulate labour-capital relations oversaw all of this.[16]

Despite the political activity of unions on a wide array of fronts, it was during the 1920s that Canadian labour suffered its most serious setbacks. Changing immigration patterns brought new ethnic and religious cleavages which when combined with the loss of skilled jobs and the lack of any centralized cohesion amongst its constituent parts created "a labour force honeycombed with divisions more complex than the older skilled-unskilled distinction which had a centuries long pedigree."[17] The economic dislocation of the Great Depression only served to further hinder the organizational and political ambitions of organized labour.

The years between 1872 and the end of World War II were marked both by alternating periods of labour quiescence and intense labour strife.[18] Of particular importance are the interwar years and the period of the Great Depression. Even though the response of the labour movement to the economic collapse of the 1930s was sporadic, localized, and uncoordinated,[19] the interwar years marked a significant change in the role played by the Canadian state which would ultimately serve to transform the Canadian labour movement.

There was, for historian Bryan Palmer, a duality to the exercise of state power in the 1920s and 1930s: interventionist, often brutally so, in defence of property and profit, and abstentionist in terms of defending those outside those social relations. Yet, out of this contradictory position the state evolved a more subtle, but at least as powerful, role. Through the interwar years the Canadian state moved slowly away from direct coercion toward a new role predicated on regulating labour-capital relations. As part of this transformation the state assumed the role of neutral arbiter. Indeed the success of this transformation relied on the state's ability to convince both parties, but especially organized labour, that it could play this role effectively.[20] To quote Bryan Palmer on this:

> Out of the dilemmas and contradictions ... [of] this period, however, would emerge a new kind of state power, one that sealed a future "compromise" between labour and capital based in industrial legality, welfare provisions, and a social Keynesianism judged affordable in the new prosperity of the post-World War Two world.[21]

Thus, this transformation in the role of the state and the eventual evolution of a system of industrial relations predicated on preserving labour peace helped pave the way for the political and ideological transformation within the labour movement. Ultimately, the integration of labour into a system of rule-based industrial relations would allow for, perhaps even demand, the kind of coalition building that would come to exemplify the contemporary Canadian labour movement in terms of its pursuit of a political and economic agenda. Throughout this time the labour movement(s) reflected a diversity of approach to the articulation of workers' interests and to political activity. McCormack, in his study of radical politics in the western provinces, makes an important distinction between the "the reformers, the rebels and the revolutionaries" that is instructive in conceptualizing the divisions within the labour movement.[22]

They were all to some extent "radicals," but there existed a continuum of political perspective running from a reformist tradition advocating traditional parliamentary politics through to a revolutionary communist strain advocating the ultimate necessity of overthrowing the economic order. The coexistence of these left analyses was often highly conflictual, with mutual denunciations being a common feature of intra-left politics. What is important to understand, however, is that it is during these years that one can begin to see the marginalization of that revolutionary critique rooted in the intellectual and political tradition of Marx. Though perhaps the most vocal element of the early labour movement, it was not necessarily the predominant one. It is a common feature of both the Canadian and American labour movements' histories that the revolutionary and even the radical perspectives within each was eventually forced to the margins by both internal and external political forces.[23]

At the same time as revolutionary class-based analyses were being drowned out in the postwar years, the political and organizational strength of labour grew at an unprecedented rate. The years following the war were the most successful in labour's history. Union membership grew to well over a third of the non-agricultural workforce, labour legislation guaranteed collective bargaining rights, employment and health and safety standards were codified, organized labour helped to shape the Keynesian welfare state that protected both the organized and the unorganized, and hundreds of thousands of Canadian workers settled into a self-perceived middle-class respectability that was as much the Canadian dream as the American. This was, in a sense, the reward for the triumph of social-democratic reformist politics on the part of the labour left. Dissent within the labour movement over strategy, ideology, and methodology was replaced with consent to a more peaceful social contract. At the outbreak of World War Two there were fewer union members in Canada than there had been two decades earlier (see Table 1), though its percentage of the non-agricultural workforce was marginally larger. Between 1945 and 1975, membership would more than quadruple and its percentage of the workforce would grow one and a half times.

Of particular importance during the period of the late 1960s and into the 1970s is that governments during this time allowed the unionization of the expanding public sector. By the mid-1970s, when the last provincial public sector was unionized in Prince Edward Island, labour had expanded its constituency to include virtually all of the public sector (as high as 85 percent in some sectors).[24] Estimates at this time put the federal and provincial public sectors as making up nearly 40 percent of the Canadian workforce.[25]

The eventual urbanization and industrialization of Canadian society that characterized an era of massive economic expansion can explain part of this. But the height of Canadian unionism arrived after the triumph of the reformist perspective within the labour movement. This "kinder and gentler" form of unionism, itself more acceptable to both the state and private capital, allowed the creation of what Panitch and Swartz have called "the great post-war compromise" — the legal protection and recognition of trade unions in exchange

Table 1: Canadian Union Membership, 1920-1993

Year	Total Membership ('000)	As % of Non- Agricultural Workers	Average Annual % Change
1920	374	16.0	—
1925	271	14.4	-6.2
1930	322	13.9	-3.2
1935	281	14.5	-2.3
1940	362	16.3	5.2
1945	711	24.2	14.5
1951	1,029	28.4	7.7
1955	1,268	33.7	5.4
1960	1,459	32.3	2.8
1965	1,589	29.7	1.7
1970	2.173	33.6	6.5
1975	2,884	36.9	5.6
1980	3.397	37.6	1.8
1985	3,666	39.0	0.4
1990	3,841	33.1	n/a
1993	3,768	32.6	0.6

Source: Adapted from Mary-Lou Coates, David Arrowsmith and Melanie Courchene, *The Current Industrial Relations Scene in Canada, 1989: Labour Movement and Trade Unionism Reference Tables* (Kingston: Industrial Relations Centre, Queen's University, 1989); and Diane Garlaneau, "Unionized Workers," *Perspectives on Labour and Income* (Ottawa: Statistics Canada, Spring 1996), p. 45.

for labour's recognition of a capital accumulation strategy based on high productivity, high wages, and the development of the welfare state (i.e., Fordism).[26]

What is of importance here is the persistence of organized labour as a constituent part of Canadian civil society. During the years of substantial union growth in the postwar era, unionism remained relatively consistent from province to province, apparently in spite of the kinds of regional, linguistic, and institutional divisions spoken of above (see Table 2). The only consistent outliers are Alberta, which is perennially lower than other provinces, and Newfoundland, which was significantly higher than other provinces from the mid-1970s through the 1980s. Not surprisingly, BC's unionization rate is also higher than average. The sudden spurt in PEI's unionization rate comes, most likely, from the unionization of the public sector in the mid-1970s which then

Table 2:   Unionization by Province, 1962-1986 as a Percentage of Paid Workers

	1962	1972	1982	1986
Canada	31.1	32.5	35.4	34.6
Newfoundland	29.0	32.2	54.2	61.4
Prince Edward Island	14.4	17.3	31.7	37.7
Nova Scotia	28.7	33.9	32.7	36.0
New Brunswick	24.7	35.5	37.4	40.1
Quebec	25.8	36.7	36.7	40.7
Ontario	32.7	32.9	31.0	31.9
Manitoba	30.7	31.3	32.5	39.2
Saskatchewan	29.5	27.5	33.9	38.2
Alberta	24.4	27.7	25.0	29.5
British Columbia	43.1	43.9	44.4	43.7

Source: Adapted from Mary-Lou Coates, David Arrowsmith and Melanie Courchene, *The Current Industrial Relations Scene in Canada, 1989: Labour Movement and Trade Unionism Reference Tables* (Kingston: Industrial Relations Centre, Queen's University, 1989).

places it firmly in the Canadian mainstream. By 1993, the figures do not change significantly with Newfoundland at a 53-percent unionization rate, followed by Quebec (39 percent) and BC and Manitoba both with 36 percent. Alberta continues to be far below the national average.[27]

There is no simple explanation for this consistency. Perhaps, most curiously, the provincial labour codes that developed in the postwar era share more similarities than differences. This is not to deny that there are some important interprovincial variations in labour law (e.g., the banning of so-called replacement workers during a strike or lock-out, which remains high on labour's legislative agenda in a majority of the provinces), but on balance there is a remarkable consistency given that there are eleven jurisdictions with ten of them also having different rules for the public and private sector unions. Similarly, there was no Canadian version, even at a provincial level, of the American *Taft-Hartley Act* that allowed the institutionalization of so-called "right to work" states and legitimized union avoidance techniques which has resulted in the clearly bifurcated nature of American industrial relations.

SOLIDARITY AND THE BUILDING OF COALITIONS

The legitimization of labour's role within the postwar political economy and its integration into civil society needs to be understood, however, as something more than simply the achievement of a political understanding with capital and the state. At the same time that labour accepted the terms of the so-called "years of consent" it was also again in the process of building political and social coalitions between itself and non-labour elements of Canadian society. As mentioned before, it was a process that began as early as the 1880s and carried through to the Progressives in the 1920s and which would, like the story of labour's growth itself, proceed in fits and starts, yielding successes and failures over the five decades following the end of World War II.[28] The success of labour's growth in the postwar economic expansion, resting as it did on the foundations of Fordism and Keynesianism, pushed labour further along this path of coalition building in an effort to overcome the institutional, political, and cultural factors that had previously mitigated against working-class organization in Canada. The marginalization of the radical and revolutionary class analyses coupled with the material benefits that unionization clearly provided in this era broke down some of this resistance to unions.

Insofar as the postwar compromise left labour as a "junior partner" in the new economic order taking shape, then labour would need such alliances if it was to continue to try to push Canada down the "parliamentary road to social democracy." In the years that followed, the labour movement, with its significant resources and its bases in all parts of the country, would eventually become the largest and most powerful element in a loosely organized coalition of social activists, environmentalists, feminists, and other elements of what might best be called the "broad left" of Canadian society that ebbed and flowed through Canadian politics from the 1960s onward. From the Solidarity Coalition that challenged the economic restraint program of the British Columbia government in the 1980s to the Days of Action protests against the policies of the Ontario government from 1996-98, organized labour has used its position as the largest component of the Canadian left to build alliances and to attempt to articulate a common agenda.

What is readily apparent, though, is that such coalition building is a double-edged sword. As noted above, by reaching out beyond the confines of its working-class base, labour necessarily altered its own conception of itself and its understanding of Canadian society.[29] At the same time, the coalitions labour built, especially those in recent times, are often fraught with internal tensions and contradictions. In fairly simple terms, there is an ongoing tension between the materialist concerns of organized labour (wages, job security, the welfare state, etc.) and what has been called the post-materialist concerns of environmentalists, feminists, and other partners within these coalitions.[30] One need only look to the ongoing battles in the forests of British Columbia to see these contradictions in operation — unionized forestry workers battling environmental groups over logging old-growth forests. In the end, the coalitions that labour has used to extend its own influence, and the support it has provided other elements of the broad left and which served to link a wide range of Canadians, have to be understood as inherently fragile. That they persist in being rebuilt and reconstituted, always in different forms and in response to different political and economic situations, speaks to the resiliency of the labour movement.

What is of interest here is the manner in which organized labour managed to secure its place within civil society while still a "minority within a minority." At the same time, labour also managed to overcome institutional and structural barriers that could have continued to keep it locally focused and fragmented. Part of the answer to this lies in labour's ability to extend the concept of solidarity, which in some sense lies at the heart of unionism, into the building of important political and social coalitions that magnified both its power and its scope. That labour was able to do this successfully may well account in part for its four decades of growth following World War II. What is still an open question is whether, in the face of the collapse of Keynesianism, the increasing importance of non-Fordist strategies of accumulation, and its own position within the Canadian left, organized labour can find new expressions of solidarity and new coalitions that will preserve its status within civil society.

Trade unionism, from its very beginning, was predicated on the notion that working people's interests were best served through collective action. Insofar as industrialization destroyed previous relations of production and challenged existing property relations, it served to make the process of production and of labouring an essentially collective act. The labour of any one individual became essentially meaningless outside its existence as part of a larger collective act of numerous other labourers.

In this way, then, the interests of individual labourers became irrevocably tied to the interests of those other workers with whom they toiled — if they laboured collectively then their interests could only be articulated and protected through collective action and mutual defence.[31] Central to collective action was the notion of "solidarity" — the recognition that one could only protect oneself if one also protected those in similar circumstances and that an assault on another was an assault on oneself.

It is easy to see how notions of solidarity can be expanded beyond simple collective action within a single workplace to include workers in other workplaces, in other parts of the country and other parts of the world. Yet with each concentric circle of inclusion the attachments between workers become increasingly abstract and come into conflict with other attachments held by individuals. "The ever expanding union of workers" of which Marx wrote was, from the very beginning, continually undercut by other calls on individuals' loyalties — to the nation, to the state, to the church, etc.

Yet given the fragmented and dispersed state of the Canadian working class and the slow and uneven process of industrialization, the Canadian labour movement was, in a sense, forced to look beyond the working class for political and social allies. The ideological and strategic divisions of the early labour movement made this process exceptionally fragile, but even the more unified labour movement of the postwar era faced similar problems. The fragility of such coalition politics is further heightened during those periods when external forces also serve to put labour on the defensive. In the interwar years, the direct, often brutal, coercion of the state and resistance on the part of capital to labour's demands created, in a sense, a two-front battle for trade unionists. In more recent years, the restructuring economy, a hostile legislative environment and reduced public support for labour's agenda only serves to make contemporary coalition building as complex, if not as physically dangerous, as in the past. The irony, of course, is that it is during those times of significant external threat that labour most needs to build political alliances and, yet, this is when such coalitions are most difficult to build and maintain.

Take, for example, the formation of the Cooperative Commonwealth Federation (CCF) in the early 1930s as, formally at least, an alliance of labour, farmers, and socialist activists. The farmer-labour alliance was always a somewhat uncomfortable one. The rural residents attracted to the alliance were more often than not the subsistence farmers (and in Atlantic Canada, fishermen) who often supplemented their farm income with wage labour. Yet their commitment to unionism was essentially instrumental — wage labour served to support their "real" lives as farmers and fisherman and was, therefore, a temporary place for them. More prosperous farmers, though they remained outside the mainstream of industrial capitalism, used casual wage-labour on a revolving basis and thus had little interest in advancing workers' interests.[32]

The ringing denunciation of capitalism that opens the *Regina Manifesto* notwithstanding, the CCF was the first major social-democratic parliamentary political force in Canadian politics. The party expressly rejected the inevitability and the desirability of class conflict in favour of a more moderate reformist politics. What is important to stress, though, is that the alliance built around the CCF was not essentially led by organized labour. The labour movement, as noted above, was still a regionally diverse, ideologically splintered and uncoordinated entity. Thus, the CCF attracted only a small portion of the labour movement's official support. It did somewhat better, at least on occasion, in attracting the votes of trade unionists. In the minds of even the more radical elements of Canadian labour, whatever the shortcomings of social democracy, it promised at least some positive reforms.[33]

The CCF's electoral success, especially in the realm of provincial politics, remains an important demonstration of successful coalition building. With such coalitions came an ongoing transformation of how labour viewed itself, its relation to Canadian society, and the advancement of its political and social agenda, even as such coalitions changed those agendas. In the end, however, the CCF remained, despite its affiliation with some labour organizations, an uncomfortable alliance for many trade unionists and a betrayal in the minds of labour's more radical minority.[34]

The history of labour's relationship with the CCF often underplays the importance of these divisions in the 1930s. Again, there really was no "house of labour" in Canada at this point that could easily be brought into a labour-farmer alliance; rather there was a myriad of organizations, parties, and movements with little coordination and much mutual antipathy. Insofar as the CCF incorporated labour into a broader coalition, it was that reformist element of the union movement that took part. As the labour movement became more institutionally and ideologically unified in the postwar era (and as both the labour movement, the state, and Canadian society generally marginalized the more radical and revolutionary elements) unions would come into a dominant role within a new political coalition.

This came about in 1961. With the CCF quickly fading into political oblivion in light of the prosperity of the 1950s and the ideological crossfire of the Cold War, it became apparent that a new party would need to carry the banner of social democracy into the 1960s. In 1961 the Canadian Labour Congress, formed in 1956, and the CCF formally joined together to form the New Democratic Party with the CLC playing a pivotal role in party strategy, policy and financing. Unlike the CCF, the NDP had organized labour as its most powerful single constituency.[35]

The coalition between the remnants of the CCF and the CLC was made possible in part because, for the first time, there was a labour organization capable and willing to speak as "the voice of labour" in Canada. The Canadian Labour Congress was formed through the merger of the Trades and Labour Congress and the Canadian Congress of Labour and included most of the major "national" and "international" unions in the country. What made the creation of the CLC possible, in part, was the successful campaign on the part of the labour movement's moderate wing to purge the radical elements from positions of influence both within specific unions and within broader labour coalitions. In short, Canadian labour was, as it entered the 1960s, more ideologically cohesive than it ever had been in the past. There is a mythology that the kinds of red-baiting and purges that devastated the radical elements of American labour did not happen in Canada.[36] Yet there was an internal struggle within Canadian labour that replicated the American experience and which saw the eventual triumph of moderate social democratic politics.[37] This would pave the way for both the consolidation of labour under the banner of the CLC and the CLC's alliance with the New Democratic Party.

As presently constituted, the CLC is in effect a confederal[38] organization structured around and ensuring representation at the centre for the 12 provincial and territorial labour federations in the country. The inclusion of the major industrial trade unions such as the United Steelworkers, the United Autoworkers and, at the time, the Teamsters meant that it was possible to talk about a Canadian house of labour. However, this confederal arrangement means that labour's house has many mansions. The CLC is both a central organization giving voice to the political agenda of Canadian labour and also a coalition of discreet unions and provincial organizations that often pursue different, if not always contradictory, agendas. Given its organizational structure the CLC experiences periods of tension and infighting as the power wielded by its constituent parts waxes and wanes. Most recently this tension has been seen in the rise to prominence of the public sector unions that have now surpassed the old-line industrial unions in size and in a potentially divisive left-right split over political strategy.

There is also an ongoing tension about the politics of Canadian labour, and especially the CLC, in terms of what is best described as its centralist orientation to Canadian politics. Like much of the Canadian left, the labour leadership has never felt entirely comfortable with the give and take of Canada's federal system and has long articulated a political and economic agenda that clearly demanded "national" solutions to "national" problems. In one sense this is consistent with a long-standing desire of the labour leadership to link together the disparate elements of the labour movement into a pan-Canadian organization. The problem, of course, is that the CLC's centralist and nationalist tendencies do not always square with its own more decentralized and confederal institutional structure. Of course, the CLC's confederal structure has allowed it to recognize the "special status" of Quebec labour by essentially institutionalizing a linguistic bifurcation within the Canadian house of labour.

From the period between the 1930s until the 1960s Quebec labour was differentiated from the rest of Canadian labour by the presence of confessional unions whose "national" focus was on the French-Canadian nation. The Quiet Revolution of the 1960s weakened and eventually virtually eliminated the political influence of the Catholic church within Quebec society generally and also within the Quebec labour movement.[39] But the decline of the church's influence within the labour movement did little to reorient its nationalist focus. Through the 1960s to the present the French-Canadian (Catholic) labour movement became the Quebec labour movement, closely tied with the politics of a reinvigorated Quebec nationalism and often with the separatist Parti Québécois. From the 1970s onward, the rest of the Canadian labour movement sought to accommodate the nationalist tendencies within Quebec labour by the gradual recognition of successive levels of independence within nominally pan-Canadian labour organizations and within specific unions (e.g., the United Auto Workers, now the Canadian Auto Workers). Thus, in a certain sense there are at least two distinct labour movements within Canada — one inside Quebec and one in the other nine provinces.[40] That is, the QFL is in many respects independent of the CLC while remaining part of the organization such that the two maintain a collaborative relationship of equals on issues of common concern.[41]

In some sense the CLC-NDP alliance that was created in 1961 has yielded significant political success. On the other hand, it can also be seen to have somewhat stifled the political activism inside the labour movement. The NDP's electoral success has been entirely on the provincial scene and, with the exception of Bob Rae's win in Ontario in 1990, limited to western Canada and the north. Other than the Rae win, it has formed governments in BC, Saskatchewan, Manitoba, and the Yukon. On the national scene it was a perennial "third party" (albeit not always third in the federal House, it was sometimes fourth or fifth). In 1993 it lost official party status, along with the Progressive Conservatives, amid the resurgence of the Liberals in Ontario and Atlantic Canada, the separatist Bloc Québécois in Quebec, and the Reform Party in the west. It has rebounded in a fashion, capturing 20 seats in the 1997 election by capitalizing on a combination of leader Alexa McDonough's profile in Atlantic Canada and that population's anger at Liberal government cutbacks, especially in the area of Employment Insurance.[42] At the same time, the NDP had maintained a high political profile as the champion of what former leader Ed Broadbent described as "ordinary Canadians." In the early 1970s the party held the balance of power during the Liberal minority government of Pierre Trudeau and proved the more effective opposition party in 1984 after the crushing defeat of the Turner Liberals at the hands of Brian Mulroney's reinvigorated Conservatives. Yet, the NDP has never fully capitalized on the political opportunities it had. David Lewis led the party to a disastrous defeat in 1974, failing to win the party credit for the popular nationalist economic policies it promoted but which the Liberals implemented. By the mid-1980s the Liberals had used the media-grabbing antics of its "Rat Pack" of parliamentary newcomers to wrest attention away from the largest ever NDP contingent in the House, effectively disguising the growing tensions within that party over Turner's leadership.

However one characterizes the success (or lack of it) of the NDP, either provincially or federally, there is one thing that is certain. For the most part the trade union membership has not traditionally voted for the NDP (or for that matter for the CCF).[43] The important role played by the labour leadership in political strategy, in the back rooms of the party and in party financing has never effectively translated into delivering even a majority of union members' votes to the NDP. Traditionally only a third of unionized electors vote for the party. Nor has the party proved to be a vehicle for trade unionists entry into electoral politics, though that has changed somewhat with the 1997 results. Traditionally, the labour movement has not sent its "best and brightest" to win office under the NDP at the federal level and only sporadically in the provincial arenas. This is not, however, unprecedented in the relationship between unions and their political wing:

> As in the British Labour Party, there appears to be a division of functions be-
> tween the parliamentary wing and the trade unions, at least with respect to
> full-time union officials. There are no prominent trade union leaders in the cau-
> cus, nor have they been candidates.... But from the point of view of economic
> policy, this is the one area which the trade union leaders guard jealously.[44]

In this area, the CLC has consistently played an important and often decisive role. When the Canadian left in the early 1970s flirted with a left-
nationalist economic analysis that was highly critical not only of the role of
US capital in the Canadian economy, but also of US-dominated international
unions in the Canadian labour movement,[45] the CLC did not hesitate to flex its
muscles to ensure that such criticisms did not become NDP policy. Known as
the Waffle Group, supporters of a party resolution calling for an "independent, socialist Canada" (a.k.a. *The Waffle Manifesto*) were not only defeated by
a labour-led response, but, in parts of the party, the Wafflers were ordered to
disband as an entity within the party. This drove some of the party's intellectual wing to leave, albeit temporarily in some cases.[46] The irony in all of this
is that little more than a decade later the same CLC would endorse a left-
nationalist critique of the *Canada-U.S. Free Trade Agreement* that could have
been written by the same people that issued the *Manifesto*.

Having united, more or less, the majority of Canadian trade unionists and
played an instrumental role in the creation of longest-surviving "third" party
in federal politics, the labour movement, or at least the CLC, seemed willing
to maintain a curious distance from the electoral process. In a sense, the NDP
became the vehicle through which labour acted within this arena. The NDP
also became the forum in which labour bumped up against the other elements
of the Canadian left — feminists, environmentalists, social activists, etc. And
in this way, there existed what appeared to be a coalition of interests that
expressed itself within the confines of the electoral system through the NDP,
and which manifested itself in a myriad of shorter term alliances when political action became extra-parliamentary.

But again, this coalition is much more complex than it first appears. It has
to be understood that labour did not enter the NDP as simply a large number
of individual trade unionists committed to social democracy, but as large, bureaucratic and, in terms of the Canadian left, economically powerful
institutions. Other constituencies within the NDP coalition, the non-labour
elements, entered as individuals. There may be a large number of Greenpeace
members within the NDP, but Greenpeace is not affiliated with the party in
the same way as the Canadian Union of Public Employees (CUPE) or the
Canadian AutoWorkers (CAW). Indeed, the affiliation of unions is much
stronger than the affiliation of unionists and thus within that coalition, the
labour movement is clearly "first amongst equals." Or, maybe more succinctly,
"first amongst unequals." It may be true that the NDP is numerically dominated by individual members and that policy convention delegates come,

mostly, from individual riding associations, but this belies power wielded behind the scenes by the labour leadership.

According to Archer and Whitehorn, though, the materialist/postmaterialist split that is supposed to be plaguing parties of the left in western nations is not evident in the NDP, at least not at the federal level. Part of this rests on the fact that economic concerns remained consistently high on the political agendas of Canadians through the 1980s and into the 1990s, thus not providing the "luxury" of concern about non-economic matters. As a result, there was no significant electoral support for "green" parties. Further, they contend, the federal NDP has accommodated support for environmental policy with little internal conflict. At the same time they admit that there a number of areas where "new politics" has the potential to divide the party, and point especially to the area of gender politics. It is, however, still a debatable proposition.[47]

Such analysis may be correct, as far as it goes. But the focus should not be on just the internal dynamics of the party, though they are important in and of themselves. The NDP is not just about those activists who attend conventions and belong to particular caucuses within the party. It is also about the much larger group of people who do not belong to the party, are not active within it, but who, nonetheless tend to vote for the NDP and whom the NDP actively courts during and between elections. These are the people Ed Broadbent called the "ordinary Canadians" and those who live on "Main Street, not Bay Street."

In addition, there needs also to be a focus on how the NDP manages the competing interests within the broad left of Canadian politics when it has to do so both in the political arena more generally and also from the position of government — when it must also confront the demands of those economic and political interests outside its traditional circle of friends and allies. It is one matter to ensure acceptance of policy resolutions calling for increased environmental protection within the confines of a party convention. It is another to try to accommodate, as a government, a labour movement (sometimes allied with employers) wanting to clear-cut a portion of the BC forests amid the protests of various environmental and aboriginal groups. This, it seems, is the real test of the resiliency of the red-green coalition.

It is true that in recent years the labour movement made important efforts to both accommodate and incorporate these competing agendas — both within the NDP as its electoral arm and within itself. The CLC has a strong history of expressing its solidarity with the goals and aspirations of the social movement left in Canada.[48] But the CLC, by virtue of its size and structure, is a long way from the shop floor where such expressions of solidarity may have little force or effect, but where they are in fact most needed. Thus, the building of solidaristic networks has fallen to individual unions and, here, the record is somewhat mixed. Much has been made of labour's inability to treat the non-labour left as equals in a common struggle, with the tendency of labour to treat the concerns of its allies as being of secondary importance.[49] At the same time, historian Kim Moody points to the significant efforts that some Canadian unions, especially the Canadian Auto Workers (CAW), have gone to in order to reach out beyond the shop floor and also to bring what were once "non-labour" issues onto the shop floor. It is a process that he calls "social movement unionism," and while he has no illusions about the inherent problems in such politics, he also recognizes that the last two decades of economic and legislative assault on labour movements across the industrialized western nations necessitates a renewed commitment to the creation of new alliances rooted in a more robust conception of social and economic solidarity.[50]

Yet, as Moody recognizes, the need for labour to seriously (re-)engage with the social movement left comes at a time when labour itself is under direct and indirect assault by both capital and the state. The 1980s and 1990s have not been easy decades for organized labour in Canada. Public sector unions were faced with massive levels of wage freezes and rollbacks as governments made them a scapegoat for the economic ills of the nation.[51] In 1983, 85 percent of all contracts in the public administration sector (which includes only a part of the public sector workforce), and 75 percent the following year, could be deemed to include significant concessions on the part of employees. Most of these were legislated by governments willing to circumvent the collective bargaining process. In the private sector, concession rates were lower, but still significant. In manufacturing, transportation, and mining sectors the concession rates in 1983 ranged from 36 to over 60 percent and between 25 and 40 percent the following year. To put this in another way, 1983 saw 41.4 percent of all contracts negotiated in Canada governed in some way by federal or provincial restraint legislation, affecting over half of the unionized workforce negotiating contracts that year.[52]

By singling out public sector workers and effectively "demonizing" them in the public's perception, governments also managed to insert a wedge between the public and private sector unions. At the ideological level, trade unionists in the private sector willingly accepted the image of the public sector as essentially parasitical — overpaid, underworked, and wasters of taxpayers' money. Even if this did not play at the leadership level within the labour movement, it made inroads at the rank and file level where private sector workers, whose real wages were declining and who faced an increasingly insecure economic future as the process of restructuring gained momentum, resented the apparently secure, high-wage workers within the public sector.

At a more concrete level, the continual subversion of collective bargaining within the public sector also threatened to bifurcate Canadian industrial relations. From 1982 through 1984, the federal Liberals effectively suspended collective bargaining within the federal public sector. The Mulroney Conservatives reintroduced the suspension in the early 1990s, and this was extended until 1997 by the Chrétien Liberals. Increasingly, public sector workers were being excommunicated from the collective bargaining process through supposedly temporary government legislation. As the suspensions of bargaining continued or were reintroduced, the temporary began to look increasingly permanent.[53] To many, it began to become obvious that the postwar compromise, the so-called "years of consent," was over and the labour movement was facing increased resistance from employers.

Thus, as labour entered the 1990s, it was facing a wide range of problems. The political coalition with the NDP was yielding little fruit. The party lost official status in Parliament after the 1993 election and its renewed strength after the 1997 election has yet to translate into an easily identifiable upswing in public support for social democratic politics. At the same time, the NDP did manage some provincial victories — in BC, Saskatchewan, Ontario, and the Yukon. But as these governments accepted the cost-cutting and deficit reduction strategies of their Liberal and Conservative rivals, the labour movement began increasingly to question their role within this political coalition. Indeed, the withdrawal of support by Ontario unions from the NDP government of Bob Rae, in the wake of the Social Contract legislation, ensured that the already very unpopular government would be defeated. In the 1995 Ontario election the NDP finished third. The irony for the labour movement in all this was that if it thought that the Social Contract was regressive, then the Conservative "Common Sense Revolution" that followed was downright draconian.

With the public sector unions under siege and the private sector unions concentrated in the old-line Fordist sectors of the economy the labour movement has had a difficult time making a clear case for its own relevance in the changing economic and social order. Unionization remained strong in the traditional areas of the trades and manufacturing, but failed to build on this base by expanding into other economic sectors, and less industrialized regions. Large sectors of the Canadian working class, especially women and immigrants, remain outside the house of labour, even though unionization appears, in wage terms, to be more beneficial to women than to men.[54] In the growing sectors of the economy, such as financial services and in much of the low-wage service sector, the labour movement barely registers on the radar.[55] As self-employment and niche-focused firms become more important in an increasingly atomized economy, trade unions are faced with finding strategies that will allow them not only to penetrate these sectors organizationally, but also to bring those workers into a newly reconstructed political and social coalition. As the 1990s draw to a close, then, labour needs to examine seriously both the challenges and opportunities that currently exist for reconstituting these coalitions.

SOLIDARITY AND COALITION BUILDING IN A NEW CENTURY

With the CCF and the NDP, organized labour had focused much of its coalition building directly on the political arena, both federally and provincially.
Yet the legislative accomplishments of that coalition, built as it was in the
1960s and 1970s, proved unable to withstand the economic and social transformations of the 1980s and the 1990s. It is no longer clear that labour's
influence within that coalition is yielding significant results in terms of government policy. It is true that NDP governments do tend to deliver more
progressive labour legislation, especially around issues like anti-scab legislation and certification rules, but labour's economic agenda has not had the
sway over NDP governments. In the 1990s all the NDP provincial governments that were elected either ran on or adopted an economic platform that, to
a greater or lesser extent, mirrored the debt- and deficit-reduction strategies
of other parties and governments. This inability on the part of labour to hold sway
over the economic agenda of supposedly friendly NDP governments, points to a
more general set of problems faced by labour throughout the 1980s and 1990s.

First, the ability of labour to create a successful set of coalitions that allowed it to put forward its reformist social-democratic agenda was, as was
noted above, predicated on its postwar accommodation with capital and the
state. That accommodation, built as it was on the twin pillars of Fordism and
Keynesianism, no longer holds. Economic transformations — the emergence
of regional trading blocs, increased capital mobility, the relative decline of
western economic dominance, and concern over the level of public debt —
and their political manifestations, such as the rise of neo-conservative and
neo-liberal politics, combined to kill it. The political coalition found itself
without a basis from which to counter the arguments for the retrenchment of
state activity; and labour found itself accepting unprecedented levels of concessions and legislative restrictions on its activities.[56]

Second, labour has failed to appreciate fully the degree to which both
Canadian society and the Canadian left (from which it drew its coalition partners, both in electoral and more broadly political and social terms) had changed
over the previous decades. The rise of new social movements, with their basis
in essentially non-material concerns — peace, the environment, sexual and
gender equality, etc. — has left labour often scratching its head. While labour
had long ago abandoned its own radical class analysis for social-democratic
reformist politics, its agenda remained consistently materialist.

Again, this is not to say that the labour leadership ignored the rise of feminist politics, environmentalism or other social movements, but rather that they
were unsuccessful in integrating those elements of the left into the political
agenda of rank and file unionists. Indeed the political and economic agenda
of labour and these elements of the left were often directly at odds, as was
noted above. In addition, other elements of the Canadian left, notably welfare

and poverty activists, went after the arrogance of a labour leadership that paid lip-service to their concerns, but failed to actively seek the organization of those left outside the house of labour.[57]

Third, there are important changes to the internal composition of labour that further weakens both its political and social position. The public and private sector unions have, for decades, had an uncomfortable relationship, but in the past few decades this relationship had become even more strained. Public sector unions have little history in the struggle that built the house of labour (their unionization having come as much at the hands of the state as through political action) and have often been characterized as the "johnny-come-latelies" of the labour movement. For their own part, public sector unions have felt uncomfortable in tying their political and social agenda with that of their industrial, more clearly "working class" brothers and sisters. This tension, which always lurked under the surface, became more apparent through the 1980s and into the 1990s.

In short, the political and social coalition that was built by organized labour has had its economic bases cut out from under it and is divided internally. Yet at the same time, there are some reasons for optimism, qualified though they may be. Understanding both these challenges and opportunities may well shed some light on labour's ability to build a more lasting political and social coalition. After nearly two decades of economic restructuring and the politics of debt-reduction, the labour-dominated coalition that was so severely strained during that period may have some reason for optimism in the post-deficit era.

One of the consistent characteristics of the history of labour in Canada, and indeed of most western countries, is that labour organizing and growth occurs most often in periods of relative economic prosperity and rising expectations.[58] Thus, as both provincial and federal governments become less obsessed with their deficits and public debt declines as the economy expands, then there exists opportunities for labour to similarly grow. As the dust settles from the upheavals of the 1980s and 1990s it becomes increasingly apparent that the "recovery" has left a society more economically divided than before. Yet as governments and industry continually tell us, the economy is expanding, debt is under control, the recession is over, and the future is rosy. But it is a rosy future for a much smaller portion of Canadian society. However one reads the economic indicators, public opinion seems to consistently indicate that Canadians feel less economically secure than ever — wages are at best stagnant, job security is a thing of the past and unemployment is persistently high. The turmoil created by the collapse of the Asian economies in the past number of months reverberated through the international political economy and the possibility that these events could trigger a worldwide economic recession is still with us.

At the same time, there appears to be an increased willingness of union members, and especially white-collar workers, to agitate for a new accommodation within the emerging political economy. Strike levels are increasing and public support is growing. In the last decade, white-collar and professional workers have become increasingly willing to use their right to strike to challenge the government — PSAC, OPSEU, and the Ontario teachers' unions, nurses and hospital workers in Calgary have all garnered significant, but admittedly not decisive, levels of public support in their job actions. The same cannot always be said for private sector workers — witness the Maple Leaf food workers who had their plant closed recently when they walked off the job. This despite the fact that it is the Ontario teachers' union pension fund that is the company's major shareholder.

While the internal divisions within the labour movement remain, they appear to have become less important than they were a few years ago. The Ontario Federation of Labour and the Ontario NDP appear to have a more congenial relationship than was the case when the NDP was actually in power — they once again have a common enemy in Mike Harris' Conservatives and the Ontario NDP no longer has to worry as much about what the Ontario Stock Exchange thinks about its policy positions. The internal challenge for organized labour will depend, to some extent, on how it deals with increased agitation for confronting both government and private capital. If the "new militancy" that Moody detects in a number of labour movements internationally is sustained in the Canadian case, then the left-right split that long simmered beneath the surface in both organized labour and the NDP could emerge on the surface. At the same time, the CLC and the provincial federations appear more united now than was the case a few years ago.

Another dilemma which labour will be forced to face is the increased decentralization of the federation. The Canadian left has, as was noted above, had a somewhat ambivalent relationship with the dynamics of federalism. The tendency on the left, at least traditionally, has been to put more faith in "national" solutions to economic and social problems where at all possible. Yet, the provinces are asserting their right to determine policy within their constitutional purview without federal interference while also pushing for an increased voice in those areas where federal action may impinge on their areas of legislative competence (e.g., environmental policy).

As federal transfers to the provinces decreased, provinces were increasingly reluctant to let the federal government determine the rules of the game as to how those remaining transfers are spent. The recent agreement on the "social union" which, on the surface at least, would move the federations toward more collaborative models of intergovernmentalism in a number of areas poses an interesting challenge to labour. If the federation does in fact become more "collaborative" in a number of policy areas, then organized labour may have to come to grips with a political reality whereby "national" solutions do not necessarily translate as "federal government" solutions. In short, organized labour could well be forced to take federalism seriously as a defining feature of the Canadian state, economy, and civil society.

Every bit as important, the labour movement must also take seriously the non-materialist concerns of not only its membership, but also that of the broader constituency it wants to reach. But this requires important moves on the part of labour: in terms of its willingness to reach meaningful coalitions with other social movements; to organize in new and expanding sectors; to accommodate a more diverse working class in terms of its gender and ethnic composition; and to begin a process of union democratization that has stagnated since the 1950s. The labour movement, as the largest, best organized, and most economically powerful element of the Canadian left, can only hope to rebuild the coalition it has lost by expanding the agenda beyond the economic to include the social and non-material concerns that it has to date given only formal acknowledgement.

Moody's analysis of social-movement unionism points to some elements of the Canadian labour movement as being worthy of imitation, especially the social and political activism of the Canadian Auto Workers.[59] Moody's point is a simple one. If the labour movements of the western liberal democracies are going to sustain themselves and even prosper in this "leaner, meaner" world, then they must simultaneously open themselves up to more inclusive and democratic practices as organizations and also begin to take notions like solidarity much more seriously than they have in the past in terms of their relationships outside the labour movement.

To be sure, such calls for union democratization are often made and labour continues to pay lip-service to the notion. But a viable new coalition for labour will necessitate labour first breaking down the bureaucratic structures that separate the rank and file from the leadership. While recognizing that such comments have a certain clichéd tone to them, there is also some indications that the rank and file, again especially within the white-collar and professional unions, are pushing for more open and responsive unions. And some of the older industrial unions, the CAW among them, have begun to address seriously the division between the rank and file membership and the labour hierarchy, but progress has been slow and uncoordinated. The expectations and interests of the membership are far more diverse today than they were in the decades after WWII and the composition of that membership is likewise different.

In short, labour faces a somewhat uncertain future in many respects. The decade and a half of concessions, legislative restrictions, and open hostility have eased somewhat. But it has also left a rather battered and weary labour movement to pick up the pieces. It faces both new and old barriers in its attempt to establish again a political and social coalition to pursue a newly articulated set of both material and non-material interests. As Canada moves toward a redefinition of the federation in a number of areas and as economic indicators remain strong, then labour has an opportunity to capitalize on the rising expectations amongst both organized and unorganized workers. In no sense is this a simple or straightforward task. There are important lessons from the four decades of growth and consolidation that need to be learned and some of these lessons are less than flattering.

NOTES

1. Paul Phillips, "Labour in the New Political Economy," in *Understanding Canada*, ed. Wallace Clement (Montreal and Kingston: McGill-Queen's University Press, 1997), p. 64.

2. See Reg Whitaker, "The Changing Canadian State," in this volume.

3. There is, of course, a story to be told about the integration of Quebec's labour movement into Quebec civil society and the process of creating linkages between elements of Quebec society. Some of that story is recounted in brief terms in this chapter, but, again, the focus here is on those factors that served to limit the inclusion of Quebec labour in the pan-Canadian labour movement and the consequences of this.

4. Diane Garlaneau, "Unionized Workers," *Perspectives on Labour and Income* (Ottawa: Statistics Canada, Spring 1996), p. 43.

5. Leo Panitch and Donald Swartz, *The Assault on Trade Union Freedoms: From Wage Controls to Social Contract* (Toronto: Garamond, 1993), pp. 1-20.

6. Bryan Palmer, *Working Class Experience: Rethinking the History of Canadian Labour, 1800-1991* (Toronto: McClelland & Stewart, 1992), ch. 6.

7. There was no recognition that working people had the right to bargain collectively over the terms and conditions of their employment or of the right to withdraw their labour in order to achieve a contract.

8. Eugene Forsey, *Trade Unions in Canada, 1812-1902* (Toronto: University of Toronto Press, 1982); and Charles Lipton, *The Trade Union Movement in Canada, 1827-1959,* 3d ed. (Toronto: New Canada Publications, 1973), pp. 39-42.

9. See, for example: H. Clare Pentland, *Labour and Capital in Canada, 1650-1860* (Toronto: James Lorimer, 1981); Stanley R. Ryerson, *The Founding of Canada: Beginnings to 1815* (Toronto: Progress, 1960); and *Unequal Union: Confederation and the Roots of Conflict in the Canadas, 1815-1873* (Toronto: Progress, 1968). It is not so much that Canada's experience with industrialization is "unique," but rather that the process of industrialization in any country needs to be understood within the specific historical circumstances in which it is rooted. It is in attempting to understand the specificity of each set of circumstances, then, that the commonalties between them become apparent. For example, the story of the American working class is dominated by the reality of a society deeply divided by the legacy of slavery and the particular property relations inherent in such a mode of production. Thus the particularities of American in-

dustrial development need to be understood within the context of the conflict with this legacy. The contemporary American labour movement is a reflection of these particular historical and social circumstances. See Mike Davis, *Prisoners of the American Dream* (New York: Verso, 1986), ch. 1; and Phillip J. Wood, *Southern Capitalism: The Political Economy of North Carolina, 1880-1980* (Durham: Duke University Press, 1986), pp. 22-58. The Canadian working class was deeply cross-cut by the reinforcing cleavages of language and religion which leaves a similar, albeit different, legacy. Beyond this division, it needs to be understood that in the pre-war era, there was much about Canada's economic, institutional and social make-up that militated against the development of a well-organized, coordinated labour movement.

10. Lipton, *The Trade Union Movement in Canada, 1827-1959*, pp. 328-32.

11. C.B. Macpherson, *Democracy in Alberta: Social Credit and the Party System*, 2d ed. (Toronto: University of Toronto Press, 1962); and Phillip J. Wood, "Marxism and the Maritimes: On the Determinants of Regional Capitalist Development," *Studies in Political Economy* 29 (1989): 123-54.

12. Craig Heron, *The Canadian Labour Movement: A Short History* (Toronto: James Lorimer, 1989), pp. xiii-xviii.

13. These economic conditions were not unique to Canada. Similar conditions existed in the United States and there are important parallels in the development of organized labour between the two countries. (See Davis, *Prisoners of the American Dream.*) However, the US with its larger population and smaller size industrialized at a much quicker rate and its urban working class remained more highly unionized than Canada's until the 1950s.

14. Heron, *The Canadian Labour Movement*, p. xv.

15. There is a significant literature on these events but the classic study remains: W.L. Morton, *The Progressive Party of Canada* (Toronto: University of Toronto, 1950).

16. Gregory S. Kealey, "Labour and Working Class History in Canada: Prospects in the 1980s," *Canadian Labour History: Selected Readings*, ed. David J. Bercuson, (Toronto: Copp Clark, 1987), pp. 232-56.

17. Ibid., p. 236.

18. Gregory S. Kealey, *Workers and Canadian History* (Kingston and Montreal: McGill-Queen's University Press, 1995), part 3; Lipton, *The Trade Union Movement in Canada, 1827-1959*, part 2; and A. Ross McCormack, *Reformers, Rebels and Revolutionaries: The Western Canadian Radical Movement, 1899-1919* (Toronto: University of Toronto, 1977).

19. Heron, *The Canadian Labour Movement*, pp. 66-77; Palmer, *Working Class Experience*, ch. 2; Irving M. Abella, *Nationalism, Communism and Canadian Labour: The CIO, the Communist Party and the Canadian Congress of Labour* (Toronto: University of Toronto Press, 1974); and Stuart Jamieson, *Times of Trouble: Labour Unrest and Industrial Conflict in Canada, 1900-1966*, Study No. 22 (Ottawa: Task Force on Labour Relations, 1968).

20. Palmer, *Working Class Experience,* chs. 5 and 6. While not wanting to over-emphasize the importance of any one individual, a great deal of the credit (or blame) for the success of the state as an "impartial umpire" policy goes to William Lyon Mackenzie King who as both minister of labour and later as prime minister sought the creation of an environment of labour peace. As he made clear in his 1918 book *Industry and Humanity,* extended periods of labour unrest and the mounting violence that accompanied repressive state tactics ultimately threatened the stability of the social order in general. In short, capitalism works better in peaceful conditions and if ensuring peace meant the integration of labour into the mainstream of the economic order (which would recognize their rights while also forcing them to accept some obligations to maintain labour peace) then so be it.

21. Palmer, *Working Class Experience,* p. 259.

22. McCormack, *Reformers, Rebels and Revolutionaries,* pp. 3-17.

23. The marginalization of the revolutionary left within the labour movements of both Canada and the United States was the result of an essentially two-pronged assault. In the first instance, the state played an indispensable role in this process through harassment and intimidation of revolutionary political activists, leading eventually to the banning of the Communist Party of Canada in the 1930s. The reformist or social-democratic elements of the labour movement sought not only to distance themselves from their revolutionary cousins politically, but also to bolster their own political legitimacy by actively pushing them out of positions of influence within the labour movement. See Norman Penner, *The Canadian Left: A Critical Analysis* (Toronto: Prentice-Hall, 1977), pp. 77-123; Palmer, *Working Class Experience,* pp. 290-98.

24. Peter Warrian, *Hard Bargain: Transforming Public Sector Labour-Managementl Relations* (Toronto: McGilligan Books, 1996).

25. See Palmer, *Working Class Experience,* pp. 320-25. The problem with these estimates is that there does not exist a common or consistent definition of what the public sector includes. Traditional industrial sector codes do not differentiate between public and private sector employees doing the same job (e.g., a teacher is a teacher regardless of whether they teach in a private school or a public one). The category of "public administration" employee covers those who work directly for the government but does not cover employees of Crown Corporations, police, firepersons, teachers or a myriad of others who would be considered public employees. Self-identification in public opinion surveys tends, though, to confirm Palmer's figure. See *Decima Quarterly Database,* Centre For the Study of Democracy, Canadian Public Opinion Archive, Queen's University.

26. One must, however, be careful in describing the history of union growth in Canada (or indeed in any nation) in a linear fashion. The story of union growth in Canada is one marked by fits and starts, gains and losses, steps forward and steps back. In the words of Craig Heron: "There was really no "golden age" when workers were more united than ever again; rather each new wave of labour resurgence brought a newly reconstituted working class into motion against quite different

odds." Heron, *The Canadian Labour Movement*, p. xvi. While there is some differences in the use of "Fordism" within the literature, it can generally be seen to be a strategy of capital accumulation based on a high-wage, high-productivity model centred on a mature manufacturing sector. There is, though, a tendency to assume a degree of universality to the Fordist model within western capitalist states. Yet, one of the important distinctions about the American political economy is the coexistence of a large Fordist sector of the economy (the so-called "industrial heartland" or "rust-belt") with an increasingly significant non-Fordist manufacturing sector centred in the south and west.

27. Garlaneau, "Unionized Workers," p. 45.

28. Again, McCormack's analysis provides some important insights into the variety of political coalitions that were built, including those that attempted to cross class boundaries, in the early years of the western labour movement. At the same time, the differences in political approach between elements of the labour left serve often to undercut such coalitions, as outbreaks of internal warfare often overtake the participants.

29. It should also be noted that cross-class alliance building is hardly a phenomenon restricted to reformist social democrats. The early revolutionary parties in Canada, especially the Communist Party of Canada, also made moves in this direction and, internationally, revolutionary leaders in Russia, China, and elsewhere built cross-class coalitions as part of a revolutionary agenda.

30. The literature on the rise of a "post-materialist" culture in western states is quite vast and beyond the scope of this paper. However, a review of the importance of these tensions, in the context of the operations of the New Democratic Party, can be found in Keith Archer and Alan Whitehorn, *Political Activists: The NDP in Convention* (Toronto: Oxford University Press, 1997), pp. 176-94.

31. Thomas A. McIntosh, *Labouring Under the Charter: Trade Unions and the Recovery of the Canadian Labour Regime*, Research and Current Issues Series No. 58 (Kingston: Industrial Relations Centre, Queen's University, 1989), ch. 2.

32. At the same time, the CCF also introduced another important element into the mix that is the Canadian left, the progressive politics of certain Christian denominations. The history of the CCF is, in some sense, the history of the social gospel movement and some of the party's most successful and important leaders were ministers who preached social justice as a means of both spiritual and material salvation. This element still exists within the contemporary New Democratic Party, but its direct influence on the party and on the Canadian left generally is more marginal than it was in the heyday of the CCF.

33. There are numerous histories of the CCF and the NDP, but they tend to suffer one similar shortcoming in that they are mostly written by party activists and insiders. This tends not to be the case with studies of other "third" parties or of the "major" parties. This is not to say that this makes these works suspect, but they do tend to be less critical than is the case with other studies of other parties. Indeed, there are some cases of what can only be termed outright "revisionism" of party history when it comes to dealing with some of the party's internal conflicts. This is certainly the case when dealing with the "Waffle" phenomenon in

the early 1970s. Among the most useful are: Walter D. Young, *Anatomy of a Party: The National CCF, 1932-1961* (Toronto: University of Toronto, 1969); Desmond Morton, *The New Democrats, 1961-1986: The Politics of Change* (Toronto: Copp Clark, 1986); Robert Hackett, "The Waffle," *Canadian Dimension* 15 (1980), nos. 1 and 2.

34. Palmer, *Working Class Experience*, pp. 302-05.

35. It is true that, in convention, the NDP is numerically dominated by individual members from the riding associations (see Archer and Whitehorn, *Political Activists*), but it is also true that organized labour plays a role in the party's "back-rooms" that to some degree belies both their numerical representation in conventions and the voting patterns of trade unionists. For example, the federal NDP caucus recently proposed a strategy on "reaching out" to small and medium-sized business interests in an effort to broaden the party's electoral base. Within a few weeks, party leader Alexa McDonough held meetings with Canadian labour leaders, angered at not having been consulted about this change of direction, to reassure them that their interests were not being abandoned. *The Globe and Mail* (national edition), 5 October 1998.

36. See Richard O. Boyer and Herbert M. Morais, *Labor's Untold Story* (New York: Cameron Associates, 1955); Arthur Preiss, *Labor's Great Leap* (New York: Pathfinder, 1974); Davis, *Prisoners of the American Dream*, pp. 82-101.

37. Much of this story is underplayed in the general histories of the CCF and NDP, but some accounts of it can be found in Cameron Smith, *Unfinished Journey: The Lewis Family* (Toronto: Summerhill, 1989); and Len Scher, *The Un-Canadians: True Stories of the Blacklist Era* (Toronto: Lester, 1992).

38. For a discussion of "confederal" arrangements and their relationship to other forms of federalism, see Ronald L. Watts, *Comparing Federal Systems in the 1990s* (Kingston: Institute of Intergovernmental Relations, Queen's University, 1997).

39. The water-shed event in history of Quebec labour in this regard is clearly the strike in Asbestos, Quebec in 1949 that led, over the next decade, to the secularization of the Quebec labour movement and saw the rise of a much more aggressive, nationalist-oriented movement. See, for example, *The Asbestos Strike*, ed. P.E. Trudeau, translated by James Bloake (Toronto: James Lewis and Samual, [1956], 1974); and Gerard Pelletier, *Years of Impatience, 1950-1960* (Toronto: McClelland & Stewart). More general histories of the Quebec labour movement can be found in Pierre Vennat, *Une revolution non-tranquille: le syndicalisme au Quebec, de 1960 a l'an 2000* (Montreal: Editions du Meridien, 1992); Louis-Marie Tremblay, *Le syndicalisme québécois: ideologies de la CSN et de la FTQ, 1940-1970* (Montreal: Presses de l'Université de Montréal, 1975); and, Black Rose Editorial Collective, ed., *Quebec Labour: The CNTU, Yesterday and Today* (Montreal: Black Rose Books, 1975).

40. Heron, *The Canadian Labour Movement*, p. 154.

41. It is worth noting that the CLC is not the only pan-Canadian labour central, though it is larger than the others combined. The largest competitor was, until recently, the Canadian Federation of Labour (CFL) which represented independ-

ent unions and remained staunchly non-partisan in its politics. The CFL also became the home of the Teamsters when that union was expelled from both the CLC and the American Federation of Labor-Congress of Industrial Organizations (AFL-CIO) amid charges of widespread corruption and links to organized crime in the US. The non-partisan stance of the CFL essentially rendered it a non-actor in the politics of the Canadian left, though it did lobby governments on issues directly related to industrial relations until its dissolution in 1997. This was triggered, in part, by the return of the Teamsters to the CLC and AFL-CIO after the electoral triumph of a reform movement within the union.

42.   It is not clear how to interpret the NDP breakthrough in the Atlantic region. It remains to be seen whether this is more than the popularity of McDonough and the unpopularity of the government. It would be grossly premature to say that the region has suddenly gone "red," but it is certainly clear that the party has managed to tap into a real frustration within the region over its position within the federation.

43.   Keith Archer, "The Failure of the New Democratic Party: Unions, Unionists and Politics in Canada," *Canadian Journal of Political Science* 18, 2 (1985): 353-66; and Penner, *From Protest to Power*, pp. 90-95.

44.   Penner, *From Protest to Power*, pp. 97-98.

45.   The left-nationalist political economy of this time (best described as the unhappy marriage of Harold Innis and Karl Marx) was an amalgam of Innisian staples theory, dependency theory, and Marxist analytic categories. Some of its policy roots can be found in the nationalism of 1960s Liberal Finance Minister Walter Gordon who first made US domination of the Canadian economy a political issue. The academic literature is best exemplified by Kari Levitt, *Silent Surrender: The Multinational Corporation in Canada* (Toronto: Macmillan, [1970] 1972); Gary Teeple (ed.), *Capitalism and the National Question in Canada* (Toronto: University of Toronto Press, 1972); and Robert M. Laxer (ed.), *(Canada) Ltd.: The Political Economy of Dependency* (Toronto: McClelland & Stewart, 1973).

46.   Hackett, "The Waffle," pp. 37-64. This remains the only book-length study of the Waffle movement (although it is a double issue of *Canadian Dimension*) and one of the few that does not lapse into either utter denunciation or misty-eyed nostalgia. See also John Ball, "The Ontario Waffle and the Struggle for an Independent Socialist Canada: Conflict within the NDP," *Canadian Historical Review* 14, 2 (1983): 188-215.

47.   Archer and Whitehorn, *Political Activists,* pp. 192-93.

48.   Rianne Mahon, "Canadian Labour in the Battles of the Eighties," *Studies in Political Economy* 11 (1983):149-75.

49.   Perhaps the most scathing criticism in this regard concerns the role of the BC Federation of Labour in the anti-government protests in the mid-1980s in that province. See Bryan Palmer, *Solidarity: The Rise and Fall of an Opposition in British Columbia* (Vancouver: NewStar, 1987). Similar doubts about labour's role in such coalitions are raised in Laurie E. Adkin and Catherine Alpaugh, "Labour, Ecology and the Politics of Convergence," in *Social Movements/Social Change, Socialist Studies No. 4*, ed. F. Cunningham *et al.* (Toronto: Between

the Lines, 1988), pp. 48-73; and, Laurie E. Adkin, *The Politics of Sustainable Development* (Montreal: Black Rose Books, 1998).

50.	Kim Moody, *Workers in a Lean World: Unions in the International Economy* (London: Verso, 1997), pp. 269-310.

51.	Panitch and Swartz, *The Assault on Trade Union Freedoms,* pp. 21-44; and, Thomas McIntosh, *The Political Economy of Industrial Relations: The State and Concession Bargaining in Canada,* Kingston: Department of Political Studies, Queen's University, PhD dissertation, 1996, pp. 139-231.

52.	McIntosh, *The Political Economy of Industrial Relations,* pp. 201-25.

53.	Gene Swimmer and Mark Thompson (eds.), *Public Sector Collective Bargaining in Canada: Beginning of the End or End of the Beginning* (Kingston: Industrial Relations Centre Press, Queen's University, 1995).

54.	In 1990 unionized women earned, on average, $4.61/hr. more than non-unionized women, whereas unionized men earned, on average, only $3.18/hr. more than non-unionized men. Of course, unionized men earned, on average, $2.57/hr. more than unionized women and non-unionized men earned, on average, $3.10/hr. more than non-unionized women. Still, unionization appears to go some of the way toward closing the gender wage gap. Garlaneau, "Unionized Workers," p. 51.

55.	Of course, unionizing in some of these sectors poses its own challenges. The workforce is often predominantly part-time, young, and transitory. Much of the service sector consists of independently owned franchises which require unionizing one shop at a time. While a great deal is made of the union victories in individual WalMarts, Starbucks, and McDonalds, those victories are very fragile and will require a huge commitment of union resources in order to secure and expand upon its position.

56.	McIntosh, *The Political Economy of Industrial Relations,* ch. 6.

57.	Palmer, *Solidarity.*

58.	See Palmer, *Working Class Experience*; and Heron, *The Canadian Labour Movement.*

59.	Moody, *Workers in a Lean World,* pp. 19-21, 239-40.

8

Interprovincial Student Mobility in Canada

Kathleen M. Day and R. Quentin Grafton

À partir de données de Statistiques Canada et de Développement des Ressources humaines du Canada, ce chapitre décrit les tendances provinciales en matière de migration étudiante, de frais de scolarité et du coût des logements pour la période de 1972-1973 à 1996-1997. Un modèle multinomial logit a été utilisé pour déterminer l'importance du coût des études universitaires, de la disponibilité des bourses d'études, du chômage, des tendances migratoires passées, de la distance entre les provinces et du climat sur le taux de migration étudiante entre les provinces. L'impact de la hausse des frais de scolarités, de l'imposition de frais plus élevés aux étudiants de l'extérieur de la province au Québec et en Colombie-Britannique ainsi que des Bourses du millénaire a été simulé en se servant de ce modèle. Les résultats indiquent que les écarts grandissants entre les frais de scolarité d'une province à l'autre — et en particulier l'imposition de frais plus élevés aux étudiants de l'extérieur de la province — auront probablement un impact sur le niveau de migration interprovinciale. En revanche, une augmentation des bourses d'étude, même généralisée à l'ensemble des provinces, n'aurait qu'un impact marginal sur les taux de migration.

Go west, young man, go west!
John L.B. Soule (1815-1891)

INTRODUCTION

From the earliest times, migration in one form or another has been one of the most enduring and important features of Canadian life. Long before the arrival of Europeans, First Nations traveled over large areas in response to the seasons and the movements of the animals upon which their survival depended. The settlement of eastern Canada by migrants from Europe and loyalists after the American War of Independence and the subsequent development of the western provinces occurred because of migration to and within Canada. Even today, migration plays a pivotal role in shaping Canada's economy and society.

An important element of migration is the movement of young Canadians from their home province to study at universities in other parts of the country. These Canadians represent a little more than 8 percent of the total full-time undergraduate student population. In some provinces, such as Prince Edward Island in 1996-97, the number of full-time undergraduate students (FTUS) studying out of province represents about 40 percent of the total number of students studying in the province itself. In Canada as a whole, the total number of FTUS studying out of province was 39,000 in 1996-97, which represents just over 0.1 percent of the total Canadian population. This relatively small number, however, obscures the importance of student migration. First, over the past 25 years about 150,000 Canadians have studied out of their home province. Second, most student migrants spend four years or more outside their home province, at a formative time in their lives. Third, the future leaders of business, the public service, and political life almost exclusively come from among the university educated. Fourth, the ability to live and study outside their home province provides young Canadians with an opportunity to connect with fellow Canadians in other provinces in a way that out-of-province vacations, visits, and business trips do not.

Using the most recent data available from the Centre for Education Statistics at Statistics Canada, the Learning and Literacy Directorate of Human Resources Development Canada, and other sources,[1] we examine the issue of student migration and mobility in Canada and address the following questions:

- What are the trends in Canadian student migration, and what is the break-down of in- and out-migration by province?

- To what extent do tuition fees, accommodation costs, student loans and other factors explain student migration in Canada?

- What will be the impact of increased tuition fees, changes in scholarship programs and the introduction of differential fees for out-of-province students on student mobility in the future?

We will present first a description of the trends and current state of student out- and in-migration.[2] The next section outlines the trends in tuition fees and accommodation costs with a focus on particular provinces, and the following section briefly summarizes the trends in Canada Student Loans and scholarship spending by province. In part five, we present estimates of a multinomial logit model that measures the impact of the many factors that may influence student mobility. Using the econometric model, we look to the future and then provide some predictions of the likely effects on student migration rates of differential fees for out-of-province students, rising tuition fees and increased funding for scholarships.

PATTERNS AND TRENDS IN STUDENT MOBILITY

The student migration data used in our study come from the Centre for Education Statistics at Statistics Canada.[3] Our analysis is restricted to FTUS in Canada, who account for over 80 percent of university students. Foreign and graduate students, and students originating in the Yukon and Northwest Territories, are excluded from consideration. The data are aggregated across institutions to the provincial level so as to examine the direction of and trends in migration.

One problem with these data is that for a few institutions in some years the province of origin of the student was not recorded.[4] These students are thus listed in a category called "not reported" and cannot be included in the analysis of migration patterns. The extent of the problem varies from year to year and province to province; it is most serious in Quebec, Saskatchewan, and British Columbia. In Quebec the two problem years are 1975-76 and 1976-77, when the "not reported" category constituted over 30 percent of Canadian students studying in the province. In British Columbia serious reporting errors were observed between 1992-93 and 1995-96, when over 50 percent of enrolled students did not report their province of origin. In Saskatchewan the problem lasted from 1976-77 to 1993-94, during which years province of origin is unavailable for between 30 and 50 percent of FTUS enrolled in the province. The discussion and analysis that follows is thus restricted to the analysis of patterns and trends in the mobility of FTUS for whom both origin and destination are known. Unfortunately these data are the only data available on university student mobility in Canada.

Despite the many changes in higher education in the past 25 years, the proportion of FTUS who study out of their home provinces has remained between 7 and 9 percent of the total. In other words, as the number of Canadian FTUS more than doubled from just over 200,000 in 1972-73 to 473,000 in 1996-97, the number of migrating FTUS increased by a similar proportion, rising from 17,000 to over 39,000 over the same period. To better understand the trends and nature of student mobility, we can examine the contribution of each province to the total number of students who leave to study out of province (out-migration) as well as the importance of each province as a destination for students (in-migration). A more detailed description of the trends in both out- and in-migration, as a proportion of the total FTUS per province, provides further insights into student mobility in Canada.[5] In our presentation, we provide a focus on Quebec, Ontario, Nova Scotia, and British Columbia,

182   *Kathleen M. Day and R. Quentin Grafton*

four provinces which combined account for most of the out- or in-migration in Canada.

OUT-MIGRATION

We begin by examining where student migrants come from. Table 1 displays the number of full-time undergraduate out-migrants from each province. While Ontario provided the greatest number of out-migrants in 1996-97, its share (about 27 percent) was far less than its 38-percent share of the Canadian population. Similarly, Quebec's 14-percent share of student migrants was less than its 25-percent share of the population. Surprisingly, almost as many migrants originated in the Atlantic provinces (approximately 27 percent of the total) as in Ontario, although the region accounts for only 8 percent of the population. The percentage of total student migrants originating in the Prairie provinces (17 percent) and British Columbia (14 percent) in 1996-97 is similar to their population shares. Thus, relative to their population size, Ontario and Quebec provide far fewer migrants than would be expected while the Atlantic provinces provide a much greater share of Canadian students who study out of province than their population share would suggest.

A closer look at the data also shows that the contribution of provinces and regions to student migration has changed markedly over the past 25 years. In particular, Quebec's contribution has not only declined as a proportion of the Canadian total, from 40 to 14 percent over the period, but it has also fallen in absolute terms such that more Quebec students were studying outside their province in 1972-73 than today. In contrast to the decline in student migration from Quebec, the number of migrants from Ontario increased from 2,300 to almost 11,000 over the past 25 years, and as a proportion of the Canadian total has more than doubled. Large increases in out-migration, as a proportion of total Canadian student migrants, were also experienced by British Columbia (from less than 6 to more than 14 percent) and Newfoundland (from 3 to 8 percent) over the period 1972-73 to 1996-97.

The relative importance of out-migration within each province is shown by the rate of migration out of the province, defined as the ratio of out-migrants to the number of FTUS originating within the province. Out-migration rates are much lower in provinces with larger populations, such as Ontario and Quebec, than in the smaller provinces. Out-migration rates are highest in the Atlantic region; the rate of out-migration was 40 percent in Prince Edward Island, 21 percent in New Brunswick, 22 percent in Newfoundland, and 14 percent in Nova Scotia in 1996-97, as compared to les than 6 percent in Ontario. In terms of trends over the period 1972-73 to 1996-97, the greatest decline in the rate of out-migration, from 21 to 5 percent, was observed in Quebec, while British Columbia has experienced the greatest increase (from 4 to 13 percent).

Table 1: Out-Migration of Full-Time Undergraduate Students, by Province

Academic Year	Nfld.	PEI	NS	NB	Que.	Ont.	Man.	Sask.	Alta.	BC	Canada
1972-73	552	704	981	1,639	6,814	2,297	742	1,192	1,350	938	17,209
1973-74	523	733	1,003	1,754	6,990	2,443	756	1,223	1,463	1,020	17,908
1974-75	522	769	1,198	1,985	7,417	2,194	888	991	1,581	1,285	18,830
1975-76	577	846	1,367	2,252	7,652	3,580	882	1,133	1,835	1,641	21,765
1976-77	608	862	1,510	2,248	7,733	3,641	911	1,054	1,902	1,908	22,377
1977-78	685	900	1,483	2,355	8,149	3,938	953	943	1,867	2,048	23,321
1978-79	704	900	1,446	2,317	7,709	3,763	919	920	1,989	2,264	22,931
1979-80	754	896	1,575	2,347	8,234	4,024	1,025	944	2,333	2,535	24,667
1980-81	728	945	1,618	2,380	7,855	4,226	1,121	1,011	2,638	2,712	25,234
1981-82	810	1,034	1,705	2,454	7,563	4,533	1,161	1,014	2,837	2,958	26,069
1982-83	838	1,094	1,742	2,474	7,272	4,867	1,176	1,065	3,161	2,964	26,653
1983-84	803	1,113	1,797	2,660	7,418	5,471	1,195	1,118	3,479	3,099	28,153
1984-85	854	1,173	1,723	2,624	6,861	5,540	1,204	1,141	3,549	3,062	27,731
1985-86	1,090	1,172	1,893	2,809	6,752	5,890	1,241	1,273	3,760	3,375	29,255
1986-87	1,315	1,176	2,016	2,950	6,406	6,273	1,296	1,422	3,747	3,591	30,192
1987-88	1,603	1,208	2,084	3,089	6,261	6,795	1,325	1,615	3,725	3,809	31,514
1988-89	1,780	1,239	2,024	3,420	6,008	7,869	1,304	1,917	3,751	3,762	33,074
1989-90	1,990	1,267	2,205	3,451	5,909	9,201	1,404	2,039	3,905	3,876	35,247
1990-91	2,078	1,252	2,330	3,580	5,645	9,935	1,417	2,140	3,930	4,112	36,419
1991-92	2,205	1,215	2,525	3,569	5,555	9,253	1,238	1,971	3,370	4,110	35,011
1992-93	2,259	1,209	2,633	3,525	5,582	9,290	1,172	1,892	3,128	4,211	34,901
1993-94	2,310	1,123	2,777	3,478	5,542	9,789	1,180	1,926	3,223	4,629	35,977
1994-95	2,611	1,064	2,884	3,478	5,468	10,198	1,300	1,895	3,489	5,185	37,572
1995-96	2,794	1,134	3,002	3,475	5,411	10,317	1,338	1,901	3,312	5,429	38,113
1996-97	3,071	1,134	3,073	3,461	5,375	10,778	1,461	1,956	3,476	5,555	39,340

Note: Students from the Yukon and Northwest Territories or whose province of origin is unknown are excluded.

IN-MIGRATION

To understand student mobility we need to examine not only the sources but also the destinations of migrants. Table 2 indicates that Ontario is the most popular destination of migrating students; in 1996-97 it welcomed over 10,000 students, representing about 27 percent of the total Canadian migrant FTUS. Quebec is also an important destination for students, receiving 19 percent of migrating students in 1996-97, while in the same year Nova Scotia and New Brunswick received 19 and 11 percent respectively of Canadian FTUS migrants. In total, 31 percent of Canadian student migrants chose to study in the Atlantic provinces, although their population share is just 8 percent. By contrast, British Columbia received only 6 percent of Canadian FTUS migrants in 1996-97 while its population share in Canada is over 13 percent. The Prairie provinces constitute the only region whose share of student migrants is comparable to their population share (17 percent).

The greatest change in student in-migration patterns over the past 25 years has been a ten-fold increase in the proportion of migrants that chose to study in Quebec, from less than 2 percent in 1972-73 to 19 percent in 1996-97. The increasing importance of Quebec as a destination for migrants is reflected in a decline in the relative importance of Ontario and British Columbia. Together they welcomed half of Canada's FTUS migrants in 1972-73, but in 1996-97 they were the destination of just one-third of migrating students.

The fact that Ontario receives more out-of-province students than any other region does not necessarily mean that its university system is the most heavily dependent on out-of-province students. In fact, rates of in-migration, calculated as a proportion of the students originating in a particular province, indicate that the Maritime provinces are the most heavily dependent on out-of-province students. In 1996-97 Nova Scotia's in-migration rate was 33 percent, New Brunswick's was 26 percent, and Prince Edward Island's was 19 percent. By contrast, the in-migration rate for Newfoundland for the same year was less than 2 percent. The largest provinces in terms of population — Ontario, Quebec, and British Columbia — also have some of the lowest in-migration rates at 5, 8, and 6 percent respectively in 1996-97.

Over the past 25 years, rates of in-migration have increased dramatically for both Quebec (from less than 1 to 8 percent) and Prince Edward Island (from 10 to 19 percent). In comparison, in-migration rates have been relatively stable in Ontario, Manitoba, and Alberta, where they have not gone below 4 percent or exceeded 10 percent over the period 1972-73 to 1996-97. Student in-migration rates in Newfoundland, British Columbia, and Saskatchewan have fluctuated over the same period, reaching a peak in Newfoundland in 1983-84 (at 4 percent), in British Columbia in 1990-91 (at 12 percent) and Saskatchewan in 1980-81 (at 13 percent). Like Ontario, Manitoba, and Alberta,

Table 2: In-Migration of Full-Time Undergraduate Students, by Province

Academic Year	Nfld.	PEI	NS	NB	Que.	Ont.	Man.	Sask.	Alta.	BC	Canada
1972-73	163	192	3,009	2,076	279	7,198	1,144	586	1,292	1,270	17,209
1973-74	172	155	2,988	2,216	351	7,289	1,066	743	1,415	1,513	17,908
1974-75	158	161	3,111	2,164	452	8,371	170	784	1,603	1,856	18,830
1975-76	231	201	3,463	2,499	1,330	8,359	1,259	874	1,668	1,881	21,765
1976-77	246	199	3,737	2,687	1,365	8,543	1,244	903	1,720	1,733	22,377
1977-78	206	223	3,886	2,740	1,670	9,056	1,193	775	1,866	1,706	23,321
1978-79	210	190	3,813	2,211	1,754	9,321	1,130	851	1,774	1,677	22,931
1979-80	214	162	3,755	2,673	1,969	9,926	1,150	1,058	1,833	1,927	24,667
1980-81	256	142	3,606	2,672	2,201	9,991	1,123	1,251	1,823	2,169	25,234
1981-82	295	137	3,856	2,655	2,553	9,978	1,122	1,292	1,909	2,272	26,069
1982-83	301	141	3,981	2,748	2,814	9,946	1,154	1,234	1,875	2,459	26,653
1983-84	328	152	4,363	2,731	3,333	10,204	1,383	1,231	1,750	2,678	28,153
1984-85	303	168	4,501	2,718	3,493	9,556	1,231	1,295	1,909	2,557	27,731
1985-86	263	195	4,724	2,698	4,161	10,014	1,192	1,233	2,058	2,717	29,255
1986-87	208	223	4,898	2,705	4,820	10,181	1,139	1,220	2,159	2,639	30,192
1987-88	186	287	5,089	2,604	5,695	10,588	1,117	1,010	2,195	2,743	31,514
1988-89	215	316	5,377	2,737	6,256	10,610	1,375	511	2,319	3,358	33,074
1989-90	292	372	5,795	2,788	7,141	10,848	1,409	773	2,201	3,628	35,247
1990-91	357	411	6,120	2,888	7,367	10,707	1,382	777	2,520	3,890	36,419
1991-92	357	458	6,597	3,062	7,412	10,693	1,491	762	2,539	1,640	35,011
1992-93	332	472	6,612	3,337	7,394	10,555	1,480	743	2,608	1,368	34,901
1993-94	319	522	6,673	3,542	7,714	10,746	1,515	810	2,799	1,337	35,977
1994-95	311	539	6,819	3,927	8,047	10,631	1,685	1,362	2,963	1,288	37,572
1995-96	177	556	7,077	4,191	7,949	10,606	1,543	1,472	3,310	1,232	38,113
1996-97	194	526	7,279	4,297	7,641	10,455	1,473	1,423	3,731	2,321	39,340

Note: Students from the Yukon and Northwest Territories or whose province of origin are unknown are excluded.

Nova Scotia and New Brunswick have enjoyed relatively stable in-migration rates over the 1972-73 to 1996-97 period.

When in-migration and out-migration rates for 1996-97 are combined to compute the rate of net in-migration to each province, the results, shown in Figure 1, are somewhat surprising. The net effect on Ontario of interprovincial movements of students is close to negligible, while Nova Scotia turns out to be the biggest net recipient in percentage terms. Net in-migration to Nova Scotia amounts to almost 19 percent of total FTUS originating in that province. New Brunswick is also a bigger net gainer than Ontario, in percentage terms. British Columbia's status as a net loser is also surprising, given that most of its universities are located in areas that enjoy relatively balmy climates for Canada. Overall, the other western provinces seem to be more successful at attracting students than British Columbia. However, British Columbia is not as big a net loser of FTUS as Newfoundland and Prince Edward Island, whose high negative rates of net out-migration are not surprising given their small populations.

Figure 1: Rates of Net Student In-Migration, 1996-1997

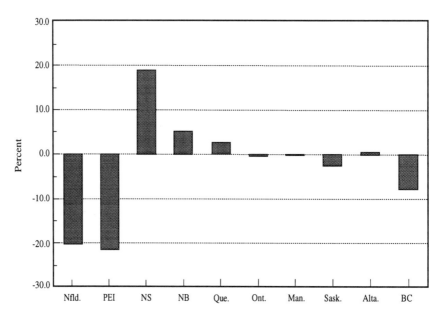

Over the past 25 years Quebec has witnessed a dramatic decline in the number of its students who choose to study outside the province. At the same time, the number of students from outside Quebec who choose to study there has increased significantly. In 1972-73 6,814 Canadian FTUS from Quebec, or 26 percent of the total FTUS in Quebec, chose to study out of province. By 1996-97 the number had fallen to 5,375 and represented just 5 percent of the total FTUS in Quebec. By contrast, in 1972-73 just 279 Canadian out-of-province FTUS chose Quebec as a destination for study, a number that represented just 1 percent of the total FTUS in the province. By 1996-97, however, the number of out-of-province Canadian FTUS studying in Quebec had risen to 7,641, or 8 percent of the Quebec total.

This dramatic increase in the enrolment of out-of-province students in Quebec has occurred almost entirely at Quebec's English-language universities, which have typically attracted the lion's share of out-of-province students over the years. In 1995-96 McGill, Bishop's, and Concordia together accounted for some 70 percent of out-of-province student migrants into Quebec, a proportion only slightly greater than it was 25 years ago. Just one university, McGill, is the destination of a little less than half of all out-of-province students studying in Quebec. Both McGill and Bishop's are heavily dependent on out-of-province students, who constitute almost 31 percent of FTUS at the former and nearly 58 percent of FTUS at the latter. Increased efforts by these two universities to recruit out-of-province students may have contributed to the increase in in-migration to Quebec.[6]

The sources of Canadian out-of-province FTUS in Quebec and the destinations of Quebec students studying out of province in 1996-97 are displayed in Figures 2 and 3. Despite the dramatic changes in the numbers of in- and out-migrants, the relative importance of the different provinces has not changed a great deal since 1972-73. The primary source of Canadian FTUS in-migrants to Quebec is Ontario, which in 1972-73 accounted for about half of all in-migrants. Twenty-five years later, in 1996-97, it provided almost two-thirds of the out-of-province students. New Brunswick supplied 28 percent of Canadian FTUS in Quebec in 1972-73, but most recently has become the source of just 9 percent of student in-migrants. In the case of out-migration, New Brunswick has become less important as a destination, falling from 14 percent to 9 percent of the total Quebec FTUS studying out of province over the period 1972-73 to 1996-97. By contrast, Ontario has become relatively more important, and is now the destination of about 80 percent of Quebec FTUS studying out of province.

Figure 2: Distribution of In-Migrants to Quebec, 1996-1997

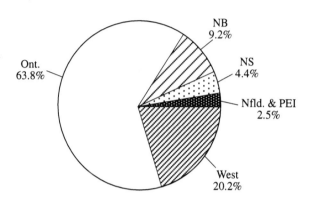

Figure 3: Distribution of Out-Migrants from Quebec, 1996-1997

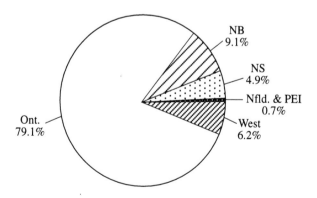

FOCUS ON NOVA SCOTIA

During the period 1972-73 to 1996-97, the number of Nova Scotians studying out of province rose from 981, or 8 percent of the total FTUS in the province, to 3,073 or 14 percent of the total. The number of out-of-province Canadian FTUS studying in Nova Scotia increased from 3,009, or 25 percent of all Canadian FTUS in the province in 1972-73, to 7,279 or 33 percent of students in 1996-97. Thus for the past 25 years, student migrants have consistently been an important component of the total student body in Nova Scotia. Most of these students attended either Dalhousie University, Acadia University, St. Mary's University, or St. Francis-Xavier University, which collectively accounted for about 80 percent of in-migrants. Dalhousie University had both the largest number (at a little less than half the total in-migrants to Nova Scotia) and the highest proportion (at over one-third of total enrolment) of out-of-province students in 1995-96.

In 1972-73, 67 percent of FTUS in-migrants to Nova Scotia came from the Atlantic region, 17 percent from Ontario, 12 percent from Quebec, and the remaining 4 percent from the western provinces. As Figure 4 shows, this decomposition has changed over time. By 1996-97, Ontario's share had almost doubled to 31 percent, while those of the other Atlantic provinces and Quebec fell to 57 and less than 4 percent of the total respectively. Over the same period, the proportion of in-migrants coming from the Prairies and British Columbia more than doubled to 9 percent of the Canadian out-of-province students studying in Nova Scotia.

Figure 4: Distribution of In-Migrants to Nova Scotia, 1996-1997

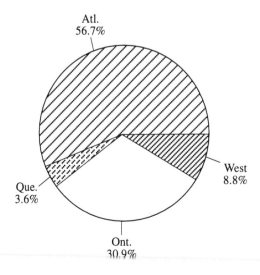

Atl.
56.7%

West
8.8%

Que.
3.6%

Ont.
30.9%

Figure 5: Distribution of Out-Migrants from Nova Scotia, 1996-1997

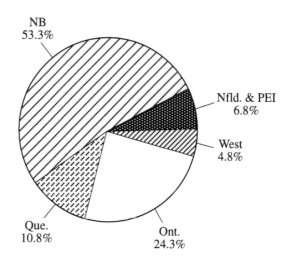

The destinations of Nova Scotia students have also changed since 1972-73. Figure 5 shows how out-going students from Nova Scotia distributed themselves across the country in 1996-97. The proportion of students choosing Quebec as a place of study was less than 1 percent in 1972-73, peaked at 22 percent in 1987-88 and then fell to 11 percent in 1996-97. The most important destinations for Nova Scotia students are New Brunswick and Ontario, which in 1996-97 accounted for 54 and 24 percent of the Nova Scotian FTUS studying out of province. The number of students going to Newfoundland and Prince Edward Island has also fluctuated over the period; in 1996-97 these provinces were the destination of about 7 percent of Nova Scotian student migrants.

FOCUS ON ONTARIO

Ontario is both the largest source and most important destination for migrating Canadian FTUS. In 1996-97, 10,778 FTUS, or about 6 percent of the total number of FTUS in Ontario, chose to study out of province, while in the same year a similar number, 10,606, of Canadian FTUS came to Ontario from other provinces. Over the period 1972-73 to 1996-97 both the number of in-migrants to and out-migrants from Ontario has increased, but the largest percentage increase has been in out-migration. The number of out-migrants increased 4.5 times (from 2,297), while the number of in-migrants has risen slightly less than 50 percent (from 7,198). Overall, in-migration has declined as a proportion of the total FTUS studying in Ontario. The two Ontario universities which rely most heavily on in-migrants are the University of Ottawa and Queen's University, where 21 percent and 15 percent respectively of the total FTUS come from outside Ontario. In 1996-97 these two institutions alone received over 40 percent of the total number of out-of-province students studying in Ontario.

Figure 6 shows the provinces of origin from which the out-of-province students studying in Ontario came. The proportion of in-migrants from Quebec was about 41 percent, a sharp decline from the 72 percent of out-of-province students that came from Quebec in 1972-73. In fact, the actual number of students from Quebec studying in Ontario has also declined in absolute terms, falling from around 5,200 to 4,250 over the period. However, the number of students from other provinces has increased over the past 25 years. In particular, the proportion of in-migrants originating from Alberta and British Columbia in the past 25 years has increased from 11 percent in 1972-73 to 31 percent in 1996-97. The Atlantic region is also sending more students to Ontario; its relative importance has more than doubled, from around 9 percent to 18 percent during the period 1972-73 to 1996-97.

Figure 6: Distribution of In-Migrants to Ontario, 1996-1997

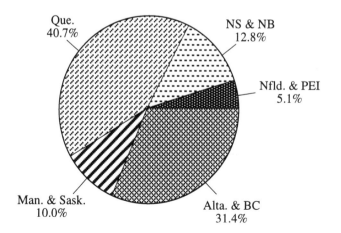

Figure 7: Distribution of Out-Migrants from Ontario, 1996-1997

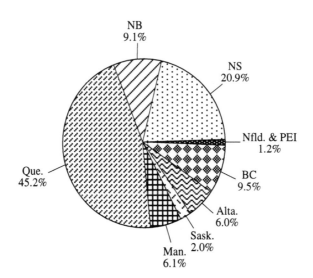

The decline in the importance of Quebec as a source of in-migrants contrasts with its increased importance as a destination for Ontario FTUS studying out of province. In 1972-73, Quebec was the destination choice of just 6 percent of Ontario out-migrants while in 1996-97, as Figure 7 shows, it was the choice of 45 percent of all Ontario students studying out of province. The increasing importance of Quebec corresponds to the decline in importance of British Columbia, which was the province of choice of 30 percent of students leaving Ontario in 1974-75 but of just 10 percent in 1996-97. A large decline in the relative importance of Manitoba was also observed over this period, with the proportion of students going to Manitoba falling from 21 percent of total FTUS from Ontario studying out of province in 1972-73, to 6 percent in 1996-97.

FOCUS ON BRITISH COLUMBIA

In 1996-97, British Columbia was second only to Ontario in terms of the number of out-migrating university undergraduates. A total of 5,555 students, a number equivalent to 15 percent of the total number of FTUS studying within the province, chose to study elsewhere. By contrast, only 2,321 students, or about 6 percent of all those students studying in British Columbia who reported their province of origin, came from outside the province. While both the number and the proportion of out-of-province students in British Columbia have fluctuated over the past 25 years, peaking in 1990-91 at 3,890 or 10 percent of students, the 1996-97 proportion is smaller than that of 1972-73. As in the case of the other provinces, the in-migrating students are not evenly distributed across universities in the province; in 1990-91, the most recent year for which migrant information was available from the University of British Columbia, it accounted for over 70 percent of total in-migration to the province.

Figures 8 and 9 provide some information about the sources of in-migrants to and the destinations of out-migrants from British Columbia in 1996-97. The principal sources of in-migrants from 1972-73 to 1996-97 were Ontario and Alberta, which together in 1996-97 accounted for 79 percent of the out-of-province FTUS going to British Columbia, up from 68 percent in 1972-73. As far as outflows of students are concerned, over the past 25 years the biggest change has been in the proportion of BC students choosing to study in Quebec. In 1972-73, Quebec was the destination choice of just 2 percent of BC students, but by 1996-97 it accounted for 15.6 percent of the total. The increasing importance of Quebec is matched by a decline in that of the Prairies, from 61 percent of the total FTUS in 1972-73 to 39 percent in 1996-97. The most important destination for out-migrants from British Columbia remains Ontario, which increased its share from 31 percent in 1972-73 to 38 percent in 1996-97.

Figure 8: Distribution of In-Migrants to British Columbia, 1996-1997

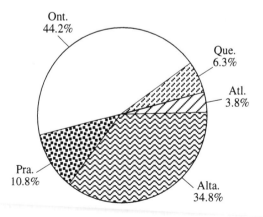

**Figure 9: Distribution of Out-Migrants from British Columbia,
1996-1997**

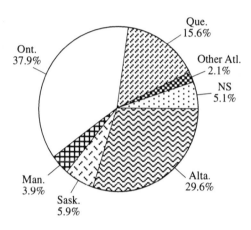

PATTERNS AND TRENDS IN TUITION FEES AND
ACCOMMODATION COSTS

An important factor affecting the choice of where to study is the cost associated with studying in a particular location. If fees and accommodation and
living costs are much more (or less) expensive in other provinces there is a
disincentive (or incentive) to study out of province. We examine the costs
faced by students in terms of their tuition fees, as approximated by the annual
full-time fees for an undergraduate in an Arts program, and yearly residence
accommodation costs charged to students by universities. Although students
in professional programs at some universities in some years (particularly recently) have faced higher fees than students registered in Arts, the majority of
undergraduates face the same fees as Arts students.[7]

TUITION FEES

In all provinces, tuition fees have increased dramatically over the past 25 years,
but significant differences in the level of fees exist among provinces. The

simple average over all provinces of full-time tuition fees in an undergraduate Arts program rose from $455 in 1972-73 to $2,954 in 1997-98. In constant 1986 dollars, Canadian average fees more than doubled from 1983-84 to 1997-98, rising from $1,074 to $2,144. Over this 15-year period, tuition fees in constant dollars rose the most in Quebec (180 percent) and the least in British Columbia (54 percent). In most provinces, however, fees have at least doubled in real terms in the past 15 years, with increases of 154 percent in Alberta, 129 percent in Manitoba, 126 percent in Newfoundland, 104 percent in Saskatchewan, and 100 percent in Ontario. Relative to the other provinces, the real tuition fee increases in Nova Scotia (87 percent), Prince Edward Island (69 percent), and New Brunswick (69 percent) have been quite low.

Table 3 presents average nominal tuition fees in Arts in the ten provinces. Despite its relatively low percentage increase in tuition, Nova Scotia had the dubious distinction of being the most expensive province in which to study in 1997-98, with fees of $3,814. In the same year, similar fees were charged by Ontario ($3,238), Newfoundland ($3,150), Prince Edward Island ($3,150), New Brunswick ($3,182), and Alberta ($3,085). The lowest fees in Canada were charged by Quebec ($2,208), despite the fact that its fees had proportionately increased the most over the past 15 years. In 1997-98 Quebec also introduced higher fees for out-of-province students. Other provinces with relatively low fees in 1997 included British Columbia ($2,308), Manitoba ($2,580), and Saskatchewan ($2,832).

RESIDENCE ACCOMMODATION COSTS

The Canadian average of residence accommodation costs (including room and board), in nominal dollars, rose from $941 in 1973-74 to $10,019 in 1997-98. But as with tuition fees, this overall trend obscures some important differences across provinces. As Table 4 indicates, the most expensive provinces in terms of residence costs in 1997-98 were Prince Edward Island ($14,588), New Brunswick ($13,366), British Columbia ($12,783), and Ontario ($12,665). Residence costs were lowest in Quebec at $4,530, followed by Manitoba ($5,861), Saskatchewan ($6,296), and Nova Scotia ($8,841). With the exception of the latter three provinces, all the provinces, including Alberta ($10,469) and Newfoundland ($10,789), had residence costs more than double those of Quebec.

In constant 1986 dollars, average residential costs in Canada have risen 178 percent since 1973-74 and 85 percent since 1983-84. The greatest increases in real residence costs betwwen 1973-74 and 1997-98 occurred in Prince Edward Island (300 percent), New Brunswick (277 percent), British Columbia (240 percent), and Newfoundland (217 percent). The lowest proportionate increases in residence costs were in Manitoba (68 percent) and

Table 3: Average Nominal Tuition Fees for Arts for Full-Time Undergraduate Canadians, by Province

Year	Nfld.	PEI	NS	NB	Que.	Ont.	Man.	Sask.	Alta.	BC	Canadian Average	SD	CV
					Dollars								
1972-73	250	550	656	603	491	558	425	313	333	366	455	130	0.29
1973-74	250	550	656	589	429	584	312	468	267	357	446	138	0.31
1974-75	250	600	522	589	430	584	312	468	267	357	438	129	0.29
1975-76	250	600	522	589	430	586	425	468	267	357	449	122	0.27
1976-77	250	660	694	687	361	586	425	468	267	357	475	162	0.34
1977-78	250	680	756	710	365	635	450	432	333	393	535	149	0.28
1978-79	600	750	770	727	361	637	513	471	367	449	567	148	0.26
1979-80	630	790	834	810	495	693	570	663	550	487	652	122	0.19
1980-81	630	865	901	822	501	774	634	709	605	587	703	126	0.18
1981-82	690	950	978	962	508	867	670	762	606	675	767	156	0.20
1982-83	850	1,120	1,130	1,112	508	993	670	832	717	855	879	200	0.23
1983-84	892	1,200	1,310	1,208	508	1,035	725	891	779	961	951	234	0.25
1984-85	936	1,270	1,404	1,292	529	1,096	798	986	842	1,243	1,039	258	0.25
1985-86	1,006	1,350	1,461	1,393	530	1,149	846	1,072	851	1,371	1,103	286	0.26
1986-87	1,056	1,480	1,536	1,507	530	1,203	886	1,134	888	1,429	1,165	315	0.27
1987-88	1,056	1,480	1,536	1,507	530	1,203	886	1,134	888	1,429	1,165	315	0.27
1988-89	1,164	1,640	1,694	1,735	516	1,414	1,171	1,340	1,018	1,514	1,321	353	0.27
1989-90	1,280	1,720	1,813	1,828	516	1,536	1,288	1,412	1,074	1,624	1,409	379	0.27
1990-91	1,344	1,840	1,973	1,977	904	1,658	1,375	1,551	1,204	1,706	1,553	330	0.21
1991-92	1,544	2,120	2,153	2,123	1,307	1,790	1,616	1,863	1,390	1,892	1,780	292	0.16
1992-93	1,700	2,280	2,425	2,368	1,461	1,915	1,946	2,314	1,771	1,892	2,007	308	0.15
1993-94	2,000	2,490	2,674	2,504	1,546	2,048	2,043	2,310	2,097	2,008	2,172	311	0.14
1994-95	2,150	2,620	2,949	2,504	1,691	2,252	2,145	2,258	2,350	2,172	2,309	317	0.14
1995-96	2,312	2,820	3,308	2,647	1,693	2,452	2,247	2,595	2,596	2,290	2,496	399	0.16
1996-97	2,670	2,920	3,580	2,978	1,694	2,931	2,473	2,655	2,830	2,290	2,702	470	0.17
1997-98	3,150	3,150	3,814	3,182	2,208	3,238	2,580	2,832	3,085	2,303	2,954	458	0.16

Note: SD is the standard deviation and CV is the coefficient of variation.

Table 4: Average Nominal Residence Accommodation Costs for Full-Time Undergraduate Canadians, by Province

Year	Nfld.	PEI	NS	NB	Que.	Ont.	Man.	Sask.	Alta.	BC	Canadian Average	SD	CV
					Dollars								
1973-74	890	950	837	926	502	1,747	911	555	1,111	981	941	322	0.34
1974-75	994	2,550	1,345	2,144	920	1,844	1,382	1,847	897	1,029	1,495	545	0.36
1975-76	994	1,125	1,383	1,194	1,110	1,898	1,630	2,035	1,061	1,173	1,360	349	0.26
1976-77	1,136	2,211	2,036	1,407	1,089	2,071	1,757	342	1,232	1,426	1,471	539	0.37
1977-78	1,903	2,408	1,897	1,944	1,194	2,169	2,148	284	1,852	1,360	1,716	588	0.34
1978-79	1,934	2,674	2,138	2,213	1,245	2,251	2,416	312	2,097	1,480	1,876	656	0.35
1979-80	1,934	2,107	2,160	1,827	1,365	2,387	2,718	332	2,984	1,609	1,942	708	0.36
1980-81	2,024	2,373	2,324	1,818	794	2,602	3,097	343	3,420	1,795	2,059	898	0.44
1981-82	3,518	2,535	2,469	3,453	872	3,193	3,953	555	3,774	2,801	2,712	1106	0.41
1982-83	4,095	2,542	2,743	4,842	1,040	3,772	4,716	657	4,517	2,859	3,178	1405	0.44
1983-84	4,326	3,861	2,898	5,178	1,133	3,999	5,330	682	4,454	2,951	3,481	1495	0.43
1984-85	4,527	4,192	3,095	7,433	1,167	4,342	4,689	733	6,503	3,021	3,970	1986	0.50
1985-86	4,784	4,459	3,516	8,055	1,199	4,891	4,877	745	5,867	4,057	4,245	2010	0.47
1986-87	5,046	4,682	3,946	8,855	1,250	5,273	5,127	835	6,595	4,301	4,591	2212	0.48
1987-88	5,329	4,966	4,341	9,438	1,274	5,569	5,318	843	7,259	3,779	4,812	2410	0.50
1988-89	5,600	5,323	6,022	9,906	1,399	5,899	5,465	789	5,134	4,100	4,964	2411	0.49
1989-90	5,818	5,556	6,341	10,237	1,466	6,418	5,300	813	5,293	5,187	5,243	2487	0.47
1990-91	6,062	5,823	6,670	10,809	1,623	7,284	5,666	839	5,649	5,400	5,583	2644	0.47
1991-92	3,111	5,605	6,795	11,391	1,959	8,705	6,001	1,514	6,346	6,346	5,777	2859	0.49
1992-93	6,956	12,038	7,616	11,859	1,712	8,641	6,497	891	6,403	6,410	6,902	3438	0.50
1993-94	10,928	14,009	8,539	11,863	2,459	10,434	6,678	5,829	10,256	9,367	9,036	3150	0.35
1994-95	11,320	13,604	8,668	12,192	2,865	11,330	6,943	5,957	10,657	11,577	9,511	3166	0.33
1995-96	11,800	13,798	8,557	12,636	2,952	11,547	6,750	6,136	9,978	12,007	9,616	3268	0.34
1996-97	10,661	14,162	8,619	12,826	4,402	12,145	6,524	6,014	10,200	12,560	9,811	3127	0.32
1997-98	10,789	14,588	8,841	13,366	4,530	12,665	5,861	6,296	10,469	12,783	10,019	3319	0.33

Note: SD is the standard deviation and CV is the coefficient of variation.

Ontario (89 percent). All other provinces, including Quebec (135 percent), Alberta (146 percent), Nova Scotia (176 percent), and Saskatchewan (197 percent), had more than doubled their residence costs.

TUITION AND ACCOMMODATION COSTS

Combining both tuition and residence accommodation costs provides an approximation of the total costs faced by students when deciding to stay in or leave their home province for higher education. The Canadian average of tuition and residence costs, in nominal dollars, was $12,973 in 1997-98. In constant 1986 dollars the combined cost rose 144 percent between 1973-74 and 1997-98; since 1983-84, there has been an increase of 88 percent.

A comparison of the total of tuition fees and residence accommodation costs across provinces reveals that students in Quebec faced the lowest costs at just 52 percent of the Canadian average in 1997-98. Thus, although Quebec has had the highest rate of increase in tuition fees since 1983, the relatively small rise in residence costs still makes it the cheapest province by far in which to study. Other provinces that in 1997-98 had combined tuition and accommodation costs below the Canadian average included Manitoba (65 percent of the average), Saskatchewan (70 percent of the average), and Nova Scotia (98 percent of the average). The most expensive province in which to study was Prince Edward Island, where costs were 37 percent higher than the average. Other provinces where costs were above average were New Brunswick (28 percent higher), Ontario (23 percent higher), British Columbia (16 percent higher), Newfoundland (7 percent higher), and Alberta (4 percent higher). Over the past 25 years, the combined tuition and residence costs of Newfoundland, Prince Edward Island, British Columbia, and New Brunswick have increased relative to the Canadian average. By contrast, the costs in Quebec, Manitoba, Saskatchewan, Nova Scotia, and Ontario have fallen relative to the Canadian average.

PATTERNS AND TRENDS IN STUDENT LOANS AND SCHOLARSHIPS

For many students, loans, scholarships, and bursaries provide a means to help finance higher education. Student loans are provided by both the federal and provincial governments, while scholarships and bursaries are available from institutions and other public sources. The extent to which these types of funding will influence student migration will depend on their terms and conditions; for example, some provincial government funding is not portable and therefore will benefit only students who choose to remain in their home province.

STUDENT LOANS

Student loans are available from the provinces and the federal government. We examine only the trends in the federal Canada Student Loan Program (CSLP) because data on provincial assistance are not available. Since 1994 Canada Student Loans (CSL) have been restricted to 60 percent of the assessed need of students.[8] Should they wish, provinces can provide additional assistance to cover the remaining needs of students. This additional assistance may take a number of forms, including grants and loan remissions as well as loans, and may exceed the remaining 40 percent of the assessed need. With the exception of New Brunswick, all the Atlantic provinces permit full portability of their provincial loans. A number of provinces, including Ontario and New Brunswick, allow portability but impose some restrictions on students studying at private schools. The provinces with the greatest restrictions on provincial loans are Alberta, Saskatchewan, British Columbia, and Quebec.

According to special tabulations provided to us by the Learning and Literacy Directorate of Human Resources Development Canada,[9] which cover all provinces excluding Quebec,[10] in 1996 Canada student loans were negotiated by over 320,000 college and university students, many of whom already had existing student loans. In some provinces, such as British Columbia and Ontario, the real average Canada Student Loan has increased by a third or more in the past 25 years, while in the Atlantic provinces there has been a decline in the loan per student. This decline in average loans in the Atlantic region has occurred despite increases in loan limits under the CSLP since 1994.

Finnie and Garneau, using data from the National Graduates Survey, provide some loan statistics for university undergraduates only.[11] They found that the overall incidence of borrowing by students in bachelor's programs in 1990 was a little less than 50 percent of all students in Canada (including Quebec). Upon graduation, the average loan per student was over $8,000.

For 1988-89 only, data are available on the province of origin and province of study of university students who were Canada Student Loan (CSL) borrowers. Interestingly, for that year all provinces except Nova Scotia had more CSL out-migrants than in-migrants. In 1988-89 the rates of out-migration of CSL borrowers in Prince Edward Island, New Brunswick, and Alberta were 46, 25, and 19 percent while the rates of out-migration as a proportion of all students enrolled were 40, 21, and 8 percent. This fact suggests that the CSLP may have helped students move to other provinces to study.[12]

SCHOLARSHIPS

Scholarships to attend institutions of higher learning have traditionally been one of the most important methods universities have used to recruit the best and the brightest into their programs. For the best students, scholarships offer an important means to study out of province. For others, bursaries, which are based on need rather than academic merit, may provide that opportunity. Given the large increase in tuition fees and accommodation expenses in recent years at most universities, scholarships and bursaries are likely to become an increasingly important factor in determining student migration.

Data on total scholarships, bursaries, and prizes awarded by institutions are available from the Financial Statistics of Universities and Colleges database of the Centre for Education Statistics at Statistics Canada. We aggregated these data across institutions to obtain total scholarships, bursaries and prizes for each province. Unfortunately, these data include both graduate and undergraduate awards, but still provide some idea of the relative generosity of institutions within different provinces.[13] In 1995 the four largest provinces in terms of total scholarship spending (in current dollars) were Ontario ($88 million), British Columbia ($36 million), Quebec ($34 million), and Alberta ($22 million). Together they accounted for over 80 percent of the Canadian total of almost $220 million. By contrast, the recently announced Canada Millennium Scholarships (CMS) will provide total funding of about $300 million/year, or on average $3,000/year, to 100,000 part-time and full-time university and college students.[14] Thus, the CMS represents more than a doubling of the current funds available for students interested in pursing higher education.

Despite the fact that Ontario universities spend by far the most on scholarships, bursaries, and prizes, Ontario ranks only fifth in terms of the real amount spent per student. In 1995 the most generous province in terms of real spending on scholarships was British Columbia. Its average expenditure of $550 per student was more than five times greater than that spent by the least generous province, Manitoba. Of all the large provinces, Quebec spent the least at $194, which was two-thirds of that spent by Ontario per student enrolled and less than 60 percent of that spent in Nova Scotia. The trend in scholarship spending also varies a great deal by province. In constant 1986 dollars scholarships, bursaries, and prizes awarded in Newfoundland in 1972 were just $20 per student enrolled, but by 1995 had increased 25-fold to almost $500. Awards per student enrolled have increased in most other provinces as well, with the exception of Nova Scotia and New Brunswick. In 1995 these two provinces spent less per student in real terms than they did in 1972.

A MODEL OF INTERPROVINCIAL STUDENT MIGRATION

In order to verify whether changes in costs and financial support have influenced student mobility, we need to estimate a model of student migration. Interprovincial migration has been studied in detail by Canadian economists, although student migration has not. Typically, models view migration as an investment in human capital or, more generally, the outcome of an individual's attempt to maximize lifetime utility. In most migration studies, students have been excluded from the analysis because their motives for migrating are believed to differ from those of the working population, despite the fact that student migration may also be viewed as an investment in human capital or the outcome of utility maximization. Variables such as wage rates which are important determinants of the migration decisions of the working population are likely to be less important to student migrants. Similarly, variables relating to the cost of a university education are unlikely to influence general migration patterns in the population as a whole.

PREVIOUS STUDIES

Among the most recent studies on the topic of student migration are Mixon and Hsing and Hsing and Mixon, but their analysis is restricted to the United States.[15] With the exception of this chapter, no models exist for explaining student migration in Canada.

Mixon and Hsing formulate a two-equation model of college student migration based on the human capital theory of migration, which hypothesizes that migrants will choose the destination in which the difference between the costs and benefits of migration over the life-cycle are maximized. The dependent variable in their first equation is out-of-state enrolment at the institution as a percentage of total enrolment and their model is, thus, a model of out-of-state enrolment rather than a model of migration per se. Out-of-state enrolment is assumed to depend on tuition fees, total enrolment at the institution, and a number of variables related to institutional quality, such as an index of entrance difficulty, the percentage of full-time professors with a PhD, and the number of students per full-time faculty member.[16] Their second equation assumes that tuition fees depend on total enrolment, the percentage of students who are from outside the state, and various measures of institutional quality; it is estimated simultaneously with the first equation using two-stage least squares.

Mixon and Hsing's 1994 results suggest that out-of-state enrolment will be higher, the higher are tuition fees at the institution. This contrary result is blamed on a lack of independence between the explanatory variables: most of the other explanatory variables in the out-of-state-enrolment equation also appear as explanatory variables in the tuition fees equation, with significant coefficients. After re-estimating their model with tuition fees deleted from the out-of-state enrolment equation, they find that nearly all the remaining variables in the equation have significant coefficients with the expected signs. The strongest conclusion to be drawn from their study is that student migration in the United States depends heavily on institutional quality, as measured by the variables included by Mixon and Hsing. Nevertheless, it is surprising that tuition fees appear to have no effect on migration decisions. Their results imply that differences in tuition fees across institutions are not large enough to have an important effect on student migration decisions.

In Hsing and Mixon, the two authors estimate an equation in which the rate of net in-migration to a state is the dependent variable.[17] Their cross-section data set includes the 50 US states in 1992. Among the explanatory variables they include tuition fees, per capita personal income in the state, the number of educational institutions in the state covered by the migration data, the lagged net migration rate of students, average expenditures per student in the state, and various state characteristics, such as the rate of growth of employment, the per capita tax burden, and the crime rate. This model resembles more closely standard models of migration applied to the labor force. The lagged migration rate is included to account for the possibility that the decisions of student migrants may be influenced by the experiences of relatives and friends who had migrated in the past, while variables such as the rate of employment growth and the tax burden are included to represent differences across states in the future payoff to education. Finally, the crime rate reflects the quality of life in a state, which may influence the mobility decisions of students. The equation is estimated using Weighted Least Squares to account for heteroscedasticity in the dependent variable.

In this study, Hsing and Mixon find that although the coefficient of tuition fees has a negative sign, it is not statistically significant, implying that tuition fees have no impact on the net migration of college students in the United States. Expenditures per student, however, do have a positive effect, as do the rate of employment growth and the lagged net migration rate, while a higher per capita tax burden and a higher crime rate will tend to deter student migrants. These results are consistent with those obtained in studies of labour market mobility; however, the finding that the coefficient of per capita income is negative and significant is not. The authors argue that in the case of student migrants, the sign of the latter variable is impossible to predict, since higher incomes may lead to more out-migration because they permit more families to finance the migration of their college-age children, or encourage more in-migration because they are an indicator of better future earnings opportunities.

A MULTINOMIAL LOGIT MODEL OF STUDENT MIGRATION

An econometric model that has been widely used in Canadian studies of migration is the conditional logit model (also referred to as the multinomial logit model) developed by McFadden.[18] It is particularly useful in the empirical analysis of problems involving a choice from among a fixed number of alternatives, and is consistent with an underlying theoretical model in which student migration decisions are based on the maximization of lifetime utility.

The multinomial logit model supposes that students have already made the decision to attend university and, conditional on this decision, it predicts the rate of migration from province *i* to province *j*. To apply the model, the important characteristics of a province that influence student migration decisions must be identified. A lifetime utility maximization model of student migration implies that these characteristics would include variables related to future incomes, the cost of an education, and personal welfare. We suppose that each student faces ten possible alternative destinations: their home province and the other nine provinces. First, we expect that the previous year's flow of student migrants from province *i* to province *j* will have a positive effect on this year's flow, not only because friends and relatives may have sent back favourable reports, but also because degree programs typically last three to four years. Further, after a student has spent at least a year in a particular institution, the costs of leaving to go elsewhere increase because students may not be able to transfer all the credits they have earned at their first institution. Second, we expect that provincial differences in the costs of a university education will influence the choice of province of study. Initially, we divide costs into two components: annual tuition fees and residence accommodation costs. Both are measured in 1992 dollars.[19] We also estimate some equations in which tuition fees and residence accommodation costs are summed to obtain a "total cost" of education. The higher is the cost of a university education in province *j*, the lower one would expect the rate of migration to that province to be. Third, the provincial average of scholarships, bursaries, and prizes awarded to students by institutions in province *j* is expected to be positively related to student migration, since scholarships constitute a form of student aid. Fourth, we expect the availability of student loans to be positively related to migration to province *j*. From a migration point of view, however, what is likely to be most important is whether loans are portable from one province to another, and whether the eligibility criteria for provincial loans include a residency requirement. These factors are more likely to influence student migration decisions than the average level of student loans in the province. Unfortunately, such data were not available for our study, so student loans are excluded from our estimating equations.

The remaining variables in the model are characteristics of the destination province *j* which might influence the student migration decision. The first characteristic is the provincial unemployment rate, which is an indicator of the ease of obtaining employment and the ability of students to supplement their income while studying. If students also wish to remain in their chosen province of study after graduation, this variable may also serve as an indicator of future employment prospects. Second, we include the distance between origin and destination, which is calculated as the road distance between major cities in each province. Distance serves as a proxy variable for both the psychic and monetary costs of moving, and has been found to be a highly significant determinant of migration flows in other studies. Because such costs are expected to increase with migration, we would expect distance to have a negative coefficient in the model. Finally, degree days above 0°C are included as a measure of the severity of the climate. The higher the number of degree days above 0°C, the milder the climate. Holding all else equal, many Canadians — and no doubt students — would prefer a milder climate to a colder one, and thus we expect the coefficient of this variable to be positive.

It is worth noting that the explanatory variables differ in the dimensions in which they vary. During the sample period used for estimation, only the lagged migration flow varies over origin, destination, and year. Tuition fees, accommodation costs, total cost, the unemployment rate, and average scholarships vary with destination and year.[20] Finally, distance varies with both origin and destination but is constant over time, while the climate variable used is an average over a period of 30 years and therefore varies only with destination. A long-term average was believed to be the best choice for the climate variable because most students expect to continue their studies in their chosen province for a minimum of three years.

RESULTS

The estimation results of the multinomial logit model, obtained using annual data for the academic years 1973-74 to 1995-96, are presented in Table 5. With 23 years of data for each of the ten provinces of origin and ten possible destinations, we have a total of 2,300 observations in the sample. The first three columns in Table 5 contain the coefficient estimates for three different equations estimated for all students, while the last two columns contain the estimates for separate equations for female and male students.

The coefficients in all the equations are statistically significant at the 1-percent level of significance; however, some of the results are unexpected in that the financial variables do not always have the expected sign. In column one, the first specification of the model, tuition fees have the expected negative coefficient but residence accommodation costs have a positive coefficient, suggesting that students are drawn to provinces where residence accommodation costs are higher. In column two we present the results with the accommodation costs variable dropped from the model. Dropping accommodation costs has no effect on the sign and little effect on the magnitude of the

Table 5: Conditional Logit Model of Student Migration: Coefficient Estimates for 1973-74 to 1995-96

Variable	All Students			Females	Males
	(1)	(2)	(3)	(4)	(5)
Lagged migration	0.0254 (0.0000273)	0.0254 (0.0000272)	0.0260 (0.0000276)	3.34 (0.00740)	3.15 (0.00649)
Tuition fees	-0.312 (0.00250)	-0.289 (0.00225)			
Accommodation costs	0.00624 (0.000289)				
Total cost			-0.0114 (0.000247)	-0.00270 (0.000730)	0.00346 (0.000725)
Unemployment rate	-21.0 (0.371)	-20.4 (0.371)	-7.68 (0.353)	-53.4 (0.791)	-55.5 (0.735)
Distance	-1.55 (0.00117)	-1.55 (0.00117)	-1.55 (0.00118)	-0.173 (0.00133)	-0.159 (0.00129)
Degree days above 0° C	0.250 (0.00208)	0.242 (0.00204)	0.255 (0.00210)	0.310 (0.00481)	0.252 (0.00471)
Average scholarships	0.393 (0.00768)	0.389 (0.00768)	0.0390 (0.00714)	-0.832 (0.0203)	-0.334 (0.0186)
Log of likelihood function	-4,115,285	-4,115,519	-4,122,544	-544,492	-597,067
R^2	0.7845	0.7844	0.7841	0.2436	0.2335
No. of observations	2,300	2,300	2,300	2,300	2,300

Notes: 1. Numbers in parentheses are asymptotic standard errors.
2. Coefficient estimates and standard errors are multiplied by 1,000.
3. All coefficients are statistically significant at the 1-percent level of significance.
4. R^2 is defined as $1-(\log L_R / \log L_U)$, where $\log L_R$ is the value of the log-likelihood function when all coefficients are assumed to be zero, and $\log L_U$ is the value of the log-likelihood function for the estimated model.

remaining coefficients. When the two cost-of-education variables are summed to obtain a total education cost, as shown in column three, the coefficient of the total cost variable has the expected negative sign. With the exception of the unemployment variable, this last specification yields coefficient estimates for the non-financial variables that are very similar to those for the other two specifications.

The coefficients of the non-financial variables in the model in all three specifications are as expected. The results suggest that the flow of student migrants from province i to province j will be higher, the higher the number of students who migrated from i to j the previous year, the milder the climate in j, the higher the average level of scholarships in j, the lower the unemployment rate in j, and the smaller is the distance between i and j.

The model was also estimated by gender over the whole period, and for francophones and anglophones in New Brunswick, Quebec, and Ontario for the period 1981-82 to 1995-96. The results by gender are reported in columns four and five of Table 5. Surprisingly, total cost has the expected negative coefficient only in the equation for females. In other equations not reported here, the coefficient of tuition fees had a positive sign for both males and females, while accommodation costs had the expected negative sign. In all the equations estimated for males and females, average scholarships had an unexpected (and significant) negative coefficient. We cannot explain these discrepancies between the results for males and females and those for all students.[21]

Overall, the results obtained were not fully consistent with our expectations, at least in terms of the financial variables relating to a university education. Nevertheless, the model suggests that several factors are important in explaining the rates of migration of university students. Notwithstanding these results, the decision to study out of province is, at least in part, influenced by the choice of university where students would like to study. For instance, the decision of a student from Ontario to study in Quebec at, say, McGill University is a function of factors such as tuition fees and distance from home, but is also influenced by the quality and reputation of the university. In other words, the decision of students to migrate may depend more on the choice of university to study at rather than the province where it is located. For the United States, Mixon and Hsing found that variables relating to institutional quality and other institutional characteristics are likely to play an important role in out-of-state enrolment.[22] Thus a more appropriate model of student migration might be one of institutional choice, rather than one of interprovincial migration. Unfortunately, such a model would not yield information about interprovincial flows of students unless data on the province of origin of students were available on an institutional rather than a provincial basis. Due to confidentiality restrictions, much of this institutional data is not available to researchers.[23]

LOOKING TO THE FUTURE

Canada is facing a number of challenges in its postsecondary education system which may have profound consequences for interprovincial student migration. The greatest challenge is to provide the financial resources for quality education while addressing the problems of provincial and federal deficits. Most provinces have tried to balance these conflicting objectives by raising fees substantially in recent years. In an attempt to prevent out-of-province students from taking advantage of much lower fees in Quebec relative to Ontario and the Atlantic provinces, Quebec is now charging higher fees to out-of-province students. Recently, the British Columbia government also announced that it is considering imposing an extra $1,500 fee on all out-of-province students, because the fees it charges are much lower than those of some other provinces, and thus it fears excessive in-migration.[24]

Underlying the question of fees is concern for the accessibility of a university education. To make university accessible to more young Canadians, the federal government announced a Canada Millennium Scholarship (CMS) in the 1998 budget. The CMS is designed to support more than 100,000 full- and part-time students each year through an endowment of $2.5 billion. For full-time students, scholarships are expected to average $3,000/year, and students are eligible to receive up to $15,000 over a four-year degree program.[25]

We examine the possible effects of rising and differential fees and the CMS on interprovincial student migration rates using simulations from the multinomial logit model. In each case, the simulation involves changing the values of one or more explanatory variables, and involves a comparison of the in- and out-migration flows relative to a base-case scenario. Variables that are not directly involved in the simulation are held constant at their 1995-96 levels.[26] The base-case scenario was constructed using the estimates in column two of Table 5 to generate the predicted migration flows for each origin and destination for the last year of the sample period, 1995-96.

When evaluating the simulation results it should be noted that the model does a better job of predicting gross migration flows for some provinces than for others, and even for a given province of origin predicts some flows better than others.[27] For example, the model grossly over-predicts inflows to Prince Edward Island from the other Atlantic provinces, Quebec, and Ontario. Similarly, the model tends to over-predict inflows to the four western provinces from each other, and thus total inflows to these provinces. While the predicted flows tend to be more accurate for Quebec and Ontario, the two largest provinces, the over-predictions of inflows to Prince Edward Island and the western provinces are offset by under-predictions of total inflows to these provinces. Further, the simulations should be viewed as short-run projections as they only predict migration rates and not the number of students deciding to attend university. In fact, changes in tuition fees and other variables are likely to affect the total number of students choosing to attend university as well as the distribution of students across provinces, but a more complex model would be required to incorporate this effect as well. Consequently, the simulations should be interpreted with caution, and thus the numbers generated cannot be regarded as definitive. Nevertheless, these errors in the predictions appear to be relatively constant across simulations, leading to percentage changes, relative to the base case, that do not seem unreasonable for each of the simulations performed.

RISING FEES

Between 1995-96 and 1997-98 the Canadian average of tuition fees in a full-time undergraduate program in Arts rose by 15 percent in real terms. In our first simulation, we assess the impact of the fee increases over these two years. In this simulation, nominal tuition fees are raised to the 1997-98 levels and converted to constant dollars using an appropriate price index.[28] The resulting percentage changes in inflows and outflows of students are presented in the first panel of Table 6. As one would expect, increased in-migration into some provinces as a result of these tuition fee increases tends to be accompanied by decreased out-migration from these same provinces. The largest percentage increases in inflows are observed in British Columbia, Prince Edward Island, Nova Scotia, and Manitoba — the provinces in which the change in tuition fees between 1995-96 and 1997-98 was lowest. These provinces also experience decreases in out-migration of students, and consequently are net gainers of students. The provinces which experience the largest decreases in in-migration are, in order of importance, Newfoundland, Ontario, Alberta, Quebec, and New Brunswick. These provinces end up as net losers of students. Thus the overall effect of the change to 1997-98 tuition fee levels is to redistribute students from provinces with high tuition fee increases to those with low tuition fee increases.

DIFFERENTIAL FEES

The consequences of differential fees in Quebec for out-of-province students and the possibility of a $1,500 fee for out-of-province students in British Columbia are examined in panels two and three of Table 6. These simulations present the effects of differential fees in addition to the effect of the 1997-98 fees on student migration. In the case of Quebec, we simulate the effect by doubling the 1997-98 fees for all students other than those whose province of origin is Quebec.

In the second panel of Table 6, the model predicts that differential fees will have a very large effect on student inflows to Quebec. In particular, the

TaEle 6: Simulation Results

Province	(1) Real tuition fees at 1997-98 levels		(2) Add to (1): Tuition fees doubled for out-of-province students in Quebec		(3) Add to (2): Nominal tuition fees raised by $1,500 for out-of-province students in BC		(4) Add to (3): Nominal average scholarships raised by $300 for migrants only	
	% Change in Inflows	*% Change in Outflows*	*% Change in Inflows*	*% Change in Outflows*	*% Change in Inflows*	*% Change in Outflows*	*% Change in Inflows*	*% Change in Outflows*
Nfld.	-8.8	8.6	-5.7	5.1	-5.7	5.1	-1.0	14.1
PEI	5.4	-2.1	8.9	-4.4	8.9	-4.4	15.7	-0.5
NS	2.3	-0.2	6.1	-3.1	6.1	-3.1	12.6	2.2
NB	-0.3	0.7	1.8	-4.2	1.8	-4.2	8.7	0.7
Que.	-0.4	-1.9	-44.0	-1.9	-44.0	-1.9	-40.1	8.1
Cnt.	-6.7	7.1	-5.6	-27.4	-5.5	-27.5	2.5	-19.3
Man.	0.3	-0.1	0.5	-1.6	2.0	-3.0	9.8	4.3
Sask.	3.4	-2.1	3.7	-2.5	5.2	-5.0	13.7	1.7
Alta.	-5.8	5.7	-5.6	5.5	-4.8	-3.5	2.5	4.7
BC	8.7	-7.5	8.8	-7.7	-25.2	-7.7	-19.1	1.4

Base case: All variables at 1995-96 levels. The total number of students originating in each province is assumed to be constant at the 1995-96 level. New values for tuition fees and average scholarships were deflated using 1997 regional city CPIs.

simulations predict that inflows will decrease by over 44 percent. It further suggests that most of these students who are deterred from studying in Quebec by higher tuition fees would have originated in Ontario, since the predicted decline in out-migration from Ontario is also high, at about 28 percent. By comparing the percentage changes in panels one and two of Table 6 we can identify the other gainers and losers, in terms of student migration, as a result of Quebec's decision to introduce differential fees. The simulation suggests that all other provinces experience greater inflows and smaller outflows as a result of the Quebec policy change. After Ontario, the four Atlantic provinces appear to benefit the most in terms of increased numbers of students.

For all provinces, the changes in migration rates are much greater than those associated with the increase in fees from 1995-96 to 1997-98. The provincial results, however, obscure the effect of differential fees on certain institutions in Quebec. For example, the policy is likely to have a pronounced negative effect on enrolment at McGill University and Bishop's University, where in 1995-96 some 31 and 58 percent of the student body were from outside the province.

We can examine the effect of differential fees in British Columbia in panel three of Table 6. The simulation supposes that fees are at their 1997-98 level and that Quebec already has in place differential fees for out-of-province students. For this simulation, the $1,500 increase is added to the nominal value of the 1997-98 tuition fees for British Columbia for out-of-province students, and then converted to constant dollars using the 1997 value of the CPI for Vancouver. The major effect of this selective tuition fee increase is to reduce inflows of students to British Columbia: inflows decrease by 24 percent relative to the previous scenario, and are 18 percent less than the base-case scenario. Virtually all of the students lost by British Columbia would have come from the west, and in particular Alberta. The percentage decreases in outflows from the six eastern provinces are virtually the same as predicted in panel two, and thus the differential fees in British Columbia have only a small impact on student migration from the east.

INCREASED SCHOLARSHIPS

Many of the details of the CMS have yet to be announced and thus it is difficult to predict how the scholarships will affect the average scholarships variable used in the student migration model. For example, it is not clear whether the program will have a differential impact on the funding available to students in different provinces, or whether all provinces will be affected in an identical fashion. Given these uncertainties, we carried out two simulations of the likely impact of the CMS. The first involved increasing the nominal value of average scholarships by $300 for all students in each province; the second consisted of restricting the $300 increase in scholarships to migrating students.[29] These changes are in addition to specifying tuition fees at their 1997-98 level and differential fees for out-of-province students in both Quebec and British Columbia.

Increasing the nominal value of average scholarships by $300 for all students in each province yielded results that were very similar to those in panel three of Table 6, and thus they were not included. In other words, the model predicts that an "across-the-board" increase in average scholarships will only have a small effect on student migration flows. Provinces that benefit in terms of slightly higher inflows and slightly lower outflows of students are Prince Edward Island, New Brunswick, Quebec, and British Columbia. However, the differences are negligible, which suggests that for the Canada Millennium Scholarships to have a major impact on the migration rates of full-time undergraduate students across the country, the funds must be targeted toward encouraging study in particular provinces. Panel four of Table 6 presents the results of the second simulation, which restricts the increase in scholarships to migrating students only. While it is unlikely that the provisions of the CMS would be this restrictive, this scenario does allow for the CMS to have a differential impact across provinces.

This alternative scenario yields considerably different results from an "across-the-board" increase in average scholarships to all students. Relative to the previous scenario in panel three, all the provinces experience increases in inflows of students, with the largest improvements occurring in the Atlantic and Prairie provinces. However, out-migration also increases relative to the previous scenario in all provinces. In short, the number of migrating students rises as a result of restricting the scholarship increase to students who are willing to move. In fact, the volume of migration is higher under this scenario than under any of the others, including the base case.

CONCLUDING REMARKS

Despite the importance of migration and tertiary education in Canada, very little work exists which both describes and explains interprovincial student migration. Using data from Statistics Canada and Human Resources and Development Canada we have tried to take a step toward filling this gap. We found that although the overall rate of student migration in Canada has fluctuated very little, the pattern of migration between provinces has changed a great deal. For example, since 1972-73 Quebec has been transformed from a province that provided almost 40 percent of all out-migrants to one that provided less than 14 percent of the total in 1996-97. Similarly, in 1972-73 Quebec was the destination of less than 2 percent of all migrating students, but in 1996-97 was the destination of about 20 percent of migrating full-time undergraduate students in Canada.

The observed changes in migration patterns can, in part, be explained by shifts in the relative costs of education, as measured by tuition fees and accommodation costs. Simulations of the model of student migration estimated here suggest that recent changes in provincial government policies regarding tuition fees are likely to bring about further changes in these patterns. As gaps widen between the fees imposed in different provinces, more and more students may move to take advantage of them. Indeed, the results of our first simulation suggest that in the absence of differential fees for out-of-province students, the 1997-98 fee structure would actually have induced greater migration of students between provinces. But if more provinces follow Quebec's lead by introducing differential fees for out-of-province students, students will likely become less mobile rather than more so, unless other sources of funding become accessible to them. This is where the Canada Millennium Scholarships and Canada Student Loan Program may be able to play an important role; if their eligibility criteria are structured so as to encourage student mobility, they may be able to offset some of the effects of differential fees for out-of-province students.

We hesitate to speculate at this point on how the provincial governments might react to an explicit attempt by the federal government to encourage student mobility through either the Canada Student Loan Program or the Canada Millennium Scholarship Fund. Even though its criteria have yet to be determined, the CMS program has been greeted with hostility by some provincial governments, who regard it as an unwanted federal intrusion into an area of provincial jurisdiction — education. But in the presence of tuition-fee differentials for out-of-province students, there may be an economic efficiency argument in favour of a scholarship program that fosters student mobility. Economists have long recognized that economic efficiency in the presence of a mobile population requires some form of transfer system when there are spillovers between regions in the consumption of public goods such as postsecondary education. It may simply be more efficient for some students from New Brunswick to study in Nova Scotia or Ontario, because New Brunswick's economy may require workers with a particular type of training that is too costly to provide within the province. However, Ontario and Nova Scotia would be unlikely to provide sufficient educational services to train New Brunswick students as well as their own in the absence of some additional funding from the federal government. Indeed, this is one of the primary justifications for federal transfers in support of postsecondary education, which currently are incorporated in the Canada Health and Social Transfer program. A scholarship program such as the CMS, although it takes the form of direct payments to students rather than to provincial governments, could be justified on similar grounds, particularly if out-of-province tuition-fee differentials exist. This line of argument raises the interesting question of whether intergovernmental transfers or transfers to individuals constitute the most efficient means of ensuring an adequate supply of postsecondary education.

While the issue of efficiency in the provision of postsecondary education is an interesting one, it should not be forgotten that student mobility may build not just human capital but social capital as well. In a country as vast and sparsely populated as Canada, it is sometimes difficult for individuals in one region of the country to understand the problems of those in other regions. Spending several years of one's life in another region is the best possible way to rectify this problem. For this reason, we should be concerned about any development that is likely to reduce student mobility, such as differential fees for out-of-province students. While more empirical work needs to be done on the effect of differential fees, our results suggest that such policies will significantly reduce the level of mobility of full-time undergraduate students in Canada.

NOTES

The authors are grateful for the financial support of the Social Sciences and Humanities Research Council of Canada and the University of Ottawa; and the assistance of the Learning and Literacy Directorate of Human Resources Development Canada. We would also like to thank two anonymous referees and the editors for their helpful comments on an earlier draft.

1. Further details about the data sources are provided in K.M. Day and R.Q. Grafton, "Interprovincial Student Mobility in Canada," Working Paper 9805E (Ottawa: Department of Economics, University of Ottawa, 1998).

2. For another recent discussion of trends in university student mobility in Canada, see G. Butlin and I. Calvert, "Interprovincial University Student Flow Patterns," *Education Quarterly Review* 3, 3 (1996): 30-41.

3. Space limitations prevented us from including many detailed tables in this section. Readers interested in additional numerical information are referred to Day and Grafton, "Interprovincial Student Mobility in Canada."

4. "Province of origin" corresponds to the variable "geographic source of student" in the University Enrolment Database. For students who enter university immediately after high school, it corresponds to the province in which they completed high school. For all other students, it corresponds to the province of permanent home address, as reported on their application for admission.

5. Throughout the chapter we restrict our attention to individuals who have already decided to go to university. For this reason percentages are generally computed in terms of total FTUS within a province, rather than the total number of university-age individuals.

6. This possibility was suggested by an anonymous referee.

7.   Space does not permit us to examine the interesting question of how fees differ across disciplines, and how those differences have changed over time.

8.   R. Finnie, and S. Schwartz, *Student Loans in Canada* (Toronto: C.D. Howe Institute, 1996).

9.   Readers interested in these data may consult Day and Grafton, "Interprovincial Student Mobility in Canada."

10. In lieu of providing direct Canada Student Loans to Quebec students, the federal government provides funding to the province which in turn maintains its own separate assistance program. For this reason, direct CSL data are not available for Quebec.

11. R. Finnie and G. Garneau, "An Analysis of Student Borrowing for Post-Secondary Education," *Canadian Business Economics* 14 (1996): 51-64.

12. See Human Resources Development Canada, "Mobility of University Students" Learning and Literacy Directorate, draft paper prepared 7 August 1997; and "Improved Reporting to Parliament — Pilot Document" (Ottawa: Minister of Supply and Services, 1997), pp. 4:13-4:21.

13. It should be noted that although the majority of university students are undergraduates, graduate student awards are typically much larger than those given to undergraduates. Thus, our average scholarship figures will likely overestimate the average award paid to undergraduates.

14. Canada, Department of Finance, "The Canadian Opportunities Strategy," http://www.fin.gc/budget98/binbe/bin2e.html (1998).

15. F.G. Mixon and Y. Hsing, "College Student Migration and Human Capital Theory: A Research Note," *Education Economics* 2 (1994): 65-73; and Y. Hsing and F.G. Mixon, "A Regional Study of Net Migration Rates of College Students," *Review of Regional Studies* 26 (1996): 197-209.

16. For the public institutions in the sample, the tuition fees are for non-resident students.

17. Hsing and Mixon, "A Regional Study of Net Migration Rates of College Students."

18. D. McFadden, "Conditional Logit Analysis of Qualitative Choice," in *Frontiers in Econometrics,* ed. P. Zarembka (New York: Academic Press, 1974). The conditional or multinomial logit model has many applications. See K.E. Grant and J. Vanderkamp, *The Economic Causes and Effects of Migration: Canada, 1965-71* (Ottawa: Minister of Supply and Services, 1976); S.L. Winer and D. Gauthier, *Internal Migration and Fiscal Structure* (Ottawa: Minister of Supply and Services, 1982); and K.M. Day, "Interprovincial Migration and Local Public Goods," *Canadian Journal of Economics* 25 (1992): 123-44 for examples of applications of the conditional logit model to migration behaviour in Canada.

19. See Day and Grafton, "Interprovincial Student Mobility in Canada," for complete details on the construction of the data used in estimation.

20. The recent introduction of fee differentials for out-of-province students by some provincial governments means that from 1997-98 on, tuition fees will depend on both origin and destination.

21. The model performed poorly for francophones and anglophones. The signs of many of the coefficients were counter-intuitive and the likelihood function did not converge for anglophones. For this reason, the results were not reported in Table 5.

22. Mixon and Hsing, "College Student Migration and Human Capital Theory."

23. The results may also be improved upon by using individual (if it were available) rather than aggregate data. Individual data would allow for the inclusion of individual characteristics that might influence the migration decision, such as family income.

24. "B.C. Fears Student Invasion,"*The Globe and Mail,* 8 June 1998.

25. Department of Finance, "The Canadian Opportunities Strategy."

26. Because the model predicts only migration rates, not migration flows, in order to generate migration flows it was also necessary to fix the number of students originating in each province at its 1995-96 level.

27. In "Interprovincial Migration and Local Public Goods," Day observed similar problems in within-sample predictive power in applying a similar model to aggregate migration data for Canada as a whole. She attributed this problem to the fact that differences across provinces in the explanatory variables tend to dominate changes over time, so that the model does a relatively poor job of predicting year-to-year changes in migration flows.

28. Conversion to constant dollars is necessary because the model was estimated using data in constant dollars.

29. College students as well as university students are eligible to receive Canada Millenium Scholarships. Dividing the estimated annual value of CMS, $300 million ($3,000 per student and 100,000 recipients), by 870,000, the approximate total of college students and university undergraduates, yields an average value of about $350. The more conservative value of $300 was suggested by an anonymous referee.

9

Canada's Political Parties in the 1990s:
The Fraying of the Ties that Bind

A. Brian Tanguay

Les partis politiques fédéraux ont joué jusque dans les années 1970 un rôle de premier plan dans l'unification du Canada et dans la neutralisation des conflits régionaux. Les résultats présentés dans ce chapitre suggèrent que le système canadien de partis fédéraux s'est effondré. Pour reprendre l'expression de David Smith, les partis nationaux ne représentent plus le nerf du fédéralisme sain. L'élection de 1997 a confirmé le triomphe du régionalisme à l'intérieur du système de partis tel que l'avait anticipée l'élection de 1993. On retrouve parmi les causes de cette fragmentation régionale : l'émergence sous Pierre Trudeau d'une vision politique pancanadienne (symbolisée par la Charte des droits et libertés, la politique nationale de l'énergie et la Loi sur les langues officielles), l'effet déformant du système uninominal à un tour et l'effondrement de la coalition maladroite entre les populistes de l'ouest et les nationalistes québécois sous Brian Mulroney. Alors que le Reform et les Conservateurs divisent le vote de droite (les Réformistes dominant à l'ouest, les Conservateurs à l'est) et se neutralisent ainsi l'un et l'autre et que le NPD s'enlise dans les dissensions internes et l'impertinence politique, les Libéraux gouvernent par défaut.

Over a decade ago, in his study of party government and national integration for the Royal Commission on the Economic Union and Development Prospects for Canada (Macdonald), David Smith remarked that "political parties have commonly been accepted as the sinews of a healthy federalism."[1] At the time, Smith complained that the federal Liberal Party under Pierre Trudeau had failed to balance the competing interests of nation and region and promoted instead pan-Canadian or centralist policies — official bilingualism, the *Charter of Rights and Freedoms*, and the National Energy Program — which "push[ed] the provinces into an exaggerated defence of provincial concerns because, unlike the era of Mackenzie King or St. Laurent ... the provinces today see no defenders of their interests at the centre."[2] This resulted in the disillusionment of important segments of the citizenry, regional alienation, and growing disaffection from all political institutions, including the parties.

A glance at an electoral map displaying the results of the 1997 federal election will confirm that the tensions described by Smith have only gotten worse in recent years. The Canadian party system has now fractured into five regional subsystems, with no party gaining significant support from all regions in the country.[3] Western alienation is as pronounced in 1998 as it was at the time of the Macdonald Commission, and the fate of Quebec is less certain than ever, despite the optimism generated in some quarters by the recent Calgary Declaration. The causes and consequences of the triumph of regionalism in our party system will be explored in the first section of this chapter.

In addition to these perennial problems of Canadian politics, our parties are affected by global forces that are transforming the structures of representative democracy in all of the industrialized nations. In the following section of the chapter, I examine two of these trends and their impact on Canada's political parties. The first is the "flattening out"[4] of political discourse in an era characterized by globalization and the exhaustion of the old Cold War ideological dualism. This manifests itself in the continuing marginalization of the traditional Left, whose large-scale economic projects and penchant for social engineering elicit widespread scepticism among the electorates of the industrialized democracies. As well, policy convergence is now an endemic feature of politics in the West: more and more, no matter what the ideological leanings of the party in power, economic and social policy seems to vary within an exceedingly narrow band. In the words of Susan Strange: "the political choices open to governments these days have been so constricted by those forces of structural change often referred to as 'globalization' that the differences that used to distinguish government policies from opposition policies are in process of disappearing."[5] At the same time, the yawning gap between what a party promises in order to win an election and its actual performance while in power serves to fuel voter hostility to parties and politics in general. Large numbers of voters, in Canada as elsewhere, seem convinced that no political party is capable of delivering the jobs and prosperity that were the hallmarks of the long postwar boom. An examination of the behaviour of Jean Chrétien and the Liberals while in power will confirm the validity of Susan Strange's observations and shed light on one of the principal causes of voter cynicism in Canada.

The second global trend to be explored below is perhaps even more far-reaching than the first: the decline of deference among today's voters, which translates into widespread mistrust of parties and politicians, along with demands on the part of ordinary citizens to be consulted on the major issues of the day. "[E]verywhere, ordinary people are now in a better position to examine what their representatives are up to, observe their errors, smirk or snarl about their sexual and financial peccadillos, and wonder whether it is really a good idea to let such a collection do so much of the business of politics."[6] These changing value orientations have promoted the rise of populist "anti-parties" like the Reform Party of Canada and have strengthened interest in institutional alternatives to parties and representative democracy, such as the use of citizen initiatives, referenda, recall, deliberative polling, televoting, and electronic town halls.[7]

CANADA'S PARTY SYSTEM IN THE 1990s: THE TRIUMPH OF REGIONALISM

It is always dangerous to posit the existence of a golden age for any institution, and this is certainly true of Canada's party system. Nonetheless, it can be argued that from the time of Confederation to the rise of John Diefenbaker's populist brand of conservatism in the late 1950s, the federal party system managed to mitigate regional tensions in the country more effectively than is the case now. There were, of course, eruptions of regional protest in federal politics — these have been a recurrent feature of Canadian political life — but federal party leaders had at their disposal a number of mechanisms to neutralize or minimize the effects of these protest movements. The effectiveness of the federal party system in attenuating regional conflict was purchased at considerable cost to representative democracy itself. Policy and ideological incoherence, for instance, was a defining characteristic of Canadian politics, a situation described in sordid detail by the French political sociologist, André Siegfried, when he visited this country in the early part of the twentieth century. Siegfried complained in his classic study of Canadian politics, *The Race Question in Canada*, that the federal parties' obsession with questions of local patronage and "public works" tended to "lower the general level of political life" in Canada.[8]

To Siegfried and other students of Canadian politics, however, the incoherence and opportunism exhibited by the federal parties were simply the price that had to be paid in order to keep Canada — a country with severe regional, linguistic, and religious cleavages — unified. According to R. McGregor Dawson, author of what was for a long time the most commonly used text on Canadian politics:

> probably the primary political generalization about Canadian parties [is] that no party can go very far unless it derives support from two or more regional areas in the Dominion, and this leads to the further consequence that a national party must take as its primary purpose the reconciliation of the widely scattered aims and interests of a number of these areas. It is chiefly for this reason that the

party leaders have been compelled to modify their principles and their policies, to favour the neutral shades rather than the highly satisfying — but politically suicidal — brighter colours.[9]

This need to balance the many competing interests in the country has also tended to place a great deal of importance on the role of the party leader in Canadian political life. In Dawson's view, "[i]t is no accident that the three prime ministers with by far the longest terms in office — Macdonald, Laurier, and King — possessed to an extraordinary degree the ability to compromise and to bring together people possessing divergent interests and beliefs."[10]

Between 1867 and 1957 two different leadership styles, two different methods of attenuating the regional and social tensions in Canada — in effect, two different party systems — existed.[11] From Confederation to the end of World War I, the two major parties were loose coalitions of local notables and elections were contests between the "ins" and the "outs" over control of constituency-based patronage. First Macdonald and then Laurier skilfully used patronage to create national party organizations in each riding and, ultimately, a national community.[12]

Social changes brought on by rapid industrialization and urbanization in the early part of the twentieth century shattered the two-party system in the years immediately after World War I (1918-21) and sparked the rise of a series of regional protest parties — first the Progressives and United Farmers, then the Cooperative Commonwealth Federation (CCF) and Social Credit in the 1930s.[13] From 1921 to 1957, however, the two most successful prime ministers, Mackenzie King and Louis St. Laurent, managed to hold in check the centrifugal forces unleashed by sweeping social and economic change. Both party leaders — King in particular — were astute practitioners of the art of *brokerage politics*, the pragmatic cobbling together of party programs designed to appeal to as broad a coalition of diverse interests as possible.[14] King, for instance, was able to blunt the effectiveness of the Progressives as the voice of agrarian protest by buying off some of the movement's leaders (T.A. Crerar, most importantly) with Cabinet posts and implementing relatively minor reforms of federal tariff and freight rate policies. By the late 1920s, the Progressives were a spent force in federal politics. King also managed to accommodate *some* of the labour movement's most pressing demands, albeit grudgingly and usually only when confronted either with worker militancy or incontrovertible evidence of the growing popularity of the CCF. The King government's adoption of the Wartime Labour Relations Regulations (PC 1003) in 1944, for instance, legally established the *Wagner Act* model of collective bargaining in Canada, thereby providing an organizational fillip to the labour movement.[15]

While some charitable observers have admired King's skilful exercise of political dexterity "through depression, drought, war and reconstruction," his many critics have been repelled by his endless vacillations and smarmy sanctimoniousness. Frank Underhill, for example, in an article written in 1944, assailed King for "patting himself on the back" for enacting progressive labour legislation. In Underhill's view, King's motives were purely cynical or manipulative — to undercut popular support for J.S. Woodsworth and the fledgling CCF, or to shore up votes among the western Progressives — and not compassionate.[16] Later critics like John Porter contended that the price paid for national unity was too high. Canada's party system, Porter charged, was distinguished among those of major industrialized societies by its entrenched conservatism and the virtual absence of real political debate (what he called "creative politics"), and this was directly attributable to our intellectual obsession with regionalism and national unity.[17]

A second tool employed by King and St. Laurent to attenuate regional conflict within the party system was to stock their respective Cabinets with influential regional chieftains — men like Jimmy Gardiner, C.D. Howe, and Ernest Lapointe. Reg Whitaker has labelled this type of party organization *ministerialist*, and he argues that:

> at the national level, it always remained true that the relationship between the cabinet ministers, and thus between the leaders of the various regions within the party, were as much relations of mutual accommodation as hierarchical, involving horizontal rather than vertical patterns of interaction.[18]

Although there were powerful ministers in the Cabinets of John Diefenbaker (Alvin Hamilton, Davie Fulton), Lester Pearson (the so-called "three wise men" — Pierre Trudeau, Gérard Pelletier, and Jean Marchand), and Pierre Trudeau (Marc Lalonde, Allan MacEachen), a combination of personal and ideological factors limited their influence and placed them in a distinctly subordinate position vis-à-vis the prime minister. In the case of Diefenbaker, for example, "instead of allowing his appointees to apply their talents, [he] acted as if he were the silent partner in every cabinet minister's office. He ignored the normal delegation of authority, and attempted to operate the federal administration through personal prerogative."[19] Ministerialist party organization essentially died with Louis St. Laurent.

The electoral defeats suffered by the federal Liberals in 1957 and 1958 laid the groundwork for a third party system, one that was "pan-Canadian," to use Smith's terminology, and therefore much less accommodating of regional interests than its two predecessors.[20] The policies pursued by each successive prime minister were moulded by a centralizing vision of the country, even if some leaders (Diefenbaker, for instance) were more sensitive to regional concerns than others (Trudeau). Diefenbaker's concept of "One Canada," combined with his championing of a Bill of Rights, drew attention to the formal equality of all citizens and "appealed to Canadians as Canadians regardless of where they lived or what language they spoke."[21] Pearson's national medicare program, the Canada Pension Plan, and the Laurendeau-Dunton Royal Commission on Bilingualism and Biculturalism, along with Pierre Trudeau's *Official Languages Act*, National Energy Program (NEP), and *Charter of Rights and Freedoms* were even more relentlessly centralizing. These initiatives were at least partly inspired by the idea of Ottawa as the laboratory for progressive social and economic policy and a counterweight to more hidebound provincial governments.

By the time Pierre Trudeau came to power, the electoral objectives of the federal Liberal Party had subtly merged with the national interest. The NEP, for example, which did so much to inflame the wounds of western alienation, had both official and tacit objectives, as Charles Doran has demonstrated. Greater energy self-sufficiency and the promotion of conservation were among the official objectives of the policy, which Doran describes as "one of the most complex energy initiatives undertaken by any of the advanced-industrial democracies."[22] The real purpose of the program, however, was political: the strengthening of Ottawa at the expense of the energy-producing provinces. Holding energy prices below world market levels was certain to shore up the federal Liberal Party's power base in central Canada (Ontario and Quebec). If the American government and the western provinces were angered by the policy, this was deemed an acceptable price to pay to bolster the "Liberal party coalition. The interests of the Liberal party and of Canada seemed to coincide."[23]

As subsequent history has demonstrated, however, this convergence of the interests of the "government party" and the country was more apparent than real. Trudeau's pan-Canadian policies patently failed to knit the country together. Official bilingualism and the NEP outraged the western provinces, and while Trudeau's constitutional reforms may have struck a responsive chord in English Canada (where the *Charter of Rights and Freedoms*, along with medicare, has become one of the defining elements of the national identity) they alienated Quebec and provided fertile soil for the growth of the sovereigntist movement. It might be argued that the pan-Canadian party system could function effectively only so long as Pierre Trudeau was at the helm of the federal Liberal Party, since only he had the ability to deliver impressive majorities from his native Quebec while successfully appealing to individual citizens in English Canada over the heads of their provincial or regional representatives.[24]

The pan-Canadian thrust of federal economic and social policy from 1957 to 1984 was parallelled by the growing regionalization of the party system. Each of the two main parties drew the bulk of its electoral support from one or two regional strongholds, and the same was true of the CCF/NDP as well. None of the these organizations was actually a *national* party with solid cross-country support. This regional fragmentation was exaggerated by the effects of Canada's first-past-the-post electoral system, to be sure. For example, the Liberals under Pierre Trudeau gained a widespread reputation for insensitivity to the west, in part because their electoral strength lay in central Canada. Nonetheless, in each of the four western provinces the Liberals managed to take at least a fifth (22 percent) of the votes in every election between 1968 and 1980. Because of the vagaries of the single-member, simple plurality electoral system, however, these respectable vote totals translated into no more than a handful of seats, aside from the 1968 "Trudeaumania" election (see Table 1). The Liberals' woes in the west were mirrored by the Conservatives' failure to make any electoral headway in Quebec: in the five elections held between 1968 and 1980, the Tories managed to win at least 13 percent of the popular vote in Quebec, but this consistently translated into two or three seats at best (see Table 2).

Alan Cairns, in an influential article on the centrifugal effects of Canada's electoral system written *before* the Trudeau era, indicted the first-past-the-post system for being

> detrimental to national unity.... The electoral system has made a major contribution to the identification of particular sections/provinces with particular parties.... By so doing, it has rendered the parliamentary composition of each party less representative of the sectional interests in the political system than is the party electorate from which that representation is derived.[25]

As will be seen below, the divisive effects of Canada's electoral system are as acutely felt in the 1990s as they were in the period from 1957 to 1984.

The disintegrative effects of Canada's first-past-the-post system have been compounded by conscious party electoral strategy. Indeed, the institutional context (the nature of the electoral system) partly determines the strategies of the various actors who contest an election. Party officials quite rationally tend to direct the bulk of their limited organizational and financial resources to those regions in which they stand the best chance of winning. This was especially obvious in the case of the federal Liberal Party during the Pearson and Trudeau years. After the massive defeat of 1958, when John Diefenbaker's Conservatives won the biggest (to that point) landslide in Canadian history, a group of young, predominantly urban reformers centred around Walter Gordon, Keith Davey, and Tom Kent (the group was known as "Cell 13") recast virtually all aspects of party organization and ideology. The party's structures were centralized; new types of candidates were attracted into the fold; new campaign techniques modelled on American practice were adopted (improved use of television and opinion polling, for example); and the focus of the party's electoral appeal shifted to the urban ridings in British Columbia, Ontario, and Quebec, rural voters being more or less conceded to the populist John

Table 1: *Liberal Party Votes and Seats (%)* in Federal Elections, 1953-1997*

Region	%	1953	1957	1958	1962	1963	1965	1968	1972	1974	1979	1980	1984	1988	1993	1997
Atlantic	Votes	56	51	43	47	51	50	43	39	45	40	46	36	47	59	36
	Seats	82	36	25	41	63	44	18	32	40	34	59	24	69	98	47
Quebec	Votes	61	58	46	39	46	46	54	46	51	61	67	35	30	33	36
	Seats	88	83	33	47	63	75	76	76	81	89	99	23	16	25	35
Ontario	Votes	47	37	33	42	46	44	47	37	45	36	42	30	39	53	49
	Seats	60	25	18	52	61	60	73	41	62	34	55	15	43	99	98
Manitoba/ Saskatchewan	Votes	39	28	21	27	29	28	35	28	29	23	26	20	27	39	30
	Seats	43	16	0	7	7	4	27	12	19	7	7	4	18	61	25
Alberta	Votes	35	28	14	19	22	22	36	25	25	22	22	13	14	25	24
	Seats	24	6	0	0	6	0	21	0	0	0	0	0	0	15	8
British Columbia	Votes	31	20	16	27	32	30	42	29	33	23	22	16	20	28	29
	Seats	36	9	0	18	32	32	70	17	35	4	0	4	3	19	18
CANADA	Votes	49	41	34	37	42	40	45	37	42	40	44	28	21	41	38
	Seats	65	40	18	38	49	49	59	41	53	40	52	14	28	60	51

Note: *Rounded to the nearest whole number.

Source: CNEWS *Federal Election Summaries 1945-1968 & 1972-1993*, http://www.canoe.ca/CNEWSFedElections/fed_elxn_1972-.html [% of seats 1953-1988]. Chief Electoral Officer, *Official Voting Results*, 35th General Election 1993 [% of seats and % of votes, 1993]. Chief Electoral Officer, *Official Voting Results*, 36th General Election 1997 [% of seats and % of votes, 1997]. Howard Penniman, ed., *Canada at the Polls: The General Election of 1974* (Washington, DC: American Enterprise Institute for Public Policy Research, 1975) Appendix [% of vote 1968, 1972, 1974]. J. Murray Beck, *Pendulum of Power: Canada's Federal Elections* (Scarborough: Prentice-Hall, 1968) [% of vote 1953-1965]. Harold Clarke *et al.*, *Absent Mandate: Interpreting Change in Canadian Elections*, 2d ed. (Toronto: Gage, 1991) Appendix, Table A2 [% of vote 1974-1988].

Table 2: Progressive Conservative Party Votes and Seats (%)* in Federal Elections, 1953-1997

Region	%	1953	1957	1958	1962	1963	1965	1968	1972	1974	1979	1980	1984	1988	1993	1997
Atlantic	Votes	40	47	55	45	42	44	53	50	44	42	39	54	41	28	35
	Seats	15	64	76	54	33	54	78	69	53	56	41	78	38	3	41
Quebec	Votes	29	31	50	30	20	21	21	17	21	13	13	50	53	14	22
	Seats	5	5	67	19	11	11	5	3	4	3	1	77	84	1	7
Ontario	Votes	40	49	56	39	35	34	32	39	35	42	36	48	38	18	19
	Seats	39	72	79	41	32	29	20	45	28	60	40	71	46	0	1
Manitoba/ Saskatchewan	Votes	19	30	54	46	48	44	34	40	42	43	39	43	37	12	13
	Seats	13	35	97	87	87	87	38	58	65	61	43	64	39	0	4
Alberta	Votes	15	28	60	43	45	47	50	58	61	67	66	69	52	15	14
	Seats	12	18	100	88	82	88	79	100	100	100	100	100	96	0	0
British Columbia	Votes	14	33	49	27	23	19	19	35	42	45	41	47	34	14	6
	Seats	14	32	82	27	18	14	0	35	57	68	57	68	38	0	0
CANADA	Votes	31	40	54	37	33	32	31	37	35	36	33	50	43	16	19
	Seats	19	42	78	44	36	37	27	41	36	48	37	75	57	1	7

Note: *Rounded to the nearest whole number.

Source: CNEWS *Federal Election Summaries 1945-1968 & 1972-1993*, http://www.canoe.ca/CNEWSFedElections/fed_elxn_1972-.html [% of seats 1953-1988]. Chief Electoral Officer, *Official Voting Results*, 35th General Election 1993 [% of seats and % of votes, 1993]. Chief Electoral Officer, *Official Voting Results*, 36th General Election 1997 [% of seats and % of votes, 1997]. Howard Penniman, ed., *Canada at the Polls: The General Election of 1974* (Washington, DC: American Enterprise Institute for Public Policy Research, 1975) Appendix [% of vote 1968, 1972, 1974]. J. Murray Beck, *Pendulum of Power: Canada's Federal Elections* (Scarborough: Prentice-Hall, 1968) [% of vote 1953-1965]. Harold Clarke et al., *Absent Mandate: Interpreting Change in Canadian Elections*, 2d ed. (Toronto: Gage, 1991) Appendix, Table A2 [% of vote 1974-1988].

Diefenbaker.[26] In the 1962 election, this meant that the federal Liberals concentrated their efforts in Ontario. In Walter Gordon's words: "'I'm an
accountant in these things. The Toronto area has more seats than Saskatchewan, and we can win them.'"[27] This strategic reorientation paid electoral
dividends, as Table 1 shows: in the 1962 election, the biggest improvements
in the Liberals' electoral fortunes were registered in British Columbia and
Ontario. In the 1963 election, which displaced Diefenbaker and brought the
Liberals back to power (albeit in a minority situation), the party continued to
make gains in Ontario and British Columbia and recovered some of its former
strength in Quebec to forge its victory.

For the federal Liberal Party, however, and for the national party system
itself, the electoral success of the Cell 13 reforms represented short-term gain
for long-term pain. The centralization of the Liberal Party organization was
intensely resented by Liberal activists in both the eastern and western "pe-
ripheries," and especially in the west. Many western Liberals doubted whether
the "bright boys" from Toronto had the desire or the ability to understand
their region's particular concerns, let alone represent their interests.[28] By the
1990s, this simmering hostility toward the Liberal Party in the west was directed against *all* of the so-called old-line parties, a resentment that facilitated
the spectacular growth of the populist Reform Party.

The 1984 and 1988 federal elections marked a brief, apparent resurgence
of parties as instruments of national integration. It was Brian Mulroney's great
achievement, no matter what his failings as prime minister, to form a federal
government in 1984 with representation from all regions of the country.
Mulroney did this by grafting onto the traditional Tory strongholds of eastern
and western Canada an unlikely alliance from Quebec, a coalition that included the vestiges of the old Union Nationale, some Liberals who were
unhappy with the federal party's decision to anoint John Turner as Pierre
Trudeau's successor, and, most important of all, nationalist and separatist sym-
pathizers of the Parti Québécois. The PQ, in fact, provided crucial
organizational support for Mulroney during the campaign. Lucien Bouchard,
a strong nationalist who had served the Parti Québécois government in a variety of capacities, acted as Mulroney's adviser on Quebec matters during the
campaign. As well, at least three Tory candidates — Pierre Ménard, Suzanne
Duplessis, and Monique Vézina — had campaigned openly for the yes side in
the 1980 referendum.[29]

Mulroney promised that a Conservative government would heal the wounds
inflicted on Quebec by Pierre Trudeau's constitutional gambit in 1982, and
this was an important factor in the Tories' remarkable success in that province
in 1984, when they took 58 seats (out of 75) and 50 percent of the popular
vote. That Mulroney won two successive majorities with this unusual coalition of western populists (who seethed at the very mention of official

bilingualism and "French power") and Québécois nationalists is testament to his partisan and brokering skills. Yet even Mulroney was unable to prevent the unravelling of the coalition over the Meech Lake Accord (along with such other issues as the imposition of the Goods and Services Tax (GST) and the awarding of the CF-18 maintenance contract to Quebec rather than Manitoba). The Progressive Conservative Party, led by an inexperienced and gaffe-prone Kim Campbell, was nearly annihilated in the 1993 election, winning a mere two seats with 16 percent of the popular vote. To employ Stephen Harper and Tom Flanagan's arresting image, the Conservative Party "became a barrel tapped at both ends," as its former supporters flooded to two new regional protest parties, Reform in western Canada and the Bloc Québécois in Quebec.[30]

The 1993 federal election masked the extent to which the national party system had broken down along regional lines. It is true that the Liberals managed to win seats in every region of the country (see Table 1). Nevertheless, their 19 seats in Quebec were mostly from Montreal ridings with heavy concentrations of anglophones and non-francophone minorities; the BQ, overwhelmingly, was the voice of francophone Quebec. Moreover, the Reform Party was clearly the first choice of voters in the two most disaffected western provinces, Alberta and British Columbia. It was only the massive Liberal sweep in Ontario (taking 98 of 99 seats, which constituted fully 55 percent of the Liberal caucus), along with a strong performance in the Atlantic region, that furnished Chrétien with his superficially convincing national victory. In the words of Alan C. Cairns, "[a]lthough the Liberals won the election, the election's overall symbolic message was of an old order tottering, of its possible replacement by one knew not what, and thus that Canadians, haltingly and apprehensively, were beginning a new era."[31]

With the 1997 election the party system fragmented into five distinct regional subsystems (see Table 3 for a provincial breakdown of the results):

- The Atlantic region, where the surprising emergence of the NDP — largely due to the coattails effect provided by the newly installed leader, native daughter Alexa McDonough — created a three-party race among Liberals, Tories, and the NDP;
- Quebec, where the Liberals managed to win seven more seats than they had in 1993 (at the expense of the still dominant BQ, which suffered from the miscues and gaffes of its new leader, Gilles Duceppe), and gain a toehold in some of the francophone regions of the province;
- the Liberal one-party state of Ontario;
- Manitoba and Saskatchewan, where three parties — Reform, Liberals, and NDP — garnered roughly equal shares of seats;
- Alberta and British Columbia, where a one and a half-party system pits a powerful Reform Party against a much weaker Liberal Party.

A. Brian Tanguay

Table 3: **1997 Election Results by Province: Popular Vote (%) and Seats Won (N)**

Province/Terrritory		Party					
		Lib	PC	Ref	BQ	NDP	Other
Newfoundland	%*	38	37	2	–	22	1
	N	4	3	–	–	–	–
Nova Scotia	%	28	31	10	–	30	1
	N	–	5	–	–	6	–
New Brunswick	%	33	35	13	–	18	1
	N	3	5	–	–	2	–
Prince Edward Island	%	45	38	2	–	15	1
	N	4	–	–	–	–	–
Quebec	%	37	22	–	38	2	1
	N	26	5	–	44	–	–
Ontario	%	50	19	19	–	11	2
	N	101	1	–	–	–	1
Manitoba	%	34	18	24	–	23	1
	N	6	1	3	–	4	–
Saskatchewan	%	25	8	36	–	31	1
	N	1	–	8	–	5	–
Alberta	%	24	14	55	–	6	1
	N	2	–	24	–	–	–
British Columbia	%	29	6	43	–	18	4
	N	6	–	25	–	3	–
Northwest Territories	%	43	17	12	–	21	7
	N	2	–	–	–	–	–
Yukon	%	22	14	25	–	30	10
	N	–	–	–	–	1	–
CANADA	%	38	19	19	11	11	2
	N	155	20	60	44	21	1

Note: *Rounded to the nearest whole number.

Source: Chief Electoral Officer of Canada, *Official Voting Results*, 36th General Election 1997, Tables 7, 9.

In addition to the fracturing of the party system along regional lines, one of the more disquieting aspects of the 1997 election result is the extent to which the Liberals owe their tenuous hold on power to the idiosyncrasies of the electoral system. As Table 4 shows, the Liberals and the Bloc Québécois benefited disproportionately from the largesse of our first-past-the-post system in both 1993 and 1997, while the Reform Party managed to win about the same share of seats as votes. The NDP and the Conservatives, meanwhile, whose support in both elections was spread thinly across the country, were severely punished by the system. Defenders of the single-member, simple plurality system invariably point out that Parliament need not be a perfect mirror of public opinion, and that the principal virtue of our system is to produce stable governing majorities. Strong parties are thus rewarded, and weak ones discouraged, with the added benefit of encouraging national parties "to be tolerant and to keep their appeal within the middle-of-the-road consensus."[32]

Although the electoral system in 1997 did transmute the Liberals' paltry 38 percent of the popular vote into a bare majority of seats in the House of Commons, it is difficult to argue either that the Liberals deserved this kind of beneficence or that the result was a boon to the political system and the country. The implicit message that voters were trying to send to the political class in the election — that a solid majority of them trusted *no* political party to govern effectively or responsibly — was lost. A party interested primarily in its own political survival now governs the country at a time when imagination and innovative policy making are desperately needed simply to ensure the

Table 4:   Effect of Electoral System on Seat Distribution, 1993 and 1997 Federal Elections

Party	1993			1997		
	% Votes	% Seats	Ratio*	% Votes	% Seats	Ratio*
Liberal	41.32	60.00	1.45	38.36	51.50	1.34
Reform	18.72	17.60	0.94	19.34	19.93	1.03
Bloc	13.51	18.30	1.35	10.73	14.62	1.36
PC	16.00	0.68	0.04	18.88	6.64	0.35
NDP	6.87	3.05	0.44	11.04	6.98	0.63
Other	3.57	0.34	0.09	1.64	0.33	0.20

Note: *Of seats to votes.

Source: Calculated from: Chief Electoral Officer of Canada, *Official Voting Results*, 35th General Election 1993, Table 8; and *Official Voting Results*, 36th General Election 1997, Table 8.

federal system's continued existence. Most disturbing of all, the regional payoffs of the first-past-the-post sytem contributed to the Reform Party's decision to play the "Quebec card" during the 1997 election campaign, with potentially dire consequences for the future of the federation. Reform's television advertisements attacking the prominent role of Quebec-born politicians in federal politics over the past 30 years may have appealed to many voters in the west and even in supposedly middle-of-the-road Ontario,[33] but they certainly reinforced the impression of most francophone Quebecers that English Canada is not likely to accede to substantive reforms of the existing federal system. It is difficult to see how this kind of election strategy could possibly serve the cause of national unity, although it is worth noting that Preston Manning seems to think of himself as a Canadian version of Abraham Lincoln. During the 1997 campaign, Manning called for additional debates on national unity, arguing that they should be "similar to the seven debates on the future of slavery that Abraham Lincoln ... held with Illinois senator Stephen Douglas three years before the Civil War." The Lincoln-Douglas debates, Manning averred, "presented ideas that became a vision and ultimately the solution" to the problem of slavery.[34] Interestingly, Manning argued that Alexa McDonough would have to be barred from the debates — since her party, the NDP, had nothing new or interesting to say on the subject of national unity — as would the separatist leader, Gilles Duceppe. These comments provided a chilling insight into the Reform Party leader's fundamentalist views on politics and national unity.

Not all of Canada's national unity problems can be attributed to the workings of its electoral system, of course. Moreover, previous elections have produced parliaments almost as regionally fragmented as the current one. The 1979 election, for example, saw Joe Clark and his Progressive Conservative Party win a plurality of seats, most of them from the Atlantic region, Ontario and the west. It took but two seats out of 75 in Quebec, at a time when the prospects for Canada's very survival as a nation seemed almost as doubtful as they are in the late 1990s. And at least one of our national parties, the CCF, has had a near-death experience (in the 1950s), only to reemerge stronger and more focused a decade later. So what is new about the present situation? Is it not possible that some semblance of normalcy will reestablish itself in the national party system? In the next section of the paper, I argue that there are at least two additional reasons for pessimism when assessing the future of Canada's national parties as instruments of integration and linkage.

THE DECLINE OF PARTIES IN CANADA

In all of the industrialized democracies in the 1990s, though to varying degrees, traditional political parties have come under attack for being corrupt, self-serving, and elitist organizations that are indifferent to the demands of the average citizen.[35] Symptoms of the widespread distrust of politicians and parties are easy enough to detect, whether in the form of vicious personal attacks on party leaders and candidates at election time organized by a welter of interest groups, or in survey data revealing that "the repute of politicians as a profession has fallen down to the lower reaches — cheek by jowl with journalists, lawyers and other systematic distorters of the truth."[36] In Canada, for example, a recent poll by Goldfarb Consultants Limited asked respondents to indicate their level of respect for various professions on a scale of 0 to 100. Doctors topped the scale with an aggregate score of 72, followed by teachers (69), journalists (46), rock musicians (45), bankers (44), car salesmen (31), and, at the bottom, federal politicians (30).[37] As faith in political parties has declined, numerous single-issue groups and social movement organizations have emerged to challenge the former pre-eminence of parties as institutions linking the individual citizen to the state. To take the Canadian example again, in the early 1990s the Royal Commission on Electoral Reform and Party Financing (RCERPF) lamented the fact that so many citizens, "especially large numbers of well-educated activists, have eschewed partisan politics, and thus political parties, as mechanisms of democratic political participation," preferring instead to work within an interest group or a social movement, where they do not have to "accommodate their goals with competing interests."[38]

It would be premature, however, to sign the death certificate of traditional political parties just yet. As their defenders point out, parties still dominate the electoral process in all of the industrialized democracies, and they continue to wield considerable influence within the modern state's policy-making structures (an influence that is, however, shared with interest groups, bureaucrats, and other institutional power centres).[39] In addition, party organizations have not withered away or collapsed; there is as yet no *general* trend of declining membership in the traditional parties, in Canada or elsewhere.[40] Finally, there is still no clearly established institutional alternative to parties and representative democracy, despite the growing enthusiasm in some quarters for citizen initiatives, referendums, electronic town halls and other tools of direct democracy.

While political parties in Canada and the other liberal democracies are obviously not in their death throes, they are facing some of the most serious challenges to their survival since they first emerged in their present form during the latter half of the nineteenth century. In the words of German sociologist Ulrich Beck, modern mass political parties resemble "dinosaurs from a fading industrial age ... [which] seem to belong more to a museum than to a government."[41] Geoff Mulgan, a British intellectual and adviser to Tony Blair's Labour government, contends that political parties "cannot avoid looking like elderly institutions that have been overtaken by more effective means of campaigning, communicating and policymaking, whether these be in the voluntary sector, the media or the research institutes."[42] Thus while the parties continue to field candidates, contest elections and provide government with decision-makers, the affective or ideological ties between them and their supporters are unravelling. To quote Mulgan again, contemporary political parties "are condemned to perpetual underachievement. Even as they offer programmes, they seem less able to offer coherent frameworks for thinking about the world."[43]

A comparison of the 1993 and 1997 federal elections, along with an examination of the actions of the Chrétien government during its first term in office, will help to show why Canada's voters, like their counterparts elsewhere in the industrialized democracies, are so disillusioned with political parties. The 1993 federal campaign was the second consecutive contest — after the 1988 free trade election — in which voters were seemingly offered a clear choice between competing party programs — something rare by the standards of Canadian politics. During the campaign, the newly installed leader of the Progressive Conservatives and short-lived prime minister, Kim Campbell, was vilified for implying that levels of unemployment would remain "unacceptably high" until the end of the century and for claiming that an election was no time to have a serious debate on social policy reform. The Tories' strategy centred on attempting to portray Campbell as the embodiment of the "new politics," and asking the electorate to trust them to deal with the deficit — their central preoccupation in the campaign — in as humane a way as possible. This allowed the Liberal Party to position itself to the centre-left of the ideological spectrum and offer the same kind of interventionist job-creating strategies (though in much less detail) that Bill Clinton had advocated in his successful campaign for the US presidency a year earlier. In stark contrast to the "heartless Tories," Jean Chrétien and other leading Liberals criss-crossed the country clutching copies of the "Red Book" like talismans, and talked of offering hope to voters whose principal preoccupation was finding and hanging onto a decent job.[44] The Liberals committed themselves to harnessing the power of the state, through a six-billion dollar infrastructure plan and other measures, to invest in people and bolster economic confidence.

What was the result of the Liberals' convincing victory in 1993? Painful and humiliating retreats by the Chrétien government on key issues trumpeted during the campaign (the Pearson Airport fiasco) and essential continuity with the Tories on other policies (like the purchase of military helicopters) were the hallmarks of their first term in office.[45] Perhaps most shocking of all was the morphing of Chrétien and his finance minister, Paul Martin Jr., into Kim Campbell clones, job-creators transformed into dogged deficit-fighters. Such was the extent of the metamorphosis of the federal Liberal Party under Jean Chrétien that two Reform Party intellectuals, Stephen Harper and Tom Flanagan, could write without a trace of irony, that the "current Liberal government is more conservative on most issues than the previous Progressive

Conservative government.... Conservative voters are getting better results as outsiders influencing a Liberal government than they did as an inside influence within a Progressive Conservative government."[46]

Even by Canada's quite remarkable standards of ideological flexibility, the Liberals' *volte-face* was a virtuoso performance. It was all the more impressive for being at least partially successful: by the time the 1997 election was called, the Chrétien government's single greatest achievement in the minds of voters was to have significantly reduced the federal deficit after years of idle talk by the Mulroney Conservatives. In their study of the 1997 election Clarke *et al.* show that a plurality of voters who thought that the deficit was the most important issue in the campaign believed that the Liberals were the party closest to them on the issue. However, the deficit still lagged far behind unemployment as the single most important issue of the campaign (health care was the second most important), and voters actually preferred "none of the parties" on five of the ten most important issues cited, including unemployment.[47] A more qualified endorsement of the existing party system would be difficult to imagine.

Although the federal Liberals have often in the past campaigned from the left and governed from the right — indeed, this was one of the keys to their remarkable longevity as a governing party in the latter half of the twentieth century — the typical voter in Canada in the 1990s seems to have a longer memory and a much more rigid notion of government accountability than was the case previously. Thus the Liberals' backsliding exacted a heavy toll in increased voter cynicism. Nowhere was this more evident than in the Chrétien government's mishandling of the Goods and Services Tax (GST). In 1990, when the populist upheaval against the widely hated GST was at its height, Chrétien pledged at a Liberal rally that " 'the Mulroney GST will disappear' under a Liberal government. 'I am opposed to the GST. I have always been opposed to it. And I will be opposed to it always.'"[48] The famed Red Book was a little less definitive on the subject, committing a Liberal government only to replacing the GST "with a system that generates equivalent revenues, is fairer to consumers and to small business ... and promotes federal-provincial fiscal cooperation and harmonization."[49] This prudence was nowhere evident in the campaign pronouncements of Sheila Copps, however: the future deputy prime minister promised to resign if the GST was not scrapped altogether, saying that " 'you've got to be accountable for the things that you're going to do and you have to deliver on it.'"[50]

Of course, the Chrétien government could not deliver on this particular promise, as Finance Minister Paul Martin Jr. admitted in his 1996 budget. Instead of replacing the GST, the Liberals managed only to harmonize the tax with the provincial sales taxes of Nova Scotia, Newfoundland, and New Brunswick. Martin apologized to Canadian voters for making an "honest mistake" on the GST, but this act of contrition was followed by a farce in three acts.

Prime Minister Chrétien, displaying a punctilious and legalistic attitude toward the English language, denied that there was any cause for apologizing, since the harmonization of the GST in his opinion fulfilled the letter, if not the spirit, of the Liberals' Red Book promise. Worse, Chrétien berated participants in an electronic town hall who had the temerity to disagree with his view. Sheila Copps, after an ill-advised attempt to joke her way out of her election campaign promise (attributing the pledge to a bad case of "loose lips"), eventually resigned her seat in the House of Commons. She subsequently won the by-election quite handily, to the dismay of the Reform Party and its allies, like the National Citizens' Coalition, who had hoped to transform the vote into a plebiscite on the Chrétien government and the issue of party accountability.

This sorry spectacle over the GST served as a foreshadowing of the dismal 1997 election, which had a thoroughly ritualistic air about it. Even Chrétien, at the press conference to launch the campaign, seemed unconvinced of the need for an election, and the voters responded with a turnout of just under 67 percent, one of the lowest levels of the twentieth century.[51] In essence, the Liberals won by default, *faute de mieux*, since a lack of enthusiasm among voters for the partisan alternatives to the Liberals is, along with the workings of the electoral system, the key to the Chrétien government's shaky grip on power. Not one of the four parties competing with the Liberals in 1997 even remotely resembled a national party with cross-country support. In the case of the Bloc Québécois, this lack of a national presence is simply a reflection of its *raison d'être*, to serve as midwife to Quebec's accession to independence. However, since the departure of Lucien Bouchard for provincial politics the BQ has been less visible and less relevant in Ottawa than at any other time during its brief existence. Gilles Duceppe's well-documented travails during the 1997 campaign were in part the result of his inexperience and wooden public demeanour, but they also reflected a deeper malaise and lack of focus within the party.

As for the Reform Party, its attempts to make a breakthrough into eastern Canada and establish itself as the national alternative to the Liberals stalled, as the party lost its only seat in Ontario.[52] In fact, the party regressed in Ontario in 1997, taking only 19 percent of the vote (in contrast to 20 percent in 1993) and coming in second in 39 ridings, as opposed to 57 in 1993. In spite of the party's overtures to Quebec, in the form of a dialogue with the Bloc Québécois on a "united alternative" and the prominent media role it gives to its young bilingual MP from Edmonton-Strathcona, Rahim Jaffer,[53] it is difficult to see how Reform could ever be a truly national party as long as Quebec remains in Canada. This fact, along with Manning's decision to play the Quebec card in a particularly divisive way during the 1997 campaign, tends to reinforce the notion that Reform and the BQ are locked in a kind of perverse symbiosis, with potentially dire consequences for the future of Canada.[54]

Reform is now experiencing the growing pains and internal bickering that typically afflict a protest movement as it attempts to adapt to the demands of Westminster-style parliamentary life. The recent squabble during the summer of 1998 that erupted when a small number of Reform MPs decided to opt back into the much scorned "gold-plated" pension plan for Members of Parliament is illustrative of the tension between the Reform's anti-party roots and the natural tendency toward professionalization and bureaucratization that occurs once a party is installed in Ottawa. To date, Reform's leadership has negotiated these organizational shoals much more successfully than some of its predecessors — the Progressives in the 1920s, most notably — and the party remains at the constituency level the most vibrant and dynamic of the five represented in the House of Commons. However, the party seems fated not to achieve the one thing its leader most desires: real power at the national level (as opposed to influence through the governing party).

Reform has all but eliminated the Tories west of Manitoba, and its ongoing efforts to break into Ontario blunt the Conservatives in that province as well. The ideological and organizational ties between Mike Harris's Conservative government in Ontario and the Reform Party also compound the federal Tories' difficulties. Indeed, of the five federal parties, it is the Conservatives that face the bleakest future. Jean Charest's departure for provincial politics to become leader of the Quebec Liberal Party[55] has left the Conservatives facing one of the worst crises of their long existence. Charest had succeeded in pulling the party back from the brink of oblivion, raising it to official party status in 1997 after the election debacle four years earlier, when the Conservatives were reduced to a pitiful rump of two in the House of Commons. But Charest as party leader was unable to exorcise the ghost of Brian Mulroney, which continues to make the party very unpopular in Ontario and the western provinces. As a result, the Conservatives managed to elect only a single member west of the Ottawa River in 1997.

The "race," such as it was, for the vacated leadership of the Progressive Conservatives in the summer and fall of 1998 was symptomatic of the party's woes. Alberta Premier Ralph Klein, the Tory with the highest national profile and the strongest support among the party rank-and-file, disavowed any interest in the job almost as soon as Charest had announced his resignation. Manitoba Premier Gary Filmon, former Reform MP Stephen Harper, and former Alberta Treasurer Jim Dinning did likewise, leaving the field to former Prime Minister Joe Clark and four relative unknowns: Hugh Segal, former adviser to Ontario's Big Blue Machine and to Brian Mulroney; Brian Pallister, who had been government services minister in Gary Filmon's Cabinet; Michael Fortier, a young bilingual lawyer from Montreal; and David Orchard, a Saskatchewan farmer who ran on an anti-free trade platform. To say that the leadership race failed to generate much enthusiasm among the voting public, or even among party militants, would be an understatement. In a vote of party members (as opposed to the traditional delegated convention), Joe Clark was crowned — once again — party leader.

Clark's moderate brand of conservatism may well appeal to a number of Ontario voters who are unhappy with the Chrétien government's "style" — the autocratic tone evinced in the debate over the hepatitis-C compensation package, for example — but who view the radical right-wing populism and Quebec-baiting of Preston Manning and Reform with considerable scepticism. He may even attract some francophone Quebec voters who are sympathetic to his flexible and decentralized version of federalism. In all likelihood, however, the Clark-led Tories are unlikely to recover their former strength in the west; nor can they count on winning many seats east of the Manitoba border. But they are capable of blunting Reform's attempts to secure an electoral beachhead in the east, and thus they appear to provide the Liberals with a formula for perpetual hegemony.

The Reform Party is aware of the electoral consequences of a fragmented opposition, and since the 1997 election has been trying doggedly to unite the right. In February 1999, Reform held a convention in Ottawa aimed at creating a "United Alternative" to the Liberals, whether through the merger of the Conservatives and Reform, the creation of an entirely new party, or the establishment of a "confederal" party with separate regional leaders. Since the unite-the-right initiative is clearly the brainchild of Manning and Reform, however, it is viewed with considerable scepticism by the Conservative Party hierarchy and many in the party's grassroots. It is therefore highly unlikely that this initiative will yield the cohesive organization necessary to dislodge the Liberals from power.

Finally, the federal NDP's apparent resurgence in 1997, when it took 21 seats with 11 percent of the popular vote, served to divert attention from the acute crisis that still wracks the party. Virtually all of the NDP's success in 1997, as noted above, can be attributed to its traditional strength in the western provinces (apart from Alberta), where it took 12 seats, and to the regional popularity of its new leader, Nova Scotia native Alexa McDonough. The NDP won a surprising eight seats in the Atlantic region in 1997, where it split the protest vote against the Liberals with the Conservatives. However, the NDP was shut out for a second consecutive election in Ontario, where it won just under 11 percent of the vote. The party was simply not viewed as a credible option by large numbers of voters in Ontario, despite the two years of turmoil and polarization engendered by Mike Harris's Common Sense Revolution. Many Ontarians, and this includes a good number of traditional NDP supporters, appear to be still suffering from the lingering after-effects of Bob Rae's five years in power.

Symptomatic of the NDP's ideological confusion was the fact that its 1997 election manifesto came with an errata sheet, as some of the numbers in the party's fiscal plan did not quite add up.[56] In truth, the party's program consists largely of warmed-over Keynesian nostrums more relevant for the 1950s than the present era. Many NDP activists seem to be engaged in a massive exercise in selective amnesia or auto-suggestion, the ultimate purpose of which is to convince themselves that the party's misfortunes can be attributed to its failure to be sufficiently left-wing and not to the demonstration effects of unpopular, overweening and less than fully competent provincial administrations in Ontario and British Columbia. Alexa McDonough has recently sparked a real debate within the party (something quite rare in recent years) by proposing that it adopt a more business-friendly approach and seek to imitate the success of Tony Blair's Labour Party and some other European social democratic parties. This long overdue move has been greeted by the predictable uproar from the usual sources — organized labour and the academic Left. Thus there is no guarantee that the party will be able to engage in the critical self-examination needed in order to stave off or simply slow down its decline into political irrelevance.

In summary, the federal party system in Canada is anything but healthy, and it is patently failing to integrate Canadians from different regions or to link citizens to the state in a durable and effective way. This conclusion is disputed by some observers, who point among other things to the continuing high levels of support enjoyed by the Chrétien government.[57] This argument misses the point, however: between elections, when most citizens pay minimal attention to politics, a party can appear to enjoy tremendous popularity — as did Chrétien and the Liberals prior to the 1997 election, or Lyn McLeod's Ontario Liberal Party before the 1995 provincial election — but this support is extremely soft. It can easily evaporate in the heat of an election campaign, as the 1997 contest demonstrated. This simply underscores one of the most prominent features of politics in the 1990s: high levels of voter volatility combined with extremely tenuous affective ties between voters and parties. As Clarke *et al.* point out, in 1997 fully 30 percent of voters did not identify with *any* political party, something "unprecedented for any election year since 1965."[58]

This decline in levels of party identification is fuelled by, and in turn contributes to, the decline in deference among voters which has been observed by Nevitte and others. Voters today are unwilling to trust politicians or political parties, and in some cases they resent the fact that these organizations presume to speak for them. This phenomenon has potentially troubling implications for the future of democracy in Canada and elsewhere, as it facilitates the rise of populist anti-parties and, in some cases, of strong leaders offering simplistic solutions to the complex problems of the late twentieth century. In Canada, there can be no doubt that the Reform Party has benefited from this anti-party sentiment, as the data in Table 5 (taken from the 1992-93 National Election and Referendum Study) show. A post-referendum

Table 5:   **Feelings Toward Politicians (Thermometer Scores, 0-100) by Party Identification, 1992**

Party ID	Mean	N	Standard Deviation
Liberal	43.46	560	20.86
PC	43.33	356	21.01
NDP	41.52	217	21.36
Reform	30.88	68	19.74
BQ	40.64	192	20.34
None	36.99	624	21.89
Total	40.53	2,017	21.41

Note: F = 9.788   Sig. = .000

Source: Data from the 1992-93 Canadian Referendum and Election Survey were provided by the Institute for Social Research, York University. The survey was funded by the Social Sciences and Humanities Research Council of Canada (SSHRCC), grant numbers 411-92-0019 and 42-92-0026, and was completed for Richard Johnston, André Blais, Henry Brady, Elisabeth Gidengil and Neil Nevitte. I am solely responsible for the analyses and interpretations presented here.

(Charlottetown) panel survey of voters indicated that Reform supporters were significantly more hostile towards political parties than supporters of other parties: their mean thermometer score was just under 31, compared to a high of about 43 for the Liberals. Interestingly, the large number of non-identifiers (approximately 30 percent of the sample), were second to the Reformers in terms of distrust of politicians. Reform Party supporters are much more sceptical about the effectiveness of our democratic system in general than are other voters.[59] It is unlikely that this situation has changed much since the early 1990s; indeed, most indications are that distrust of parties and politicians has increased since that time.

CONCLUSION

The evidence presented in this chapter suggests that the federal party system in Canada has broken down. The national parties no longer serve as the sinews of a healthy federalism, to use David Smith's expression, and the 1997 election served to confirm the triumph of regionalism in the party system, something that had been foreshadowed by the 1993 election. Among the principal causes of the regional fragmentation of the party system are the emergence of a pan-Canadian political vision (embodied in the *Charter of Rights and Freedoms*, the National Energy Program, and the *Official Languages Act*, among other policies) under Pierre Trudeau; the centrifugal effects of the first-past-the-post electoral system; and the collapse of Brian Mulroney's ungainly coalition of western populists and Quebec nationalists. With Reform and the Conservatives dividing the right-of-centre vote along regional lines (Reform dominant in the west and the Tories in the east) and neutralizing each other in the strategic electoral battleground of Ontario, and with the NDP trapped in a spiral of irrelevance and internal dissension, the Liberals essentially govern by default.

Political parties in Canada and the other industrialized societies are also under attack as the primary vehicles of democratic representation, the most important links between citizen and state. The causes of this trend are complex, but two in particular can be cited. In the first place, there is a growing perception among voters that no matter what the ideological stripe of the party in power, it will be powerless to protect the domestic economy against the forces of globalization or to guarantee the economic prosperity — and in particular stable, high-paying jobs in the manufacturing sector — that characterized the long postwar boom. An examination of Jean Chrétien's government during its first term in office confirms that there are rational grounds for voter scepticism, since the gap between promise and performance in this particular case was huge. Secondly, voters have lost a large measure of their trust for politicians and parties, and are less inclined than ever to allow them to speak on their behalf. This decline of deference has helped fuel the rise of populist anti-parties like Reform, which have been quick to exploit voter cynicism with the existing party system.

Are Canada's federal parties doomed to underachievement, as Mulgan has argued? There are possible reforms that might revitalize the party system — a change in the electoral system being an obvious place to start. Perhaps the biggest obstacle to such necessary reforms, however, is the incumbent prime minister and his distinctly old-style approach to politics: at a time when innovative thinking is required, it is "politics as usual" in Ottawa.

NOTES

1. Peter Aucoin, ed., "Party Government, Representation and National Integration in Canada," in *Party Government and Regional Representation in Canada* (Toronto: University of Toronto Press, 1985), p. 1.

2. Ibid., p. 50.

3. The fragmentation of our federal party system has been exaggerated and intensified by our first-past-the-post electoral system, a problem that will be discussed in greater detail later in the chapter.

4. François Furet describes the flattening out of public life in his article, "Europe After Utopianism," *Journal of Democracy* 6, 1 (1995): 81-83.

5. Susan Strange, "The Limits of Politics," *Government and Opposition* 30, 3 (1995): 291.

6. "The Future of Democracy," *The Economist*, 17 June 1995, p. 13. For an insightful treatment of this topic, see Neil Nevitte, *The Decline of Deference* (Peterborough, Ont.: Broadview Press, 1996).

7. For interesting and cautiously enthusiastic overviews of the new technologies of direct democracy, see "Democracy and Technology," *The Economist*, 17 June 1995, pp. 21-23; and "Happy 21st Century, Voters! A Survey of Democracy," *The Economist*, 21 December 1996.

8. André Siegfried, *The Race Question in Canada*, ed. Frank Underhill (Toronto: McClelland & Stewart, Carleton Library edition, 1966 [originally published in French in 1906]), p. 114.

9. R. McGregor Dawson, *The Government of Canada*, 5th ed., revised by Norman Ward (Toronto: University of Toronto Press, 1970), p. 430.

10. Ibid., pp. 430-31. R.K. Carty also underscores the crucial importance of the party leader in Canadian politics in his article, "For the Third Asking: Is There a Future for National Political Parties in Canada?" in *In Pursuit of the Public Good: Essays in Honour of Allan J. MacEachen*, ed. Tom Kent (Montreal and Kingston: McGill-Queen's University Press, 1997), p. 149. According to Carty, "party leadership has been ... much more important to the survival and health of Canadian parties than those elsewhere."

11. The next few paragraphs draw on the analysis in Smith, "Party Government, Representation and National Integration," pp. 2, 15-25. See also R.K. Carty, "Three Canadian Party Systems: An Interpretation of the Development of National Politics," in *Party Democracy in Canada*, ed. George Perlin (Scarborough Ont.: Prentice-Hall, 1988), pp. 15-24.

12. See Jeffrey Simpson, *Spoils of Power* (Toronto: Collins, 1988), chs. 3 and 4 for a detailed historical account of the Macdonald and Laurier administrations' uses of patronage.

13. This transformation of Canadian society and polity is skilfully examined by John English in his book, *The Decline of Politics: The Conservatives and the Party System, 1901-1920* (Toronto: University of Toronto Press, 1977). See also W.L. Morton, *The Progressive Party in Canada* (Toronto: University of Toronto Press, 1950).

14. John McMenemy defines brokerage politics as "[p]olitical behaviour based on practical actions best suited to achieving and maintaining power. Brokerage politics is justified as the proper management of social tensions in a heterogeneous society through pragmatic decision-making to maintain social harmony." *The Language of Canadian Politics*, rev. ed. (Waterloo Ont.: Wilfrid Laurier University Press, 1995), p. 14.

15. As some critics have legitimately pointed out, the *Wagner Act* model of industrial relations has been a double-edged sword in Canada: while it may have

encouraged unionization in its early years, it also established "one of the most restrictive and highly juridified frameworks for collective bargaining in any capitalist democracy." Leo Panitch and Donald Swartz, *The Assault on Trade Union Freedoms: From Wage Controls to Social Contract* (Toronto: Garamond Press, 1993), pp. 12-13.

16.   Frank H. Underhill, *In Search of Canadian Liberalism* (Toronto: Macmillan, 1961), pp. 114-15.

17.   John Porter, *The Vertical Mosaic* (Toronto: University of Toronto Press, 1965), ch. 12. See also Janine Brodie and Jane Jenson, "Piercing the Smokescreen: Stability and Change in Brokerage Politics," in *Canadian Parties in Transition*, 2d ed., ed. A. Brian Tanguay and Alain-G. Gagnon (Scarborough: Nelson, 1996).

18.   Reg Whitaker, *The Government Party* (Toronto: University of Toronto Press, 1977), pp. xxii. See also pp. 407-14 for a more detailed discussion of the concept and the actual practices of King and St. Laurent.

19.   Peter C. Newman, *Renegade in Power: The Diefenbaker Years* (Toronto: McClelland & Stewart, 1973), p. 92.

20.   In "Three Canadian Party Systems," Carty refers to this third party system as the era of "electronic politics." Rather than focusing on federal-provincial dynamics in the party system, Carty explores the impact of new campaign technologies — the media, pollsters, consultants, and spin doctors — on parties as organizations and as the pre-eminent linkage institutions in liberal democratic society. These trends will be examined in greater detail in the next section of the chapter.

21.   Smith, "Party Government," p. 27.

22.   Charles Doran, *Forgotten Partnership* (Toronto: Fitzhenry & Whiteside, 1984), p. 221.

23.   Ibid.

24.   As I argue below, Brian Mulroney and the federal Conservatives were able to duplicate Trudeau's success, but only for six or seven years at most.

25.   Alan C. Cairns, "The Electoral System and the Party System in Canada, 1921-1965," in *The Canadian Political Process*, rev. ed., ed. O. Kruhlak, R. Schultz and S. Pobihushchy (Toronto: Holt, Rinehart and Winston, 1973), p. 140. The article was originally published in the *Canadian Journal of Political Science* in 1968.

26.   These reforms are examined in great detail by Joseph Wearing in his excellent book, *The L-Shaped Party: The Liberal Party of Canada, 1958-1980* (Toronto: McGraw-Hill, Ryerson, 1981). See also Tom Axworthy, "Innovation and the Party System: An Examination of the Career of Walter L. Gordon and the Liberal Party," unpublished MA thesis, Queen's University, 1971.

27.   Quoted in Peter C. Newman, *The Distemper of Our Times* (Toronto: McClelland & Stewart, 1968), p. 79.

28.   See Wearing, *L-Shaped Party;* and David E. Smith, *The Regional Decline of a National Party* (Toronto: University of Toronto Press, 1981).

29.   John Sawatsky, *Mulroney: The Politics of Ambition* (Toronto: Macfarlane Walter and Ross, 1991), pp. 46-47.

30.   "Our Benign Dictatorship," *Next City* (Winter 1996/97): 39. In spite of its obvious right-wing bias, this article contains a very perceptive analysis of the current crisis and future prospects of the federal party system.

31.   Alan C. Cairns, "An Election to be Remembered: Canada 1993," *Canadian Public Policy* 20, 3 (1994): 226.

32.   David Butler, "Electoral Systems," in *Democracy at the Polls*, ed. David Butler, Howard R. Penniman and Austin Ranney (Washington and London: American Enterprise Institute for Public Policy Research, 1981), p. 18.

33.   See Harold Clarke, Peter Wearing, Allan Kornberg and Marianne Stewart, "The Contest Nobody Won: The 1997 Canadian Federal Election and the National Party System," paper presented to the biennial Association for Canadian Studies in the United States (ACSUS) Conference, Minneapolis, 20 November 1997, p. 3. The authors estimate that Reform gained approximately 8 percent in Ontario in the last week of the campaign, after "going negative" and "airing television commercials suggesting that it was time that Canada had a prime minister who was not a Quebecker."

34.   *The Globe and Mail*, 21 May 1997. Michael Fellman, a professor of history at Simon Fraser University, wrote a withering critique of Manning's alarming views, arguing that the Lincoln-Douglas debates did not resolve the issue of slavery but merely heightened tensions in the United States. Fellman concluded that "[t]he degree to which Canadian politicians muddle the sovereignty issue is the degree to which they can prevent separation. Sharpening our indecisive polity in another Lincoln-Douglas debate is precisely the wrong way to handle our fundamental divide." See *The Globe and Mail*, 22 May 1997.

35.   For especially eloquent expressions of this view, see Hans Magnus Enzensberger, *Europe, Europe* (New York: Pantheon Books, 1989), p. 81; and Martin Jacques, "The End of Politics," in *Comparative Politics 94/95*, ed. Christian Søe (Guilford CT: Dushkin Publishing Group, 1994), p. 100. Jacques, the former editor of *Marxism Today*, first published his article in *The Sunday Times* of London in November 1993.

36.   Geoff Mulgan, *Politics in an Antipolitical Age* (Cambridge: Polity Press, 1994), p. 9.

37.   Reported in *Maclean's*, 1 June 1998, p. 12. Details of the sample size and the margin of error were not reported in the article. These survey results mirror data published in *The Gallup Report* throughout the 1980s. For a discussion of the declining levels of trust in Canada's political parties, see A. Brian Tanguay, "Reflections on Political Marketing and Party 'Decline' in Canada ... or, A Funny Thing Happened on the Way to the 1988 Election," in *Democracy with Justice/ La juste démocratie: Essays in Honour of Khayyam Zev Paltiel*, ed. Alain-G. Gagnon and A. Brian Tanguay (Ottawa: Carleton University Press, 1992), pp. 391-406.

38. Canada, Royal Commission on Electoral Reform and Party Financing [RCERPF], *Reforming Electoral Democracy*, Volume I (Ottawa: Minister of Supply and Services, 1991), p. 222.

39. Angelo Panebianco, *Political Parties: Organization and Power*, trans. Marc Silver (Cambridge: Cambridge University Press, 1988), p. 268.

40. See Per Selle and Lars Svåsand, "Membership in Party Organizations and the Problem of Decline of Parties," *Comparative Political Studies* 23, 4 (1991) for evidence about the European case.

41. *The Reinvention of Politics*, trans. Mark Ritter (Cambridge: Polity Press, 1997), p. 145.

42. *Politics in an Antipolitical Age*, p. 29.

43. Ibid.

44. Liberal Party of Canada, *Creating Opportunity: The Liberal Plan for Canada* (Ottawa: Liberal Party of Canada, 1993).

45. One of the first actions of the Chrétien government was to cancel the contract for purchasing 50 EH-101 helicopters, a deal that the Liberals had roundly denounced during the election campaign as a symbol of Tory profligacy and of its penchant for putting guns before butter, hardware before people. The Liberal government was forced to pay over $470 million in compensation to the Anglo-Italian consortium that manufactured the EH-101. Ultimately, the Liberals ended up purchasing a smaller number of what was essentially a modified EH-101. See Jeffrey Simpson, "The government spins its own propellers over the helicopter deal," *The Globe and Mail*, 6 January 1998, p. A12.

46. "Our Benign Dictatorship," p. 39. For a useful account of the metamorphosis of the Chrétien government, see Edward Greenspon and Anthony Wilson-Smith, *Double Vision* (Toronto: Doubleday Canada, 1996).

47. "The Contest Nobody Won," p. 5 and Table 3.

48. Quoted in Greenspon and Wilson-Smith, *Double Vision*, p. 373.

49. Liberal Party of Canada, *Creating Opportunity*, p. 22.

50. Quoted in Greenspon and Wilson-Smith, *Double Vision*, p. 374.

51. The lowest turnout for any federal election in the twentieth century was 66 percent (in 1925); in 1953 only 67 percent of voters actually cast their ballots. See Munro Eagles, "Voting and Non-Voting in Canadian Federal Elections: An Ecological Analysis," in *Voter Turnout in Canada*, ed. Herman Bakvis (Toronto: Dundurn Press, 1991), p. 6.

52. The party had won Simcoe-Centre in the 1993 election, but that riding was lost to redistribution and the incumbent chose not to run again. Reform's best result in Ontario in 1997 was in the riding of Bruce-Grey, where it managed to take only 33 percent of the vote.

53. Jaffer is regarded by some in the Quebec media as an appealing politician who might have a chance of establishing some sort of beachhead in Quebec or, at the

very least, of getting the party noticed by the province's voters. See Michel
Vastel, "L'armée secrète du Reform Party," *L'Actualité*, 15 mars 1998.

54. See A. Brian Tanguay, "The Transformation of Canada's Party System in the
1990s," in *Canadian Politics*, 2d ed., ed. James P. Bickerton and Alain-G. Gagnon
(Peterborough Ont.: Broadview Press, 1994), pp. 124-31, for a more detailed
examination of the "symbiotic" relationship between Reform and the Bloc.

55. A party that finds itself frequently at odds, both organizationally and philosophi-
cally, with its federal counterpart in Ottawa. Tensions between the two wings of
the Liberal Party were most evident during the recent Quebec provincial election (held on 30 November 1998, and resulting in a virtual photocopy of the
results of the 1994 contest). At the very outset of the campaign, Prime Minister
Chrétien gave a press interview in which he claimed that no more "goodies"
would be forthcoming for Quebec, since "all" of the province's historical constitutional demands had been met. Jean Charest and the provincial Liberals
understandably felt as though their federal counterparts had betrayed them and
needlessly hobbled them during the campaign; the fact that they were able to
take a slightly larger share of the popular vote than the Parti Québécois, even if
they lost the election, was viewed as a moral victory in the face of enormous
odds.

56. NDP, *A Framework for Canada's Future* (Ottawa: New Democratic Party, 1997).

57. An Angus Reid poll published on 10 July 1998, for example, shows that "Chrétien
continues to ride high in public esteem," with a 65-percent approval rating. Forty-
nine percent of those surveyed indicated that they would vote for the Liberals if
an election were held the next day; the next highest level of support was for the
Tories, with a mere 15 percent. The poll is available on Angus Reid's web-site,
www.angusreid.com.

58. "The Contest Nobody Won," p. 4. The authors write: "Prior to 1997, the largest
percentage of nonidentifiers in any election year was 14% (in 1993), and the
average was 12%."

59. On this topic see the interesting research done by Colleen Nichols in her MA
major research paper, "Responding to Postindustrialism: The Case of the Reform Party of Canada," Department of Political Science, Wilfrid Laurier
University, September 1997.

V

Identity,
Citizenship
and Culture

10

Redress Politics and Canadian Citizenship

Matt James

Ce chapitre s'appuie sur une étude de cas des mouvements canadiens demandant réparation. À partir de la notion d'honneur civique, on y suggère que les demandes de changements symboliques à l'histoire gagnent à être vues comme autant d'efforts de la part de groupes marginalisés pour être respectés publiquement. Je soutiens que la capacité à être respecté est une caractéristique essentielle de la citoyenneté. En effet, la participation à la vie politique requiert le respect des autres. Bien que les demandes de réparation aient été décrites comme une menace à la citoyenneté canadienne, elles apparaissent plutôt posséder une fonction intégrative lorsqu'elles sont considérées comme des efforts pour gagner le respect. Bref, demander réparation devrait être vu comme une tentative de construire une identité sociale permettant la participation dans l'arène publique.

En conclusion de ce chapitre, les demandes de réparation sont inscrites dans le processus d'apprentissage politique à travers lequel les mouvements sociaux du XXᵉ siècle ont mis en lumière les conditions nécessaires, au-delà de l'égalité formelle, à l'exercice de la citoyenneté. À l'intérieur de cette perspective où le non-respect constitue un obstacle majeur à la participation politique, les conflits symboliques représentent, aux yeux des mouvements demandant réparation et des «nouveaux» mouvements sociaux, un moyen important de transformer les modes traditionnels d'allocation du respect. Je soutiens, en terminant, que le retour des communautés affligées sur les injustices passées peut conduire à l'élaboration d'une citoyenneté capable de canaliser les loyautés et les énergies de ces communautés.

All people share the universal need to gain the respect or esteem of others, since without it they can not as easily elicit the help of others.

William J. Goode, *The Celebration of Heroes*

INTRODUCTION

Groups seeking redress for past injustices have made historical symbolism a crucial focal point for contemporary Canadian debates about citizenship.[1] This role is fitting, for revisiting wrongs that were inflicted in the past can help elevate group status in the present. When a community forces removal of the historical stigma under which it previously laboured, it improves its capacity to influence the political dialogues and struggles whose outcomes will help to shape its future.

The significance of redress for debates about Canadian citizenship has been established by Alan Cairns, who situates redress campaigns as responses to Canada's postwar experience of constitutional introspection. As Cairns argues, a country undergoing a prolonged period of constitutional rethinking — in Canada's case, a process of altering inherited practices and understandings in favour of ones better able to attract support from a multinational and pluralistic society — is likely to face demands that devising an acceptable common future requires reinterpreting the past.[2] The controversies over symbolism that have featured so prominently in this process of rethinking have also been remarkably controversial and stressful.[3] Redress politics is certainly no exception: Cairns describes it as an "adversarial, accusatory history [that] challenges the majority society through its government to reprove what are now viewed as nefarious acts committed by its ancestors."[4]

The symbolism of redress attracts the energies of social movements that seek to replace the stigma, and even the more subtle civic invisibility, produced by past humiliations with images of group honour to deploy in future civic endeavours. Historical episodes that violate contemporary standards of equal citizenship become potent political tools when they can be made to symbolize what others must learn about, understand, and then repudiate in order to produce a more satisfactory future. In 1988, for example, Japanese Canadians won an authoritative reversal of the verdict of dishonour imposed by their World War II internment. The federal government proclaimed that "the shame on [Japanese Canadians'] honour, their dignity, their rights as Canadians is now removed forever."[5] More recently, in January 1998, the Assembly of First Nations forced Ottawa to apologize for its past policy of forcing native children to attend residential schools. This struggle produced the official admission that "the contributions made by all aboriginal peoples to Canada's development ... have not been properly acknowledged."[6]

In this chapter, I focus on symbols as power resources,[7] as political signifiers that are prized or reviled for what they tell others about a collectivity's worthiness and virtue. In particular, I draw upon an ancient notion that features extensively in redress politics, the concept of honour. Until well into the early modern era, to speak of honour in citizenship was to invoke the additional judgement of respect that formally-entitled participants required if they were to be accepted by their peers as legitimate civic interactants. By invoking a conservative concept from a past era, my aim is twofold. The first is to show how "dishonour" can still be associated with an informal exclusion from the public sphere of citizen interaction. The second aim is to establish campaigns for redress as vehicles that the informally excluded employ in order to better enjoy the participation rights that citizenship aims to confer. Key to understanding the politics of redress, I argue, is the movement's attempt to accumulate a "symbolic capital"[8] of honour with which to convince suspicious or indifferent others that members of the formerly denigrated or marginalized group are worthy civic participants.

The chapter begins by surveying the various redress claims and the historical episodes from which they derive. It then proceeds to situate redress movements as campaigns of identity transformation that respond to problems of civic interaction experienced by historically stigmatized communities. Although these campaigns are often confrontational, I argue that they are potentially crucial vehicles of civic integration. As the examples of South Africa's Truth and Reconciliation Commission and the ongoing Jewish-Catholic dialogues about the Holocaust well attest, to demand apologies for past wrongdoing is also to seek more harmonious future relations with former antagonists. This point is important to consider in the case of First Nations peoples, to whom the desirability of Canadian citizenship has often seemed less than obvious. But neither can the differences between the residential schools campaign and the other redress movements be ignored. Thus, my analysis distinguishes between demanding historical atonement as an unambiguous project of citizenship inclusion and doing so as a means of assessing more cautiously the desirability of achieving such inclusion in the future.

The chapter concludes by characterizing the redress movement's emphasis on eliciting respect as an illustration of the impact of equality-seeking social movements on the twentieth-century evolution of liberal-democratic citizenship. Like the social democrats of the interwar period, who argued that the inequities of *laissez-faire* capitalism made a mockery of liberalism's promise of political equality, such "new" social movements as feminism and anti-racism offer a probing focus on how denials of respect mitigate the ideal of equal civic participation. Building on this evolutionary account, I suggest that the debate between redress movements and their critics offers a useful lens through which to consider a larger conflict between two understandings of citizenship in which Canadians have increasingly become embroiled.

One understanding emphasizes the importance of securing for previously excluded or marginalized actors the social conditions upon which meaningful opportunities for the practice of citizenship depend. Critics of this view, who have become increasingly influential in Canada as populist opponents of "special status," resent the burdens of adjustment imposed upon them by contextually-informed approaches to citizenship and, accordingly, demand the return of a rigorously formal approach to equality. The chapter concludes by arguing that the increasingly successful backlash against the egalitarian emphasis on the prerequisites of citizenship, while understandable, poses an extreme danger because it encourages Canadian citizens and their governments to avoid undertaking the important society-level work of reconciliation upon which a more inclusive and durable citizenship must rest.

REDRESS POLITICS IN CANADA

Among non-aboriginal redress movements, the successful campaign waged on behalf of the approximately 22,000 Japanese Canadians internees of World War II is the most well known. In September 1988, the National Association of Japanese Canadians received a Parliament Hill ceremony, $450 million in financial compensation and an official apology from the Conservative federal government.[9] Other movements have also demanded redress for historical wrongs, wrongs that include the World War I internment of roughly 5000 Ukrainian Canadians and the racist policies (of which the notorious "head tax" is the most widely remembered) that, until 1947, severely restricted Chinese immigration to Canada.[10]

These movements have not matched the success of their Japanese-Canadian counterpart. The National Congress of Italian Canadians was forced in 1990, after failing to win financial redress for the World War II internment of approximately 1,000 Italian Canadians, to settle for an informal, out-of-Parliament apology from Conservative Prime Minister Brian Mulroney.[11] The Congress continues to lobby the federal government for an official apology, the establishment of university chairs in Italian-Canadian studies and the payment of unspecified amounts of compensation to remaining survivors.[12] In 1993, the other non-aboriginal redress movements — most notably Canadians of Chinese and Ukrainian ancestry — ended collective redress negotiations with the Mulroney administration when it became clear that no financial compensation would be forthcoming.[13]

These groups were rebuffed entirely a year later, when the government announced its policy of refusing to offer monetary restitution or apologies of any sort.[14] In protest, the Chinese Canadian National Council has taken its claim to the United Nations, to make Ottawa face the "spectacle of elderly pioneers ... bringing forth their individual cases of human injustice before the world community."[15] The Ukrainian Canadian Civil Liberties Association, like its Italian-Canadian counterpart, continues to press its case with the federal multiculturalism ministry. The association seeks the erection of memorial plaques at all 24 former internment sites (it has persuaded Ottawa to establish two such memorials), an official parliamentary acknowledgement and $563,000 to cover the costs of documenting the internment experience.[16]

In contrast to Italian Canadians, who received an apology but no compensation, the movement seeking redress for the hundreds of Inuit who were relocated under federal government auspices in the 1950s recently experienced a setback of the opposite sort.[17] In March 1996, the Department of Indian Affairs agreed to offer $10 million in monetary compensation for the coerced relocation — which buttressed Canadian sovereignty in the High Arctic by sending the Pond Inlet and Grise Fiord Inuit thousands of kilometres north as "human flagpoles"[18] — but refused to apologize.[19] The Inuit, who wished "to try putting their misery behind them," accepted what appeared to be the government's final offer.[20] Ottawa also adopted the compensation-without-apology approach in response to First Nations' demands for atonement and restitution for a residential schools policy that, for many survivors, issued in the near-destruction of their families and languages. In December of 1997, the Department of Indian Affairs agreed to set up a $200 million fund (raised subsequently to $350 million) to help meet the health-care and counselling needs of survivors, but refused steadfastly to apologize or to accept responsibility for the residential schools fiasco.[21] But after extremely difficult negotiations with the Assembly of First Nations, the Chrétien government relented on the eve of the January 1998 reconciliation ceremony, which was its planned forum for offering its long-awaited response to the recommendations of the Royal Comission on Aboriginal Peoples. "To those of you who suffered this tragedy at residential schools," said Minister Jane Stewart, "we are deeply sorry."[22]

PAST WRONGS AND CONTEMPORARY CITIZENSHIP

Many of the past discriminatory federal policies for which redress has been sought are ones that, solely on the basis of group identity, excluded particular Canadians from some of the most basic rights of citizenship. In the case of the federal government's World War II internment operations, the denial was almost total. The vast majority of the interned "Japanese" and "Italians" were Canadian citizens who, with absolutely no proof of their disloyalty, were removed from their communities, incarcerated, forced to work without compensation and, in many cases, stripped of their homes and possessions.[23] Little wonder that Italian Canadians in World War II doubted "that they were dealing ... with a democratic state,"[24] or that Japanese Canadians now consider internment as "a betrayal of democracy itself."[25]

Like internment, other past federal policies for which redress has since been claimed also shattered communities by separating innocent individuals and their families against their will. These state actions seem clear violations of liberal citizenship's historic concern to respect the "life, liberty and security of the person." For instance, until the early 1970s the federal government's residential schools policy aimed at eliminating what authorities viewed as "backward" native cultures by, each year that the policy was in place, effecting the forcible removal of thousands of aboriginal children from their homes.[26] The 1994 Assembly of First Nations report, *Breaking the Silence*, has spoken powerfully about the damage inflicted by this policy on First Nations families and communities. Even excepting the horrific experiences of physical and sexual abuse that are now the schools' most well-known legacy, prolonged periods of near-total familial separation under authoritarian and degrading conditions meant that children who attended residential schools "found themselves becoming alone — silent and isolated and without any hope of belonging to a sensible world."[27] The ban on speaking aboriginal languages, which all the residential schools enforced, though with varying degrees of brutality, is further testimony to how thorough was this assault on First Nations communities and identities.[28]

The Inuit who were relocated from their northern Quebec homes to the High Arctic also experienced the shock of an unexpected community breakup brought about by state policy. As survivor John Amagoalik has recounted, "we just went into a panic because [the RCMP] had promised that they would not separate us."[29] Rather than fracturing an already existent Canadian community, Canada's "Chinese exclusion" policy (1885-1947), which made "married bachelors"[30] of two generations of Chinese men drawn to Canada by the lure of work and wages, worked to prevent viable Chinese-Canadian communities from forming. The onerous head tax and subsequent ban on Chinese immigration consigned these men, many of whom found themselves abandoned by the same employers who had urged them to come to Canada, to permanent separation from their wives and families. With a ratio of 2,790 men for every 100 women, there would be virtually no second Chinese-Canadian generation until well after World War II.[31]

Redress movements remember these episodes as unjust assaults launched by a hostile government and society against the very existence of their communities. As former residential school student Gilbert Oskaboose wrote "To the Government of Canada" in 1996: "when we returned to our own communities we had become strangers.... [T]he policies of assimilation ... brought pain, suffering, lost lives, vicious in-fighting, divisions, waste and sorrow."[32] Unsurprisingly, redress-seekers find it difficult to discharge with any enthusiasm the concomitant obligation that accompanies the enjoyment of citizenship; loyalty to the state within which the status has been assumed.[33] In 1984, for example, an angry Roy Miki of the National Association of Japanese Canadians told Jack Murta, the federal minister then responsible for multiculturalism: "your government instituted a policy which was meant to destroy the community, and that policy worked."[34] To seek official atonement for past injustices may thus be one way of endeavouring to reconcile citizenship's demands of loyalty with the undimmed awareness of equal citizenship denied. As one Japanese-Canadian internee remarked four years prior to the historic redress settlement of 1988: "A sense of incompleteness gnaws at me. I need to feel right about my country."[35]

Redress may also be valued for reasons of an even more purely private nature. In particular, individuals who trace severe personal and family difficulties back to past injustices may seek apologies and restitution in order to help further their often painful recoveries. Representative of this latter focus is Inuit leader Martha Flaherty's query to the Royal Commission on Aboriginal Peoples: "whether the High Arctic exiles do not deserve some recognition so that they can start the healing process and rebuilding their lives?"[36] Official repudiation of the relevant historical wrong is welcomed as evidence that the victims will find support from the wider society in their rehabilitation. One survivor, for instance, reacted to Ottawa's apology for the residential schools disaster by saying: "It's a nice feeling ... to think that the government was listening. It's certainly a better day today than it was yesterday."[37]

Although internment burdened many Japanese-Canadian survivors with psychiatric problems, and winning redress has been described as akin to having "a tumour removed,"[38] the focus on redress as an aid to personal recovery has been most evident in the residential schools campaign. With so many First Nations people suffering problems of low self-esteem and family dysfunction because of the abuse and mistreatment they experienced in residential schools, recognition of their undeserved suffering, according to the Assembly of First Nations, is valued as the "beginning of respect, of feeling that [they] are capable of making a contribution to the world."[39] This focus on the personal needs of survivors has also driven demands on behalf of former residential students for monetary compensation, which, as native filmmaker Phil Lane has argued, is necessary "to start healing, because we don't have adequate therapy, addiction treatment, child care or education."[40] Such indeed is the major emphasis of the $350 million healing package included as part of Ottawa's response to the residential schools redress campaign.[41]

REDRESS AND THE SYMBOLIC CAPITAL OF HONOUR

Demands for redress are thus in part the reaction of traumatized persons who feel that the entity responsible has now an obligation to help them overcome their suffering's ongoing contemporary manifestations. However, this focus on personal motivations leaves unexplored other important aspects of redress politics, such as the involvement in the various campaigns of persons other than the immediate victims themselves. As one business opponent of redress has rather harshly put it: "Precious few [survivors] returned to their homelands because of their treatment by Canada. It is their children and grandchildren who are claiming that redress must be made."[42] The fact that the residential schools, High Arctic relocation, World War II internment and "Chinese exclusion" redress campaigns have all been driven, if not actually led, by survivors of the relevant episodes does not mollify their critics. Nor does the fact that descendants of the immediate survivors have often spoken eloquently about the impact of their parents' torment on their own lives.[43]

More specifically, critics find it difficult to understand why, particularly given the gaps of time extending between the original occurences and the present in which redress is now sought, claimants do not seek reconciliation through the more customary routes of psychiatry or forgiving-by-forgetting. Puzzlement on this question seems to lead opponents to reduce redress politics to a cynically orchestrated attempt to raid the public purse.[44] Thus, *Winnipeg Free Press* editor John Dafoe has complained: "The theory used to be that time healed all wounds. Now there is a growing belief that time plus about $30 million might just do the job."[45] Prominent columnist Jeffrey Simpson has depicted the emphasis on financial compensation similarly, as "crass multicultural politics" that aims at forcing "today's generation to pay for policies and attitudes of generations past."[46]

But redress politics is a more complex phenomenon than such comments leave room to admit. Certainly, redress movements aim at more than simply meeting the personal needs of survivors — but noting their pronounced monetary emphasis falls glaringly short of considering adequately what these other aims may be. More useful for understanding the powerful attraction of redress is Cairns's point, that redress movements see historical contestation as their means to a "more dignified future."[47] This perspective highlights the political specificity of redress movements, as attempts to employ the unique visibility of highstakes battles over past injustices as vehicles for transforming damaged civic identities. Pursuing it further should help to bring out more clearly the relevance of redress politics for contemporary Canadian citizenship.

The advocacy literature on redress abounds with references to the public humiliation that can attach to a community even after the original episode or policy that gave rise to its initial official stigmatization has passed. According to the Chinese Canadian National Council, "having been singled out by law for unequal treatment," Chinese Canadians have been labelled as "inferior and undesirable."[48] The anniversary of 1 July 1923, the date the *Chinese Immigration (Exclusion) Act* was passed, is remembered by survivors and their descendants as "Humiliation Day."[49] For the National Congress of Italian Canadians, "Canadians of Italian origin were denigrated and discriminated against in their own country.... For that stigma there can never be sufficient compensation."[50] And Japanese Canadians, as community leader Maryka Omatsu explains, have been "scarred by our history in this country," by a "debilitating virus that ... filled me with a shame that I could not understand as a child."[51]

These comments call attention to how acts of official stigmatization, which communicate authoritatively that the stigmatized community is "disloyal" or "backward," can leave even future members of the groups so tagged with a profound feeling that their equal worth is denied, or accepted only superficially, by their "normal" anglo-celtic counterparts. The reaction of redress movements to the specifically civic dimension of this problem of social interaction is captured usefully by the concept of honour.[52] Although honour is a "protean concept, capable of many social and personal applications,"[53] here the term is most important in the former sense. As opposed to personal, or inner honour — that "most sublime of virtues" — social understandings of honour are concerned with the nature and function of perceived virtue rather than with the moral issue of whether a given person is or is not truly virtuous.[54] In the civic context, honour as a reputation for virtue designates a socially produced good whose possessors enjoy what Frank Henderson Stewart describes as a "losable right to respect."[55]

The losable right to respect that civic honour confers can be contrasted with the non-losable right to respect associated traditionally with liberalism's concern to uphold the innate dignity of the person, which, as Charles Taylor points out, recognizes and respects "a universal human potential, rather than anything a person may have made of it."[56] Thus critical theorist Axel Honneth, for instance, describes the civic honour so important in the early modern age as "what each individual [had to] *further accomplish* in order to actually attain the level of social standing collectively accorded to his or her estate."[57] This understanding of honour emphasizes that a reputation for virtue allows those so favoured to command a respectful hearing from others, while "dishonour," even for the formally included, can help to effect an informal exclusion from the circle of persons accepted as worthy partners in collective action. This notion of honour as a losable right to respect, in which demonstrated accomplishment is key, provides a useful conceptual model for explaining why receiving official atonement for past injuries has become so politically important today.

Undeserved dishonour can be experienced as an extreme form of misrecognition, which makes "outsiders," even "foreigners," of persons whose citizenship histories ought to support a quite different response. For example, Chinese-Canadian redress-seekers blame the exclusion, disfranchisement, and head-tax legislation for preventing other Canadians from relating to them as civic partners. One member of the Chinese-Canadian redress movement has remarked that despite being able to trace his Canadian family history to 1906, his children were still told to "go back to Hong Kong" while attending Simon Fraser University some 80 years hence.[58] As the Chinese Canadian National Council put it, "the bitter legacy of the Canadian government's 62 years of legislated racism is a Chinese Canadian community that is still seen as a new immigrant community."[59] A similar point has been made by the National

Association of Japanese Canadians, which found during its redress campaign that it "still had a long way to go in making ... Canadians aware that [internment] was carried out against Canadians who happened to be of Japanese ancestry, and not against Japanese nationals who happened to find themselves in Canada."[60]

From this misrecognition redress movements can trace a legacy of barriers that inhibit their ability to become, in more than a merely legal sense, equal civic participants. They speak bitterly of group histories marred by orientations to public action strikingly similar to that evinced singly by Erving Goffman's prototypically stigmatized individual, who "may perceive, usually quite correctly, that whatever others profess, they do not really 'accept' him and are not ready to make contact with him on 'equal grounds'."[61] This is a retrospective bitterness that resents the lesson of quietism drawn by the affected community from its initial experience of official stigmatization. Such episodes are often taken as cues to abstain from civic interaction, to "play it safe" lest the original harm become the basis of future experiences of disrespect. Goffman explains this fearful orientation by saying that "the very anticipation" of receiving disesteem in social encounters leads "the stigmatized to arrange life so as to avoid them."[62]

Thus, as novelist Joy Kogawa remarked during the Japanese-Canadian redress campaign, "internment worked beyond the wildest dreams of politicians. [F]orty years later, most of the people of my generation are still hiding in the woodwork and wanting to speak."[63] Omatsu, too, has written of a "passivity ... fashioned by our history in this country, that, like some invisible undertow, pulls us down on bended knees."[64] A similar reaction among Ukrainian Canadians was noticed after the World War I internment. One school principal remarked at the time that his Ukrainian-Canadian pupils, who had felt before internment that "they were really becoming Canadians[,] ... are now hurt, bewildered, shy and drawing back into their halfdiscarded alien shells."[65] Internment, according to Ukrainian Canadian Civil Liberties Association research director Lubomyr Luciuk, "conditioned the entire community to be very apprehensive about their ... status as Canadians."[66] Above all, these remembrances indicate how a citizen's formal right to public participation can be compromised significantly by the (historically justified) perception that accepted actors do not regard them with respect.

Achieving redress is thus prized as highly public and authoritative proof that the historical stigmatization of the redress movement's constituency was ill-deserved. For example, the federal government's "Statement of Reconciliation," the outcome of extensive negotiations with the Assembly of First Nations, spoke of "the assistance and spiritual values of the Aboriginal peoples who welcomed the newcomers to this continent," of "diverse, vibrant Aboriginal nations" and of "the strength and endurance of Aboriginal people"

— contributions and characteristics that "too often have been forgotten."[67] For the National Congress of Italian Canadians, redress would "restore the positive image of Italian Canadians as significant contributors to this country of ours in this century."[68] Focused particularly on securing lasting reminders of extraordinary contributions to Canada's development was the 1988 Chinese Canadian National Council redress proposal. It urged the "symbolic community redress [of] commemorative plaques dedicated to our elderly true pioneers at the site of the last spike of the Canadian Pacific Railway [and at the] House of Commons Railway Committee Room."[69]

Pursuing redress also allows the movement to display evidence of its present virtue. To display public-spirited virtue can be crucial in the arena of citizenship politics, where a heavy burden of suspicion often faces actors susceptible to construction as "special interests."[70] Accordingly, one of the most prominent themes in the advocacy literature on redress is the movement's insistence that its aim is to prevent similar racist acts from being visited on others. The National Association of Japanese Canadians emphasized that "it is as an act of citizenship and because we refuse to see democracy betrayed that we seek an honourable resolution to the injustices of the war years."[71] Similar confirmations that redress is valued as an opportunity to display altruism include the Chinese Canadian National Council's call for "a trust foundation ... to ensure that similar discriminatory government actions do not happen again"[72] and the Ukrainian-Canadian redress movement's plea to "ensure that no other ... minority in Canada will in the future experience the injustices Ukrainian Canadians did in the past."[73] Like the bygone duel of honour, in which combatants strove to demonstrate certain prized traits in order to defeat threats to their status as "gentlemen,"[74] redress campaigns seek to elicit the respect accorded "worthy" participants by demonstrating virtue.

Striking is the contrast between unrepudiated past policies that work as what Goffman calls "stigma symbols"[75] and the positive symbolism that a redress settlement may convey. Processes or events that replace negative symbolism with images of undeserved suffering overcome by group virtue are truly forms of social alchemy which, at their strongest, transform the stigma of dishonour into a symbolic capital of honour.[76] Unveiled in a moving 1988 Parliament Hill ceremony, the Japanese-Canadian redress settlement symbolized the transformation of a shamed group tagged with a reputation for disloyalty into a proud community of Canadian citizens whose activism had elicited their prime minister's "solemn commitment" that the "injustices of the past ... will never again be countenanced or repeated."[77]

The social alchemy of redress follows from its capacity to provide a capital of symbols that ratify a group's political response to its experience of historical wrongs as potent evidence of its past and present honourability. The successful Japanese-Canadian campaign produced lasting signifiers of Japanese-

Canadian honour, reminders symbolizing that the community's struggle was motivated by a concern to enhance the future well-being of other Canadians. For example, because the 1988 *Emergencies Act* — which replaced the old *War Measures Act* that had enabled the various internments — was largely a federal government response to Japanese-Canadian protests, the *Nikkei Voice* newspaper could call the new act the Japanese-Canadian community's "Gift to Canadians."[78] The establishment of the Canadian Human Rights Foundation as part of the terms of the 1988 redress settlement stands similarly as usable proof of Japanese Canadians' concern to help protect other Canadians from potential future acts of racist oppression. By no means irrelevant to its 1986 argument that a "Japanese-Canadian human rights foundation" would "help other groups ... encountering similar difficulties" in the future[79] was the imperative to present other Canadians with an ongoing and visible reminder of Japanese-Canadian virtue.

However, critics of redress ask (often with angry cynicism), why do redress movements seek "conscience money ... to appease,"[80] why do they demand "cash to expiate the perceived sins?"[81] Despite the rather narrow preoccupation that tends to animate such complaints, the question is important. After all, Conservative Multiculturalism Minister Gerry Weiner's 1993 offer of a parliamentary ceremony and formal apologies for the various movements seeking redress through his office was refused by all the groups involved, on the ground that redress without money was not redress at all.[82] The need for better health and addictions services in First Nations and Inuit communities has of course given an understandably consistent monetary emphasis to the two redress claims dealt with by the Ministry of Indian Affairs. But money is not necessarily the "concrete" opposite of symbolism in redress politics — it is in fact integral to that symbolism.

The insistence that any sincere repudiation of the racist policies of the past requires paying financial restitution in the present can be understood as a contemporary instance of money's ancient symbolic role, as a universally exchangeable equivalent used to authenticate agreements when trust is lacking.[83] With this monetary emphasis, redress movements indicate that they are willing to forgive the wrongs of the past, but only if they can elicit a persuasive indicator that those wrongs will not be repeated. One cannot, after all, be brutally robbed, accept a casual "sorry" from the absconding thief and feel with confidence that the exchange augurs well for the future. As the National Association of Japanese Canadians insisted in 1988, "significant individual compensation acknowledges the severity of the injustices [and provides] an honourable and meaningful settlement."[84] Indeed, the federal government itself emphasized at the 1988 Japanese-Canadian redress ceremony that the sincerity of its anti-racist regret was underwritten financially. The $450 million compensation package, Prime Minister Mulroney declared, "is symbolic of our determination to address this issue, not only in the moral sense but also in a tangible way."[85]

The symbolic contribution of money to redress also stems from the medium's ability to lend to an apology a certain symmetry with which to match the original misdeed. Groups whose past victimization caused them direct and significant financial hardship[86] insist that an honourable apology, one that does credit to both offender and victim, must contain an equally significant financial component. Thus, the Chinese Canadian National Council deplored the federal government's failure to offer "a symbolic sum to acknowledge the injustice of the [head] tax,"[87] while the Ukrainian Canadian Civil Liberties Association protested that a proposed memorial at a former internment site was utterly insufficient: "a small plaque, valued at $15,000, is not enough. The internees suffered substantial economic losses."[88]

But money's symbolic importance in redress is by no means exhausted by its role as the proof movements demand in order to be convinced, in their own minds and hearts, that Canada's repudiation of past wrongs is sincere. Struggles for financial redress are also oriented toward showing others that the movement's dedication and power have been sufficient to force the government to respond to the injustices of the past with more than just rhetorical declarations of future good intent. To return to the mugging analogy, accepting apologies from absconding thieves is only likely to boost one's reputation in circles where masochism is a particularly cherished value. Redress movements, then, view the importance of financial compensation through two lenses. The first sees the willingness to pay restitution as a symbol of the integrity of the state's apology: this lens seeks to determine whether governmental regret is sufficiently profound to have dictated a course of action that repudiates past misdeeds with the appropriate symmetry. The second lens through which the question of financial restitution is considered attempts to ascertain what a particular proposed settlement is likely to tell other Canadians about the movement to whom the apology has been proffered. In short, it judges the settlement's adequacy as potential symbolic capital.

Financial restitution as a form of symbolic capital became particularly important after the precedent set by the 1988 Japanese-Canadian settlement. It is, of course, commonplace to deride the "imitation factor" so often apparent in the field of what is called "ethnic" politics.[89] Redress, which has often been criticized for its potential economic cost, on the ground that "more [claimants] will probably join the queue,"[90] is certainly no exception. The notion of civic honour, which links the nature of the future social reception a group can anticipate to its externally perceived virtue, can help more adequately to explain the significance of this competitive aspect of financial restitution in redress politics. As a nineteenth-century defender of the duellist's honour so violently put it: "anyone who turns into a worm has no right to complain if

they are crushed underfoot ... [I]n this world, complete independence from
the opinions and prejudices of others is a mere chimera."[91] The point, of course,
is that being seen as successful in eliciting respect in the present can bear
crucially on how one fares in social interaction in the future.

In the wake of Japanese-Canadian success, winning financial redress has
come to be viewed as a measure of whether the group is regarded by other
Canadians as sufficiently worthy to deserve an "honourable and meaningful
settlement."[92] Failure to elicit financial compensation, it is feared, will inaugurate an unflattering symbolism that contrasts the apparent disregard with
which the unsuccessful movement's constituency has been handled with the
concrete demonstration of respect already accorded one's more successful
counterparts. Indicating how common this fear has been among redress movements are remarks such as: "redress offered to ... Japanese Canadians would
be discriminatory if it ignored the experience of the Ukrainians in Canada";[93]
"compensation [was] given to the Japanese[,] the Inuit ... deserve the same
recognition";[94] "how could the federal government redress ... other past wrongs
but not the ... Chinese Head Tax?"[95]

Other redress movements know that it is the Japanese-Canadian campaign,
and not their own, that will be recognized when visitors read the inscription
announcing that the Canadian Race Relations Foundation was established "on
behalf of the Japanese Canadian community, in commemoration of those who
suffered injustices during and after World War II."[96] Certainly, the vehement
reaction of the Chinese Canadian National Council to the Liberals' 1994 refusal to offer redress would have been inconceivable absent the backdrop of
Japanese-Canadian success. The anger of Council representative Victor Wong
resembled the 1960s reaction of those non-British anglophones who felt that
the Royal Commission on Bilingualism and Biculturalism's proposed recognition of dualism would effect a damaging symbolic erasure of their
contribution to Canadian development: "We need to respond very strongly to
this measure. It's unacceptable, unfair and racist."[97]

REDRESS AND CITIZENSHIP INCLUSION

Critics who condemn this combative emphasis argue that "the search for restitution for past wrongs ... risks piling up more division in a country already
quite divided,"[98] that "this rush for compensation for past slights and indigni-
ties is likely to open old wounds."[99] At the extreme, they see redress-seeking
as a vehicle of vengeance rather than of reconciliation: "Everybody has a hor-
ror story to tell about what used to go on. The time has now come to get
even."[100] But focusing on the notion of civic honour, which mediates "between individual aspirations and the judgment of society,"[101] suggests a more
integrative function to this conflict. In their bids for honour, redress movements

see a potential lever with which to transform the formal right to participate into a far more potent right, which they have seen so often redeemed by more fortunate others — the informal right to be heard.

A leader of the Japanese-Canadian movement has written that "the winning of redress restored honour to my community."[102] The political response of the Japanese-Canadian community to this restoration demonstrates how the social alchemy of redress can promote civic integration and increased political participation. For example, the energetic and thorough contribution made by the National Association of Japanese Canadians to the 1991-92 parliamentary hearings on the ill-fated Charlottetown constitutional proposals contrasts with the failure of most of the unsuccessful redress-seeking organizations to appear at all. The Japanese-Canadian organization presented on three different occasions to argue in support of, among others, its positions in favour of entrenching Aboriginal peoples' inherent right to self-government and recognizing Quebec as a distinct society.[103]

Crucial to this participation was a new confidence about their civic status on the part of citizens who, in Omatsu's words, had sought previously a safe public identity by adopting an "invisibility" of "fatalistic resignation" and maintaining a "low crime rate."[104] Because the successful redress campaign had replaced undeserved stigma with official acknowledgment of its constituency's virtue, the National Association of Japanese Canadians could use redress to convey in shorthand its status as a powerful organization carrying an almost unique authority with which to speak on civil liberties issues. Thus, President Art Miki began: "We were the organization that was deeply involved in achieving the redress settlement on behalf of our community."[105] As Miki suggested, because of "the things [that have] occurred to Japanese Canadians ... there may be some suggestions we can offer to strengthen the ensuring of minority rights."[106]

Most significant is that the National Association of Japanese Canadians connected explicitly the successful outcome of its redress campaign to, in President Miki's words, a growing desire on the part "of Canadians of Japanese ancestry [to contribute] to the development of a better and stronger Canada."[107] One appearance the association concluded by declaring: "We are thankful that the Canadian government has recognized the past injustices ... We feel it is now our role to ensure that other past injustices will be acknowledged and that our new Constitution will protect all of us from future violations."[108] The National Association of Japanese Canadians has indeed extended "moral support and advice" to the other redress movements,[109] which, most recently, have included participating in a conference held by the British Columbia Union of Indian Chiefs, in which the former organization provided useful and frank advice as to how the First Nations campaign might replicate Japanese-Canadian success.[110]

The stigma of dishonour can be a powerful obstacle to healthy civic involvement: viewing their stigmatization as a warning of future disrespect from others, the "dishonoured" are prone to retreat to the ostensibly safer posture of withdrawal. Therefore, to understand redress campaigns as bids to elicit a more active acceptance from others is to argue that redress-seeking may be a more healthy phenomenon than its critics suppose. Redress politics calls our attention to the presence in contemporary Canada of groups of citizens, emerging from prolonged periods of relative disengagement from civic life, that are now engaged in a course of action that aims at helping to promote the more broadly-based citizen participation whose absence contemporary analysts bemoan.[111] Far from being fissiparous threats to a common Canadian citizenship, redress movements seek to participate more effectively in the common affairs of a society in which they find history has placed them at a significant symbolic disadvantage. Indeed, for the previously dishonoured, honour in its public sense assumes value primarily as a means of forging more acceptable future relationships with former detractors. Struggles to gain the respect of past antagonists are meaningless unless one desires to undertake with them common projects in the future. Even in the case of the duel, because it was employed as an alternative to the far more uncompromising strategy of retribution, the challenged party was not only an enemy, but also a potential friend.[112]

Strategies that have securing an apology as their object reveal with particular clarity that the aim in question is reconciliation rather than rupture. An apology allows the offended party to relate positively to the offender in a way that would not be possible if the latter refused to convincingly disavow their actions. Where, for instance, a person may signal a desire to sever relations with a tormentor by demanding punishment, the apology-seeker demands reassurance that the attitudes that gave rise to the past offence have now been decisively repudiated. Like the crime victim whose condition for undertaking future relations with the mugger is receiving persuasive evidence that the former wrongdoer no longer harbours piratical intentions, redress movements premise their search for apologies on the desire to engage in future interaction with other Canadians, not on the impulse to renounce it.

This is a particularly important point to make about the residential schools redress campaign. But the caveat must first be registered that this movement cannot be portrayed unequivocally as a push for integration within the larger Canadian society. The quite different approach to the question of honour taken by the residential schools movement is a helpful guide to understanding its specificity. On those occasions when the movement has described itself as a vehicle for attaching honour to First Nations people, the context of interaction most often cited has been that of particular status Indian communities. This focus contrasts with that of the High Arctic Inuit, who stressed that the respect they sought to garner through redress was respect from non-native Canadians: prominent spokesperson Martha Flaherty has described the relocated Inuit as "Canadians who suffered for Canadian sovereignty and deserve ... recognition."[113]

This theme has not been as conspicuous in the residential schools campaign, which has been more overtly concerned to use redress as a remedy for interaction problems that it sees within First Nations communities. As the Assembly of First Nations has summarized the consensus among residential schools survivors: "people realized they needed to work on themselves first, help family next, and then their communities."[114] Recalled with painful regret are the tendencies of many abuse survivors to either shun interaction with their families and former neighbours[115] or to return only to inflict their own suffering on significant others.[116] Thus, the Assembly of First Nations has viewed *Breaking the Silence* as a means of ending a cycle of "dishonourable behaviour"[117] so as to create stronger and more healthy native communities. Encapsulating this project of achieving community solidarity through healing has been the phrase, "the honour of one is the honour of all."[118]

This tendency to focus primarily on the movement as a vehicle for producing respect and healing within First Nations communities, and to place less stress on accumulating honour as a means of achieving more effective participation within Canadian institutions, helps to point up the immense difficulty that Canada's historical legacy poses for native peoples. Canadians cannot expect First Nations to view redress in the same way as non-aboriginal movements, which have seen atonement unequivocally as a symbol of their more fully-fledged inclusion within the political community. For the First Nations campaign, redress does not inaugurate necessarily or unanimously a new chapter of integration within the Canadian polity. At least equally significant for the residential schools movement has been the understanding of redress as a precedent for bolstering future court attempts to make the federal government financially accountable to individual abuse survivors.[119]

Pointing to the immense problems bequeathed native communities by past federal policies underscores one of the most important reasons for the equivocation with which many First Nations persons view Canadian citizenship. As Darlene Johnston argues, federal government policies (like the early ban on traditional practices such as the potlach and the assimilative thrust of the residential schools policy and 1970 White Paper proposals) have produced cumulatively the lesson that achieving equal Canadian citizenship requires repudiating — or simply becoming dispossessed of — aboriginal lands, heritages, connections, and identities. It is only against this background, Johnston writes, "[that] the ambivalence and resistance that First Nations display toward Canadian citizenship [can] begin to be understood."[120]

But those who worry that the native stress on past wrongs augurs poorly for a common Canadian future should consider the potential implications if First Nations stopped attempting to discuss history with other Canadians. The analogy ought not be pushed too far, but the near-total breach in Canada Quebec

relations following the 1990 collapse of the Meech Lake Accord has also been
accompanied by a marked shift in the role played by historical grievances in
Quebec nationalism. Complaints directed at English Canada about historical
attitudes and policies toward Quebec, and particularly about the "betrayal" of
1982, were extremely prominent in the Meech debates.[121] But since Meech's
failure, angry remarks about Quebec's history in Canada seem much less appealing to English-Canadian consciences than bids to consolidate
pro-independence sentiment among Quebecers. As Charles Taylor writes:
"With the demise of Meech, something snapped.... A certain kind of compromise was for ever over."[122]

Of course, aboriginal nationalism lacks the economic and institutional advantages that make independence a far more immediate prospect for its Quebec
counterpart. But there are other alternatives to joint historical discussion that
First Nations may come increasingly to find as the only honourable basis from
which to create future relationships with Canada. These alternatives could
include, and indeed have included, engaging in campaigns of civil disobedi-
ence, launching embarassing complaints in international fora, or even — more
subtly but also indicative of an increasing apartness that would bode ill for a
common future — adopting the sullen posture of inauthentic acceptance with
which inhabitants of the former Soviet empire awaited their captor's demise.

Therefore, it is important to note that the Assembly of First Nations has
indeed sought redress as part of an attempt to "forge a more conciliatory relationship with the federal government."[123] Similarly, the co-chair of the
Nuu-chah-nulth Tribal Council, Nelson Keitlah, told the Royal Commission
on Aboriginal Peoples that an apology "would go a long way toward patching
up the differences between Canada's Indians and the federal government. When
a person hurts another person, the first thing that comes about before a friendship can start again is that [they] say, 'I'm sorry'."[124] *Breaking the Silence* has
also drawn a connection between redress and seeking greater inclusion within
the Canadian polity: "Today, First Nations are reclaiming their history and
affirming their place in Canada, a trend which includes speaking out about
their residential school experience."[125] Individual survivors, too, have recognized that pursuing redress is a move that involves the risk of adopting a certain
openness toward non-aboriginal Canadians and the federal government. At a
British Columbia redress meeting, one woman expressed this feeling by saying: "Sometimes we have to reach out.... I guess that's what we're doing here.
Trusting the government that somehow things are going to be ... dealt with."[126]

Certainly, such aboriginal organizations as the Metis National Council,
Native Women's Association of Canada and Native Council of Canada have
been angered by the fact that the program proposals contained in the reconciliation agreement seem designed primarily for on-reserve status Indians.[127]
Comparing Minister Stewart's 1998 reconciliation statement with the stronger
apology given Japanese Canadians by Prime Minister Mulroney in 1988 has

also occasioned bitterness.[128] Willie Blackwater, a former student of the Port Alberni Indian Residential School, expressed his dissatisfaction by saying: "If any kind of apology is going to have any meaning, it's got to come from the top. It meant nothing because one of Prime Minister Chrétien's flunkies gave it."[129] Others have pointed out that Stewart apologized only to those who actually attended residential schools and thus ignored the related suffering of the former students' friends and families.[130] The fact that Ottawa failed to admit responsibility and remorse for undertaking policies whose intent was cultural assimilation, and simply expressed "regret" for the abuse associated with the schools, has also invited the important criticism that the Statement of Reconciliation was intended more to assuage the guilt of non-aboriginal Canadians rather than to signal a genuine repudiation of racism and colonialism.[131] And for many, doubtless that the enormity of Canadian wrongs and aboriginal suffering simply militated against receiving the agreement with undue enthusiasm in any case.

But it is also clear that redress has been understood as a means of reaching out, of attempting to gauge the sincerity of a polity that claims to want partnership with Aboriginal peoples.[132] Thus, it is important to note that many First Nations individuals did react to the apology and healing package as an appropriate basis from which to begin reconciliation with non-native Canadians: "I felt that we didn't have hope, that this was ever going to materialize. And today it did";[133] "It's a nice feeling — after listening to the pain and hurt of so many people for so many years — to think that the government was listening. It's certainly a better day today than it was yesterday";[134] "It's a good first step";[135] "[it's] a historic step to break from the past."[136] An editorialist for the publication *Windspeaker* has summarized well the mixed First Nations reaction to Minister Stewart's Statement of Reconciliation: "The minister went miles ahead of where other colonial governments have gone. That much is true. But ... if the goal was really to put paternalism to bed and call an end to cultural suppression, we've still got miles and miles to go.... But it's a start and it's about time."[137]

Ottawa's previous refusal to admit that the residential schools policy constituted an injustice for which it would accept responsibility meant that survivors seeking healing would have to do so without Canada's recognition and active assistance. To survivors, therefore, redress symbolizes a welcome shift in non-aboriginal thinking about the residential schools issue. In the wake of Minister Stewart's apology, a First Nations person scanning the pages of *The Vancouver Sun* could find that the quotation marks used formerly to signify journalistic doubts about the veracity of his or her grievances, as in, "'Atrocities' alleged in mission schools,"[138] had now been replaced with a forthright admission: "Residential schools: A sad history of abuse."[139] It is unwarranted to expect that such symbolism will in itself alleviate the anger

and mistrust with which many First Nations people regard non-native society
and Canadian institutions. But Canada's official acceptance of responsibility
and communication of belief has already begun to make a small but not insignificant difference. In British Columbia, for instance, calls to a provincial
sexual abuse helpline from First Nations persons have doubled (up from 12 to
25 calls a day) since Minister Stewart's announcement, while approximately
50 to 60 additional former residential schools students have initiated new formal abuse complaints with the RCMP.[140] This does not mean that redress is a
workable substitute for settling land-claims agreements or that it can solve
the political impasse between demands for self-government and populist opposition to anything smacking of "special status." But it does show that a
willingness to deal with history by addressing past wrongs can help First Nations people to connect with Canadian institutions on a footing of respect. By
encouraging residential schools survivors to contact, in an environment that
portends trust and support, institutions and authorities that history has given
them good reason for distrusting, Canada has earned an opportunity to show
Aboriginal peoples that a common citizenship can provide a basis from which
to address pressing problems in concert with other Canadians.

CONCLUSION

By making respect a politicized issue of citizenship, redress movements tel-
escope into a shorter time frame (and thus make more vivid to the observer)
key elements of the project in which the so-called new social movements have
been engaged over a much longer period. Movements such as feminism, anti-
colonialism and gay rights have all sought to demonstrate the inaccuracy of
past judgements of their constituencies as "unworthy" or "incompetent," to
recover for public consideration their neglected past accomplishments and to
undertake courses of action that demonstrate their contributions to building a
better future.[141] Pithy testimony to the relevance of this comparison is the
work of symbolic contestation undertaken by lesbians and gay men, which
has furthered the transformation of former "deviants" into the inheritors of a
proud tradition that claims as members such eminent historical figures as
Sappho, da Vinci, and others. Like redress campaigns, equality-seeking social
movements have come to react against legacies of civic stigmatization by struggling to achieve the elusive status of honour, which is prized for its ability to
elicit the concrete judgement of respect that makes the promise of equal participation rights more meaningful.

Today's "identity politics" of historical revision and symbolic contestation
is the product of a long process of political learning, through which social
movements have come increasingly to look behind the formally equal participation rights of liberal-democratic citizenship to emphasize the prerequisites

of participation.[142] This was a focus pioneered by the social democrats of the mid-twentieth century, who argued for understanding social rights as necessary to extend to working-class and poor people the participation opportunities enjoyed by more fortunate actors.[143] Social movements that are organized explicitly around the politics of respect bring this emphasis on the prerequisites of equal citizenship into the sphere of symbolism, culture, and identity.[144] For instance, many feminists are concerned about sexism in language because they understand demeaning references to women in particular arenas of social interaction as signals that women are not accepted actors in those contexts. Like redress movements, the fear is that leaving prevailing symbolic repertoires unaltered will only serve to prevent one's constituency from taking its rightful place in the public sphere. Whether they argue forthrightly for symbolic recognition as a vehicle of citizenship inclusion or, as in the case of the First Nations campaign, do so in order to better gauge their prospects of achieving honourable inclusion in the future, Canadian redress movements are clearly part of an historical movement toward more demanding understandings of what equal citizenship entails.

Situating redress politics as part of the great postwar social movement against racism and colonialism might seem implicitly to suggest the ready existence of clear-cut criteria according to which the frivolous redress movement may be separated from the worthy. One might, for instance, distinguish redress claims animated by lingering, and perhaps unwarranted, perceptions of disrespect from those that aim to confront actual contemporary experiences of racism. From this perspective, then, redress claims such as those of the Italian- and Ukrainian-Canadian communities might be viewed as unjustified to the degree that their members tend no longer to face forms of disrespect that extend to direct instances of public discrimination or experiences of outright civic rudeness.[145] But it is important to understand that actors may also find their putative civic equality mitigated by a comparatively benign form of subordinate status. As Hobbes points out, "to neglect is [also] to Dishonour."[146]

Inhabiting a polity in which so many important conflicts are understood in terms of linguistic dualism, "third force" ethnic minorities often find their collective civic identities collapsed into a near-faceless membership in a larger "English Canada," an entity whose British traditions of constitutionalism and responsible government are credited for Canada's ascent from colony to nation. In the terms of a dramaturgical metaphor, the English-Canada narrative assigns leading civic roles to anglo-celtic identities while relegating, say, Eastern or Southern European players to peripheral parts irrelevant to the main line of action. Or, as one prominent Italian Canadian framed his objection to the Meech Lake Accord's emphasis on dualism: "not all the people of this country have been dealt the same constitutional card, nor have they been equally credited with being a dignified and contributing part of this country."[147] Thus, while racism and colonialism may properly be understood as proxy signals for the urgency of responding to redress claims, it is also important to keep in mind that "third force" demands for redress constitute an attempt to confront an often subtle politics of prioritization that, for these actors, impairs their civic visibility. In short, the tendency of historical patterns of inequality to furnish some groups of citizens with more promising symbolic bases of civic participation than others poses a problem that the government and citizens of Canada, if they take the notion of equal participation seriously, have a responsibility to address.

Yet the apparent widespread public opposition to the concept of "special status" indicated by the 1993 referendum defeat of the Charlottetown Accord seems part of a more general revolt in Canada against the demands imposed by contextually-informed approaches to practising citizenship. The rallying cry, "equal rights for all, special rights for none," which is now brought to bear on issues ranging from welfare "entitlements" to aboriginal fishing rights and gay-positive information in the schools, bespeaks a thoroughgoing impatience with any approach to equality that looks beyond the formal. It reacts to the postwar adjustments that have sought to make Canadian citizenship a more hospitable environment of interaction for women, French-speakers and others by saying: "No more adjustment. We've adjusted far too much already."

The chapter in this volume by Frank Graves warns powerfully against the mistake of understanding hardened citizen attitudes on issues such as wealth redistribution and official multiculturalism as a simple reflex of economic recession. I want to suggest similarly that depicting this rise in hard-line orientations as a temporary product of fiscal crisis is to ignore a phenomenon of long-run significance. Business-cycle explanations of "get-tough" attitudes are attractive, for they suggest that increased future harmony awaits only the employment boom of whose imminence finance ministers and free-market pundits seem certain. But, as I have tried to suggest by situating Canadian redress movements within the evolution of twentieth-century understandings of citizenship, the increasingly adamant opposition to any accommodation with "special interests" has far deeper roots than the current jobs crisis. Key among these roots is the tendency of newer, more challenging approaches to citizenship to place heavy demands on historically privileged actors, who have lost not just their own former "special status" in the explicit sense but find under attack the informal social honour that once attended their exalted public role as well. Indeed, the fear that politically charged historical revision might engender such a reaction can even produce opposition within the redress-seeking group itself. As one member of the National Association of Japanese Canadians explained about redress: "It's a painful subject which many [Japanese Canadians] want nothing to do with ... They fear confrontation and recrimination."[148]

Applying this evolutionary perspective on citizenship to Canada's recent proliferation of redress politics and the often hostile reactions it has received highlights a conflict between two understandings of citizenship that the balm of future prosperity is unlikely to salve. One understanding argues for including respect as a prerequisite necessary to realize the promise of equal citizen participation. Accordingly, its demands of adjustment target those who once derived valorized civic identities from the exclusion or stigmatization of "outsiders." The other understanding of citizenship emphasizes the advantages of simplicity that follow from more formalistic notions of citizenship-as-legal-status. But these advantages are not neutral in their manner of distribution. By rejecting action that aims at easing the burdens of citizen participation for marginalized actors, formalist conceptions make their own demands of adjustment, which weigh most heavily on those whose identities, accomplishments, and histories have not been traditional components in the West's stereotypical rendering of the virtuous citizen.

In this clash between formalist and more radical views of citizenship, the sympathies of the present administration in Ottawa seem increasingly clear. The federal government's 1994 refusal of the remaining non-aboriginal redress claims, the extreme reluctance with which Ottawa apologized for the residential schools policy and the prime minister's remarkable absences from the 1998 First Nations reconciliation and Nisga'a land claims ceremonies (to say nothing of his obvious antipathy to social movement protest more generally), all suggest the growing influence of the backlash against the demands imposed by contextually-informed approaches to practising citizenship. This is not to say that it is wrong to question how far the recognition of context and group histories in citizenship should go, any more than it is to argue that all redress claims are equally meritorious and that automatic acceptance is invariably the most appropriate way to respond. The respect desired by stigmatized or marginalized groups wishing to become citizen actors would be almost meaningless were it dispensed in uniform doses from above against the protests of a recalcitrant majority.

Indeed, it would be unwise to conclude without sounding a certain note of scepticism about the capacity of redress to serve as a recipe for a more inclusive citizenship. One reason for such scepticism is the unfortunate paradox that actors who lie outside Canada's anglo-celtic and francophone bourgeois male elites, but who are also unable to call upon the potential symbolic capital furnished by extraordinarily visible episodes of past oppression, may lack the historical levers of sympathy to which some comparably less discriminated-against groups have access. As Cairns points out, for example, communities that only began to immigrate to Canada in significant numbers after World War II do not have legacies of internment or head taxes for which now to claim redress and, thus, may face even greater barriers in seeking to impress forcefully their claims for recognition on the public consciousness.[149] Thus, this problem of inequality in symbolic resources amongst non-dominant actors points up the shortcomings of using redress alone as a strategy for producing a public sphere more amenable to equal citizen participation.

But such problems and shortcomings ought not to lead Canadians into dismissing redress politics as an opportunistic form of psychological irredentism that only confirms the wisdom of Trudeau's insistence that "we can only be just in our own time."[150] For accepting too readily the merits of formal equality while emphasizing the contrasting drawbacks of "special status" and a preoccupation with past sins offers a powerful stimulus to the dangerous belief that history has no moral bearing on our present. Contemporary conservatives exhibit a "like-it-or-lump-it" approach to historical grievance, which, with no small irony, denies Edmund Burke's understanding of citizenship as a partnership between the dead and the living. Wondering if "anyone [has] told France that England is sorry it burned Joan of Arc?"[151] critics of redress mutter darkly about a wrong-headed fixation on "long-forgotten administrations"[152] and "claims that go back to the Dark Ages."[153] Opposition to the recent Nisga'a land claim deal in British Columbia betrays a similar amnesia, which contrasts the "Pandora's box ... of attempting to resolve historical 'wrongs'" against the justice of living "as equals without special status for anyone."[154] Thus do some opponents of native land claims pose as defenders of "the integrity of Canadian democracy."[155]

In short, the attractive simplicity of formalism is helping to justify an often self-serving indifference toward the contemporary outcome of a legacy of oppression and conquest. When exhibited in relation to Aboriginal peoples, such indifference is more than just unseemly. But even if only the redress claims of the comparatively fortunate Italian- and Ukrainian-Canadian communities are one's object of critique, the insistence that past wrongs are unreasonable items of political discussion involves a refusal to confront a significant problem of contemporary Canadian democracy. This problem is that Canadians wishing to participate on the civic stage are to a significant extent faced with a preexisting allocation of roles according to which members of some groups enjoy a much greater capacity to command civic notice than do others. To the degree that it is through participation in democracy that we shape our futures, this question of civic honour carries an importance that goes far beyond psychological issues of self-esteem.

How, then, can Canadians better connect? The country's sheer bigness indicates an important need for instruments of connection capable of transcending the basic physical obstacles of population density and geographic scope. Citizenship can serve precisely as such an instrument of connection. It provides a basic framework of equality within which people can relate as normative equals. Its democratic rights provide the basis for creating broad communities of action that can help to found solidarities and understandings, even if these are only provisional, where none existed before. Indeed, citizenship constitutes the only terrain on which it is possible for all the adult members of the polity to participate in the querying, refining and shaping of the rules and norms by which they are to collectively live. Yet for individual citizens, redeeming equal citizenship's promise depends, in an important and too often unacknowledged sense, on being able to command the positive regard of others. For without this crucial prerequisite of successful interaction, the civic arena is a remarkably intimidating, and in extreme cases even unthinkable, forum in which to enter.

For the federal government, therefore, demands that Canada must revisit unflattering episodes and practices of its past afford an opportunity. This opportunity is to seek to realize in a more thorough and inclusive manner the potential of the most basic instrument of connectedness that we have. Struggles over respect and recognition are often discomforting, but they are premised on the desire to pursue the project of a common citizenship. Meeting this desire by seeking to foster a respectful and considered dialogue about past wrongs is a far more promising basis for lasting unity than is the growing refusal to entertain minority-group grievances about the limitations of existing Canadian modes of togetherness.

NOTES

A quite different version of this paper was presented at the annual meeting of the Canadian Political Science Association at St. Catherines, Ontario, 1996. Financial support from the Social Sciences and Humanities Research Council of Canada is gratefully acknowledged. For helpful comments, thanks go to Avigail Eisenberg, Julie Fieldhouse, F.L. Morton, John O'Grady, Veronica Strong-Boag, and to the editors and anonymous reviewers of the *State of the Federation*. Special thanks go to Alan Cairns, who first suggested redress politics as a research topic and offered generous help and encouragement along the way. The paper's defects are the author's sole responsibility.

1. Alan C. Cairns, "Whose Side is the Past On?" in *Reconfigurations: Canadian Citizenship and Constitutional Change*, ed. by Douglas E. Williams (Toronto: McClelland & Stewart, 1995). Also see Veronica Strong-Boag, "Contested Space: The Politics of Canadian Memory," Presidential Address, *Journal of the Canadian Historical Association* (1994).

2. Cairns, "Whose Side is the Past On?" pp. 20-25.

3. See, for example, C.E.S. Franks, *The Myths and Symbols of the Constitutional Debate in Canada* (Kingston: Institute of Intergovernmental Relations, Queen's University, 1993).

4. Cairns, "Whose Side is the Past On?" p. 24.

5. "Speaking Notes for the Honourable Gerry Weiner, Minister of State for Multiculturalism and Citizenship, at the Japanese Canadian Redress Agreement Press Conference," 22 September 1988. "Speaking Notes" loaned by Alan Cairns.

Subsequent materials from this source, which are also on file with the author, will be indicated by the designation, (AC).

6.   Jane Stewart, Minister of Indian and Northern Affairs, "Statement of Reconciliation: Learning From the Past," 8 January 1998. Reprinted in *The Globe and Mail* (Toronto), 8 January 1998, p. A19.

7.   Here I apply to symbolic conflict a term from Walter Korpi, *The Democratic Class Struggle* (London: Routledge and Keagan Paul, 1983).

8.   See Pierre Bourdieu, *Outline of a Theory of Practice*, trans. by Richard Nice (Cambridge: Cambridge University Press, 1977), ch. 4, "Structures, Habitus, Power: Basis for a Theory of Symbolic Power."

9.   On Japanese-Canadian internment, see Roy Miki and Cassandra Kobayashi, eds., *Justice in Our Time: Redress for Japanese Canadians* (Vancouver: National Association of Japanese Canadians, 1988). The redress agreement and Minister Weiner's and Prime Minister Mulroney's apologies are reprinted in Miki and Kobayashi, eds., *Justice in Our Time: The Japanese Canadian Redress Settlement* (Vancouver: Talon Books, 1991), pp. 138-39.

10.   On Ukrainian-Canadian internment, see Lubomyr Luciuk, *A Time for Atonement: Canada's First National Internment Operations and the Ukrainian Canadians, 1914-1920* (Kingston: The Limestone Press, 1988). On the "Chinese exclusion" policy, see B. Singh Bolaria and Peter S. Li, *Racial Oppression in Canada* (Toronto: Garamond Press, 1985), pp. 85-95. German, Sikh and Jewish Canadians have also sought redress for World War II internment, the Komagatamaru incident, and the refusal to accept Jewish refugees during World War II, respectively. Because of their comparatively low profile (they attracted very little press coverage and produced no publications on redress), these movements are not discussed here.

11.   For the apology, see "Notes for an Address by Prime Minister Brian Mulroney to the National Congress of Italian Canadians and the Canadian Italian Business Professional Association," Toronto, 4 November 1990 (AC). Details of Italian-Canadian internment are found in the National Congress of Italian Canadians, "A National Shame: The Internment of Italian Canadians" (1990) (AC). A more readily available account, though dealing only with the Quebec case, is Bruno Ramirez, "Ethnicity on Trial: The Italians of Montreal and the Second World War," in *On Guard for Thee: War, Ethnicity, and the Canadian State, 1939-1945*, ed. Norman Hillmer *et al.* (Ottawa: Minister of Supply and Services, 1988).

12.   Agata de Santis, "Canada's unknown PoWs," *Montreal Gazette*, 14 April 1997, p. A4.

13.   "Hefty price tag delays settlements," *Calgary Herald*, 1 June 1993, p. A12.

14.   Ministry of Canadian Heritage News Release, "Sheila Finestone Tables and Sends Letter on Redress to Ethnocultural Organizations," 14 December 1994 (on file with author).

15.   Victor Yukmun Wong, "An old wrong stays wrong," *The Vancouver Sun*, 13 January 1995, p. A15.

16. Eva Ferguson and Jim Cunningham, "Ukrainians [sic] to get federal hearing," *Calgary Herald*, 1 February 1997, p. B7. The complete proposal is Ukrainian Canadian Civil Liberties Association, "The Ukrainian Canadian Case for Acknowledgment and Redress," A submission to the Honourable Gerry Weiner, PC, MP, minister of state for multiculturalism and citizenship, 28 October 1988 (AC).

17. On the relocation, see Canada, Royal Commission on Aboriginal Peoples, *The High Arctic Relocation: A Report on the 1953-55 Relocation* (Ottawa: Minister of Supply and Services, 1994).

18. Jack Aubry, "Compensation urged for 'coercive' move of Inuit to High Arctic," *The Vancouver Sun*, 14 July 1994, p. A6.

19. Under the terms of a "reconciliation agreement," Ottawa "acknowledges" the "hardship" caused by the relocation and agrees to set up a $10 million High Arctic Trust to benefit the affected Inuit. The relocatees are required to agree that federal planners "were acting with honourable intentions," Ministry of Indian Affairs and Northern Development News Release, "High Arctic Relocation Reconciled," 28 March 1996 (on file with author).

20. Emanuel Lowi, "A shameful episode," *Montreal Gazette*, 6 April 1996, p. B5.

21. Erin Anderssen, "Natives to get $200-million fund," *The Globe and Mail* (Toronto), 16 December 1997, p. A1.

22. Minister Stewart, "Statement of Reconciliation."

23. Miki and Kobayashi, eds., *The Japanese Canadian Redress Settlement*, pp. 17-49; National Congress of Italian Canadians, "A National Shame," pp. 7-12.

24. Ramirez, "Ethnicity on Trial," p. 80.

25. National Association of Japanese Canadians, *Democracy Betrayed: The Case for Redress* (Vancouver: National Association of Japanese Canadians, 1984), p. 1.

26. Assembly of First Nations, *Breaking the Silence: An Interpretive Study of Residential School Impact and Healing as Illustrated by the Stories of First Nations Individuals* (Ottawa: First Nations Health Commission, 1994), pp. 13-19. More generally, see J. R. Miller, *Shingwauk's Vision: A History of Native Residential Schools* (Toronto: University of Toronto Press, 1996).

27. Assembly of First Nations, *Breaking the Silence*, p. 34.

28. On the federal government's "assimilative linguistic campaign," see Miller, *Shingwauk's Vision*, p. 200; and Celia Haig-Brown, *Resistance and Renewal: Surviving the Indian Residential School* (Vancouver: Tillacum Library, 1988), esp. pp. 51-54.

29. Quoted in Alan R. Marcus, *Out in the Cold: The Legacy of Canada's Inuit Relocation Experiment in the High Arctic* (Copenhagen: International Work Group for Indigenous Affairs, 1992), p. 21.

30. Bolaria and Li, *Racial Oppression in Canada*, p. 94.

31. Chinese Canadian National Council, *It is Only Fair! Redress for the Head Tax and Chinese Exclusion Act* (Toronto: Chinese Canadian National Council, 1988) (AC), p. 14; Bolaria and Li, *Racial Oppression in Canada*, p. 95.

32. Gilbert Oskaboose, "To the Government of Canada," *The First Perspective*, December 1996, p. 4.

33. See Derek Heater, *Citizenship: The Civic Ideal in World History, Politics and Education* (London: Longman, 1990), p. 2.

34. Quoted in Miki and Kobayashi, eds., *The Japanese Canadian Redress Settlement*, p. 132.

35. Frank Moritsugu, quoted in Miki and Kobayashi, eds., *Redress for Japanese Canadians*, p. 15.

36. Quoted in Canada, Royal Commission on Aboriginal Peoples, *The High Arctic Relocation: Summary of Supporting Information* (Vol. I) (Ottawa: Minister of Supply and Services, 1994), p. 77.

37. Charlene Belleau, quoted in Janet Steffenhagen, "Apology to abused natives elicits powerful emotions," *The Vancouver Sun*, 8 January 1998, p. A3.

38. Joy Kogawa, *Itsuka* (Toronto: Penguin, 1992), p. 276.

39. Assembly of First Nations, *Breaking the Silence*, p. 125.

40. Quoted in Suzanne Fournier, "Abused natives seek $1 billion," *The Province* (Vancouver), 4 December 1997, p. A3.

41. See Peter O'Neil, "Natives say Ottawa's apology may sway judges in civil suits," *The Vancouver Sun*, 8 January 1998, p. A1.

42. Arthur Drache, "Little basis for redress of long past injustices," *The Financial Post*, 6 September 1990, reprinted in Lubomyr Luciuk, ed., *Righting an Injustice: The Debate Over Redress for Canada's First National Internment Operations* (Toronto: The Justinian Press, 1994), p. 84.

43. A good example is Omatsu's discussion of how internment affected her relationship with her father, *Bittersweet Passage*, p. 39.

44. A particularly hostile reaction to the residential schools campaign, "Residential schools and the electric chair," can be found in *Western Report*, 22 August 1994, p. 37.

45. John Dafoe, "The cash that heals wounds," *Winnipeg Free Press*, 19 August 1994, p. A6.

46. Jeffrey Simpson, "The trouble with trying to compensate groups for historical wrongs," *The Globe and Mail* (Toronto), 14 June 1990, reprinted in Luciuk, ed., *Righting an Injustice*, p. 78.

47. Cairns, "Whose Side is the Past On," p. 24.

48. Chinese Canadian National Council redress pamphlet, "Then, Now and Tomorrow," September 1988 (AC), 11. Quoted in Cairns, "Whose Side is the Past On?" p. 23.

49. F.J. McEvoy, "'A Symbol of Racial Discrimination': The Chinese Immigration Act and Canada's Relations with China, 1942-1947," *Canadian Ethnic Studies* 3 (1982), p. 26. Also see Chinese Canadian National Council, *It is Only Fair*, p. 13. The 1923 legislation replaced the earlier $500 head tax with a ban on Chinese immigration, mandatory registration of all persons of Chinese ancestry in Canada and severe restrictions on Chinese-Canadian mobility within Canada, ibid., pp. 12-13.

50. National Congress of Italian Canadians, "A National Shame," p. 21.

51. Omatsu, *Bittersweet Passage*, p. 39.

52. Honour's obsolescence has been proclaimed by (among others) sociologist Peter Berger ("On the Obsolescence of the Concept of Honor," in Peter Berger, Brigitte Berger and Hansfried Kellner, *The Homeless Mind: Modernization and Consciousness* [New York: Vintage Books, 1973]), a judgement with which Charles Taylor has recently concurred ("The Politics of Recognition," in Charles Taylor and Amy Gutmann, eds., *Multiculturalism: Examining the Politics of Recognition* [Princeton: Princeton University Press, 1994]). It is hoped that the examples and arguments contained herein are at least sufficient to register persuasively a certain qualification to these judgements.

53. Geoffrey Best, *Honour Among Men and Nations: Transformations of an Idea* (Toronto: University of Toronto Press, 1982), p. xi.

54. Social and personal conceptions of honour are often, of course, closely related: Clinton's apparent lack of honourability may augur poorly for how the American electorate perceives his presidency. But, as Machiavelli is most famous for observing, too much personal honourability can ruin one's honour in the socio-political sense; Joe Clark's prime ministership seemed plagued by this problem.

55. Frank Henderson Stewart, *Honor* (Chicago: University of Chicago Press, 1994), pp. 21-23.

56. Taylor, "The Politics of Recognition," p. 41.

57. Axel Honneth, *The Struggle for Recognition: The Moral Grammar of Social Conflicts*, trans. by Joel Anderson (Cambridge: Polity Press, 1995), p. 123, my emphasis.

58. Gim Wong, quoted in Kim Bolan, "Liberal's [sic] refusal to redress head tax 'betrays' Chinese-Canadians' trust," *The Vancouver Sun*, 15 December 1994, p. A3.

59. Quoted in Kim Bolan, "Chinese group [sic] asks UN to act on redress," *The Vancouver Sun*, 22 March 1995, p. B3.

60. Miki and Kobayashi, eds., *The Japanese Canadian Redress Settlement*, p. 80.

61. Erving Goffman, *Stigma: Notes on the Management of Spoiled Identity* (New York: Touchstone, 1986), p. 7.

62. Ibid, p. 12.

63. Quoted in Miki and Kobayashi, eds., *Redress for Japanese Canadians*, p. 10.

64. Omatsu, *Bittersweet Passage*, p. 69.

65. Quoted in John Herd Thompson, "The Enemy Alien and the Canadian General Election of 1917," in *Loyalties in Conflict: Ukrainians in Canada During the Great War,* ed. Frances Swyripa and John Herd Thompson (Edmonton: Canadian Institute of Ukrainian Studies, 1983), p. 40.

66. Quoted in "Ukraine: In the shadow of Lenin: 'Enemy aliens' remember," *Edmonton Journal*, 8 October 1988, p. F5 (AC).

67. Minister Stewart, "Statement of Reconciliation."

68. National Congress of Italian Canadians, "A National Shame," p. 21.

69. Chinese Canadian National Council, "Resolution of Chinese Canadian National Council at 1991 National Meeting" (AC).

70. See Iris Marion Young, *Justice and the Politics of Difference* (Cornell: Cornell University Press, 1990), ch. 4, "The Ideal of Impartiality and the Civic Public."

71. National Association of Japanese Canadians, *Democracy Betrayed*, p. 1.

72. Chinese Canadian National Council, *It is Only Fair*, p. 21.

73. Ukrainian Canadian Civil Liberties Association brief, "A Time for Atonement" (1988) (AC).

74. The duel must not be confused with vengeance, for its most important function was to provide a means of reconciliation and reputation-saving for persons — usually, though not always, men — involved in potentially unseemly public disputes. On the duel of honour in the antebellum American South, see Kenneth Greenberg, *Masters and Statesmen: The Political Culture of American Slavery* (Baltimore: The Johns Hopkins University Press, 1988), ch. 2, "The Duel as Social Drama." For Germany, where duelling was, well into the nineteenth century, employed as a potential vehicle of upward mobility by ambitious middle-class men, see Ute Frevert, *Men of Honour: A Social and Cultural History of the Duel*, trans. by Anthony Williams (Cambridge: Polity Press, 1995).

75. Goffman, *Stigma*, p. 43.

76. On symbolic capital as a medium of social alchemy, see Bourdieu, *Outline of a Theory of Practice*, p. 192.

77. "Notes for an Address by the Right Honourable Brian Mulroney, P.C., M.P., Prime Minister of Canada, on Japanese-Canadian Redress," House of Commons, 22 September 1988 (AC).

78. See Miki and Kobayashi, eds., *The Japanese Canadian Redress Settlement*, p. 121.

79. National Association of Japanese Canadians, Presentation to the House Standing Committee on Multiculturalism, *Minutes of Proceedings and Evidence*, No. 9, 27 May 1986, p. 10.

80. "Post no bills," *The Ottawa Sun*, 10 November 1988, reprinted in Luciuk, ed., *Righting an Injustice*, p. 50.

81. Drache, "Little basis for redress," in Luciuk, ed., *Righting an Injustice*, p. 84.

82. "Hefty price tag delays settlements," *Calgary Herald*, 1 June 1993, p. A12.

83. Noting the historic existence of closed communities with highly developed modes of production but no money, Marx argues that money "originally appears, rather, in the connection of ... different communities with one another, not in the relations between the different members of a single community," Karl Marx, *Grundrisse*, in *The Marx-Engels Reader*, ed. Robert C. Tucker (New York: Norton, 1978), p. 239. Also see Bourdieu, *Outline of a Theory of Practice*, p. 173.

84. Miki and Kobayashi, eds., *Redress for Japanese Canadians*, p. 7.

85. "Notes for an Address by the Right Honourable Brian Mulroney on Japanese-Canadian Redress."

86. To give just two examples, the Chinese Canadian National Council has reported that between 1885 and 1923, Chinese immigrants to Canada paid $23 million in head taxes, or over $1 billion in current dollars, *It is Only Fair*, p. 23. The Price-Waterhouse accounting firm has estimated that the federal government confiscated $450 million in current dollars from interned Japanese Canadians, see Miki and Kobayashi, eds., *The Japanese Canadian Redress Settlement*, p. 93.

87. Chinese Canadian National Council, quoted in "Hefty price tag delays settlements," *Calgary Herald*, 1 June 1993, p. A12.

88. Lubomyr Luciuk, "Time to correct injustice," *Winnipeg Free Press*, 17 October 1994, p. A7.

89. A sensitive discussion of inter-group comparisons in Canadian constitutional politics is Alan C. Cairns, "Political Science, Ethnicity, and the Canadian Constitution," in *Federalism and Political Community: Essays in Honour of Donald Smiley*, ed. David Shugarman and Reg Whitaker (Peterborough, Ont.: Broadview Press, 1989), pp. 120-26.

90. Patrick O'Flaherty, "Grievances from the grave," *Western Report* 34, September 1993, p. 15.

91. Heinrich Alexander von Oppen, quoted in Frevert, *Men of Honour*, p. 22.

92. Miki and Kobayashi, eds., *Redress for Japanese Canadians*, p. 7.

93. Lubomyr Luciuk, Civil Liberties Commission of the Ukrainian Canadian Committee, Presentation to the House Standing Committee on Multiculturalism, *Minutes of Proceedings and Evidence*, No. 11, 12 August 1987, p. 49.

94. Martha Flaherty, quoted in Royal Commission on Aboriginal Peoples, *The High Arctic Relocation: Summary of Supporting Information* (Vol. I), p. 77.

95. Victor Yukmun Wong, "An old wrong stays wrong," *The Vancouver Sun*, 13 January 1995, p. A15.

96. On the foundation, see Audrey Kobayashi, "The Japanese-Canadian Redress Settlement and its Implications for 'Race Relations'," *Canadian Ethnic Studies* 1 (1992): 1-19.

97. Quoted in Kim Bolan, "Liberal's [sic] refusal to redress head tax 'betrays' Chinese-Canadians' trust," *The Vancouver Sun*, 15 December 1994, p. A3. On the commission and the reaction of the "third force" minorities, see Raymond Breton, "Multiculturalism and Canadian Nation-Building," in *The Politics of Gender,*

Ethnicity and Language in Canada, ed. Alan C. Cairns and Cynthia Williams (Toronto: University of Toronto Press, 1985), p. 44.

98. Simpson, "The trouble with trying to compensate groups for historical wrongs," in Luciuk, ed., *Righting an Injustice*, p. 79.

99. Christopher Dafoe, "Lining up for compensation," *Winnipeg Free Press*, 22 October 1988, reprinted in Luciuk, ed., *Righting an Injustice*, p. 40.

100. Ibid.

101. Julian Pitt-Rivers, "Honor," *International Encyclopedia of the Social Sciences*, Vol. 6, (New York: Macmillan, 1968), p. 503.

102. Omatsu, *Bittersweet Passage*, p. 9.

103. The National Association of Japanese Canadians appeared before the Special Joint Committee on a Renewed Canada on 31 October 1991, 4 November 1991, and 11 December 1991. The Ukrainian Civil Liberties Association and the Chinese Canadian National Council failed to appear, while the National Congress of Italian Canadians, in a joint appearance with the Canadian Jewish Congress and Hellenic Canadian Congress, spoke only for half a page, and then only in response to a committee members' question (see Special Joint Committee on a Renewed Canada, *Minutes of Proceedings and Evidence*, No. 58, 3 February 1992). The as-then unsuccessful Inuit Tapirisat of Canada and Assembly of First Nations did appear, no doubt because of the crucial aboriginal interests at stake.

104. Omatsu, *Bittersweet Passage*, p. 67.

105. National Association of Japanese Canadians, Presentation to the Special Joint Committee on a Renewed Canada, *Minutes of Proceedings and Evidence*, No. 16, 4 November 1991, p. 53.

106. Ibid., No. 29, 11 December 1991, p. 16.

107. Ibid., p. 18.

108. Ibid.

109. Bob Bergen, "Plea for redress," *Calgary Herald*, 30 March 1997, p. A1.

110. Art Miki, "Japanese Canadian Redress Strategy," in Provincial Residential Schools Project, *Chiefs' Special Assembly on Residential Schools*, proceedings held in Vancouver, BC, 25-26 March 1996.

111. See Will Kymlicka and Wayne Norman, "Return of the Citizen: A Survey of Recent Work on Citizenship Theory," *Ethics* 2 (1994): 352-81.

112. Frevert, *Men of Honour*, p. 24.

113. Martha Flaherty, quoted in Royal Commission on Aboriginal Peoples, *Summary of Supporting Information, Volume I*, p. 77.

114. Assembly of First Nations, *Breaking the Silence*, p. i. Also see the views of survivors canvassed in Nuu-chah-nulth Tribal Council, *Indian Residential Schools: The Nuu-chah-nulth Experience* (Vancouver: Nuu-chah-nulth Tribal Council, 1996), pp. 172-89.

115. See Assembly of First Nations, *Breaking the Silence*, on "running away" as a response to "shaming and humiliation," pp. 93-97.

116. See, for example, the abuse survivors quoted in Susan Lazaruk, "77-year-old pedophile sentenced to 11 years," *Windspeaker* 2 (June 1995), p. 3.

117. Assembly of First Nations, *Breaking the Silence*, p. 55.

118. Ibid., p. 159.

119. See Peter O'Neil, "Natives say Ottawa's apology may sway judges in civil suits," *The Vancouver Sun*, 8 January 1998, p. A1; Paul Barnsley, "Minister anticipates changes in department," *Windspeaker* 8 (December 1997), p. 3.

120. Darlene Johnston, "First Nations and Canadian Citizenship," in *Belonging: The Meaning and Future of Canadian Citizenship,* ed. William Kaplan (Montreal and Kingston: McGill-Queen's University Press, 1993), p. 349.

121. See Alan C. Cairns, "Passing Judgement on Meech Lake," in *Disruptions: Constitutional Struggles, from the Charter to Meech Lake,* ed. Douglas Williams (Toronto: McClelland & Stewart, 1991), pp. 226-29.

122. Charles Taylor, "Shared and Divergent Values," in *Options for a New Canada,* ed Ronald L. Watts and Douglas M. Brown (Toronto: University of Toronto Press, 1991), pp. 65-66.

123. Erin Anderssen and Edward Greenspon, "Federal apology fails to mollify native leaders," *The Globe and Mail* (Toronto), 8 January 1998, p. A4.

124. Quoted in "Apologize for residential schools says Indian leader," *The First Perspective* 1 (March 1997), p. 1.

125. Assembly of First Nations, *Breaking the Silence*, p. 2.

126. Phyllis Chelsea, quoted in Penny Gummerson, "Residential school inquiry releases report," *Raven's Eye*, 3 July 1997, p. 3.

127. "The money will be used to finance healing centres, native-language training and counselling programs on reserves," Erin Anderssen, "Natives to get $200-million fund," *The Globe and Mail* (Toronto), 16 December 1997, p. A1. For the reaction, see Erin Anderssen and Edward Greenspon, "Federal apology fails to mollify native leaders," *The Globe and Mail* (Toronto), 8 January 1998, p. A4.

128. "Aboriginal leaders also criticized the statement for not being nearly as strong as the apology former prime minister Brian Mulroney offered to Japanese [sic] interned in Canada during the Second World War," Peter O'Neil, "Natives say Ottawa's apology may sway judges in civil suits," *The Vancouver Sun*, 8 January 1998, p. A1.

129. Quoted in Paul Barnsley, "Apology, a compromise," *Windspeaker* 10 (February 1998), p. 4.

130. "Ottawa acknowledges mistakes," ibid., p. 2.

131. Psychologist Roland Chrisjohn has expressed this criticism: "Nowhere in the *Statement of Reconciliation* does the government admit it was the intention of the federal policies to assimilate. [It] is an attempt to turn that page before anyone can read it," quoted in Paul Barnsley, "*Gathering Strength* not strong enough," ibid., p. 3.

132. For evidence of this dynamic, see the account of Indian Affairs Minister Jane Stewart's advocacy of partnership and of the suspicious response of the First Nations journalists to whom Stewart was speaking, in Paul Barnsley, "Minister anticipates changes in department," *Windspeaker* 8 (December 1997), p. 3.

133. Jeri Sparrow, quoted in Janet Steffenhagen, "Apology to abused natives elicits powerful emotions," *The Vancouver Sun*, 8 January 1998, p. A3.

134. Charlene Belleau, quoted in ibid.

135. Ron Arcand, quoted in Brian Laghi, "Residential school left lasting scars," *The Globe and Mail* (Toronto), 8 January 1998, p. A4.

136. Phil Fontaine (head of the Assembly of First Nations), quoted in Janet Steffenhagen, "Apology to abused natives elicits powerful emotions," *The Vancouver Sun*, 8 January 1998, p. A3.

137. "Give us strength," *Windspeaker* 10 (February 1998), p. 6.

138. Jack Aubry, "'Atrocities' alleged in mission schools," *The Vancouver Sun*, 8 August 1994, p. A1.

139. "Residential schools: A sad history of abuse," *The Vancouver Sun*, 8 January 1998, p. A3.

140. Stewart Bell, "Abuse claims soar in wake of apology," *The Vancouver Sun*, 27 January 1998, p. A1. "Some of the callers want to know how they can get their share of the $350 million, but most are asking what counselling help is available and how to initiate criminal charges against their abusers," ibid.

141. See, for example, Young, *Justice and the Politics of Difference*, ch. 6, "Social Movements and the Politics of Difference"; Paul Colomy and J. David Brown, "Goffman and Interactional Citizenship," *Sociological Perspectives* 3 (1996):371-81; Cairns, "Whose Side is the Past On?" pp. 27-28.

142. Honneth, *The Struggle for Recognition*, pp. 115-17.

143. The classic scholarly statement of this position is T.H. Marshall, "Citizenship and Social Class," in *Class, Citizenship and Social Development*, ed. Seymour Martin Lipset (Garden City, NY: Doubleday, 1964).

144. This is not to say that culture and identity have been irrelevant to working-class movements, only that the explosion of identity-oriented social movements in the postwar West has made the emphasis far more pronounced and explicit. On the role of culture in Canadian socialist and working-class politics, see Bryan Palmer, *Working-Class Experience: The Rise and Reconstitution of Canadian Labour, 1800-1980* (Toronto: Butterworth, 1983).

145. Thanks to one of this publication's anonymous reviewers for pointing out this important implication of the distinction between perceived and actual disrespect.

146. Thomas Hobbes, *Leviathan* (Cambridge: Cambridge University Press, 1991), p. 64.

147. Liberal MP Sergio Marchi, quoted in Cairns, "Political Science, Ethnicity, and the Canadian Constitution," p. 124.

148. Dr. Wesley Fujiwara, quoted in Alfred Holden, "Backlash feared by Japanese [sic] over compensation bid," *Toronto Star*, 21 January 1985, p. A2.

149. Alan Cairns, personal communication with author.

150. Pierre Trudeau, defending the 1969 White Paper, quoted in Sally Weaver, *Making Canadian Indian Policy* (Toronto: University of Toronto Press, 1981), p. 179.

151. "Good Guys," *The Ottawa Sun*, 23 May 1991, reprinted in Luciuk, ed., *Righting an Injustice*, p. 100.

152. Drache, "Little Basis for Redress of Long Past Injustices," reprinted in ibid., p. 85.

153. Progressive Conservative MP Don Blenkarn, quoted in Tom Philip, "Haunted by history: Ukrainians, Italians and Chinese [sic] seek redress for historical ill-treatment by Ottawa," *Alberta Report*, 17 December 1990, reprinted in ibid., p. 94.

154. Adrian Lipsey, letter to the editor, *The Vancouver Sun*, 28 July 1998, p. A10.

155. Trevor Lautens, "Let's preserve the integrity of Canadian democracy," *The Vancouver Sun*, 1 August 1998, p. A23.

11

English and French and Generation X: The Professional Values of Canadian Journalists

David Pritchard and Florian Sauvageau

En s'appuyant sur les résultats d'un sondage conduit auprès de 554 journalistes canadiens choisis au hasard, on s'attarde dans ce chapitre aux différences entre les journalistes anglophones et francophones, entre ceux travaillant pour Radio-Canada/ CBC et ceux oeuvrant dans les médias privés de même qu'entre ceux appartenant à la génération X et leurs aînés. Les résultats semblent indiquer l'existence d'un «credo» journalistique largement partagé par les journalistes canadiens. La précision du traitement et la rapidité à communiquer l'information sont les principaux éléments de ce credo. Les résultats du sondage montrent que les journalistes anglophones et francophones posent un regard fort semblable sur leur profession, bien qu'aucun groupe ne démontre d'intérêt envers les médias de l'autre langue. Les résultats du sondage soulignent d'importantes différences entre les journalistes de Radio-Canada/CBC et ceux travaillant dans les médias privés, notamment quant à l'aspect commercial du journalisme. Les différences les plus importantes se trouvent entre les journalistes de la génération X et leurs aînés. Les plus jeunes tendent à être plus conservateurs, moins scolarisés, moins orientés vers les médias de prestige et accordent moins d'importance à la précision dans le traitement de l'information.

At the end of World War II novelist Hugh MacLennan published *Two Solitudes*,[1] a story about relationships between French and English Canadians whose title has become a familiar metaphor for what many Canadians believe is the country's principal cultural fault line.

At the end of the Cold War another Canadian, Douglas Coupland, published a novel that described cleavages in the world he perceived. The book, *Generation X: Tales for an Accelerated Culture*,[2] not only gave a name to a generation of young adults but suggested that generations were a fundamental source of social and cultural identity.

Social scientists have confirmed the importance of generational affiliations. Pollster Michael Adams, in a 1997 book analyzing Canadian social values, went so far as to write: "Far greater divisions exist among the generations than between anglophones and francophones. If there are in fact two solitudes in Canada, they are the young and the old."[3]

As Canadian society changes, of course, so does Canadian journalism. The people who reported on the tumultuous (and, to many, exciting) 1960s and 1970s are leaving newsrooms, and a younger generation with a somewhat different conception of journalism is moving into positions of prominence. The passing of the torch is taking place during a time of increasing concentration of ownership in privately owned media and at the end of a decade of major budget cuts at the Canadian Broadcasting Corporation/Société RadioCanada, an institution created in part to help Canada's various "solitudes" understand each other.

These changes have important social and political implications, because journalists play major political roles in democratic societies by serving as vital communication links not only between the governors and the governed but between different groups and regions. This linking function of journalism (and of the mass media generally) has special relevance to Canada, where the ties that bind citizens together are strained by the immense size of the country, its strong regional nature, and its lack of a common language and culture. More broadly, the news stories journalists choose to tell influence how a society comes to understand itself. It is not an overstatement to assert that Canadian society cannot fully be understood unless its journalism and journalists are understood.

Unfortunately, very few national surveys of journalists have been conducted in Canada, and those that do exist are limited in scope. One striking fact that emerges from a review of the existing studies is that scholars of journalism in Canada tend to speak only to members of their own linguistic community. Quite literally none of the national or regional studies of journalists published before 1998, for example, cited research on Canadian journalists that was published in the other official language — a stark example of how Canada's media scholars tend to exist in two solitudes. Such mutual ignorance not only impedes a full understanding of Canadian journalism but increases the likelihood that scholars from one linguistic community will fail to grasp the richness and complexity of journalism in the other.

In the absence of representative data about Canada's news people, it is inevitable that ideas about the country's journalists will be based largely on subjective impressions, often those of politicians or pundits who have strong (and generally critical) opinions about why the news media covered a given issue in a given way. As interesting and entertaining as the subjective impressions may be, the lack of systematic evidence makes it difficult to assess the validity of widely held notions about Canadian journalists. For example, is it true, as many believe, that French-Canadian journalists are less devoted to factual reporting than their English-language counterparts? Or that "lefties pervade its [CBC's] producer ranks," as Diane Francis, editor of *The Financial Post*, put it?[4]

We designed a survey to help answer such questions with evidence. Our data came from telephone interviews with 554 randomly selected journalists,[5] including an oversample of 50 francophone journalists from Quebec.[6] The sample included journalists from all kinds of news organizations — those who work at weekly newspapers as well as those who work at metropolitan dailies, those who work at tiny radio stations as well as those who work for CBC/Radio-Canada. Journalists turned out to be willing survey respondents. Only 36 refused to take part in the survey, resulting in a response rate of 94 percent. We ended up with 51 respondents from news organizations in the Atlantic provinces, 146 (including the oversample of 50) from Quebec, 206 from Ontario, 88 from the Prairie provinces and the territories, and 63 from British Columbia.

OVERALL RESULTS

We estimated that Canada had about 12,000 full-time journalists at the time our survey was conducted in 1996. About half of them worked in print journalism, the other half worked in radio or television. Specifically, 30 percent of Canada's journalists work at daily newspapers, 27 percent in radio, 22 percent in television, 18 percent at weekly newspapers, and 3 percent at other kinds of news organizations (represented in our survey by wire services and news magazines). No previous survey of journalists included those at weekly newspapers and most have ignored radio journalists, two groups who together account for 45 percent of Canada's journalists.[7] A substantial proportion of Canada's journalists — about 19 percent, according to our survey — work for CBC/Radio-Canada.

Table 1 provides a brief description of Canada's journalists. The typical journalist is a man (72 percent) at the beginning of middle age (about 40 years old) who has a university degree (56 percent), works in a unionized newsroom (63 percent), and who in 1995 made a little more than $49,000 from his news work. Like Canadians in general, journalists as a group perceive themselves to be politically left of centre (rating themselves at 36 on a 100-point scale where 0 means "very progressive" and 100 means "very conservative").[8] We also found Canadian journalists to be less cynical than many observers believe. Although most journalists say it is important to be sceptical of public officials and business, most also said that the chance to help people and the opportunity to make a community a better place were important.

Table 1:   Profile of Canadian Journalists, by Media Sector

	Dailies	Weeklies	TV	Radio	Other	Overall
Age (years)	42.0	36.2	41.1	38.2	38.6	39.7
Experience (years)	17.6	11.6	17.0	14.1	13.3	15.3
Sex (% male)	77%	66%	64%	76%	70%	72%
Conservative (max=100)	31	39	36	40	33	36
News room is unionized	83%	9%	87%	53%	89%	63%
Income from media (1995)	$57,150	$30,150	$59,100	$43,950	$55,050	$49,050
University degree	65%	41%	61%	49%	87%	56%
N (weighted)	151	91	113	134	15	504

Men outnumber women in all media sectors, but by the biggest margin in daily newspapers (77 percent male) and radio (76 percent male) and by the smallest in television (64 percent male) and weekly newspapers (66 percent male). Daily newspaper journalists are the most politically progressive journalists, those who work in radio and at weekly newspapers the least progressive (but still perceiving themselves to be left of centre). Weekly newspaper journalists place the greatest emphasis on helping others and making the community a better place.

Salaries are highest in television ($59,100) and daily newspapers ($57,150) and lowest in weekly newspapers ($30,150). Salaries are closely related to whether a newsroom is unionized. Levels of unionization in daily newspapers, television, and "other" (wire services, magazines) range from 83 to 89 percent; average salaries in those places ranged from $55,000 to nearly $60,000. Only about half of radio newsrooms, where salaries average $43,950, are unionized. Fewer than 10 percent of weekly newspapers are unionized, helping to explain the very low average salaries at such papers.

We also found that Canadian journalists share a set of core beliefs which can be construed as constituting a sort of unwritten "credo" of Canadian journalism. Our survey asked journalists to rate each of 14 journalistic functions on a 1-to-4 scale, where 1 meant "not at all important," 2 meant "somewhat important," 3 meant "quite important," and 4 meant "very important." Table 2 not only shows the average scores on each function, but provides the proportion of journalists who considered each function to be very important.

Table 2:   *Respondents' Views of the Importance of 14 Journalistic Functions*

	Proportion who Say it Is "Very Important" to:	Average Score on the Item (Maximum=4)
Accurately report the views of public figures	86.2%	3.82
Get information to the public quickly	79.6%	3.75
Give ordinary people a chance to express views	77.6%	3.70
Investigate government and public institutions	73.5%	3.68
Provide analysis of complex problems	68.0%	3.58
Discuss policy while it is being developed	57.2%	3.41
Focus on news of the widest possible interest	48.8%	3.24
Be sceptical of the actions of public officials	48.5%	3.20
Be sceptical of the actions of businesses	44.1%	3.12
Develop the public's cultural interests	26.0%	2.71
Increase circulation or ratings	25.3%	2.70
Provide entertainment and relaxation	21.7%	2.60
Influence public opinion	7.2%	2.04
Set the political agenda	3.5%	1.73
N (weighted)	504	504

Five functions were clearly more important than the others: (a) accurately reporting the views of public figures, (b) getting information to the public quickly, (c) letting ordinary people express their views, (d) investigating the activities of government and public institutions, and (e) providing analysis and interpretation of complex problems. These are the concepts that two-thirds or more of Canadian journalists believe to be very important. Heading the list is accurate reporting. If there is a single unshakable article of faith among Canadian journalists it is accuracy.

TWO CULTURES, TWO JOURNALISMS?

The conventional wisdom in much of Canada is that French-language journalists are more likely than their English-speaking *confrères* to allow their personal opinions to guide the content of news stories. A more nuanced variation on this theme comes from Lysiane Gagnon, well-known columnist at *La Presse* in Montreal. Gagnon has written that the French-Canadian press inherited a style and direction from France's journals of opinion, resulting in a "predominance of analysis, as opposed to simple reporting of events" and "the tendency to treat matters conceptually rather than in terms of people and events."[9]

In an important university textbook, political scientist Arthur Siegel provides a similar view. He notes that "the newspaper system in Quebec today is, by and large, North American in style, with an emphasis on objective journalism." Nevertheless, Siegel also highlights presumed differences between French- and English-language newspapers: "Whether under the surface or quite openly, it [the French-language press] retains its intense political involvement. The press of opinions may have disappeared, but the opinions remain; the great journalists of the French-language press are more editorialists than reporters, in a continuation of the need to 'form' rather than 'inform.'"[10] In 1981, the Royal Commission on Newspapers stated as fact that "French-language journalists — like the priest or politician — saw themselves as invested with a certain nationalist mission."[11]

Differences in style between anglophone and francophone journalists might be nothing but a curiosity except for the emergence of a powerful independence movement in Quebec in the 1970s. By the time the Parti Québécois (PQ) won power in the 1976 elections, it was no secret that many francophone journalists in the province supported independence.[12] Many observers came to believe that the personal preferences of journalists explain the well-documented fact that anglophone and francophone news organizations cover issues relating to the Parti Québécois (and constitutional matters in general) quite differently.

Since the 1995 referendum on sovereignty, which resulted in a razor-thin victory for the federalists, charges and countercharges about biased reporting have become more heated. In 1997, for example, influential *Globe and Mail* columnist Jeffrey Simpson wrote that *Le Devoir*, where he had been a regular contributor, had become "the house organ for the Parti Québécois."[13] The reaction by *Le Devoir* publisher Lise Bissonnette was bitter in tone: "The only reasonable explanation for this sudden transition from friendship to slander is a decision to consider us as political adversaries, and to use any means to win."[14]

Although many of the accusations of biased reporting about constitutional issues have focused on the French-language media, in the late 1990s it may be the English-language media that have become more opinionated. Starting about 1995 Gérald Leblanc, a reporter who covers English Canada for *La Presse,* began to notice a qualitative change in the treatment Quebec received in the English-Canadian media. Columnists and editorial writers increasingly express open animosity toward Quebec, he writes, and this "militant antagonism sometimes finds its way into what are supposed to be news stories."[15] Leblanc says "pamphleteering" replaces journalism in the English-Canadian media "when the subject is one that can hurt the separatists." *Toronto Star* journalist Robert McKenzie, who has covered Quebec politics for more than 30 years, also has noted what he called "un durcissement" — a harder line about Quebec — in the anglophone media in recent years.[16] It seems that most English-language journalists are convinced that their francophone colleagues are all separatists[17] while most French-language journalists have been convinced for a long time that their anglophone colleagues are blinded by their fear of Canada breaking up.[18] Can it be that the presumed nationalist mission of francophone journalists has found its counterpart in the presumed patriotic mission of anglophone journalists to save Canada?

The future of Canada and Quebec is such an emotional issue that some journalists may shed the impartiality that characterizes their work on other topics when they write about it. Nonetheless, our findings contradict certain long-lived stereotypes that exaggerate the differences between how journalism is practised in English-language and French-language news organizations in Canada.[19] As Table 3 shows, the five functions that anglophone journalists consider most important are the same five that francophone journalists consider most important.

Accuracy is the most important function of journalism for both anglophones and francophones. Contrary to the stereotype of opinionated French journalism, francophone journalists are significantly more likely than anglophones to consider accuracy very important ($p<.01$).[20] Similarly, while Gagnon's observation that the French-language press emphasizes analysis more than the English-language press may have been true when she wrote it in 1981, the evidence from our survey suggests that in the late 1990s journalists from both language groups are equally interested in analysis. The differences in anglophones' and francophones' responses to the question about the importance

Table 3:   **English- and French-Language Respondents' Views of 14 Journalistic Functions**

	Proportion who Say it Is "Very Important" to:		Average Score on the Item (Maximum=4)	
	English	French	English	French
Accurately report the views of public figures	84.5%	93.2%	3.79	3.93[2]
Get information to the public quickly	81.0%	73.6%	3.76	3.73
Give ordinary people a chance to express views	78.8%	72.3%	3.70	3.70
Investigate government and public institutions	75.1%	66.9%	3.69	3.62
Provide analysis of complex problems	67.5%	69.6%	3.56	3.67
Discuss policy while it is being developed	59.9%	45.3%	3.43	3.33[1]
Focus on news of the widest possible interest	46.1%	60.8%	3.17	3.53[4]
Be sceptical of the actions of public officials	45.8%	59.9%	3.13	3.52[4]
Be sceptical of the actions of businesses	40.6%	59.2%	3.03	3.50[4]
Develop the public's cultural interests	21.7%	43.9%	2.57	3.30[4]
Increase circulation or ratings	26.3%	21.1%	2.67	2.83[1]
Provide entertainment and relaxation	22.9%	16.2%	2.58	2.68
Influence public opinion	7.0%	8.2%	1.96	2.35[4]
Set the political agenda	2.5%	7.4%	1.59	2.33[4]
N	406	148	406	148

Notes: [1]$p < .05$, [2]$p < .01$, [3]$p < .001$, [4]$p < .0001$

of providing analysis and interpretation of complex problems are small and insignificant.

Although anglophones and francophones agree on the most important functions of journalism, the survey did reveal differences with respect to functions of journalism respondents considered less important. Francophones, for example, rate developing the cultural and intellectual interests of the public as a much more important function of journalism than do anglophones (p<.0001). They also are much more sceptical than their English-media counterparts, both of public officials and of businesses (p<.0001 for both items).

In addition, francophone journalists are more likely than their anglophone counterparts to think that it is important to influence public opinion and to set the political agenda (p<.0001 for both items). There is evidence, in other words, that francophone journalists are more likely than anglophone journalists to see political action as a valid journalistic function. It would be a mistake, however, to make too much of this finding. Both for francophones and for anglophones, influencing public opinion and setting the political agenda were by far the least important functions of journalism.

For all practical purposes, then, the results of our study contradict the image of opinionated and politically activist journalism traditionally associated with francophones and increasingly with anglophones. It is likely, we believe, that the images of journalistic activism are based on flawed assumptions about the reasons why major French-language media cover national issues differently than do the major English-language media. Many politicians and pundits assume that differences in coverage are caused by journalists slanting the news to match their personal opinions or by major differences between anglophones and francophones about fundamental conceptions of the roles journalism should play in society. We found no evidence to support either assumption.

That said, it is not surprising that anglophone and francophone media do not cover subjects relating to federalism in the same way. What is important to understand is that the differences result not from any lack of "objectivity,"[21] but rather from the fact that English- and French-language news organizations must speak to their respective communities, which have markedly different orientations toward the Canadian federation. As Siegel notes:

> Since the 1960s, nearly every provincial election in Quebec has had a referendum element, a matter of particular interest for English Canadians. Quebeckers, for their part, want coverage of the campaigning politicians' views on policies that may be of little interest outside the province. Thus, the differences in coverage across linguistic lines can be attributed in part to the specific interests of different audiences.[22]

Other observers suggest that the legitimacy granted to the PQ by francophone journalists flows from their near-unanimous belief that it is important to faithfully report the actions of important public officials — such as major figures in the Parti Québécois, which has held the reins of the Quebec government for more than half of the past 25 years — to a population that is split more or less evenly in its views on possible Quebec independence.[23] Whatever the causes of the differences in coverage, it is clear that the conditions which create a context for respectful coverage of the independence option in Quebec are not present in English Canada, where, needless to say, the PQ does not have much support.

To a great extent, francophone and anglophone journalists work in two separate worlds. Content analyses of news, especially news dealing with constitutional issues, demonstrate this phenomenon, and our study found evidence of it as well. Although most francophone journalists (85 percent) say they speak English, relatively few read English-Canadian newspapers: 28 percent read *The Globe and Mail*, 13 percent *The Gazette* of Montreal. The reverse is even worse; less than 5 percent of anglophone journalists read a francophone newspaper. Only 14 percent of English-Canadian journalists say they speak French. Most anglophone journalists would have a very hard time gaining first-hand information about the francophone culture in Quebec.

Our survey contained a question about which magazines journalists regularly read. The responses suggested that Canadian journalists are interested most by their own society (English Canadian or French Canadian), somewhat by US society, and least by the Canadian culture to which they do not belong. The magazines most likely to be read by Canadian journalists are Canadian: A clear majority of francophone journalists (62 percent) read *L'Actualité*, and a near majority (49 percent) of anglophone journalists read *Maclean's*. Next in popularity for both language groups are US news weeklies. *Time* is read by 24 percent of francophones and 20 percent of anglophones; *Newsweek* is read by 10 percent of francophones and 14 percent of anglophones. Only 11 percent of francophone journalists read *Maclean's*, the most important news magazine in English Canada. Only 2 percent of anglophone journalists read *L'Actualité*, the most important news magazine in French Canada.

Canadian journalists share a common conception of their profession, one that places them squarely in the mainstream of North American journalism. But anglophone and francophone journalists practise their profession in separate worlds, as their media consumption habits show. Neither group pays much attention to what happens in the other's culture. In this sense, the two solitudes are alive and well.

JOURNALISM AT CBC/RADIO-CANADA

The government's creation of CBC/Radio-Canada in the 1930s was part of its efforts to build a nation and then to hold it together. As Walter Stewart noted: "History, custom and necessity have led us to recognize that, with so few people and so much geography, we had to use government agencies as major instruments of national development."[24] It is to promote national development that CBC/Radio-Canada is legally required to "reflect Canada and its regions to national and regional audiences" and to "contribute to shared national consciousness and identity."[25] With the weakening of the Canadian Press as a national news agency in recent years, the public broadcaster's multiple networks — which include television news, radio news, and around-the-clock cable news, all in both English and French — stand alone as sources of comprehensive, nationwide news for Canadians anywhere in the country.

CBC/Radio-Canada was modeled on the fabled British Broadcasting Corporation (BBC). Like the BBC, it has developed an international reputation for high-quality journalism. Even judges, not necessarily known for being admirers of the media, have noted the importance of CBC/Radio-Canada. In an opinion about a libel case, for example, the British Columbia Supreme Court noted:

> In terms of prestige, power and influence ... [CBC/Radio-Canada] is at the opposite end of the spectrum from the sleazy scandal sheet. Created and maintained by Parliament to inform the Canadian public, its news services are accorded great respect throughout Canada. They have a well-merited reputation for reliability.[26]

Over the years, CBC/Radio-Canada has acquired what journalist George Bain has called "the mystique of leadership," especially among government officials and people in the media.[27] Bain was certainly right about the public broadcaster's reputation in media circles. More than half of the anglophone journalists in our survey who identified a news organization as Canada's best chose either CBC (54 percent) or Radio-Canada (1 percent) as Canada's best news organization. The proportion of francophone journalists choosing the public broadcaster approached those levels, with 41 percent identifying Radio-Canada and 5 percent identifying CBC as the best news organization. No other news organization, print or broadcast, came close to CBC/Radio-Canada's status among journalists.

In addition, CBC/Radio-Canada and its 24-hour-a-day cable networks, *Newsworld* in English and RDI in French, are by far journalists' preferred sources for television news. Among anglophone journalists, 57 percent say they get most of their television news from the CBC, 8 percent from *Newsworld*, and 1 percent from Radio-Canada. Among francophones, the proportions are even higher, with 69 percent getting most of their television news from Radio-Canada, 14 percent from RDI, and 1 percent each from CBC and *Newsworld*. Overall, one CBC/Radio-Canada service or another is the principal source of television news for 69 percent of Canadian journalists who watch television news (a handful do not watch television news, and were excluded from these calculations).[28]

CBC/Radio-Canada's reputation for high-quality journalism notwithstanding, the fact that it is financed principally by the Canadian government coupled with the fact that its parliamentary mandate is somewhat ambiguous has led some politicians to make questionable interpretations of its mission, especially in the context of news coverage of Quebec. No news organization has been criticized as often as Radio-Canada for alleged pro-separatist bias. One Cabinet minister said publicly that he believed that Radio-Canada journalists should be unequivocally pro-Canada.[29] After all, CBC/Radio-Canada was created to help build a country, not to help tear it apart. Or so the argument goes.

And what an argument it can be, with important federalist public figures blaming Radio-Canada for the victory of the Parti Québécois in the 1976 elections. The charges that Radio-Canada's news coverage was slanted in favour of the PQ were investigated by the CRTC and ruled to be unfounded,[30] but the suspicions remained. They resurfaced at the time of the 1995 referendum on sovereignty, when Prime Minister Jean Chrétien suggested that Radio-Canada's coverage was failing to promote national unity. Chrétien may have forgotten that the *Broadcasting Act* of 1968, which required the CBC to "contribute to the development of national unity"[31] was replaced in 1991 by a new *Broadcasting Act* that has the less politically charged mandate to "contribute to shared national consciousness and identity."[32] Federalists are not the only critics of Radio-Canada, however. Some supporters of Quebec independence cannot see a positive Radio-Canada report from English Canada without perceiving propaganda in favour of federalism or national unity.

Another illustration of the tension between CBC/Radio-Canada and politicians was Brian Mulroney's 1991 appointment of University of Toronto professor John Crispo to the Corporation's board of directors. Just before being appointed, Crispo had harshly criticized news and public affairs programming on the CBC, saying that it was a "lousy, left-wing, liberal-NDP-pinko network."[33] The presumed domination of leftists at CBC/Radio-Canada's English-language services is as frequent a criticism as is the presumed domination of separatists at the French-language services. Crispo, Diane Francis, the Vancouver-based Fraser Institute and others regularly denounce what they consider to be the pro-labour, pro-NDP, anti-free trade and anti-United States bias of CBC coverage. Crispo even called the CBC "Radio Iraq" for its coverage of the Gulf War.[34]

Although our survey shows that CBC journalists are somewhat more left of centre than other Canadian journalists, they are far from the agitprop activists described by Crispo and others. The English-language journalists for the CBC averaged a score of 31 on the 100-point scale of conservatism, while English-language journalists for private media rated themselves at 37 — still to the left of centre, but not as far left as the CBC journalists (the difference between CBC and private media journalists in English-language news

Table 4: ***Private-Media and CBC/Radio-Canada Journalists'***
Views of 14 Journalistic Functions

	Proportion who Say it Is "Very Important" to:		Average Score on the Item (Maximum=4)	
	Private	*CBC/R-C*	*Private*	*CBC/R-C*
Accurately report the views of public figures	85.3%	90.2%	3.80	3.90
Get information to the public quickly	80.8%	74.4%	3.77	3.68
Give ordinary people a chance to express views	77.7%	76.8%	3.70	3.70
Investigate government and public institutions	70.0%	89.1%	3.63	3.89[3]
Provide analysis of complex problems	64.0%	85.9%	3.52	3.84[4]
Discuss policy while it is being developed	53.4%	73.7%	3.36	3.65[3]
Focus on news of the widest possible interest	51.5%	36.8%	3.29	3.00[2]
Be sceptical of the actions of public officials	46.3%	57.9%	3.17	3.33
Be sceptical of the actions of businesses	40.9%	58.2%	3.07	3.32[2]
Develop the public's cultural interests	24.3%	33.3%	2.69	2.83
Increase circulation or ratings	28.8%	9.9%	2.79	2.28[4]
Provide entertainment and relaxation	24.3%	10.3%	2.71	2.11[4]
Influence public opinion	6.5%	10.3%	2.03	2.09
Set the political agenda	2.5%	8.0%	1.71	1.80
N (weighted)	410	94	410	94

Notes: [1]$p < .05$, [2]$p < .01$, [3]$p < .001$, [4]$p < .0001$

organizations was significant at p < .05). A similar, though statistically non-significant, tendency was found among francophone journalists. Those who work for Radio-Canada averaged 32 on the conservatism scale, those who work for private media 35. There is nothing unique about the left-of-centre views of CBC/Radio-Canada journalists, however. Journalists who work at daily newspapers are even a shade farther to the left, according to our survey.

In addition to their somewhat different political orientations, news people at CBC/Radio-Canada are different in other ways. CBC/Radio-Canada journalists tend to be older. They are more likely to be female, and much more likely to have a university degree. Further, they are quite a bit higher paid than their private-media counterparts. These tendencies hold both for anglophones and for francophones.

Despite such differences, the ideas that form what we have called the "credo" of Canadian journalism are widely shared, at CBC/Radio-Canada as well as in the private sector. Although CBC/Radio-Canada journalists prioritize their functions somewhat differently than do private-media journalists, both groups have the same five functions at the top of their list, as Table 4 shows.

Not surprisingly, private-media journalists are more concerned than are CBC/Radio-Canada journalists with the commercial aspects of journalism. Private-media journalists place significantly higher importance on focusing on news of interest to the widest possible audience (p<.01), on increasing audience size (p<.0001), and on providing entertainment and relaxation (p<.0001). CBC/Radio-Canada journalists, in turn, focus more than do the private-media journalists on investigative reporting (p<.001), on analysis and interpretation (p<.0001), and on discussing public policy while it is still being developed (p<.01). CBC/Radio-Canada journalists also are more sceptical of business than are journalists in the private media (p<.01). Neither group expresses much interest in influencing public opinion or in setting the political agenda, two functions that would be expected to be associated with activist journalism.

GENERATION X JOURNALISTS

The story we have told to this point suggests that Canadian journalists, regardless of language and regardless of whether they work for CBC/Radio-Canada, to a great extent share a single conception of journalism that highlights functions which are central to journalism's role in democratic societies — accurate reporting, rapid transmission of news, letting ordinary people express their views, investigative reporting, and analysis and interpretation of the news. What is more, Canadian journalists overwhelmingly get their news from and admire the media organizations that embody that kind of journalism, especially CBC/Radio-Canada.

The above statements are true of journalists over 30 years old. Younger journalists, however, have somewhat different views. To explore those differences we divided our sample of journalists into three generations: Generation X, defined as journalists 30 years old and younger; Baby-Boomers, defined as everyone over 30 but less than 50; and Elders, everyone 50 years or older.[35] Initial analyses showed very little difference between Baby-Boomer and Elder journalists, so we collapsed those two categories into one. Although Gen-Xers make up only about 20 percent of the Canadian journalistic workforce, understanding them is important because their professional values offer a hint at the future of Canadian journalism.

Our study shows Gen-X journalists to be different in several ways from their colleagues over 30 years old. The younger journalists are slightly more conservative (averaging 39 on the conservatism scale compared to 35 for their elders), less likely to have a bachelor's degree (45 percent of Gen-Xers have such a degree compared to 59 percent of journalists over 30), more likely to be female (45 percent to 24 percent), and much less likely to work in a unionized newsroom (32 percent to 71 percent). In 1995 they earned, on average, about half of what journalists over 30 earned ($27,150 to $54,600).

Gen-Xers are less oriented to the traditional media elite than are their elders. They are less likely to get their television news from CBC/Radio-Canada and less likely to read prestige newspapers, phenomena especially pronounced among young francophone journalists.[36] Anglophone Gen-Xers are almost as likely as older English-language journalists to say that they get most of their television news from one of the CBC services (58 percent to 63 percent). A majority of francophone Gen-Xers, however, prefer private networks (mostly TVA) as their principal source of television news. Only 37 percent say they get most of their television news from Radio-Canada, compared to 88 percent of their elders.

Less than a third of young anglophone journalists (31 percent) read *The Globe and Mail*, Canada's only national newspaper at the time of our study, compared to 54 percent of the English-language journalists over 30. Among the newspapers widely available throughout Quebec, francophone Gen-Xers are less likely than their elders to read *La Presse* (58 percent to 81 percent) and *Le Devoir* (11 percent to 40 percent), and quite a bit more likely to read the tabloid *Le Journal de Montréal* or its Quebec City cousin, *Le Journal de Québec* (47 percent to 22 percent). Journalists' assessments of quality do not necessarily match their patterns of media consumption. Although younger journalists are less likely to watch CBC/Radio-Canada for news, roughly equal proportions of young and old journalists in both linguistic communities rate CBC/Radio-Canada as Canada's best news organization.

The most striking difference between Generation X and the older journalists is that a substantial proportion of the younger journalists do not rate accurate reporting of the views of public figures as a very important journalistic function, as Table 5 shows. Gen-X journalists were almost three times as likely as their elders to rate accurate reporting in a category other than "very important," a difference that was highly significant ($p<.0001$). This generational gap in the importance of accuracy appears to be an anglophone phenomenon; only about two-thirds of anglophone Gen-X journalists (69 percent) think accuracy is "very important," compared to 88 percent of their elders. Among francophone journalists, 90 percent of the Gen-Xers and 94 percent of the others say accuracy is very important, a difference that is not statistically significant. Gen-X journalists also place less importance than their elders on virtually all kinds of reporting related to government. As Table 5 shows, not only are the younger journalists less interested in accurately reporting the views of public figures, but they place less importance on investigative reporting ($p<.01$), on discussing public policy while it is under consideration ($p<.001$), and on being sceptical of public officials ($p<.01$).

There are indications that Gen-X journalists are not atypical of their generation, one that distrusts absolutes, sees everything as relative, and feels less connected to traditional institutions such as the news media and government. In addition, there is evidence that young people in general tend to reject conventional definitions of news and treat the hallowed distinction between information and entertainment as artificial and irrelevant.[37] Many Gen-Xers focus more on style than on substance; for them, style is substance. "Why do so many young people watch MTV and not the news?" a Gen-X keynote speaker asked a broadcast journalism conference in 1996. The answer, according to the speaker: "Because they would rather watch that style of picture design." His recommendation to the broadcast news executives? "TV news needs to be design driven."[38]

There is no denying the importance of visual design in today's world, especially among the young. Design-driven journalism will have different strengths and weaknesses than content-based journalism that many veteran news people hold dear, but it will not necessarily be "worse" journalism. It will simply be different journalism, managed by journalists who may have somewhat different priorities.

Our finding that 28 percent of Gen-X journalists do not consider it to be very important to accurately report the views of public figures will be seen as a portent of doom by supporters of classical "objective" journalism. Some might go so far as to see the lower level of interest in accurate reporting among younger journalists as a threat to democracy, which after all relies upon a citizenry accurately informed about public affairs. However, the fact that one of the most important functions of journalism for Gen-X news people is giving ordinary people a chance to express their views is somewhat reassuring. Certainly the desire to give ordinary people the chance to express their views

Table 5: *Generation X and Older Respondents' Views of 14 Journalistic Functions*

	Proportion who Say it Is "Very Important" to:		Average Score on the Item (Maximum=4)	
	Younger	*Older*	*Younger*	*Older*
Accurately report the views of public figures	71.3%	89.7%	3.59	3.87[4]
Get information to the public quickly	79.5%	79.7%	3.75	3.75
Give ordinary people a chance to express views	79.2%	77.2%	3.77	3.68
Investigate government and public institutions	61.4%	76.4%	3.53	3.72[2]
Provide analysis of complex problems	64.4%	68.9%	3.52	3.59
Discuss policy while it is being developed	45.4%	59.9%	3.19	3.46[2]
Focus on news of the widest possible interest	48.0%	49.0%	3.28	3.23
Be sceptical of the actions of public officials	35.9%	51.4%	2.96	3.26[2]
Be sceptical of the actions of businesses	31.4%	47.1%	2.88	3.17[2]
Develop the public's cultural interests	17.3%	28.0%	2.48	2.77[1]
Increase circulation or ratings	22.0%	26.1%	2.59	2.72
Provide entertainment and relaxation	25.5%	20.8%	2.65	2.59
Influence public opinion	3.2%	8.2%	1.66	2.13[4]
Set the political agenda	0.7%	4.2%	1.63	1.75
N (weighted)	95	409	95	409

Notes: [1]$p < .05$, [2]$p < .01$, [3]$p < .001$, [4]$p < .0001$

is a democratic impulse, perhaps even more so than the desire to parrot the views of public figures. One thing is certain: Gen-X journalists are less interested than their elders in imposing anything on their audiences. They place much less importance, for example, on developing the cultural and intellectual interests of the public (p<.05) and on influencing public opinion (p<.0001).

DISCUSSION

We conducted this survey in large part to gather representative evidence that would enable us to assess the validity of some commonly held assumptions about Canadian journalists. Our finding that the similarities between anglophone and francophone journalists are greater than the differences will surprise those who have accepted the old stereotype that English-Canadian journalism is more factual and French-Canadian journalism more opinionated. The survey uncovered no evidence to support the stereotype. Journalists from both language groups hold very similar conceptions about the relative importance of various journalistic functions. Accurate reporting is at the top of the list for anglophones and francophones alike; influencing public opinion and setting the political agenda are at the bottom for both groups.[39] What is interesting about anglophone and francophone journalists was the extent to which they are uninterested in each other's media and culture. In this respect, Canadian journalists reflect their news organizations. With the exception of CBC/Radio-Canada and a very few other news organizations, neither English-language nor French-language media show much interest in regular in-depth coverage of the other linguistic community.

We also examined differences between CBC/Radio-Canada journalists and journalists who work in private news organizations. We did find some evidence to support the assertion often made by conservative pundits that CBC/Radio-Canada journalists (especially those at the CBC) are more left of centre than journalists in the private sector, though daily newspaper journalists are even a bit more left than their counterparts at the public broadcaster. However, just as we found no evidence that francophone journalists insert their opinions into news stories, we found no evidence that CBC/Radio-Canada news people are more likely than their private-media counterparts to view journalism as a tool of political activism. A huge majority of CBC/Radio-Canada journalists and private-media journalists alike say that accurate reporting is very important. And both sets of journalists rank influencing public opinion and setting the political agenda as the least important functions of the 14 functions of journalism explored in the survey.

There is no reason to believe, in other words, that a federalist journalist cannot write a fair and accurate news story about a Parti Québécois convention, or that a journalist who regularly votes for NDP candidates cannot write a fair and accurate story about the Reform Party's policy proposals. These findings are consistent with research that has demonstrated that the content of news stories is determined principally by organizational needs, not individual journalists' personal opinions about the topics of the news stories.[40]

It is true that journalists whose stock in trade is flamboyant opinions are becoming increasingly visible in Canada. The mission of such journalists is to win the loyalty of their audience members by "entertaining, amusing, outraging, goading,"[41] even if their inflammatory comments sometimes impede rather than enhance public understanding of issues in the news. Such journalists often are invited to appear on radio and television precisely because they have clearly identifiable biases that they express without subtlety. Their visibility and vociferousness can give the misleading impression that journalists in general allow their personal biases to guide their decisions about how to report the news. By focusing on a representative sample of journalists, not just the loud minority of journalists who are in the business of selling their opinions, we believe our study paints a more valid picture of the reality of Canadian journalists.

The vast majority of Canadian journalists say that accurately reporting the views of public figures is very important; indeed, all groups subscribe to what we have called the credo of Canadian journalism. That said, Generation X journalists — and especially English-language Gen-Xers — are significantly less likely than their elders to consider accurate reporting to be very important. In addition, they place less importance than do their elders on several of the traditional tenets of public affairs reporting, including investigative reporting, discussing public policy while it is being developed, and being sceptical of public officials and businesses.[42]

Will Gen-X journalists remain relatively uninterested in traditional public affairs journalism as they age and advance in their careers, or will age and experience make them more like their elders? It is a question that a single survey cannot answer. Research on US journalists suggests that professional values associated with an individual's generation are somewhat resistant to change as the individual moves through familiar cycles of life — a steady job, marriage, home ownership, a family.[43] In contrast, professional values not directly tied to one's generational membership do evolve as individuals gain experience and responsibility in life as well as in journalism. The key question, then, is whether today's Gen-X journalists will, as a group, ascribe more importance to the traditional ideals of public affairs reporting as they grow older, or whether their hesitancy to make an unambiguous commitment to those ideals is a hallmark of their generation. Future research should track the professional values of Gen-X journalists as they age and gain experience.

If today's Gen-X journalists continue to place less importance on accurately reporting the views of public figures — indeed, if they share the views of some young US journalists that news is an "obsolete artifact"[44] — it is valid to ask whether the public's trust in news about politics and government, already challenged by spin doctors and entertainment values, will erode even more. Roger Bird recently wrote in a book with the ominous title *The End of News* that the important political role of the news media in democratic societies depends on the public's trust in the accuracy of what the news media report: "If the news is not believed to be 'the truth,' even in a naive sense, by a majority of the public, it is drained of its importance."[45]

A related question is whether it makes sense to talk about "the news" in an increasingly fragmented political, social, and media environment. As Adams wrote in *Sex in the Snow*: "More and more, Canadians refuse to be constrained by the specifics of their demographics; instead, they are determined to be the authors of their own identities and destinies."[46] They are not just French Canadians or English Canadians or even Gen-Xers or Baby-Boomers. Instead, there are countless solitudes constructed from individual Canadians' values. New modes of communication — electronic and print "zines," the interactive and information-rich Internet, ever more specialized cable channels — make it possible to "narrowcast" to each of the "values tribes," as Adams calls them. In fact, it is possible for individuals to choose only the news and information they want from the wealth of sources available to them.

The *Broadcasting Act* not only requires CBC/Radio-Canada to "contribute to shared national consciousness and identity"[47] but requires all radio and television to be "a public service essential to the maintenance and enhancement of national identity."[48] Many major newspapers also cloak themselves with a public service mission linked to democracy. However, in a society increasingly characterized by the pursuit of individual interests it is valid to ask whether the concepts "public service" and "national identity," when applied to the media, have the same meanings they had in a world where most of the nation gathered at 10 p.m. every evening to watch news provided by CBC/Radio-Canada. Can Canada even be considered to have a "public" if fewer and fewer of its citizens share common knowledge of public issues?

Such questions, which essentially are questions about the meaning of citizenship, have no clear answers at this point. Nor is there any clear consensus about what, if anything, journalists can do or should do to foster citizenship and national identity. Canadian journalism and democracy, like those of many other industrialized nations, are entering a period of uncertainty.

NOTES

1.   Hugh MacLennan, *Two Solitudes* (Toronto: Collins, 1945).

2.   Douglas Coupland, *Generation X: Tales for an Accelerated Culture* (New York: St. Martin's Press, 1991).

3. Michael Adams, *Sex in the Snow: Canadian Social Values at the End of the Millennium* (Toronto: Penguin Books, 1997), pp. 30-31.

4. Diane Francis, "Analysis Reveals CBC's Regional and Philosophical Biases," *The Financial Post*, 25 February 1997, p. 21.

5. We defined journalists as salaried full-time editorial personnel (reporters, writers, correspondents, anchors, columnists, news directors, and editors) responsible for the information content of daily and weekly newspapers, more-than-monthly news magazines, wire services, broadcast networks, and individual radio and television stations. Photographers and camera operators were excluded because their function is more to illustrate news than to decide what will be news. For a complete description of the survey, see David Pritchard and Florian Sauvageau, "The Journalists and Journalisms of Canada," in *The Global Journalist: News People Around the World,* ed. David H. Weaver (Cresskill, NJ: Hampton Press, 1998), pp. 373-93.

6. We oversampled francophone journalists from Quebec so that we would have a sufficient number for statistical analyses of that group. In analyses of anglophone and francophone journalists, we use a weighting factor of 0.64 for the francophone journalists from Quebec.

7. One scholar, George Pollard, has studied Canadian radio journalists in some depth. See citations of his work in Pritchard and Sauvageau, "The Journalists and Journalisms of Canada," p. 390.

8. A survey of the Canadian adult population a year before our survey showed that 30.6 percent of Canadians consider themselves to be "liberal" or "extremely liberal," 51.8 percent consider themselves to be "moderate," and 17.6 percent consider themselves to be "conservative" or "extremely conservative." Figures compiled from data in Reginald W. Bibby, *The Bibby Report: Social Trends Canadian Style* (Toronto: Stoddard Publishing, 1995), p. 118.

9. Lysiane Gagnon, "Journalists and Ideologies in Quebec," in *The Journalists*, Research Studies on the Newspaper Industry, vol. 2, Royal Commission on Newspapers (Ottawa: Minister of Supply and Services, 1981), p. 28.

10. Arthur Siegel, *Politics and the Media in Canada*, 2d ed. (Toronto: McGraw-Hill Ryerson, 1996), p. 219.

11. Royal Commission on Newspapers (Kent Commission), *Report* (Ottawa: Minister of Supply and Services, 1981), p. 31.

12. Pierre Godin, "Qui vous informe," *L'Actualité*, May 1979, pp. 31-40.

13. Jeffrey Simpson, "Léon Dion: A Man who Kept Searching for a New Canada," *The Globe and Mail*, 21 August 1997, p. A-18.

14. Lise Bissonnette, "La semence de la colère," *Le Devoir*, 27 August 1997, p. A-6.

15. Gérald Leblanc, "The English Canada Media and Quebec," *Inroads* 7 (1998): 23-30.

16 Quoted in Gérard Roy, "De l'autocensure et un plus grand contrôle des patrons," *Le 30*, October 1995, p. 7.

17. *Globe and Mail* journalist Graham Fraser, quoted in Vincent Marissal, "Les deux solitudes," *Le 30*, October 1997, p. 11.

18. Marissal, "Les deux solitudes," pp. 11-12. See also Michel Cormier, "The amazing double standard," *Media* 2, 4 (1995): 16-17; and Fred Langan, "Charges of media bias run two ways as Quebec votes today on separation," *Christian Science Monitor*, 30 October 1995, p. 1.

19. This is not to suggest that there are no differences between anglophone and francophone news media. A journalist at *La Presse* recently wrote that English-language newspapers produce better stories than French-language papers because editors at the former are more heavily involved in working with reporters on stories. Marie-Claude Lortie, "Que le meilleur gagne!" *Le 30*, June 1998, p. 18.

20. The terms "significant" or "meaningful," when applied to the quantitative results of this survey, refer to differences that are statistically significant at the traditional $p<.05$ level. Levels of statistical significance are two-tailed probabilities from the Mann-Whitney U test (also known as the Wilcoxon test). See Alan Agresti and Barbara Finlay Agresti, *Statistical Methods for the Social Sciences* (San Francisco: Dellen, 1979), pp. 175-79.

21. We use the word "objectivity" with caution, for while we favour detachment and impartiality in reporting we share many of the reservations others have expressed about the ideological biases of so-called "objective" journalism. Hackett and Zhao, for example, note that the regime of journalistic objectivity "systematically produces partial representation of the world, skewed towards dominant institutions and values." Robert A. Hackett and Yuezhi Zhao, *Sustaining Democracy? Journalism and the Politics of Objectivity* (Toronto: Garamond Press, 1998), p. 161.

22. Siegel, *Politics and the Media in Canada*, p. 222.

23. This view is widely held by members of the Quebec journalistic community, be they federalists or supporters of Quebec independence. There have been some attempts to make Canadians outside Quebec understand. See, for example, the text of a speech to the Empire Club of Toronto and the Canadian Club of Toronto by Roger D. Landry, the staunchly federalist publisher of *La Presse*. The text of the speech, "Media and the Unity Issue," was published in *The Media Series: A Special Collection of Luncheon Addresses* (Toronto: Canadian Journalism Foundation, 1997).

24. Walter Stewart, "The Seven Myths of Journalism," in *The Forty-Ninth and Other Parallels,* ed. David Staines (Amherst: University of Massachusetts Press, 1986), p. 103.

25. *Broadcasting Act,* 1991, art. 3 (1) (m) (ii) and (vi).

26. *Vogel v. Canadian Broadcasting Corp.*, [1982] 3 W.W.R. 97 (B.C.S.C.) at 178.

27. George Bain, *Gotcha: How the Media Distort the News* (Toronto: Key Porter Books, 1994), p. xi.

28. It is interesting to note that journalists differ from the Canadian public in their preferred sources for television news. In English Canada at the time of our sur-

vey, *CTV News* was drawing ratings about 50 percent higher than CBC's *The National.* In Quebec, the rating of the TVA evening news were slightly ahead of Radio-Canada's *Le Téléjournal.*

29. André Ouellet, quoted in Graham Fraser, *Le Parti québécois* (Montreal: Libre Expression, 1984), p. 147.

30. Arthur Siegel, "Une analyse du contenu: Similitudes et différences entre les nouvelles des réseaux anglais et français de la Société Radio-Canada (unpublished paper prepared for the CRTC, July 1977).

31. *Broadcasting Act,* 1968, art. 2 (g) (iv).

32. *Broadcasting Act,* 1991, art. 3 (1) (m) (vi).

33. Quoted in Wayne Skene, *A Requiem for the CBC* (Vancouver: Douglas and McIntyre, 1993), p. 218.

34. Skene, *A Requiem for the CBC,* p. 219.

35. We defined generations as did Adams in *Sex in the Snow.*

36. Conclusions about francophone Gen-Xers should be regarded as tentative because they are based on the responses of only 19 journalists. We have greater confidence in conclusions about anglophone Gen-Xers, which are based on 83 responses.

37. See, e.g., Carl Sessions Stepp, "The X Factor," *American Journalism Review,* November 1996, pp. 34-38.

38. Stephen Marshall, quoted in Felix Vikhman, "Video Killed the TV News Star," *Ryerson Review of Journalism,* Spring 1998, p. 16.

39. The functions that Canadian journalists rate highly are those also rated highly by US journalists. David H. Weaver and G. Cleveland Wilhoit, *The American Journalist in the 1990s* (Mahwah, NJ: Lawrence Erlbaum Publishers, 1996).

40. The research is summarized nicely in Pamela J. Shoemaker and Stephen D. Reese, *Mediating the Message: Theories of Influences on Mass Media Content,* 2d ed. (White Plains, NY: Longman, 1996).

41. David Taras, "The Winds of Right-wing Change in Canadian Journalism," *Canadian Journal of Communication* 21 (Autumn 1996): 485-95, esp. 487.

42. Because young journalists are especially likely to work at weekly newspapers and radio stations, we wondered whether it might be the kind of news organization rather than the age of the journalist that was the principal factor in the differences. Analyses of the data, however, showed that Gen-X journalists are systematically different than their elders in the ways described regardless of where they work. As far as we can tell, in other words, the differences are not a function of where young journalists work; they seem to be a function either of their age or of the unique generation to which they belong.

43. Jian-Hua Zhu, "Recent Trends in Adversarial Attitudes Among American Newspaper Journalists: A Cohort Analysis," *Journalism Quarterly* 67 (Winter 1990): 992-1004.

44. Stepp, "The X Factor," p. 35.

45.   Roger Bird, *The End of News* (Toronto: Irwin Publishing, 1997), p. 7.

46.   Adams, *Sex in the Snow*, p. 16.

47.   *Broadcasting Act,* 1991, art. 3 (1) (m) (vi).

48.   *Broadcasting Act,* 1991, art. 3 (1) (b).

12

Identity and National Attachments in Contemporary Canada

Frank L. Graves with Tim Dugas and Patrick Beauchamp

Ce chapitre remet en question l'opinion reçue selon laquelle le nationalisme canadien serait affaibli par les transferts de pouvoirs aux provinces, la réduction de la taille du gouvernement fédéral et les pressions de la mondialisation. On y soutient que les facteurs économiques n'épuisent pas le nationalisme. Cette recherche sur les structures sous-jacentes de l'identité canadienne s'appuie sur les données colligées par les Associés de Recherche Ekos dans leurs sondages Rethinking Government. Des comparaisons interna-tionales de même que des tendances canadiennes à long terme sont aussi présentées. Depuis 1994, les opinions de plus de 12 000 Canadiens ont été sondées par Ekos. En s'attardant aux attitudes récentes des Canadiens vivant en Ontario et au Québec, on avance que le sentiment d'appartenance au Canada demeure fort au Canada anglais. Au cours des quatre dernières années, l'attachement au pays est demeuré stable alors que l'attache-ment à la province a diminué. Même au Québec, où l'attachement au Canada est beaucoup plus faible, l'attachement à la province a subit un recul important au cours de la même période. En dernière analyse, il appert que l'identité canadienne demeure importante pour une majorité de Canadiens, en particulier au Canada anglais. L'attachement au Canada est aussi présent au Québec où il rivalise avec un nationalisme ethnolinguistique. L'État-nation est peut-être en déclin, mais ce déclin ne se manifeste pas dans l'opinion publique selon les données d'Ekos.

INTRODUCTION

Many people are making claims about the fragile state of Canadian national-ism. There is a significant lineage of work predicting the inevitable weakening and possible demise of Canada.[1] More recently, the works of Thomas Courchene and Robert Kaplan have captured considerable popular attention.[2] Our ongoing research on public attitudes shows that anxieties about the integ-rity and viability of Canada are shared by many members of Canadian society. Outside Canada, others have commented on the impending demise of the nation-state. Often these popular and academic arguments are linked to the economic, social and political consequences of globalization in general and the liberalization of international trade in particular.

Although the integrity of nation-states cannot be reduced solely to the domain of identity and attachment, a strong sense of identification and belonging to country is a necessary (if not sufficient) condition for its survival. Therefore, any discussion of the future of Canada should give explicit consideration to empirical evidence of levels of identification and attachment. In many instances, recent popular and academic discussions are conspicuously lacking evidence in this domain. The macrosociological consequences of economic or political change are often taken as a given. For example, if Canadians are less economically interdependent, will they then be less loyal or committed to Canada (and more committed to their local, regional interests or those of their new more significant trading partners)? These forms of arguments are expressions of a materialist or economic determinist model of history, and they may well be true. It is, however, essential to pause and consider the available direct evidence on identity and attachment to see if it supports or contradicts these broad theses.

In this chapter, we examine the current status and future prospects for national identity and attachment in Canada. We are broadly evaluating the hypothesis that national attachment is weakening under the pressures of devolution, federal diminution, and globalization. Is Canada an anachronism unravelling under the combination of regionalist frustrations arising from its historical roots and the contemporary pressures of globalization?

Our empirical evidence is imperfect. On some indicators, we can measure Canada against other countries and compare changes over the past three decades. Our most extensive data, however, comes from the EKOS Research Associates' *Rethinking Government* project which provides a broad range of indicators measured over the past four years.

AIMS AND STRATEGY

The purpose of this chapter is to examine current and evolving levels of national attachment with a view to describing and interpreting the role of shifting political and economic forces in Canada. Recent empirical data measuring strength of attachment to Canada are drawn largely from the ongoing *Rethinking Government* project.[3] The first part of the chapter provides a fairly straightforward description of identification and attachment in order to situate the other chapters in this volume within the realm of current public attitudes and beliefs.

The topic of identity and attachment is hopelessly broad and ambitious. For purposes of focus and tractability, we will examine the issues of identification and attachment as they have unfolded recently in Canada as a whole but with a special focus on Quebec and Ontario.

We selected Quebec as a special case because our research suggests that attachment to Canada is qualitatively different in intensity and form in Quebec than in the rest of Canada. This is clear from the basic descriptive analysis. A more sophisticated analysis of both the underlying structure of identity and belonging attitudes (using factor analytic techniques) and the multivariate factors which explain or predict strength of attachment, shows that Quebec is really a distinct phenomenon. For example, in our best multivariate models predicting overall strength of belonging to Canada, a variable representing whether one resides in Quebec or not accounts for 27 percent of the overall variation in the ratings of sense of belonging to Canada; roughly ten times the influence of all other predictors. In other words, the sheer impact of living in Quebec overwhelms the influence of all other factors on how strongly one feels attached to Canada. We will also see later in the analysis that Quebecers reveal a somewhat different value structure and that different values are linked to Canadian nationalism in Quebec than in the rest of Canada.

Our interest in Ontario is also keen, but for different reasons. Here we want to examine at least part of Tom Courchene's thesis that Ontario is moving from being the heartland of Canada to becoming a North American region/state. The thesis is provocative and important, not just for Ontario but, by implication, for the rest of Canada. Courchene's thesis is by no means restricted to the realm of Ontarians' perceptions of these shifts and indeed most of his elaborate argument is offered in the realm of historical analysis and political-economic shifts. However, Courchene also speaks of the "social" transition of Ontario. Although he moves broadly across the political-economic, geographic and constitutional-legal levels of analysis, there is little question that a central component of his argument comes from the realm of perceptions, attitudes and other psychological states. As such, his thesis collides squarely with our topic of identity and attachment.

In his introduction, for example, he speaks of "recent dramatic changes in Ontario and Ontarians' perceptions of their role in Canada."[4] Elsewhere, he speaks of "Ontarians' views," the "Ontario psyche," their "attention and loyalties." These are not parenthetical components of his argument but are cited as "defining characteristics" of Ontario (*qua* heartland). These themes permeate the book, but there is little if any direct evidence to support his explicit and implicit conclusions regarding this domain.

We intend to (roughly) test a range of hypotheses with a view to exploring anomalies/contradictions in the current public landscape and offer some tentative explanations. Our ultimate questions are: (i) What are current levels of attachment to Canada? (ii) How have they been changing? and (iii) Why are these changes (or lack of changes) occurring?

METHODOLOGICAL ISSUES

We have extended the basic statistical analysis in several directions as a partial fix for some of the weaknesses of a simple univariate and bivariate analysis.

These do not eliminate the weaknesses of our research design, but they do redress some of the threats to validity.

First, we test whether or not changes in recent time series of expressed strength of attachment (belonging) to Canada and province are statistically significant. We then control for the influences of age and region using analysis of variance.

Second, we conduct factor analysis of selected identity indicators and related attitudinal concepts. Factor analysis is a technique which identifies the extent to which groups of variables tend to vary together.[5] If the patterns of common variability are found to be reliable, the variables are interpreted to reflect a common underlying variable or trait. This analysis was used both to evaluate the measurement quality (particularly construct validity) of the identity indicators and related concepts and to discern the underlying patterns of meaning evident in the data. These analyses have been reproduced for different years of the database using the same indicators in order to assess whether the data are reliable (intersubjectively repeatable) and valid (plausibly linked to the underlying theoretical concepts). In both cases, we find usable reliability and validity. We also find interesting patterns of regional variations in the underlying structure of identity and attachment to Canada.

Third, we conduct a series of correlative tests (using simple bivariate correlation coefficients and cross-tabulations) which are then extended to more carefully identified multivariate models. These multivariate models have been constructed to test theoretically plausible structures of influence and refined to deal with some of the typical problems that confront this type of analysis.

We use secondary data reported by Neil Nevitte to compare Canada to other western countries on primary source identification.[6] We reproduced this question on a new random sample of the Canadian population last spring. This allows us to make broad comparisons about relative identification with Canada, province, world, North America and local community over a nearly 30-year time span. Although this analysis is weak in terms of ability to cross-tabulate and link to other data, the extended period of the time series does redress one of the key weaknesses of the *Rethinking Government* database (i.e., fairly short time series: 1994-98).

Finally, our analysis relies on both self-conscious accounts of the public (e.g., we believe Canada is disappearing because of government withdrawal) and indirect analysis of patterns of covariation in the data (e.g., people who are more frequent users of new technology are less attached to Canada). The data and our research design are decidedly non-experimental. There are major risks involved in drawing causal inferences about the factors producing attachment or change in attachment.[7] Our extended multivariate analysis provides some limited controls for these difficulties but we caution the reader that our ability to draw firm causal conclusions is quite limited.

DEFINITIONAL DISCUSSION: THE CONCEPTS

Identity is one of those rare terms which can mean its exact opposite — either absolute similarity or individuality. That identity can mean both that which is unique *and* that which is common reflects one of the ironies of the social world. The construction of a sense of *personal* identity is negotiated from interaction with the external social world.

Attachment is used here in the vernacular sense of belonging or devotion. One can identify with something without feeling an affective bond but this is not typically the case. Although identity and attachment are conceptually distinct, they tend to blur under empirical observation (although there are notable exceptions). For the purposes of this chapter, we will focus on the issue of sense of attachment or belonging while occasionally examining the separate issue of identity. For most respondents in social surveys, the terms evoke similar responses.

Human beings have always felt a need to identify themselves according to various social group memberships. In preliterate societies, marriage and kinship delineated not only identity but the bases for all social and economic exchange. Family and consanguineal kinship provided the roots of we versus others. From preliterate hunting and gathering societies we see increasingly complex forms of economic and political organization, but this powerful instinct to affiliate on the basis of blood and belonging is still the most potent source of identity and attachment to this day.[8] Identities still serve powerful social and economic functions — they guide how we think, who we associate with, and who we have conflicts with. Even economic and artistic pursuits are highly conditioned by one's set of social identities.

Most national identities are rooted in blood and belonging or minimally based on common ethno-linguistic foundations and strong shared historical or mythic narrative. Canada is relatively unique in featuring an ahistoric, multi-ethnic society. Some have argued that in the absence of traditional levers of nation-building the federal state has assumed a special role in constructing a sense of national identity.[9] In a period of turbulent debate concerning the role of the state and its connection to identity, it may be helpful to review the recent empirical evidence.

Against the backdrop of devolution and decentralization, diminution of federal role, the apparent inevitability of another Quebec referendum, continued western disaffection, shifting trade patterns from east-west to north-south, and inexorable globalization which some relate to the end of the nation-state, the answers to these questions may appear obvious. Our data and analysis will bring into question some of the current wisdom about the inevitability of these forces (while confirming other parts).

CANADIANS' CURRENT AND SHIFTING LEVELS OF ATTACHMENT

ATTACHMENT TO CANADA AND RECENT SHIFTS

The following two figures show how Canadians rate their sense of belonging to Canada and the provinces. The wording of the question is fairly straightforward and the stimuli (e.g., family, country) are presented in random order to the respondent. In this sample, a mean difference of about 0.2 on a seven-point scale is statistically significant.

Figure 1 shows that people do discriminate different sources of belonging and that family is the most important source of belonging. Of the political-geographic sources of belonging, Canada is strongest by a highly significant margin. This varies significantly by region, particularly in Quebec where only 55 percent express strong positive belonging to Canada. Overall, Canadians' high identification with country is unusual and many other advanced western countries reveal relatively stronger attachments to community and region. When this list of sources of belonging is extended to include North America or the world, these sources score the weakest of all sources.

Figure 1: Sense of Belonging for Canada

"Some people have a stronger sense of belonging to some things than others. Please tell me how strong your own personal sense of belonging is to each of the following. Use a 7-point scale where 1 means not strong at all, 7 means extremely strong and the midpoint 4 means somewhat strong."

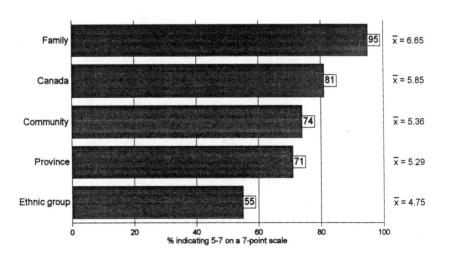

Note: n=1824
Source: EKOS Research Associates Inc., *Rethinking Citizen Engagement,* March 1998.

Figure 2 shows recent shifts in belonging to Canada and province. Overall, there have been no significant changes in strength of attachment to Canada over the nearly five-year period tested.[10] The fact that it remains so robust is interesting and important. Recall that this period straddles the Quebec referendum, growing levels of free trade, the federal deficit crisis, and the diminution and withdrawal of many key federal programs. It is not surprising given the range and depth of these shocks to federalism that many would predict the weakening of bonds connecting Canadians to Canada. It is, however, the case that attachments remained strong and stable.

The same figure shows a significant (tested using analysis of variance) shift in attachment to province.[11] Attachment to province is significantly weaker and more turbulent, and it actually declined over this same period. This trend will be even more revealing when we break it down by Ontario and Quebec.

Figure 2: Tracking a Sense of Belonging to Canada vs. Province

"Some people have a stronger sense of belonging to some things than others. Please tell me how strong your own personal sense of belonging is to each of the following. Use a 7-point scale where 1 means not strong at all, 7 means extremely strong and the midpoint 4 means somewhat strong."

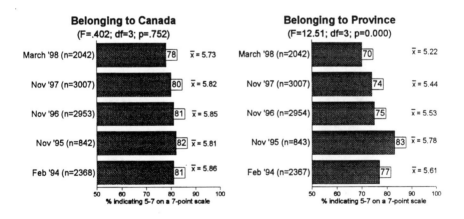

Source: EKOS Research Associates Inc., *Rethinking Government,* 1994-1997; *Rethinking Citizen Engagement,* March 1998.

COMPARATIVE IMPORTANCE OF NATIONAL ATTACHMENT AND
LONGER-TERM TRENDS

Neil Nevitte presents comparative survey evidence which supports the thesis
that national attachment is both relatively more important in Canada than other
western countries and has strengthened over the period he measures from 1981
to 1990 (Figure 3).[12] Our updates of this indicator show that identification
with a country has remained the most popular source of belonging in Canada
with locality declining further since 1990 (Figure 4).

Interestingly, Nevitte's data also show little support for the view that localism is rising as a source of attachment. In fact, town and region have declined
significantly everywhere. Conversely, more cosmopolitan sources of attachment (i.e., continent and world) increased over the period from 1981 to 1990.
The sizable advantage which Canada reveals in terms of identification with nation would undoubtedly be larger still if we were to focus only on English Canada.

Figure 3: *Percentage Belonging to Given Geographical Units, 1981-1990*

"To which of these groups would you say you belong, first of all? And what would come next?"

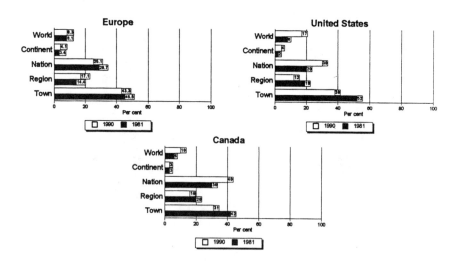

Source: International Comparative Research Group, 1981; and 1990 World Values Surveys.

Figure 4: Tracking Sense of Belonging for Canada

"To which of these groups would you say you belong, first of all?

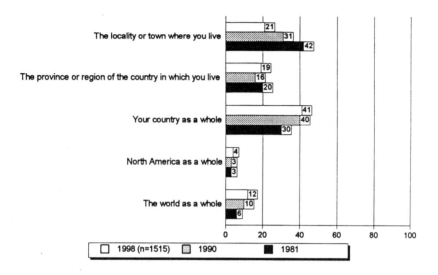

Source: EKOS Research Associates Inc., World Values Survey; and *Rethinking Government,* March 1998.

It is noteworthy that the international belonging advantage which Canada reveals does not extend to pride. Our data tracking "pride in Canadian culture" show no significant changes over the past 15 years. Canadian nationalism tends to be less chauvinistic and quieter than that of a country like the United States. Nevitte shows similar results in his review of the World Values Survey.[13] A more detailed cross-national analysis of national pride by Smith and Jarkko of NORC provides a much more detailed but consistent analysis of this phenomenon.[14]

Based on data from 1989 and 1990, Nevitte has suggested that the Canadian public is becoming less parochial and more cosmopolitan. Our newer findings suggest that these trends are continuing in Canada in 1998 (see Figure 4).

The proportion of Canadians who select a subnational unit (i.e., town or region) as their primary source of belonging has decreased steadily from 62 percent in 1981 to 40 percent in 1998. Over the same time period those who select a more cosmopolitan source of belonging (i.e., North America or the world) has also steadily increased, from 9 percent in 1981 to 16 percent in 1998. Belonging to country increased steadily from 1981 to 1990 (30 percent and 40 percent) but has stabilized over the past several years (41 percent in 1998). It still is, however, the most popular source of identity by a margin of over two to one for the next most popular source.

SUMMARY

Sense of belonging to Canada is quite high, second only to family. Sense of belonging to Canada is higher than for all other geographic levels and it has remained very high with no significant shifts over the past four years. Province and local community show lower levels of attachment and they show significant decline over same period. Comparatively, Canada has the highest levels of belonging to country of those areas tested in the World Values Survey. Longer-term trends show national attachment strengthening, local attachment declining, and cosmopolitan attachment rising but still clearly subordinate to national attachment.

EXAMINING RECENT SHIFTS IN QUEBEC AND ONTARIO

Focusing on Ontario and Quebec helps underline some important findings (Figure 5). First consider Ontario.

ONTARIO

For reasons noted in our introduction, Ontario provides an interesting point of focus for recent shifts in identity and attachment. Courchene argues that Ontario is moving away from its traditional role as the heartland of Canada to becoming a North American region/state. Although his thesis is by no means restricted, or even focused on the perceptions of Ontarians, it definitely strays into this area. Whether this reflects political or economic reality is debatable, but the evidence on attachment (and sense of role and status in Canada) flies in the face of this part of his thesis. Ontarians' sense of attachment to province has declined significantly since 1995. In 1995, 81 percent of Ontario residents expressed a strong sense of belonging to their province. By the spring of 1998, only 64 percent still felt this way. Meanwhile, Ontarians' attachment to Canada has remained largely stable over the past several years (and much higher than for province). Following the Quebec referendum, 95 percent of Ontario residents indicated a strong sense of belonging to Canada; in 1998, 87 percent still expressed this strong attachment to country. The fact that attachment to both Canada and province rose sharply in 1995 is an interesting phenomenon. We also saw a sharp rise in attachment to province in Quebec.

Figure 5: Tracking a Sense of Belonging for Ontario and Quebec

"Some people have a stronger sense of belonging to some things than others. Please tell me how strong your own personal sense of belonging is to each of the following. Use a 7-point scale where 1 means not strong at all, 7 means extremely strong and the midpoint 4 means somewhat strong."

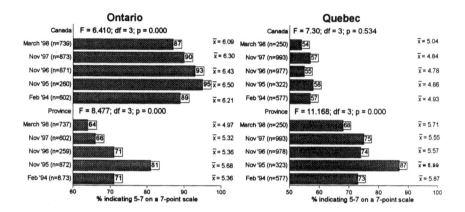

Source: EKOS Research Associates Inc., *Rethinking Government*, 1994-1997; *Rethinking Citizen Engagement*, March 1998.

Although it may be a statistical anomaly or "outlier," we suspect that it was conditioned by cultural insecurity linked to the trauma of the Quebec referendum debate (contemporaneous with this data collection). The sense of potential loss or profound change in identities associated with this event may have produced a temporary strengthening of attachments.

These Ontario findings bring into question the age-old dispute about the relative role of culture and economy in shaping each other (e.g., Marx's base and superstructure). Courchene clearly supports a materialist conception where economic arrangements (e.g., trade flow) will determine consciousness and identity. The data, at least in the short term, are difficult to reconcile with this perspective. We have seen no decline in affiliation to Canada as the vested economic interests of Ontarians shift from an east-west to north-south trade axis.

We will show later that nationalism is linked more strongly to idealism, values, and culture than to the economic realm. Economics and political economy are related to attachment, but more weakly. For example, we find that those who believe that their province does not receive its fair share are significantly less attached to Canada. Paradoxically, however, Ontarians are much less likely to feel this sentiment compared to respondents in other provinces. No doubt vested economic interests influence beliefs but they do not appear to determine them. Another possible explanation is that the extent of these shifts in economic interests may well be overstated. Helliwell's chapter in this volume argues that the vast majority of economic flows are still east-west in Canada.

For Ontario, Figure 5 reveals two key conclusions. First, attachment to province is substantially lower than attachment to Canada (and the national advantage is even larger focusing on the most intense level of attachment). Second, and particularly problematic for the Courchene thesis, attachment to Canada has remained fairly stable and high (95 percent to 87 percent), while provincial attachment has declined sharply (81 percent to 64 percent) over the past three years. This decline has occurred in spite of a period of unprecedented federal diminution and a relatively concentrated period of protest about Ontario's "fair share" from the past two premiers of Ontario.

The failure to grow, let alone even sustain, a serious regionalist identity alternative to Canada during this period, in spite of obvious political economic forces favouring such growth, provides cause for serious scepticism of the region-state hypothesis. These surprising trends are not unique to Ontario, although they are more apparent there.

QUEBEC

Quebec is different again. The most striking feature of the Quebec data is the profound difference in level of attachment to Canada. At 54 percent, attachment to Canada is much lower than attachment to province and tests of statistical significance indicate that over the time period examined, it is highly stable. Attachment to province is mercurial and the analysis of variance confirms highly significant fluctuations. The most recent sounding from last spring shows attachment to province at 68 percent down fully 19 points from the 87 percent registered in 1995 (post-referendum). Identification with Canada or Quebec is directly linked to sovereignist fortunes as Maurice Pinard and others have argued.[15]

A couple of further features of Quebec identity and attachment are worth noting. Quebecers' attachment to province (or "Quebec" in random wording experiments) is no higher than attachment to province in the rest of Canada. In fact, Newfoundlanders and Nova Scotians show significantly higher levels of attachment to province than Quebecers. What really distinguishes Quebecers is a lower attachment to Canada and a higher attachment to ethnic group than other Canadians. For example, Quebecers attachment to their ethnic group or national ancestry is the highest in Canada at 71 percent, while Ontarians attachment is at 58 percent. The lowest attachment to ethnic group or national ancestry is found in Alberta at 43 percent.[16]

Quebecers' identities are more plural and diffuse. Quebec identity is also rooted more in a sense of consanguinal community (what Michael Ignatieff refers to as the sense of "blood of belonging" characterizing ethnic nationalism[17]). But Quebec identity is more complex and pluralistic than this. Our subsequent multivariate analysis shows that not only is Quebec qualitatively different in terms of overall levels of identification and attachment but that the underlying structures and causal influences of identity are very different in Quebec. There are also some significant differences in the value structures of Quebecers.

PERCEIVED BASES OF NATIONAL IDENTITY AND UNDERLYING DIMENSIONS

In this section we present two types of analysis. First, we examine Canadians' self-reported perceptions and images of Canadian identity. Next, we conduct dimensional analysis using factor analytic tools to help discern the underlying patterns of meaning latent in the interconnections of the data.

PERCEPTIONS OF NATIONAL IDENTITY

It may be helpful to examine a couple of defining features of Canadian identity which are drawn from our recent research (Figure 6). There is a consensus within the Canadian public that there is a Canadian culture and that it is a positive source of pride and accomplishment: fully 83 percent agree that Canadian culture is something we can "all take pride in." Furthermore, participants in focus group sessions are explicit in their feelings of pride and nationalism about Canadian culture (although these feelings are much more pronounced in English Canada than in Quebec).

Canadians also believe that Canadian identity is elusive and complex. Seventy-six percent agree that it may be difficult to identify precisely but there definitely is a unique Canadian culture. The extent of the vagaries of Canadian identity is evident in the fact that 47 percent disagree with the suggestion that there really is no distinct Canadian identity, but fully 40 percent agree. Canadians also believe that identity is rooted in diversity. This almost Zen koan-like belief that unity lies in diversity is a recurring feature of qualitative research as well. This somewhat ambiguous notion that unity is stimulated by diversity does produce mixed responses. Amongst francophones and younger Canadians this positive unity-diversity linkage is viewed much more sceptically.

Figure 6: Perceptions of Canadian Identity

"Please rate the degree to which you agree or disagree with the following statements using a 7-point scale where 1 means you strongly disagree, 7 means you strongly agree and 4 means neither."

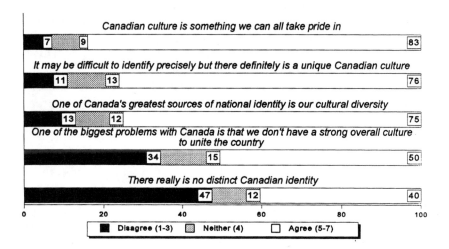

Note: n=1204
Source: EKOS Research Associates Inc./Les Associés de recherche Ekos inc., November 1995.

DIMENSIONAL ANALYSIS

A series of factor analyses were conducted using a battery of attitudinal variables from *Rethinking Government*, 1996.[18] Factor analysis is used to analyze multiple measures, identify a common underlying theme, and create a summary measure. This summary measure reduces the amount of data and the complexity of subsequent analysis. The summary measure also provides a more reliable measure than any single variable measure would provide.[19] Factors are now variables created by linking together the original variables used in the analysis to produce higher order factors. They reflect patterns of association which reflect the underlying structures or themes uniting various individual variables. Because they are based on observed correlations rather than direct questioning some argue that they detect underlying latent structures of meaning.

We chose 1996 because it had the most complete set of data related to this topic. Since some data were obtained on different waves of the 1996 *Rethinking Government* survey, only cases where there were valid observations for all variables were used in the analysis. Three core dimensions or summary measures emerged from the factor analysis which were relatively stable when tested using all cases or cases from only Ontario and Quebec. These three dimensions or factors represent an intuitively plausible organization of the original variables. After observing the configuration of the factor analysis, we labelled these dimensions (or factors) "liberalism," "conservatism," and "nationalism."[20] The variables which are most strongly related to each of these dimensions are presented in Tables 1 to 3. The correlation coefficients are a simple measure of the strength of relationship between two variables. The coefficient ranges between 1.0 (a perfect positive relationship) and -1.0 (a perfect negative or inverse relationship), with zero meaning no relationship at all. Each "loading" (coefficient) is a measure of the strength of connection between the original variable and the factor. Technically, a factor loading is a regression coefficient between the variable and the factor.

It is quite interesting to see the liberalism, conservatism, and nationalism factors emerging so distinctly. They also reveal different socio-demographic correlates, and they perform independently and meaningfully in models predicting strength of belonging to Canada. The theoretically plausible structure suggests that the data have usable validity and reliability. The loadings for the sense of belonging questions, however, varied substantially between Canada overall, Ontario, and Quebec.

Table 1: Factor Analysis for All Cases: "Liberalism" Factor

Variables Correlated with the LIBERALISM FACTOR	*Correlation Coefficients*
How important... social equality	0.744
How important... collective human rights	0.723
How important... distribution of wealth among poor and rich	0.639
How important... tolerance for different people, cultures, and ideas	0.624
How important... clean environment	0.602
How important... preservation of heritage	0.592
How important... social cohesion	0.565
How important... healthy population	0.561
How important... distribution of equality among all regions of Canada	0.513
How important... freedom	0.492

Table 2: Factor Analysis for All Cases: "Conservatism" Factor

Variables Correlated with the CONSERVATISM FACTOR	Correlation Coefficients
How important... thriftiness	0.646
How important... respect for authority	0.587
How important... prosperity and wealth	0.568
How important... security and safety	0.566
How important... hard work	0.536
How important... minimal government intrusions	0.502

Table 3: Factor Analysis for All Cases: "Nationalism" Factor

Variables Correlated with the NATIONALISM FACTOR	Correlation Coefficients
Sense of belonging... Canada	0.721
How important... national unity	0.668
How important... Canadian identity	0.666
All in all, government is a positive force in my life	0.579

Table 1 shows the individual variables that loaded (linked) on the liberalism factor. The strongest items, social equality, collective human rights, wealth redistribution and tolerance reflect popular small "l" liberal values. On the other hand, the key items in the separate (statistically independent) conservatism factor are quite recognizably small "c" conservative values (*viz.,* thriftiness, respect for authority, prosperity, security, hard work, and minimal government). The final factor clearly reflects national attachment or belonging to country, and the values of national unity and national identity. Interestingly, government as "a positive force in my life" is also incorporated in this factor. This reflects an interesting and stable linkage between identity and the role of the state; a linkage which we suspect is stronger in Canada than in most other countries.

In order to focus more narrowly on the underlying structure of the sense-of-belonging questions, a restricted factor analysis was conducted using only the five "sense-of-belonging" questions. When the questions were run alone

Table 4: Factor Analysis for All Cases: Sense-of-Belonging Variables

	Correlation Coefficients	
Sense of Belonging Variables	*Factor 1*	*Factor 2*
Sense of belonging... Canada	0.816	
Sense of belonging... your family	0.622	
Sense of belonging... your community	0.594	0.433
Sense of belonging... your ethnic group or national ancestry		0.796
Sense of belonging... your province		0.752

Table 5: Factor Analysis for Quebec Only: Sense-of-Belonging Questions

	Correlation Coefficients	
Sense of Belonging Variables	*Factor 1*	*Factor 2*
Sense of belonging... your ethnic group or national ancestry	0.713	
Sense of belonging... your community	0.667	
Sense of belonging... your province	0.649	-0.587
Sense of belonging... your family	0.554	
Sense of belonging... Canada		0.870

for all cases, two factors emerged, one with Canada, family, and community loading together and the other with ethnic group and province with some over-lap with sense of belonging to community as well (Table 4). The Quebec-only analysis revealed two different factors, one with ethnic group, community, province, and family loading together and on the second factor, province again loaded, *negatively* this time, with Canada (see Table 5). For Ontario, Table 6, only one factor resulted (also true for the Atlantic provinces and the west).

Recalling our earlier discussion, it appears that the underlying structure of identity in Quebec is more complex than in Ontario. We see a separate dimension of ethnic nationalism linked to province and family (blood and belonging?) and a separate Canadian identity, which competes with, and is negatively related to provincial identity. In Ontario, and the rest of Canada, nationalism is more unidimensional and exclusively "Canadian" in nature.

Table 6: Factor Analysis for Ontario Only: Sense-of-Belonging Variables

	Correlation Coefficients
Sense of Belonging Variables	*Factor 1*
Sense of belonging... your province	0.767
Sense of belonging... your community	0.716
Sense of belonging... Canada	0.672
Sense of belonging... your family	0.532
Sense of belonging... your ethnic group or national ancestry	0.511

EXPLAINING BELONGING TO CANADA

The analysis now turns to the problem of "explaining" sense of belonging to Canada. As noted earlier, we make no claims for rigorous causal explanation. We do, however, offer and test a number of hypotheses using simple bivariate cross-tabulations and correlations. These are drawn from our existing data using strength of belonging as our dependent variable. Our independent variables include: (i) measures of the perceived role of the state in general and the federal government in particular, (ii) rated values, and in particular, values rated most important for national government, and (iii) age (as a rough proxy for possible generational shifts). These variables are closely linked to some of the forces putatively underlying broader socio-economic changes discussed in our introduction. The bivariate analysis is easier to illustrate to the lay reader but it is susceptible to a number of methodological flaws; most notably the possibility of spurious causal relationship. Properly identified multivariate models can serve as a partial correction for this and other problems. We will present and discuss three final multivariate models which emerged from a much larger set of tested models.

GOVERNMENT

Tables 7a and b show a strong positive bivariate connection between a sense that strong national government is important, and a belief in the need for strong national standards. It is impressive to note the very small minorities who disagree. Moreover, agreement with the importance of strong national government and strong national standards is positively linked to a stronger sense of belonging to Canada. This may be somewhat obvious and slightly tautologous. Table 7c is less obvious.

Table 7a: Connection Between Attachment to Canada and Role of State

"Because of our vast geography and the diversity of our people, Canada cannot survive without a strong national government to provide shared goals and values."

	No Strong Attachment to Canada		Moderate Attachment to Canada		Very Strong Attachment to Canada		Total	
Disagree	52%	49	22%	34	8%	96	12%	179
Neither	15%	16	23%	34	10%	129	12%	179
Agree	32%	31	56%	83	82%	1022	76%	1136
Total	6%	96	10%	151	83.5%	1247	100%	1494

Notes: (Chi²=213, df=4, P<0.001)
     n=1494.
Source: EKOS Research Associates, *Rethinking Government,* November 1996.

Table 7b: Connection Between Attachment to Canada and Role of State (cont'd)

"How important is it to have strong national standards in the area of medicare?"

	No Strong Attachment to Canada		Moderate Attachment to Canada		Very Strong Attachment to Canada		Total	
Not important	13%	30	3%	19	2%	46	3%	85
Moderately important	10%	21	14%	39	5%	116	6%	176
Very important	76%	170	82%	219	93%	2299	91%	2688
Total	8%	221	9%	267	84%	2461	100%	2949

Notes: (Chi²=150, df=4, P<0.001)
    N=2949.
Source: EKOS Research Associates, *Rethinking Government,* November 1996.

Table 7c: Connection Between Attachment to Canada and Role of State (cont'd)

	"All in all, government is a positive force in my life"						
	No Strong Attachment to Canada		*Moderate Attachment to Canada*		*Very Strong Attachment to Canada*		*Total*
Disagree	62%	138	50%	134	33%	823	37%	1095
Neither	25%	57	29%	80	25%	625	26%	762
Agree	12%	27	21%	55	41%	1008	37%	1080
Total	8%	222	9%	269	83%	2456	100%	2947

Notes: (Chi^2=14, df=4, P<0.001)
n=2947.

Table 7d: Connection Between Attachment to Canada and Role of State (cont'd)

	"In the past three months, approximately how often have you personally had direct contact with the federal government, either initiated by yourself or a government official, including in-person, mail and telephone contacts?"						
	No Strong Attachment to Canada		*Moderate Attachment to Canada*		*Very Strong Attachment to Canada*		*Total*
Never	66%	147	69%	186	62%	1528	64%	1861
1-2 times	22%	50	16%	41	19%	460	19%	551
3+ times	11%	25	13%	34	18%	440	17%	499
Total	8%	222	9%	261	83%	2428	100%	2911

Notes: (Chi^2=14, df=4, P<0.001)
n=2911.

Belief that government (any government) is a "strong positive force in my life" produced highly polarized responses (37 percent agree, 37 percent disagree). A positive view of the state is strongly linked to strength of belonging to Canada. This effect remains robust in the multivariate models and is one of the few terms which has the same strength and direction of effect in Quebec and the rest of Canada. Recall that the factor analysis linked this variable to Canadian nationalism. Table 7*d* shows another linkage which is not attitudinal but behavioural. Those who have had more direct contact with the federal government are more likely to feel a significantly stronger sense of belonging to Canada. The effect is modest but important. It survives in some of our multivariate models (although not the one we chose for the conclusion of this chapter).

It is possible that stronger nationalism produces a greater desire to contact the federal government but the reverse is more likely. Contact, particularly meaningful, successful contact strengthens belonging. This leads to interesting questions about the future prospects for nationalism in a devolved universe where the lion's share of delivery and contact are shifted downwards to the provinces and municipalities with increased use of commercial and third sector delivery.

The broad underlying question is: What is the role of the federal state in constructing a sense of national belonging? Others have commented that the federal government has played an unusual role in constructing a sense of national identity in Canada.[21] Our data suggest that it is not only the role of the federal government but government in general which underlies a sense of national attachment in Canada. This dynamic appears to have persisted during a period where the federal role has withered somewhat. The prospects for the future, however, are less clear.

VALUES AND IDENTITY

Further reinforcing the connection between the state and identity is a random test of preferred values for society versus the federal government. Some *Rethinking Government* respondents were (randomly) asked to rate the most important values for society as opposed to the most important values that should guide the federal government. The comparison of results obtained using each version yields the important conclusion that these values are seen as basically identical. The federal ratings are generally slightly lower but the overall ranking and intensity ratings are virtually identical. Moreover, when factor analyzed, the underlying structures are identical for each level (federal, societal). This finding is similar to earlier research we have conducted randomizing societal priorities versus federal priorities. Often a conclusion of no difference in a test is seen as banal. In this case, the finding of no difference may be significant.

One possible interpretation is that Canadians largely equate societal values (and priorities) with the federal government. Another interpretation is that respondents simply answer the question with a focus on values rather than values for whom. Other evidence and analysis leads us to believe it is a little of each. For example, "family values" loads differently in the "social" version of the question than the "government" version which suggests that people do discriminate between different values for government and society, where appropriate. This is consistent with our earlier research and Richard Gwyn's notion of Canadian identity as constructed from "state-nationalism."[22] It also explains some of the anxiety and intensity of debate related to federal withdrawal. As discussed earlier, Canadians reveal a very strong attachment to Canada (particularly in English Canada). They worry about the fragility and viability of Canada in light of federal retrenchment, devolution, protracted unity troubles over the Quebec issue, and an increased sense of Americanization. Here we see evidence that Canadians see their societal values as inextricably connected to the federal state: the societal level is seen as slightly more important than the federal, but Canadians may have difficulty conceiving of a methodology for nation-building that excludes the federal government.

LINKS TO ECONOMY, POLITICAL ECONOMY AND CULTURAL INSECURITY

Table 8 summarizes selected correlations between strength of attachment to Canada and attitudes toward the economy and political economy.

*Table 8: **Connection Between Belonging to Canada and Selected Economic Attitudes***

	Pearson Correlation	Significance
I'm confident that I have the knowledge and skills to move easily in today's labour market (*Rethinking Government*, November 1997; n=2814)	-0.137	0.000
The most important things in life don't depend on money (*Rethinking Government*, April 1996; n=1385)	0.117	0.001
How would you rate your ability to access the Internet? (*Rethinking Government*, December 1996; n=1475)	-0.085	0.001
My province puts more into confederation than it gets out (*Rethinking Government*, November 1997; n=1471)	-0.089	0.001

The following variables are linked to *lower* levels of attachment to Canada: (i) those expressing the greatest confidence in their skills; (ii) those who are more materialistic are less attached to Canada; (iii) those who are most comfortable with technology; and (iv) those who do not feel that their province receives its fair share from Confederation. Attachment to Canada is inversely related to economic security. The most economically secure have the higher levels of attachment to Canada and the economically insecure have lower levels of attachment.

In our past analysis, we have also identified a cultural insecurity factor which is linked to economic insecurity. Cultural insecurity combines a sense of nostalgia and regret for the passage of old Canada with a sense of anxiety and trepidation about the pace of change. It is more deeply felt amongst more economically insecure, older, less educated, English-speaking Canadians. It is linked to a stronger attachment to Canada, almost as a desire to hang onto some symbolic anchors or roots in a bewildering world which is changing too quickly.

By corollary, and these correlations support this, those who feel confident and poised to meet the challenges of globalization and the new economy are less rooted in national identity. This may be a reflection of the more cosmopolitan ethnic characteristic of what Robert Reich referred to as the symbolic analyst class.[23] Symbolic analysts are techo-literate; and we also find that youth goes hand in hand with technological literacy. This may eventually weaken the viability of a unique Canadian identity in an increasingly information-driven global economy. These forces may eventually weaken attachment to Canada in a future where today's young Canadians dominate and look to symbols, narrative and economic interests less and less rooted in Canada.

One final point of interest from Table 8 is the positive correlation between self-expressed idealism and attachment to Canada. This correlation may indicate that economism, rationalism, and materialism are not the key drivers of attachment, and hence explain, in part, the improbable persistence of strong national attachment in a world where there is less and less of an economic reason to feel this way.

ATTACHMENT TO CANADA AND PROVINCE BY AGE

Examining how attachment to province and country vary by age reveals possible generational effects with young Canadians being much less attached to Canada (and other sources of identity) than their parents and grandparents (Figure 7). These may simply be reflections of patterns of aging effects rather than generational shifts but the possibility of a generational shift also exists and must be considered.

Analysis of variance demonstrates statistically significant age effect on the sense of belonging to Canada. Overall, between 1994 and 1997 the attachment to Canada for Canadian youth was considerably lower compared to the evidence

Figure 7: Sense of Belonging for Canada

"Some people have a stronger sense of belonging to some things than others. Please tell me how strong your own personal sense of belonging is to each of the following. Use a 7-point scale where 1 means not strong at all, 7 means extremely strong and the midpoint 4 means somewhat strong."

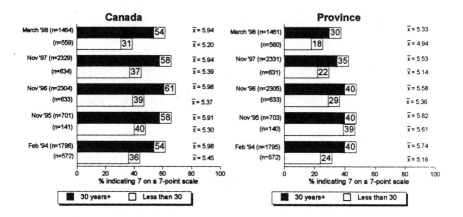

Source: EKOS Research Associates Inc., *Rethinking Government,* 1994-1997; *Rethinking Citizen Engagement,* March 1998.

for their parents and grandparents. Overall, however, the sense of belonging to Canada did not vary significantly according to the year of our study. To put it in other words, changes in belonging means over years are too small to be considered as statistically significant shifts. When exploring the interaction effect of age and year, the interaction effect was non-significant, which indicates that there was no difference in average ratings over time for each of the two age groups. So, overall, young people are less attached to Canada in each year but attachment to Canada has not changed.

Different results are produced by the analysis of variance for the sense of belonging to province. As in the case of belonging to Canada, generation plays a statistically significant effect on the variance of overall scores with young Canadians feeling less attached to their province than their older counterparts. Moreover, the sense of belonging to province decreases significantly according to the year of the study. Finally, there is a statistically significant interaction effect between respondents' age and year of the study. There is some evidence that the overall attachment advantage which Canada enjoys over province is much smaller for young people and is narrowing. We have seen this phenomenon expressed in a range of parallel analyses that we have conducted.

This sheds interesting light on the issue of the "self-sustaining thesis" which suggests that even though identity was constructed through state-nationalism it can now persist independently. Whereas, clearly, there is some inertia to Canadian nationalism, these potential generational splits bring into question the idea that nationalism will persist indefinitely without state intervention. This conjecture becomes more troublesome still for Canadian nationalists when it is linked to the symbolic analysts-globalization trends discussed earlier. In other words, the mutual influences of aging, technology, and globalization could well lead to a Canada which engenders much lower levels of attachment in the future.

MULTIVARIATE ANALYSIS

If factor analysis can help identify latent mental maps used to cognitively organize different values and attitudes, regression analysis can help isolate the relative contribution of these forces to attachment and belonging. We are attempting to roughly isolate the relative explanatory power of different forces. We utilize the factors of liberalism and conservatism, as well as other demographic and behavioural variables in order to model the strength of belonging. These models are better approximations of causal tests than the simple bivariate tests examined in the preceding section.

A series of regression models[24] were run using the conservatism and liberalism factors described earlier,[25] the rating for the perception that government is a positive force in the respondent's life, and the four remaining sense-of-belonging questions (family, community, province, and ethnic group) as predictors. The results of this model for all cases are presented in Table 9. Based on these models, the best predictors of a sense of belonging to Canada were sense of belonging to your community (beta = 0.22), government is a positive factor in my life (beta = 0.22), and the conservatism factor (beta = 0.19); — all with positive coefficients. The positive coefficients indicate that higher levels of sense of belonging to community, the perception that government is a positive factor in one's life, and higher levels of conservatism were all correlated with higher levels of a sense of belonging to Canada. Weaker, but still significant, linkages are evident between sense of belonging to province and ethnic group. These variables had a negative impact on a sense of belonging to Canada, while sense of belonging to family had a positive coefficient. The only insignificant variable was the liberalism factor of trying to incorporate the very different structure of the Quebec and rest-of-Canada (ROC) data. Testing separate models for Quebec and ROC proved more useful.

Once this model had been developed, the impact of including a variable representing Quebec versus all other regions was tested. The inclusion of this variable was highly significant and once a dummy variable for Quebec entered the equation, ethnic group became highly non-significant.[26] All in all,

Table 9: Multivariate Analysis of Belonging to Canada for All Cases

Independent Variables	Dependent Variable: Sense of Belonging to Canada				
	B	Std. Error	Beta	t	Sig.
Sense of belonging... your community	0.242	0.003	0.224	7.243	0.000
Sense of belonging... your family	0.177	0.053	0.100	3.378	0.001
Sense of belonging... your ethnic group and national ancestry	-0.0896	0.025	-0.107	-3.563	0.000
Sense of belonging... your province	-0.0759	0.033	-0.071	-2.317	0.021
Liberalism	0.0045	0.004	0.035	1.087	0.277
Conservatism	0.0258	0.004	0.194	5.950	0.000
All in all, government is a positive force in my life	0.207	0.027	0.220	7.713	0.000
Constant	1.084	0.446	—	2.430	0.015

the attempt to construct an overall model of attachment to Canada is quite difficult, particularly because of the stress of trying to incorporate the very different structure of the Quebec and ROC data. Testing separate models for Quebec and ROC proved more useful.

Was the structure of the equation different for Quebec versus the rest of Canada? To answer that question, a formal test of the interaction between Quebec and all the attitudinal variables was conducted. The test revealed that there was a strong statistically significant interaction effect. The significant interaction effect indicates that the structure of the Quebec model (compared to other regions) was substantially different, and the model coefficients for all of Canada presented in Table 9 could not be applied to Quebec and the other regions equally. To refine the nature of these structural differences, a segmented model was run for Quebec and Ontario using the exact same variables used in the model for Canada overall. The differences are both significant and revealing. As seen from Table 10, for Quebec, the most important predictors of sense of belonging to Canada were a sense of belonging to province (beta = -0.35), overall government is a positive force (beta = 0.26) and a sense of belonging to community (beta = 0.18). The key difference is the very strong negative influence of a sense of belonging to province, compared to the weaker (but

Table 10: Multivariate Analysis of Belonging to Canada for Quebec

Independent Variables	Dependent Variable: Sense of Belonging to Canada				
	B	Std. Error	Beta	t	Sig.
Sense of belonging... your community	0.220	0.064	0.182	3.437	0.001
Sense of belonging... your family	0.042	0.094	0.024	0.442	0.659
Sense of belonging... your ethnic group and national ancestry	0.086	0.066	-0.073	1.297	0.196
Sense of belonging... your province	-0.452	0.072	-0.353	-6.281	0.000
Liberalism	0.017	0.011	0.097	1.653	0.099
Conservatism	0.023	0.009	0.148	2.477	0.014
All in all, government is a positive force in my life	0.313	0.060	0.264	5.182	0.000
Constant	1.070	0.955	—	1.120	0.264

still negative) coefficient in the overall model. Of the remaining variables, the only significant predictor was the conservative factor (a positive coefficient). Ethnic group, family, and liberalism were all non-significant.

The Ontario model (see Table 11) was substantially different from the Quebec model. First, the most important predictors were a sense of belonging to province (beta = 0.31) and a sense of belonging to family (beta = 0.29). The strong *positive* relationship between sense of belonging to province and sense of belonging to Canada for Ontario residents stands in marked contrast to the strong *negative* relationship for Quebec residents. While this was probably the most extreme difference between the Quebec and Ontario models, it was not the only significant difference. Unlike the Quebec model where the conservatism factor was a significant predictor, for the Ontario model the conservatism factor was highly non-significant and the liberalism factor showed a significant positive relationship to sense of belonging to Canada. Government as a positive force remained significant, however, sense of belonging to community and ethnic group were non-significant.

To summarize, Quebecers' sense of attachment to Canada is not only qualitatively much lower than in other parts of Canada but the underlying structure is quite different. Moreover, the factors producing attachment in Quebec are

Table 11: Multivariate Analysis of Belonging to Canada for Ontario

Independent Variables	Dependent Variable: Sense of Belonging to Canada				
	B	Std. Error	Beta	t	Sig.
Sense of belonging... your community	0.0104	0.038	0.014	0.273	0.785
Sense of belonging... your family	0.436	0.075	0.288	5.822	0.000
Sense of belonging... your ethnic group and national ancestry	-0.015	0.026	-0.031	-0.602	0.547
Sense of belonging... your province	0.197	0.035	0.309	5.610	0.000
Liberalism	0.0117	0.004	0.160	3.087	0.002
Conservatism	-0.0036	0.005	-0.035	-0.670	0.503
All in all, government is a positive force in my life	0.0993	0.027	0.172	3.615	0.000
Constant	1.362	0.513	—	2.653	0.008

quite different. In Ontario, (and the ROC) attachment to provinces *reinforces* belonging to Canada; in Quebec it is the other way around. In Ontario belief in liberal political culture reinforces attachment to Canada; in Quebec it is conservatism that stimulates attachment to Canada. Interestingly, the key unifying factor across both Quebec and ROC is positive attitudes to the role of the state.

CONCLUSIONS: WHITHER CANADIAN NATIONALISM?

This review and the analysis shed fairly clear light on two of the three originating questions "What are current levels of attachment to Canada?" and "How have they been changing?" These answers are relatively straightforward and pose significant challenges to theories of ongoing or imminent national disintegration. We also provide some helpful, but much less definitive evidence regarding the question "Why are these changes (or lack of changes) occurring?"

For those who have waded through the statistical manipulation in the middle of this paper, and more pointedly, for those who have skipped to the substantive conclusion we will try to make some sense of this exercise.

THE CORE QUESTIONS

Let us first consider the less controversial conclusions of this analysis.

National Trends. We find that sense of belonging to Canada is quite high, second only to family. Sense of belonging to Canada is higher than for all other geographic units and it has remained very high with no significant shifts over the past four years. Province and local community show lower levels of attachment and they have experienced significant decline over the same period.

International Comparisons. Comparatively, Canada has the highest levels of belonging to country of all areas tested in the World Values Survey. Longer-term (30 year) trends show national attachment strengthening, local attachment declining and cosmopolitan attachment rising, but still clearly subordinate to national attachment.

Ontario. Ontario does not show any significant evidence of declining attachment to Canada over the past five years and attachment to region has actually declined in a statistically and substantively significant fashion. These conclusions are true in spite of a declining federal presence, shifts in the density of interprovincial versus international trade flows and growing critique of fair share and other federalism issues from provincial leaders from the left and right of the political spectrum.

Quebec. In terms of the underlying structure of identity and attachment Ontario is similar to the rest of Canada. Quebec on the other hand is quite different. Although there are some cross-cutting loyalties and patterns of similarity Quebec really is distinct in its patterns of attachment and identification. Quebecers reveal *much* lower levels of attachment to Canada, but they have also shown sharply declining attachment to the province over the past four years. In fact, what distinguishes Quebecers from other Canadians today is *not* higher levels of attachment to Quebec but lower attachment to Canada (and significantly higher attachment to ethnic group). Quebecers' attachment to province has been quite mercurial and this turbulence is greater than in any other part of Canada. The sharp decline in attachment to province is also linked to a sharp decline in the intention to vote yes in a future referendum.[27]

IS THERE A CANADIAN IDENTITY? DOES IT MATTER?

Our data indicate that there is a Canadian identity, that Canadians believe that there is a national identity, and that it is a source of pride and belonging. Moreover, there is also a Quebec identity which coexists with this Canadian identity, although Quebecers reveal mixed allegiances. In English Canada, *Canadian* identity is clearer and more important to the citizenry. This identity is somewhat vague and amorphous; it is a loose combination of diversity, values, political-geography, and state-nationalism. In Quebec, identity is more pluralistic and split across ethno-linguistic nationalism for Quebec and allegiance to Canada.

Canadian identity, although confused, is extremely important, particularly for English Canadians. It engenders powerful attachment (even against international comparison) and it outstrips all other sources of belonging (save family). Canadian identity is strongest in older, less secure anglophones. By corollary, identity is weaker amongst the more secure, younger and agile portions of Canadian society. Our data also suggest that identities do not compete; they reinforce each other, particularly at the local/regional level. Quebec is an exception to this reinforcement rule: country and province do compete. However, the Canada-province link is strong throughout the rest of the country. For most Canadians, the province-Canada question is not an issue of either/ or. In fact, they tend to mutually reinforce each other.

DESCRIBING NATIONAL IDENTITY AND ATTACHMENT

Dimensional analysis of linked attitudinal data reveals a theoretically plausible underlying structure of national identity. The key ingredients are values, which separate clearly into conservative and liberal values; attachment to other geographic and social groups; attitudes to government; and attitudes to skills, technology, and globalization (the latter is less reliable). This structure can be applied (loosely) on a pan-Canadian basis.

If we restrict attention to sources of belonging (i.e., family, province, community, and ethnic group) we are incapable of developing a Canada-wide model. Quebec splits into two dimensions with province, ethnic group, community and family all forming one factor (blood and belonging?) and belonging to Canada on its own, with a strong negative loading for province. In Ontario, and the rest of Canada, the belonging variables are unidimensional with each tending to reinforce the other.

EXPLAINING NATIONAL ATTACHMENT

The explanatory analysis suggests that attitudes and interaction with government positively correlates with Canadian nationalism. The overall analyses suggest that government in general and the federal government in particular are key sources of national attachment. Although Canadians do not reduce Canada to government, the state is inextricably linked to the future of Canadian nationalism. The relationship is clearly not a simple linear relationship. One can reasonably speculate that the response of the federal state is the key conditional variable underlying the future of nationalism in Canada (and Quebec).

Values are connected to sense of belonging although the intensity and direction of these connections varies by the value considered the social setting. For example, conservative values are positively linked to Canadian nationalism in Quebec whereas liberal values are positively linked in Ontario. We also find that in general, self-professed idealism and non-economic values are more strongly linked to the sense of belonging. This connection may help explain the partial failure of economistic-materialistic theories to account for recent trends, although there is evidence that perception of vested interests are separately linked to nationalist sentiments in a rational manner.

Another key conclusion is that blending Quebec with Ontario or the rest of Canada tends to obscure certain important dynamics of nationalism. Although some forces work the same way (e.g., a positive perception of the role of governments in general), other key forces work in opposite directions. For example, belonging to province *reinforces* belonging to Canada in Ontario, but sharply *reduces* belonging to Canada in Quebec. In general, sense of belonging to one level reinforces sense of belonging to all other levels and by corollary disconnection at one level is linked to broader alienation.

LOOKING FORWARD: WHITHER CANADA?

The preceding conclusions are firmly rooted in our empirical analysis. We can also speculate about broader issues which are too important to be left to the purely empirical realm. We believe that we can construct reasoned conjectures about the forces driving levels of attachment. This provides an alternative picture of nationalism which is at least as firmly rooted in logic and evidence as some of the more dramatic accounts of the ongoing weakening and demise of Canadian nationalism. Our analysis leads to some areas of broad agreement, with some of the pressures on Canadian attachment, but leaves open the strong possibility of the persistence of a strong, dominant national identity (in English Canada) albeit with significant alterations.

So are we really witnessing the end of the nation-state as a source of salient identification? Is national affiliation fading against the backdrop of globalization and an anachronistic federal state? Somewhat surprisingly, there was a general rise in national attachment in Canada (and even the United States) between 1980 and 1990; meanwhile, attachment to communities went down despite the rising localism claims of some theorists (e.g., Courchene's "globalism"). In Canada, the trend in favour of country was even more pronounced. The nation-state may be fading, but the empirical attitudinal evidence shows that this has yet to express itself in the realm of public attitudes.

The key conditional question lies in the future response of the federal state. In Canada, the state has played a crucial role in constructing national identity. This linkage is clearly evident in several lines of the analysis presented here. If the Canadian federal state does not offer a vigorous and different vision of Canada to younger Canadians then the seeds of dissolution evident in our analysis may take root. On the other hand, there is ample evidence of strong demand and preference for the construction of a new twenty-first century Canadian identity. Although hazardous social forecasting is a tempting exercise, those seeing one clear future path poses either more skill or courage than this analyst. Certain trends and conditional outcomes are more plausible than others.

The recent crisis of federalism linked to fiscal and unity woes has had the ironic impact of strengthening national attachments while weakening provincial attachments. The long-term viability of this crisis effect as a boon to Canadian nationalism is highly questionable, as is the thesis of how self-sustaining it is. In our survey research, Canadians themselves discount the possibility of a rudderless, standardless Canada surviving. Moreover, generational shifts suggest weakening attachment amongst the youngest cohort (who have experienced diminished federalism during this period).

One of the more important but less obvious conclusions that we draw is that the production of a national identity is more strongly linked to ideals and values than programs and policies (although these two interact). Material interests and political economy appear to exert a significant but modest influence on national attachment. It appears, however, that values and ideals are even more potent forces. In particular, the case of Ontario vividly contradicts the thesis that sentimental attachments will follow political/economic interests.

It may well be that the desire for a sense of place, community and meaning in a too-rapidly changing world is more important than the rational calculus of benefits and costs. The elusiveness of these conclusions to many elites may lie in class differences in acknowledging the role of idealistic and materialistic factors. Our ongoing research in the *Rethinking Government* project shows that elites give far greater prominence to economic-material factors than do the general public. These polarizing trends may be reinforced by the role of globalization, technology and the new class (of cosmopolitan symbolic analysts). Our analysis reveals that participation in the new class, use of new information technology and feeling well-equipped to negotiate globalization all lead to a diminished need for a national identity. Insecurity, however, both cultural and economic, is at least as prevalent as security. Perhaps this is why the putative collapse of nationalism, tribalism, and ideology, predicted by various post-industrial theorists has failed to materialize.

Localism, regionalism, and cosmopolitanism may all blend to displace nationalism in the next millennium. Canada may well disappear and citizens may even be happier under this new order. After all, state nationalism and multi-ethnic federalism are merely ephemeral blips in the evolution of human sources of identity and community. In the meantime, however, we must consider that the very recent trends based on empirical analysis of claimed identities and attachments of citizens themselves do not follow these patterns or predictions. Moreover, Canadians demonstrate an intense penchant for maintaining this somewhat improbable model of identity and attachment.

NOTES

I would like to acknowledge the very helpful comments of Tom McIntosh and especially Harvey Lazar, both from the Institute of Intergovernmental Relations. Whereas the author is responsible for any errors, there is also a need to share any credit with several others, including two earlier anonymous reviewers who offered criticisms which were both blunt and fair. I received helpful editorial assistance from Sheila Redmond of EKOS and additional helpful comments from Matthew Mendelsohn, Department of Political Studies, Queen's University, Donna Nixon of the Canada Information Office and Dana-Mae Grainger of Canadian Heritage.

1.   For example, see George Grant, *Lament for a Nation: The Defeat of Canadian Nationalism* (Toronto: Macmillan, 1965)

2.   Thomas Courchene with C. Telmer, *From Heartland to North American Region State* (Toronto: Centre for Public Management, University of Toronto, 1998); Robert D. Kaplan, *An Empire Wilderness: Travels into America's Future* (New York: Random House, 1998).

3.   The methodology for each year of the *Rethinking Government* study typically involves the following components: an initial telephone interview of over 200 questions with a random sample of 3,000 Canadians 16 years and over;

   • a second detailed telephone interview (over 150 questions) with approximately 1,500 of the original 3,000 public survey respondents;
   • a third survey of the general public (over 150 questions) with approximately 1,300 of the original 3,000 panel respondents, and 200 general public respondents;
   • six follow-up focus group sessions with respondents from "Rethinking Government"; and
   • a survey of the top governing and economic decisionmakers in Canada.

   Question wording and sampling will be provided as data are introduced. Additional methodological information is provided in Appendix B.

4.   Courchene, *From Heartland to North American Region State*, p. 14.

5.   For a solid introduction to factor analysis, see Chapter 12 in Marija I Norusis/ SPSS Inc., *SPSS Base System User's Guide* (Chicago: SPSS Inc., 1990).

6.   Neil Nevitte, *The Decline of Deference* (Toronto: Broadview Press, 1996).

7.   For an introductory discussion of these issues, see Frank Graves, "The Changing Role of Nonrandomized Research Designs in Assessment," in *Action Oriented*

Evaluation in Organizations, ed. Joe Hudson, John Mayne and Ray Thomlison (Toronto: Wall and Emerson Inc., 1992), pp. 230-54.

8.   For a contemporary treatment of the topic, see Michael Ignatieff, *Blood and Belonging* (Toronto: Viking, 1993).

9.   Richard Gwyn, *Nationalism Without Walls* (Toronto: McClelland & Stewart, 1995).

10. The F statistic reported in the figure is essentially the ratio of the variance in the dependent variable (in this case the sense of belonging) that can be explained by the predictor or independent variable (in this case time) relative to the variance that can be explained using only the mean of the dependent variable as the predictor. The p value is the likelihood or probability that a statistic occurred by chance. A p value of less than 0.05 is generally used to reject the hypothesis that the observed statistic could have occurred by chance.

11. Analysis of variance was conducted on the *Rethinking Government* data from 1994 to 1997. The March 1998 data presented in this and subsequent exhibits is drawn from EKOS Research Associates Inc.'s *Rethinking Citizen Engagement* study.

12. Nevitte, *The Decline of Deference.*

13. Ibid.

14. Tom W. Smith and Lars Jarkko, "National Pride: A Cross-National Analysis," CSS Cross-National Report No. 19 (Chicago, IL: National Opinion Research Center/University of Chicago, 1988).

15. Maurice Pinard and Robert Bernier, *Un combat inachevé* (Sainte-Foy: Presses de l'Université du Québec, 1997).

16. EKOS, *"Rethinking Government IV."*

17. Ignatieff, *Blood and Belonging.*

18. The analyses were performed using a principal components extraction with a varimax rotation.

19. See H.H. Harmon, *Modern Factor Analysis*, 2d ed. (Chicago, IL: University of Chicago Press, 1967).

20. A fourth factor consisted of measure of confidence in skills and self-rated ability to work with computers. However, the reliability coefficient for this factor was relatively low.

21. For example, see Gwyn, *Nationalism Without Walls.*

22. Ibid.

23. Robert Reich, *The Work of Nations: Preparing Ourselves for the 21st Century* (New York: Vintage Books, 1992).

24. Regression models allow the testing of the relationship between one independent variable or predictor and the dependent variable while holding the effect of all other variables in the model constant. A Beta coefficient measures the amount of change in the dependent variable as a result of one standardized (e.g., using

two scores, which are the result of subtracting the mean from each value of a variable and dividing the result by its standard deviation, having a mean of zero and a standard deviation of one) unit of change in the independent or predictor variable, controlling for or holding constant all other variables in the regression model. Since both the dependent and independent variables are standardized, the coefficients between different variables can be compared. The Bs, or unstandardized regression coefficients, measure the amount of change in the dependent variable as a result of a change of one unit in predictor. But since the units of measurement are not standardized, the coefficients for different variables cannot be compared unless they have the same unit of measurement. For example, comparing an unstandardized coefficient for total household income and the age of the respondent would be meaningless since one variable has a unit of measurement in the thousands and the other virtually never exceeds 100. Since the unstandardized coefficients (Bs) in the model are sensitive to differences in the units of measurement for each predictor, the standardized coefficients (Betas) should be used to compare results between different predictors used in the models. Fred N. Kerlinger and Elazar J. Pedhazur, *Multiple Regression in Behavioral Research* (New York: Holt, Rinehart, and Winston, 1973).

25.   The scales were simple additive scales which were the sum of each variable listed in Tables 1 to 3. To maintain the original seven-point scale measurement, each summary measure was divided by the number of variables used to create the measure, yielding an average score that ranged between one and seven.

26.   The dummy variable for Quebec is a variable which is coded one if the respondent is from Quebec, and zero otherwise. This variable measures how much higher or lower on the dependent measure residents of Quebec tend to be compared to respondents from all other regions, all other variables in the equation being held constant.

27.   See EKOS Research Associates Inc, *Press Release*, "Sovereignty Movement at Ebb Point as Charest Enters Quebec Theatre," 1 April 1998.

APPENDIX A
Correlation Between Sense of Belonging to Canada and Attitudinal Variables

Table A-1: Correlation Between Sense of Belonging to Canada and Values — Canada

	Sense of Belonging... Canada	
Attitudinal Variables	*Pearson Correlation*	*Two-Tailed Significance*
Liberal factor	0.180	0.000
Neo-conservative factor	0.248	0.000
Nationalism factor	0.577	0.000
Sense of belonging... your community	0.276	0.000
Sense of belonging... your ethnic group and national ancestry	0.014	0.600
Sense of belonging... your family	0.195	0.000
How would you rate your ability to work with computers?	-0.086	0.001
I'm confident that I have a knowledge and skills necessary	-0.175	0.000
How important... Canadian identity	0.519	0.001
How important... national unity	0.484	0.000
How important... hard work	0.286	0.000
How important... distribution of equality among all regions of Canada	0.242	0.000
How important... security and safety	0.214	0.000
How important... respect for authority	0.201	0.000
How important... clean environment	0.165	0.000
How important... tolerance for different people, cultures, and ideas	0.163	0.000
How important... thriftiness	0.129	0.000
How important... healthy population	0.132	0.000
How important... social cohesion	0.135	0.000
How important... family values	0.135	0.000
How important... freedom	0.112	0.000
How important... collective human rights	0.083	0.002
How important... social equality	0.085	0.001
How important... minimal government intrusions	0.062	0.020
How important... prosperity and wealth	0.061	0.023
How important... preservation of heritage	0.053	0.044
How important... distribution of wealth among poor and rich	-0.010	0.712
How important... integrity and ethics	0.198	0.000
All in all, government is a positive force in my life	0.227	0.000

Table A-2: Correlation Between Sense of Belonging to Canada and Values — Quebec

Attitudinal Variables	Sense of Belonging... Canada	
	Pearson Correlation	Two-Tailed Significance
Liberal factor	0.230	0.000
Neo-conservative factor	0.268	0.000
Nationalism factor	0.698	0.000
Sense of belonging... your community	0.180	0.001
Sense of belonging... your ethnic group and national ancestry	0.070	0.181
Sense of belonging... your family	0.100	0.055
How would you rate your ability to work with computers?	-0.106	0.044
I'm confident that I have a knowledge and skills necessary	-0.194	0.000
All in all, government is a positive force in my life	0.260	0.000

Table A-3: Correlation Between Sense of Belonging to Canada and Values — Ontario

Attitudinal Variables	Sense of Belonging... Canada	
	Pearson Correlation	Two-Tailed Significance
Liberal factor	0.292	0.000
Neo-conservative factor	0.196	0.000
Nationalism factor	0.382	0.000
Sense of belonging... your community	0.277	0.000
Sense of belonging... your ethnic group and national ancestry	0.190	0.000
Sense of belonging... your family	0.383	0.000
How would you rate your ability to work with computers?	-0.105	0.034
I'm confident that I have a knowledge and skills necessary	0.035	0.485
All in all, government is a positive force in my life	0.272	0.000

APPENDIX B
Survey Marginals

Frequencies

The following frequencies are drawn from *Rethinking Government 1994 to 1997* and *Rethinking Citizen Engagement 1998 Surveys.* Included are the complete questions with preambles as well as frequencies, means, standard deviations, and number of respondents.

RG94-1

FAM

Your family

01	Not strong at all	1	0%
02		2	0
03		3	1
04	Moderately strong	4	2
05		5	4
06		6	9	$\bar{x}=6.71$
07	Extremely strong	7	84	s=0.81
08	DK/NR	9	0	n=2369

COMM

Your community

01	Not strong at all	1	2%
02		2	2
03		3	3
04	Moderately strong	4	13
05		5	17
06		6	24	$\bar{x}=5.62$
07	Extremely strong	7	37	s=1.47
08	DK/NR	9	0	n=2369

PROV1

Your province

01	Not strong at all	1	3%
02		2	2
03		3	4
04	Moderately strong	4	15
05		5	17
06		6	23	$\bar{x}=5.57$
07	Extremely strong	7	37	s=1.51
08	DK/NR	9	0	n=2369

COUN

Canada

01	Not strong at all	1	3%	
02		2	2	
03		3	3	
04	Moderately strong	4	11	
05		5	11	_
06		6	18	x=5.85
07	Extremely strong	7	51	s=1.55
08	DK/NR	9	0	n=2369

RBEL4

Some people have a strong sense of belonging to some things than others. Please tell me how strong your own personal sense of belonging is to each of the following. Please use a 7-point scale where 1 means not strong at all, 7 means extremely strong and the mid-point 4 means moderately strong.

YFAM4

Rotation => YRELG

MESSAGE: HOW STRONG...TO YOUR OWN PERSONAL SENSE OF BELONGING ON A 7-POINT SCALE

Your family

01	Not strong at all	1	1%	
02		2	1	
03		3	1	
04	Moderately strong	4	3	
05		5	6	_
06		6	16	x=6.47
07	Extremely strong	7	72	s=1.10
08	DK/NR	9	0	n=1204

YCOM4

MESSAGE: HOW STRONG...TO YOUR OWN PERSONAL SENSE OF BELONGING ON A 7-POINT SCALE

Your community

01	Not strong at all	1	3%	
02		2	2	
03		3	4	
04	Moderately strong	4	16	
05		5	23	_
06		6	25	x=5.39
07	Extremely strong	7	28	s=1.47
08	DK/NR	9	0	n=1204

YPROV

MESSAGE: HOW STRONG...TO YOUR OWN PERSONAL SENSE OF BELONGING ON A 7-POINT SCALE
Your province

01	Not strong at all	1	2%	
02		2	2	
03		3	3	
04	Moderately strong	4	11	
05		5	17	_
06		6	25	x=5.76
07	Extremely strong	7	40	s=1.38
08	DK/NR	9	0	n=1204

YCANA

MESSAGE: HOW STRONG...TO YOUR OWN PERSONAL SENSE OF BELONGING ON A 7-POINT SCALE
Canada

01	Not strong at all	1	3%	
02		2	2	
03		3	2	
04	Moderately strong	4	6	
05		5	10	_
06		6	22	x=5.99
07	Extremely strong	7	54	s=1.51
08	DK/NR	9	0	n=1204

YETHC

MESSAGE: HOW STRONG...TO YOUR OWN PERSONAL SENSE OF BELONGING ON A 7-POINT SCALE
Your ethnic group or national ancestry

01	Not strong at all	1	4%	
02		2	3	
03		3	5	
04	Moderately strong	4	17	
05		5	19	_
06		6	22	x=5.25
07	Extremely strong	7	29	s=1.63
08	DK/NR	9	0	n=1204

RG96-1

P8

Some people have a stronger sense of belonging to some things than others. Please tell me how strong your own personal sense of belonging is to each of the following. Please use a 7-point scale where 1 means not strong at all, 7 means extremely strong and the mid-point 4 means moderately strong.

YFAM8

Rotation => YETH8

MESSAGE: HOW STRONG IS YOUR OWN PERSONAL SENSE OF BELONGING TO ...
Your family

			Quebec		All	
01	Not strong at all	1	1%		1%	
02		2	1		0	
03		3	1		1	
04	Moderately strong	4	5		3	
05		5	4	_	3	_
06		6	11	x=6.5	10	x=6.7
07	Extremely strong	7	77	s=1.1	82	s=1.0
08	DK/NR	9	1	n=984	0	n=2961

YCOM8

MESSAGE: HOW STRONG IS YOUR OWN PERSONAL SENSE OF BELONGING TO ...
Your community

			Quebec		All	
01	Not strong at all	1	6%		3%	
02		2	4		3	
03		3	6		5	
04	Moderately strong	4	21		17	
05		5	19	_	19	_
06		6	16	x=5.0	22	x=5.4
07	Extremely strong	7	27	s=1.8	31	s=1.6
08	DK/NR	9	1	n=984	0	n=2961

YPRV8

MESSAGE: HOW STRONG IS YOUR OWN PERSONAL SENSE OF BELONGING TO ...
Your province

			Quebec		All	
01	Not strong at all	1	3%		3%	
02		2	2		2	
03		3	3		4	
04	Moderately strong	4	18		16	
05		5	14	_	18	_
06		6	18	x=5.6	21	x=5.4
07	Extremely strong	7	41	s=1.6	35	s=1.6
08	DK/NR	9	0	n=984	0	n=2961

YCANA

MESSAGE: HOW STRONG IS YOUR OWN PERSONAL SENSE OF BELONGING TO ...

Canada

		Quebec	All			
01	Not strong at all 1	11%		3%		
02	 2	6		2		
03	 3	5		2		
04	Moderately strong 4	22		9		
05	 5	13	_	10	_	
06	 6	14	x=4.7	19	x=6.0	
07	Extremely strong 7	28	s=2.0	55	s=1.5	
08	DK/NR 9	1	n=726	0	n=2961	

YETH8

MESSAGE: HOW STRONG IS YOUR OWN PERSONAL SENSE OF BELONGING TO ...

Your ethnic group or national ancestry

		Quebec	All			
01	Not strong at all 1	4%		9%		
02	 2	4		7		
03	 3	3		5		
04	Moderately strong 4	21		22		
05	 5	15	_	16	_	
06	 6	17	x=5.3	14	x=4.8	
07	Extremely strong 7	36	s=1.7	27	s=1.9	
08	DK/NR 9	1	n=984	0	n=2948	

RG97-1

Some people have a stronger sense of belonging to some things than others. Please tell me how strong your own personal sense of belonging is to each of the following, using a 7-point scale where 1 means not strong at all, 7 means extremely strong and the mid-point 4 means moderately strong.

BFA10

MESSAGE: HOW STRONG IS YOUR OWN PERSONAL SENSE OF BELONGING TO ...

Your family

01	Not strong at all 1	1%	
02	 2	1	
03	 3	1	
04	Moderately strong 4	4	
05	 5	5	_
06	 6	11	x=6.53
07	Extremely strong 7	76	s=1.07
08	DK/NR 9	0	n=3007

BCO10

MESSAGE: HOW STRONG IS YOUR OWN PERSONAL SENSE OF BELONGING TO ...

Your community

01	Not strong at all	1	3%	
02		2	3	
03		3	4	
04	Moderately strong	4	19	
05		5	23	_
06		6	21	x=5.24
07	Extremely strong	7	27	s=1.56
08	DK/NR	9	0	n=3007

BPR10

MESSAGE: HOW STRONG IS YOUR OWN PERSONAL SENSE OF BELONGING TO ...

Your province

01	Not strong at all	1	3%	
02		2	3	
03		3	4	
04	Moderately strong	4	17	
05		5	19	_
06		6	21	x=5.37
07	Extremely strong	7	32	s=1.58
08	DK/NR	9	0	n=3008

BCA10

MESSAGE: HOW STRONG IS YOUR OWN PERSONAL SENSE OF BELONGING TO ...

Canada

01	Not strong at all	1	4%	
02		2	2	
03		3	3	
04	Moderately strong	4	10	
05		5	10	_
06		6	19	x=5.89
07	Extremely strong	7	52	s=1.57
08	DK/NR	9	0	n=3010

BRT10

MESSAGE: HOW STRONG IS YOUR OWN PERSONAL SENSE OF BELONGING TO ...

Your ethnic group or national ancestry

01	Not strong at all	1	9%	
02		2	5	
03		3	6	
04	Moderately strong	4	20	
05		5	17	_
06		6	14	x=4.87
07	Extremely strong	7	27	s=1.89
08	DK/NR	9	1	n=2979

Rethinking Citizen Engagement

POV1

MESSAGE: HOW STRONG IS YOUR SENSE OF BELONGING TO ...
Your province

01	Not strong at all	1	4%	
02		2	3	
03		3	5	
04	Moderately strong	4	18	
05		5	22	
06		6	22	x̄=5.22
07	Extremely strong	7	27	s=1.58
08	DK/NR	9	0	n=2042

CAN1

MESSAGE: HOW STRONG IS YOUR SENSE OF BELONGING TO ...
Canada

01	Not strong at all	1	3%	
02		2	2	
03		3	4	
04	Moderately strong	4	12	
05		5	12	
06		6	19	x̄=5.73
07	Extremely strong	7	47	s=1.61
08	DK/NR	9	0	n=2042

CCI

Please tell me how you feel about each of the following statements using a 7-point scale where 1 means you strongly disagree, 7 means your strongly agree, and the midpoint 4 means neither.

OCUL4

Rotation => GRED4

MESSAGE: HOW DO YOU FEEL ABOUT ...
One of the biggest problems with Canada is that we don't have a strong overall culture to unite the country.

01	Strongly disagree	1	12%	
02		2	11	
03		3	12	
04	Neither	4	15	
05		5	19	
06		6	15	x̄=4.31
07	Strongly agree	7	17	s=1.96
08	DK/NR	9	0	n=1204

PRID4

MESSAGE: HOW DO YOU FEEL ABOUT ...
Canadian culture is something we can all take pride in.

01	Strongly disagree	1	2%
02		2	2
03		3	3
04	Neither	4	9
05		5	13
06		6	25	x=5.85
07	Strongly agree	7	47	s=1.45
08	DK/NR	9	0	n=1204

NCID4

MESSAGE: HOW DO YOU FEEL ABOUT ...
There really is no distinct Canadian identity.

01	Strongly disagree	1	19%
02		2	16
03		3	13
04	Neither	4	12
05		5	14
06		6	12	x=3.78
07	Strongly agree	7	13	s=2.06
08	DK/NR	9	0	n=1204

CCUL4

MESSAGE: HOW DO YOU FEEL ABOUT ...
It may be difficult to identify precisely but there definitely is a unique Canadian culture.

01	Strongly disagree	1	3%
02		2	4
03		3	4
04	Neither	4	13
05		5	21
06		6	26	x=5.39
07	Strongly agree	7	29	s=1.54
08	DK/NR	9	0	n=1204

GRED4

MESSAGE: HOW DO YOU FEEL ABOUT ...
One of Canada's greatest sources of national identity is our cultural diversity.

01	Strongly disagree	1	4%
02		2	3
03		3	5
04	Neither	4	12
05		5	23
06		6	27	x=5.31
07	Strongly agree	7	25	s=1.56
08	DK/NR	9	0	n=1204

RG96-1

Next I am going to read you a number of statements. Please rate the degree to which you agree or disagree with these statements using a 7-point scale where 1 means you strongly disagree, 7 means you strongly agree and the midpoint 4 means you neither agree nor disagree.

GEOG8

Because of our vast geography and the diversity of our people, Canada cannot survive without a strong national government to provide shared goals and values.

01	Strongly disagree	1	5%	
02		2	4	
03		3	4	
04	Neither	4	12	
05		5	15	_
06		6	23	x=5.5
07	Strongly agree	7	38	s=1.7
08	DK/NR	9	0	n=1508

SNS8M

Rotation => SNS8W

MESSAGE: HOW IMPORTANT IS IT TO HAVE STRONG NATIONAL STANDARDS IN THE AREA OF ...

Medicare

01	Not at all important	1	1%	
02		2	1	
03		3	1	
04	Somewhat important	4	6	
05		5	9	_
06		6	21	x=6.3
07	Extremely important	7	61	s=1.2
08	DK/NR	9	0	n=2961

GPOS8

All in all, government is a positive force in my life.

01	Strongly disagree	1	15%	
02		2	10	
03		3	12	
04	Neither	4	26	
05		5	17	_
06		6	11	x=3.9
07	Strongly agree	7	10	s=1.8
08	DK/NR	9	8	n=2959

Q61

In the past three months, approximately how often have you personally had direct contact with the federal government, either initiated by yourself or a government official, including in-person, mail and telephone contacts?

01	Never	1	
02	DK/NR	9	x=1.9, s=6.6, n=2963

RG97-1

I am going to read you a number of statements. Please rate the degree to which you agree or disagree with these statements using a 7-point scale where 1 means you strongly disagree, 7 means you strongly agree and the mid-point 4 means you neither agree nor disagree.

KN10

I'm confident that I have the knowledge and skills necessary to move easily in today's labour market.

01	Strongly disagree	1	6%	
02		2	4	
03		3	5	
04	Neither	4	16	
05		5	15	
06		6	21	x=5.07
07	Strongly agree	7	25	s=1.79
08	DK/NR	9	7	n=2814

RG95-3

I am going to read you a number of statements. Please rate the degree to which you agree or disagree with these statements using a 7-point scale where 1 means you strongly disagree, 7 means you strongly agree and the mid-point 4 means you neither agree nor disagree.

IMPO6

MESSAGE: DO YOU AGREE OR DISAGREE WITH THE FOLLOWING STATEMENT?

The most important things in life don't depend on money.

01	Strongly disagree	1	6%	
02		2	5	
03		3	7	
04	Neither	4	11	
05		5	17	
06		6	22	x=5.2
07	Strongly agree	7	32	s=1.8
08	DK/NR	9	0	n=1385

RG97-2

I am going to read you a number of statements. Please rate the degree to which you agree or disagree with these statements using a 7-point scale where 1 means you strongly disagree, 7 means you strongly agree and the mid-point 4 means you neither agree nor disagree.

ACC11

How would you rate your ability to access the internet? Please rate your answer on a 7-point scale where 1 is extremely poor, 7 is excellent and 4 is average.

01	Extremely poor	1	33%	
02		2	6	
03		3	5	
04	Average	4	16	
05		5	7	
06		6	11	x=3.71
07	Excellent	7	19	s=2.35
08	DK/NR	9	0	n=1475

RG96-1

I am going to read you a number of statements. Please rate the degree to which you agree or disagree with these statements using a 7-point scale where 1 means you strongly disagree, 7 means you strongly agree and the mid-point 4 means you neither agree nor disagree.

PROV8

My province puts more money into confederation than it gets out.

01	Strongly disagree	1	7%	
02		2	6	
03		3	6	
04	Neither	4	29	
05		5	11	
06		6	13	x=4.7
07	Strongly agree	7	23	s=1.8
08	DK/NR	9	5	n=1471

VI

Chronology

13

Chronology of Events July 1997 – June 1998

Melissa Kluger

An index of these events begins on page 393

3 July 1997 *Aboriginal Peoples*	A report is released by the BC legislature's aboriginal affairs committee indicating that the cost of settling the province's land claim issues could be up to $1.4 billion. The year-long study advocates a streamlined treaty process as the best direction for settling land claims. The report includes: a call to the BC and federal governments to apologize for injustices that the native people have suffered, elimination of native tax-free status, and the implementation of native self-governments. Their jurisdiction will include: local health and education, language, land use, and taxation. The report endorses the Nisga'a land-claim agreement, the only major treaty near completion; but a minority statement from Opposition members criticizes the agreement for being too vague and urges a provincial referendum before any treaties are signed.
7 July 1997 *Fisheries*	Federal Fisheries Minister David Anderson announces that the government will continue to aid East Coast fishermen and plant workers after the $1.9 billion Atlantic Groundfish Strategy, established in 1994, runs out a year early than expected. Anderson, new to his portfolio, says he is aware of the necessity of transitional measures but does not offer details as to how the new aid will be distributed.

9 July 1997 *Unity*	The federal government supports a move to put national unity on the agenda at the upcoming annual Premiers' Conference. The meeting will include a brief from the Business Council on National Issues. Representing high-powered business groups, this package emphasizes the need for a rebalancing of federal and provincial powers, equality of the provinces and recognition of the distinct needs of Quebecers. On 10 July Premier Lucien Bouchard dismisses the proposal, saying that there is nothing in it that has not already been rejected.
12 July 1997 *Premiers*	Nova Scotia Liberals choose federal MP Russell MacLellan as their new leader and premier. MacLellan has promised Nova Scotians that his government will work to ease the burden of the blended sales tax, eliminate proposed tolls for the new provincial highway and work toward a better deal for the province on pipeline tolls from Sable Island's natural gas.
14 July 1997 *Sovereignty*	Andre Joli-Coeur is appointed by the Supreme Court of Canada to participate in the legal arguments to determine whether or not Quebec has the right to secede unilaterally. Known as a sovereignist, the Quebec City lawyer will act as a friend of the court in the case that will be brought in the fall. While representing separatist interests, Joli-Coeur will not formally represent the Quebec government, as the province maintains that any decision about secession must be determined by a vote of the people and not through the courts.
14 July 1997 *Energy*	Nova Scotia's premier-designate, Russell MacLellan, introduces a new toll proposal for the Sable Island natural gas development. MacLellan wants to scrap the June agreement which gives Nova Scotia's gas distributors a 10-percent discount on tolls for the first eight years and New Brunswick 4 percent for three years, and to establish a new agreement in which tolls are determined by volume.
18 July 1997 *Premiers*	Nova Scotia's new premier, Russell MacLellan, and his Liberal Cabinet are sworn in.
23 July 1997 *Quebec*	Federalist and sovereignists clash over the unveiling of a statue at the entrance to the Plains of Abraham of Charles de Gaulle. It was paid for by the Quebec government.

25 July 1997 *Health*	Four Canadian hepatitis C victims file a class action suit against the Red Cross, the federal government, and eight provinces for failing to test the blood supply for the dangerous virus. Federal Health Minister Allan Rock says that, if he can get support from the provinces, he will consider compensation. The suit seeks damages of $3.5 billion.
29 July 1997 *Fisheries*	The Fisheries Resource Conservation Council issues a warning about the future of the East Coast fishing industry. The report indicates that not enough action has been taken to improve the cod stocks. While some small commercial cod fishing has resumed, the report warns that there is hardly any opportunity for the industry to grow. The council urges the federal government to work with industry to reduce and restrict fishing activity.
30 July 1997 *Premiers*	Alberta Premier Ralph Klein and Ontario Premier Mike Harris meet in Edmonton. The premiers agree that Ottawa must hand over some of its power to the provinces in the areas of health, education, and welfare. They suggest that such a rebalancing of power would help in convincing Quebec that federalism is viable.
30 July 1997 *National Unity*	Gordon Wilson, head of the BC Progressive Democratic Alliance Party, submits the results of his "National Unity Project" to the BC government which had commissioned the study. The report suggests that BC should play a proactive role in the non-constitutional renewal of the federation while also developing contingency plans in the event of Quebec's secession. The government of BC distances itself from Wilson's report which results in his resignation as constitutional advisor to Premier Glen Clark.
31 July 1997 *Aboriginal Peoples*	At an Assembly of First Nations meeting, leader Phil Fontaine speaks of new partnerships with Ottawa as well as with businesses, community, and interest groups which share native concerns. Indian Affairs Minister Jane Stewart assures delegates that the Royal Commission on Aboriginal Peoples will not be ignored and that the report is being studied in order to decide how its recommendations will be implemented.

1 August 1997 *Health*	The British Columbia Supreme Court rules that the province's decision to cut the pay of new doctors who refuse to practise in remote areas contravenes the *Charter of Rights and Freedoms* and the *Canada Health Act.* BC is just one of a number of provinces that has introduced a policy of this nature to prevent doctors from opening new practices in the major cities where there are already more than enough.
6 August 1997 *Unity*	Quebec Premier Lucien Bouchard writes a letter to New Brunswick Premier Frank McKenna reprimanding McKenna for supporting a Quebec partitionist group. This prompts a response from Intergovernmental Affairs Minister Stéphane Dion, who then exchanges letters with Quebec in order to show Quebecers the potential consequences of separation. Dion warns that Quebec will not have international respect without Canada's support and says that separatists cannot use Canadian law only when it is to their advantage. On 28 August, Prime Minister Jean Chrétien praises Dion's letters, saying that they have earned Ottawa increased support in the west and have encouraged debate within Quebec.
7-8 August 1997 *Premiers' Conference*	Premiers and territorial leaders meet in St. Andrews, NB. The leaders urge Ottawa to reduce Employment Insurance premiums by 25 percent and create a youth employment strategy. Led by Ontario, the provinces agree to ask Ottawa to hand over some of its control in areas such as health, education, and welfare — areas that are constitutionally under the jurisdiction of the provinces. Quebec Premier Lucien Bouchard says his province will not be a part of the other leaders' agreement, explaining that no Quebec premier would accept the premise that Ottawa has jurisdiction over social programs. Also at the meeting, the nine federalist premiers and two territorial leaders agree to meet again in the next few months to discuss Canadian unity without representation from Quebec or from Ottawa. Bouchard calls the planned meeting a waste of time and says that it will lead nowhere.
13 August 1997 *Health*	The Ontario Health Services Restructuring Commission announces that Ottawa's Monfort Hospital will not be shut

down, as had been announced previously, but will continue to operate with reduced services. The announcement follows a politically charged campaign to save the province's only francophone hospital.

13 August 1997 *Aboriginal Peoples/* *Natural Resources*	The Alberta government approves the proposal for a $250-million coal mine on the boundary of Jasper National Park. Local people file a treaty and land claim in an attempt to block the development. The approval, which is waiting for federal sanction, is consistent with recommendations that were put forth by a federal-provincial panel in June.
14 August 1997 *Fisheries*	In an attempt to prevent British Columbia from escalating the salmon war between Canada and the United States, the federal government files a law suit in the BC Supreme Court. BC Premier Glen Clark had threatened that on 22 August he would terminate the navy's lease on the Nanoose Bay testing site if the dispute over salmon quotas was not resolved. The federal government argues that BC does not have a legitimate reason for terminating the lease and that its cancellation would violate an international defence treaty with the United States. Clark writes to Prime Minister Jean Chrétien that Ottawa has performed "a great disservice to BC" by undermining the province's decision and failing to represent national interests.
14 August 1997 *Health/Children*	In response to recent deaths of children in Ontario, Quebec, and British Columbia, the federal Health Department launches its first national study on child abuse. The three-year, $500,000 study will investigate reported cases of neglect and abuse. It will also study the relationship between child abuse and socio-economic factors.
18 August 1997 *Aboriginal Peoples*	The federal government agrees to buy land from the Quebec community of Oka. The 12,000 square metres of land will be used to expand a Mohawk cemetery. The agreement resolves one of the outstanding issues left over from the 1990 crisis at Oka, in which police raided barricades erected by the Mohawks in protest over the expansion of a golf course in and around the native cemetery. This most recent agreement is part of an ongoing effort by Ottawa to create a continuous land base for the 1,200 Mohawks.

19 August 1997 *Unity*	New Brunswick Premier Frank McKenna announces that Canada's premiers, minus Quebec's Lucien Bouchard, will meet to discuss national unity. The meeting, scheduled for September, will be held in Calgary in an attempt to confront the controversial issue.
20 August 1997 *Aboriginal Peoples*	The General Council of the United Church of Canada expresses its sorrow for its role in the native residential school system, but fails to offer an apology. The Church has gone to court to hold the federal government responsible for its role in the operation of residential schools in British Columbia.
20 August 1997 *Health*	Federal Health Minister Allan Rock acknowledges that the cuts in health-care transfer payments have hurt. Speaking to the Canadian Medical Association in Victoria, Rock did not promise new money, but did say that the reduction in transfer payments to the provinces is over – leaving $6 billion more than expected over the next five years. Representatives vote against a BC motion for private health care and urge the government to restore adequate health-care funding in order to prevent a two-tiered system.
20 August 1997 *Quebec*	Leon Dion, dean of Quebec constitutional experts and father of federal Intergovernmental Affairs Minister Stéphane Dion, dies in Sillery, Quebec at the age of 74.
22 August 1997 *Aboriginal Peoples*	The Sechelt Indian band of British Columbia is offered $48.2 million and 348 hectares of land to settle its land claim. The deal also includes the transfer of 11 commercial fishing licences and a commitment to giving the band municipal powers. In exchange for this offer, the Sechelt band will be required to start paying sales and income taxes within 12 years.
25 August 1997 *Quebec/Premiers*	Dr. Vivan Rakoff, former director of the Clarke Institute admits that the psychological profile he drew of Quebec Premier Lucien Bouchard was unscientific and influenced by his own political biases. Commissioned by Liberal MP John Godfrey, Rakoff had concluded that Bouchard might suffer from "esthetic character disorder" – emotional zoning in which a person can be passionate about a project only to then drop it and take up an entirely different cause.

26 August 1997 *Aboriginal Peoples*	The Newfoundland Court of Appeal grants an injunction to Labrador Innu and Inuit to stop Inco Ltd's construction of a temporary road and airstrip near Voisey's Bay. The injunction is established pending an appeal of an earlier decision that allowed the construction after determining that the road and airstrip were for exploratory purposes only.
2 September 1997 *Sovereignty/Unity*	The Supreme Court of Canada grants lawyer Guy Bertrand his request to present partitionist resolutions as part of his intervention in the federal government's case regarding the legality of Quebec secession. Bertrand says, "we can't talk about separation without talking about partition."
5 September 1997 *Education*	After 73 percent of Newfoundlanders voted in a referendum to move to a non-denominational school system, legislators pass a resolution that asks Ottawa to allow the reform. The Pentecostal and Roman Catholic churches, which have traditionally controlled the province's church-run school system, vow to continue their fight against the reforms.
9 September 1997 *Sovereignty/ Aboriginal Peoples*	Quebec Premier Lucien Bouchard announces that he has resumed talks on self-government with Quebec's Inuit community. The talks began four years ago, but were pushed aside by the 1995 provincial referendum. The talks are just one of a number of efforts by the premier to improve relations with native communities as debate grows about the partitioning of the Quebec. Quebec's aboriginal community has opposed separation.
9 September 1997 *Aboriginal Peoples*	Ottawa introduces third-party management on Alberta's Stoney Reserve, appointing management firm Coopers and Lybrand to take control of the reserve's finances. This new arrangement comes in the wake of accusations of mismanagement and corruption on the reserve. In 1996-97, the Stoneys had a $5.6 million deficit, even though they had received $50 million from Ottawa and natural gas royalty revenue. On 13 September the federal Indian Affairs Department turns financial information about the reserve over to the RCMP for a criminal investigation.

11 September 1997
Health

Canada's health ministers meet in Fredericton to draft an agreement for a new national blood agency. Federal Health Minister Allan Rock announces that Ottawa will contribute $81 million over the next two years for the establishment of the agency. The ministers agree to establish an interim transition bureau to oversee takeover negotiations with the Red Cross. The bureau will include federal and consumer members and will have representation from all provinces except Quebec, as the province has decided to create its own blood agency. Also at the meeting, provincial health ministers call on Ottawa to grant more power over health care to the provinces since Ottawa is providing less funding. Rock says Ottawa will not surrender any of its power but agrees that the federal and provincial powers should be more cooperative on issues regarding the future of public health care.

11 September 1997
Fisheries

British Columbia's Premier Glen Clark accuses the federal government of treason for undermining the province's attempt to force the United States to abide by treaty negotiations established to conserve salmon stocks. Also, on 10 September, BC accused the government of trespassing onto provincial territory off Vancouver. The territory is a weapons-testing site used by the American navy. BC threatened to evict the navy, which, in turn, led to a suit filed by Ottawa.

12 September 1997
Social Services

Social services ministers from the federal, provincial, and territorial governments, except for Quebec, release a paper that outlines steps to reduce the depth and extent of child poverty in Canada and to help low-income parents to remain in the workforce. The new National Child Benefit will by implemented in July 1998 in an effort to improve support for families with net incomes below $26,000. The paper defines the roles of the federal, provincial, and territorial governments in the development and administration of the new system, and reaffirms their commitment to building a better future for Canada's children.

14 September 1997
Unity

The nine federalist premiers of Canada agree to consult their citizens in order to determine a way in which to recognize Quebec's unique status. At the Calgary meeting, the premiers declare that Quebec's unique character is essential to the makeup of the country, but also insist that all Canadians and provinces are equal and therefore any constitutional amendment that confers powers to one province must be conferred to all. The premiers also schedule a 18 November meeting with aboriginal leaders, who were excluded from the Calgary meeting. Quebec's minister of intergovernmental affairs, Jacques Brassard, sees no improvement for his province in the premiers' declaration and explains, "The only thing that could give full satisfaction to Quebecers ... is to recognize Quebec as a people." On 16 September, Quebec Premier Lucien Bouchard rejects the Calgary Declaration, calling it "insipid" and "banal." Meanwhile, the grand chief of the Assembly of First Nations, Phil Fontaine, complains that Quebec has been afforded more attention than Aboriginal peoples and that they have been "lumped in" with all of Canada's multicultural groups and have therefore not been given a high enough priority in the new unity framework.

16 September 1997 *Natural Resources*	Heritage Minister Sheila Copps rejects a commercial development plan put forward by the Banff town council. Copps concludes that the plan, which would increase commercial development by 25 percent, would put the national park in grave danger.
17 September 1997 *Sovereignty*	In response to the rising partitionist movement, Quebec Intergovernmental Affairs Minister Jacques Brassard announces the introduction of a new group in Quebec. This group, which may be called Democracy Quebec, will promote secession without partition and will work to counter the federal government's strong stand against separation.
19 September 1997 *Education*	Federal Minister of Intergovernmental Affairs, Stéphane Dion, says that the government still intends to introduce a constitutional amendment to change the Quebec school system from religious-based to language-based, but adds that opponents to the change will still have the opportunity to raise their concerns before the final decision is made.
23 September 1997 *Throne Speech*	Prime Minister Jean Chrétien's Liberals begin their second mandate by announcing that the federal budget will be balanced by 1998-99, but leave open the possibility of eliminating the deficit even earlier. It is announced that

half of future surpluses will go toward social programs and the other half will go toward tax and debt reduction. More specifically, the government pledges to improve health-care services, increase financial assistance to students, invest in technology partnerships, increase the child-tax benefit, expand programs that provide aboriginal assistance, and work with the provinces to develop a framework for financing a national drug plan.

23 September 1997
Senate

Prime Minister Jean Chrétien restores a Liberal majority in the upper chamber by appointing four new senators. The new members of Senate are: former Liberal MP Fernand Robichaud of New Brunswick, who gave up his seat to Chrétien; former premier of Prince Edward Island, Catherine Callbeck; social worker Marisa Ferratti Barth of Quebec, and Sister Mary Alice Butts of Nova Scotia, a Roman Catholic nun. The Senate now comprises 52 Liberals, 48 Conservatives and 3 Independents.

25 September 1997
Health

Ontario Premier Mike Harris announces that his government will delay next year's proposed $507 million budget cut for hospitals for at least a year. The announcement comes after the Ontario Hospital Association went public with two studies that indicated the dangerous effects of health-care cuts. Since the Conservative government has been in power, hospitals have seen their budgets cut drastically, first by $365 million in 1996-97 and then by $435 million in 1997-98. The association says that hospitals have been forced to close, merge or alter services at such an alarming speed that they have been unable to cope.

25 September 1997
Aboriginal Peoples

Indian Affairs Minister Jane Stewart cancels planned changes to the *Indian Act*. The changes, which died on the order paper when the June election was called, were put forward by former Indian Affairs Minister Ron Irwin. The changes were met with dissent by aboriginal leaders who called for the abolition of the Act rather than an overhaul. Stewart is applauded by the grand chief of the Assembly of First Nations, Phil Fontaine, for her statement that she will not make changes to the Act without the support of Canada's Aboriginal people.

29 September 1997
Sovereignty

French President Jacques Chirac holds a private meeting with Quebec Premier Lucien Bouchard in which he tells Bouchard that "whatever path Quebec chooses, France will accompany it" and that "Quebec can count on the friendship and solidarity of France." Bouchard interprets this to mean that France would recognize an independent Quebec if it voted to secede from Canada. The following day, French Prime Minister Lionel Jospin clarifies France's position by saying that his country does not intend to meddle in Canada-Quebec affairs. Also, on 30 September, Canada welcomes France's decision to cancel a postage stamp that marks former President Charles de Gaulle's visit to Quebec in 1967. The visit, in which de Gaulle proclaims "Vive le Quebec libre," fed the Quebec separatist movement.

2 October 1997
Environment

Federal Fisheries Minister David Anderson gives the go-ahead for the establishment of an open-pit coal mine within 2.8 kilometres from Jasper National Park. Environmentalists, concerned about the impact the mine will have on the park's wildlife, threaten a court challenge.

6 October 1997
Sovereignty

Quebec City lawyer Guy Bertrand announces he is going back to court to earn the right to pay his taxes to Ottawa if Quebec tries to secede unilaterally.

7 October 1997
Premiers

Exactly ten years after he won every seat in the provincial legislature, Frank McKenna announces his resignation as New Brunswick's premier. Treasury Board President Marcel Massé calls the resignation "a loss for national unity," since McKenna played a key role in the development of the Calgary Declaration.

8 October 1997
Unity

Saskatchewan Premier Roy Romanow takes over New Brunswick Premier Frank McKenna's lead role in the unity discussion. Romanow says he wants to deal with issues of national unity more quickly in order to build enthusiasm for the ideas put forth in Calgary. Romanow plans to hold a conference call among the premiers, who are in the midst of consulting their provinces about unity, to see what progress has been made since the Calgary Declaration on 14 September. Romanow hopes that each provincial government will introduce unity resolutions into their legislatures by the spring. The resolutions would be non-constitutional statements of intent that would acknowledge Quebec's "unique" character and deal with the difficulties of unity. In the meantime, Romanow says it is important to remind Canadians of the everyday issues that prove that Canada works.

8 October 1997
Health

Alberta's first private hospital starts treating patients. The hospital, which Federal Health Minister David Dingwall threatened to shut down, offers services not currently insured by the province's health plan, such as cosmetic and dental surgery. The hospital is still waiting for permission to perform operations that would require an overnight stay.

9 October 1997
Sovereignty

The Supreme Court of Canada rules the spending restrictions of Quebec's referendum law to be an unconstitutional restriction of freedom of speech. Under the law, only Yes and No camps can authorize spending. Quebec Premier Lucien Bouchard considers using the constitution's notwithstanding clause to preserve the provincial law.

9 October 1997
Fisheries

Federal Fisheries Minister David Anderson says the government will continue to provide transitional support to East Coast fishermen after the Atlantic Groundfish Strategy (TAGS) expires. One option would be for the government to buy back fishing licences, since there are not enough cod stocks to support the number of fishermen. Future income support seems less likely. After Auditor-General Denis Desautels declared TAGS a failure, the Liberal government says it does not intend to "extend, renew or replace" the aid program. Newfoundland Fisheries Minister John Efford warns that, without a clear alternative, many fishermen will be forced to fish illegally.

10 October 1997
Atlantic Canada

Prime Minister Jean Chrétien makes his first visit to Atlantic Canada since the 2 June federal election in which the Liberals lost 20 of the 31 seats it held previously in the region. Speaking in Moncton, Chrétien acknowledges that the Atlantic provinces were the hardest hit by federal spending cuts and defends the losses as necessary.

17 October 1997
Education

Education ministers representing every province, except Quebec, agree to broad guidelines for science education.

20 October 1997
Health

Quebec Health Minister Jean Rochon says that his ministry will manage the province's blood supply when the Red Cross is replaced. Canada's nine other provinces have agreed to create a new national agency. Doctors, advocacy groups, and patients who depend on the blood supply warn that Quebec's decision to exclude itself from the agency could lead to life-threatening shortages for the province and for Canada. Currently, Quebec collects about one-quarter of the country's blood supply. While Quebec itself uses most of that blood, provinces have traditionally shared blood in times of shortages.

21 October 1997
Emergency Aid

Estimates suggest that the total cost of the Manitoba flooding of last spring amounts to $300 million, a cost to be shared by the provincial and federal governments. Manitoba Finance Minister Eric Stefanson says that up to $100 million will have to be withdrawn from the province's Fiscal Stability Fund.

23 October 1997
Premiers

Prime Minister Jean Chrétien invites Canada's premiers and territorial leaders to a First Ministers' Meeting to be held 11-12 December in Ottawa. Unlike the recent meeting in Calgary, unity will not be on the agenda. Instead, the main topics of discussion will be youth employment, health care, and social policy renewal. Quebec Premier Lucien Bouchard says he plans to attend the conference because the issues on the table affect his province.

27 October 1997
Energy

A federal-provincial panel led by the National Energy Board approves the Sable Offshore Energy Project and endorses a plan to build a pipeline through Nova Scotia and New Brunswick into Maine. Pending federal and Nova Scotia approval, the $3 billion project and pipeline will pump 85 billion cubic metres of gas from fields near Sable Island.

30 October 1997
Health

Federal representatives meet with BC Health Minister Joy MacPhail in order to assess the best way to deal with soaring rates of HIV among injection drug users in Vancouver. MacPhail accuses Ottawa of neglecting a public health crisis and says that BC spends more on AIDS and AIDS education, prevention, and treatment than the federal government spends across Canada. Reports suggest that up to half the 6,000-10,000 addicts in the city could be HIV positive.

30 October 1997
Gun Control

The final details of Canada's gun control law are introduced in the House of Commons. The details are a supplement to Bill C-68, passed in the House in 1995, which mandates that all gun owners register and license their weapons. The new regulations set standards for gun clubs and target ranges, establish a national firearm registry, and set fee structures and timetables for the registry. Alberta, Ontario, Manitoba, Saskatchewan, and the two territories have gone to court to challenge the registry, charging that it is unconstitutional.

31 October 1997
Education

Ontario's 126,000 primary and secondary-school teachers walk off the job. The walkout, which is the largest teacher's strike in Canadian history, is in protest to Bill 160 which would allow the government to decide class sizes, reduce teacher preparation time, extend the school year, and allow non-certified people to teach some classes. The bill will also remove principals and vice-principals from the teachers' unions.

5 November 1997
Aboriginal Peoples

The Newfoundland government announces that the province's Inuit will be given direct ownership of 15,700 square kilometres, or 5 percent, of Labrador. The Inuit will also receive 25 percent of revenues from the province's mining, oil and gas production. A cap is also introduced, stipulating that once the Inuit per-capita annual income reaches that of the Canadian average, provincial royalty payments will be cut off. The Inuit hope that this deal will lead to a land-claims agreement within the year.

5 November 1997
Energy

The Federal Fisheries Department asks the Justice Department to clarify the fact that Sable Island, southeast of Halifax, is federal territory and not part of Nova Scotia. The ownership dispute began in 1971 when undersea oil and gas were first discovered surrounding the island. The dispute has renewed itself since a federal-provincial panel gave the green light to Mobil Oil for the construction of a pipeline from the Maritimes to New England.

7 November 1997 *Infrastructure*	New Brunswick Premier Ray Frenette and federal Solicitor-General Andy Scott unveil a $300-million package to improve the Trans-Canada highway in the province.
10 November 1997 *Aboriginal Peoples/* *Environment*	The British Columbia Court of Appeal rules that the province does not have sole control over its forests until aboriginal land claims have been settled. Earlier in the month, the New Brunswick Court of the Queen's Bench ruled that Aboriginal peoples have the right to cut down trees on Crown land. The Court declared that they have ownership of those trees and that they maintain their title to the property.
12 November 1997 *Environment*	Federal and provincial environment and energy ministers, excluding Quebec, agree to set a target of reducing carbon-dioxide emissions to 1990 levels by 2010. Quebec hopes to make an even more significant reduction.
18 November 1997 *Unity*	Premiers from every province except Newfoundland, Alberta, and Quebec meet in Winnipeg with native leaders to develop a companion document for the Calgary Declaration. Native leaders had complained that while the declaration recognizes Quebec as having "unique character," Aboriginal peoples were lumped in with the rest of Canada's multicultural citizens. The companion document recognizes natives as constituting a distinct society of their own with a separate order of government. The premiers agreed to include aboriginal leaders in future constitutional and social policy talks.
18 November 1997 *Education*	A motion is passed, with overwhelming support, in the House of Commons to amend the constitution in order for Quebec to replace its denominational school boards with linguistic boards.
24 November 1997 *Supreme Court*	Supreme Court Justice John Sopinka dies at age 64.
26 November 1997 *Senate*	Former federal Cabinet minister Serge Joyal and Alberta Metis leader Thelma Chalifoux are appointed to the Senate by Prime Minister Jean Chrétien. With the new appointments, 53 of the 104 seats belong to the Liberals, 47 to the Conservatives, and 4 to Independents.

| 30 November 1997 *Sovereignty* | At a Parti Québécois meeting in Quebec City, Premier Lucien Bouchard says he will hold an election, rather than a referendum, if the Supreme Court of Canada rules against the province's right to secede unilaterally. |

1 December 1997
Health

To mark World AIDS Day, federal Health Minister Allan Rock announces that Ottawa will give $211 million to a new national AIDS strategy. AIDS groups attack Rock for providing insufficient funds, as the number of people infected with HIV continues to rise.

2 December 1997
Health

The Quebec legislature calls on the federal and provincial governments to consider a compensation package for victims of hepatitis C. Quebec is the first government to extend compensation to these victims.

5 December 1997
Justice

At a meeting of justice ministers, the federal government agrees to consider the establishment of a public national registry of serious offenders and pedophiles. The ministers also discuss giving victims of crime a stronger voice, toughening the *Young Offenders Act* and cracking down on domestic violence.

8 December 1997
Finance

Legislation is introduced in the House of Commons to stabilize social and health transfer payments. Fulfilling an election promise, the bill sets a $12.5 billion floor on money to be sent annually to the provinces, thereby giving the provinces an extra $143 million this year and about $6 billion over the next five years.

9 December 1997
Finance

Provincial finance ministers express discontent over the cuts that Ottawa has made in order to reduce the federal deficit. They decide on ways they would like to see a future surplus spent. The ministers say that they would like to see the reduction of provincial tax burdens and of Employment Insurance rates, as well as the restoration of transfer payments for health, education, and social programs. The ministers urge Ottawa not to introduce any new social programs until traditional funding has been restored. Federal Finance Minister Paul Martin agrees to think about giving the provinces more flexibility in setting tax rates and tax brackets, and in providing tax credits.

| 9 December 1997
Education | A constitutional amendment is passed in the House of Commons to allow for the elimination of church-run school boards in Newfoundland. |

10 December 1997
Unity

Members of the Alberta legislature vote unanimously to support the Calgary Declaration on national unity. In a recent government questionnaire, 75 percent of Albertans supported the general framework of the accord, while 33 percent objected to the recognition of Quebec's "unique character." On 2 December, the Newfoundland legislature unanimously adopted the same resolution.

11 December 1997
Aboriginal Peoples

The Supreme Court of Canada rules unanimously that native peoples have a constitutional right to own their ancestral lands in areas where treaties have not been signed. The decision has a great impact on parts of Atlantic Canada and most of British Columbia

11 December 1997
Sovereignty

After a week-long tour of western Canada, in which he promoted a post-separation partnership between Canada and Quebec, Bloc Québécois Leader Gilles Duceppe says that if sovereignists win the next referendum, the Bloc will still run candidates in the next federal election in order to provide a separatist voice during negotiations between Canada and an independent Quebec.

12 December 1997
Premiers'
Conference

Canada's federalist premiers win an agreement from Ottawa to negotiate the country's social framework. Quebec Premier Lucien Bouchard had agreed to participate in the conference but his conditions, including the right of his province to opt-out of any new national program with compensation, could not be met. The nine other premiers demand that Ottawa reinstate some of the $6 billion cut from federal transfer payments for health and other social programs, but Ottawa commits to nothing more than its previous $12.5 billion promise. The premiers also agree to continue to find ways to reduce students' debt burdens, make youth employment a national priority, and to launch a national child benefit system by 1 July 1998. Ottawa says it is willing to double its $850 million commitment to poor families and children when the provinces establish matching programs to help parents get off welfare.

12 December 1997
Aboriginal Peoples

Indian Affairs Minister Jane Stewart signs an agreement that will compensate British Columbia's Osoyoos Indian band for land that they lost in 1870, when it was sold after a clerical error failed to indicate that it was part of the reserve. Accompanying the deal is $7 million from the federal government and $3.1 million from the province. The band will also be allowed to use $9.5 million of the settlement money to purchase unspecified land to be added to their reserve.

12 December 1997
Ontario

The megacity of Toronto learns that under changes to municipal finances, the provincial government's efforts to download services and their costs will leave the municipality with a $163 million shortfall. Toronto Mayor Mel Lastman campaigned for mayor on a platform that promised a tax-freeze, and accuses Ontario Premier Mike Harris of lying when he said that the service exchange would be "revenue neutral." Under the new bill, which was passed 2 December, local governments will now cover the costs for transit, public health, and social housing and will contribute more toward welfare and child care. In exchange, the Ontario government will take over $2.5 billion in education funding and transition funds.

15 December 1997
Education/Language

A motion to amend the constitution to allow for Quebec to have language-based school boards, rather than religious-based boards, is passed by the Senate in a 52-17 vote.

15 December 1997
Environment

Following a ten-day environmental summit in Kyoto, Japan, Natural Resources Minister Ralph Goodale announces a three-year, $60 million energy efficiency program. During the conference, Canada pledges to reduce its emissions of greenhouse gases by 6 percent — a tougher agreement than the provinces and Ottawa had agreed to when federal and provincial environment ministers met in November. Alberta Premier Ralph Klein complains that the new efforts to reduce emissions are too harsh for his oil-dependent province, while environmentalists complain that the new pledge does not go far enough.

16 December 1997
Fisheries

The federal government announces that the $1.9 billion Atlantic Groundfish Strategy will not be exhausted as early as expected. Since fewer people than anticipated have required financial assistance, Human Resources Minister Pierre Pettigrew says that the funds will be extended until 31 August instead of only until mid-May. More than 25,000 people in Atlantic Canada will qualify to receive the extended funds.

18 December 1997 *Sovereignty*	Quebec Intergovernmental Affairs Minister Jacques Brassard says that the Quebec government will ignore lawyer Andre Joli-Coeur's attempts to challenge the Supreme Court of Canada's authority to rule on Quebec's right to secede.
19 December 1997 *Unity/BC*	The *Vancouver Sun* releases a survey indicating that 25 percent of British Columbians believe that their province would be better off without Canada.
27 December 1997 *Emergency Aid*	The total estimated cost of the flooding in Manitoba exceeds $400 million, thereby doubling the initial estimation.
30 December 1997 *Energy*	The Canada-Nova Scotia Offshore Petroleum Board approves the province's $3 billion gas project. The board stipulates that certain environmental conditions must be met and that preference must be given to Nova Scotian and Canadian bids for work. The Sable Island's partners estimate that 5,000 jobs will be created, mostly during the development of the six energy fields.
6 January 1998 *Emergency Aid*	An ice storm cripples Quebec and continues both east and west, leaving over 1.4 million people in Quebec, Ontario, and the Maritimes without electricity for up to a month. The Canadian Armed Forces send over 14,000 soldiers to aid the devastated areas. The federal government pledges $50 million in aid for Quebec and $25 million to assist Ontario. The Quebec government promises cash payments to residents without power and Ontario announces that it will provide $50 million in emergency relief. In order to respond to the crisis, Prime Minister Jean Chrétien and Ontario Premier Mike Harris delay their trip to Mexico City for the Team Canada trade mission and Quebec Premier Lucien Bouchard cancels altogether. Estimates indicate that the storm could cost approximately $2 billion

dollars and that the reparation of fallen hydro lines could cost as much as $500 million in Quebec and $100 million in Ontario.

6 January 1998
Health

The Red Cross disables Quebec's plan to establish a blood agency independent of the rest of Canada by announcing that it is not interested in transferring its blood-related assets to the province.

7 January 1998
Aboriginal Peoples

The federal government issues an historic "statement of reconciliation," apologizing to Canada's Aboriginal peoples for more than a century of mistreatment. Indian Affairs Minister Jane Stewart extends a specific apology to those who suffered abuse at residential schools; and she introduces a $350 million healing fund for treatment and counseling of victims. She announces another $250 million will be spent to improve housing and health conditions on impoverished reserves. Stewart also announces that an independent land claims body will be established to ease the current backlog. The Assembly of First Nations grand chief, Phil Fontaine, welcomes the apology.

7 January 1998
Sovereignty

The English-speaking Catholic community of Quebec becomes angry when Jean-Claude Cardinal Turcotte, archbishop of Montreal, says that Quebecers have the right to decide their future and that the Supreme Court of Canada should not stop Quebec from seceding if the majority of its citizens vote for separation.

8 January 1998
Supreme Court

Prominent Bay Street lawyer, Ian Binnie, is appointed to the Supreme Court of Canada.

9 January 1998
Unity

Saskatchewan Premier Roy Romanow expresses his optimism for the Calgary Declaration and points out that Newfoundland, New Brunswick, Prince Edward Island, Saskatchewan, Alberta, and the Northwest Territories have already passed resolutions to support the unity declaration.

15 January 1998
Energy

The Canada-Newfoundland Offshore Petroleum Board approves Newfoundland's second offshore oil project to develop an oilfield about 350 kilometres southeast of St. John's. The board's approval was the project's last hurdle, having already been cleared by Ottawa and the province.

15 January 1998 *Justice*	Four provinces send a proposal to federal Justice Minister Anne McLellan urging Ottawa to crack down on young offenders. Alberta, Ontario, Manitoba, and Prince Edward Island propose a ten-point plan including: lowering the age of criminal accountability, publishing the names of convicted youth, and sending 16-year-olds who have committed serious or violent crimes to adult court.
22 January 1998 *Finance*	Federal Finance Minister Paul Martin surprises the provincial governments by announcing that a bonus in transfer payments will be distributed to each province in March. The extra $236 million comes as a result of a revision in Statistics Canada figures for economic growth.
23 January 1998 *Aboriginal Peoples*	The Aboriginal Human Resources Development Council is established as part of the government's response to the Royal Commission on Aboriginal Peoples. The council, made up of cabinet ministers, aboriginal leaders, and corporate heads will work to seek partnerships with business and thereby improve employment for Indians, Metis, and Inuit. Ottawa commits $1.5 million to the council, in addition to $200 million already set aside for aboriginal employment programs.
28 January 1998 *Education*	University students across Canada protest rising tuition costs. Education costs have gone up, on average, 9 percent since the federal government slashed $6 billion in education and health-care transfer payments to the provinces.
29 January 1998 *Environment*	The nine federalist premiers sign an Accord on Environmental Harmonization — a controversial agreement established to reduce federal-provincial overlap in dealing with particular environmental issues. Quebec Environment Minister Paul Begin criticizes the agreement for not going far enough to eliminate duplication, while environmentalists fear that the provinces have been given too much responsibility.
31 January 1998 *Emergency Aid*	65,000 Quebec residents, hardest hit by the ice storm in Eastern Ontario, Quebec, and the Maritimes head into their twenty-seventh day without power. Hydro-Québec plans to spend $650 million to improve its damaged power

distribution network and Ontario Hydro expects to spend between $100 and $200 million in repairs. On 16 January, the federal government gave out $45 million in aid to hire unemployed people to clean up the wreckage of the storm. This pledge comes in addition to $75 million already announced for relief in Quebec and Ontario.

6 February 1998
Labour

Ottawa and Saskatchewan sign a labour market agreement. The pact, designed to decrease federal-provincial duplication and improve delivery of services, will put the province in charge of current federal employment programs and over 100 federal employees.

8 February 1998
Emergency Aid

Quebec Premier Lucien Bouchard accuses the federal government of trying to sabotage the province's plan to eliminate its deficit by the year 2000, after federal Treasury Board President Marcel Massé says that ice-storm ravaged Hydro-Québec does not qualify for federal disaster compensation. Massé explains that like Ontario Hydro, Hydro-Québec is a Crown corporation with its own financial resources. Quebec is seeking more than $1 billion in federal compensation, approximately two-thirds of which would go toward Hydro repairs.

12 February 1998
Budgets

Alberta Premier Ralph Klein provides evidence that the years of fiscal restraint are ending by including a $123 million tax break in the provincial budget. The budget also includes an increase in spending of $222 million for education, $136 million for health and social services, and $260 million for public works. Other budgeted expenditures include a $100 million for municipal grants and $24 million for incentive bonuses to government employees. Much of the surplus from the 1997-98 fiscal year will be used toward the province's accumulated debt.

12 February 1998
Unity

British Columbia's national unity panel says that 90 percent of the province's citizens consider national unity important and that the majority endorses the premiers' Calgary Declaration.

14 February 1998
Taxes

Cigarette taxes go up by $1.20 per carton in Ontario, Quebec, Nova Scotia, and Prince Edward Island. The hike, levied by both the provinces and the federal government, is expected to discourage young Canadians from smoking.

15 February 1998
Sovereignty

Bloc Québécois leader Gilles Duceppe announces that a series of protests will take place surrounding the Supreme Court's hearing on Quebec's right to secede. The case begins 16 February.

17 February 1998
Health

Federal and provincial health ministers fail to agree on a system for compensating Canadians who contracted hepatitis C from tainted blood. Federal Health Minister Allan Rock says that if no agreement is reached, Ottawa is prepared to go it alone in compensating hepatitis C victims.

17 February 1998
Aboriginal Peoples

The Innu Nation of Betsiamites files a $500 million lawsuit in the Quebec Superior Court. The band claims that they were cheated in a land deal with Ottawa and Quebec. The deal, struck in 1973, authorized the government to use the band's land for a major hydroelectric project. The band, which received $150,000 for the land, thought that they were negotiating a right-of-way for a power line, not a hydro dam. The Betsiamites want compensation for the infringement on their rights and also hope to stop the development of the dam.

17 February 1998
Agriculture

A controversial bill that changes the face of the Canadian Wheat Board is passed in the House of Commons. Under the new legislation, the board will be able to expand its monopoly of grains beyond barley and wheat. In addition, the makeup of the board will change from a few government-appointed commissioners to a 15-person body. The new body will be made up of ten individuals elected by Prairie farmers and five, including the president, to be selected by Ottawa.

19 February 1998
Senate

For the first time in 131 years, the Senate suspends a senator. After coming to work only 47 times in the last 13 years, and only 14 times since 1990, senators say that Liberal Andrew Thompson is in contempt, not only of the Senate, but also of the Canadian people. Just over half the Senate was present for the historic vote, leaving the Senate under much scrutiny. On 27 February, Liberal Senator Len Marchand announces he is resigning from the Senate, leaving the standings in the red chamber at: Liberals 50, Conservatives 45, Independent 4, and 5 vacancies.

24 February 1998
Budgets

For the first time in a 28-year history of federal deficits, the budget balances at zero. Finance Minister Paul Martin presents this landmark budget with a focus on social spending, tax relief, and debt reduction. In the area of social spending, students make the most gains. Most significantly, Martin announces the establishment of a $2.5 billion millennium scholarship fund to help over 100,000 postsecondary students based on financial need and merit. Tax relief focuses on the lower and middle classes. 400,000 low-income Canadians will be exempt from taxes altogether, while another 46 million will see a tax cut; $9 billion will go toward paying down the $583 billion national debt.

Opposition parties criticize the budget for not providing enough tax relief to middle-income Canadians and, on 25 February, the Quebec government seeks the right to opt out of the education fund with compensation, explaining that education is a provincial responsibility.

25 February 1998
Fisheries

British Columbia Premier Glen Clark sends a letter to federal Fisheries Minister David Anderson, urging Ottawa to keep Alaskans away from coho salmon stocks. Calling for a Pacific treaty on salmon quotas, Clark says the stocks in BC's northern waters are on the verge of extinction as a result of Alaskan fishing. Anderson responds by saying that while a renewed agreement with the United States would be useful, it would only be a small step in dealing with a larger problem — citing El Nino and habitat destruction as the major threats to both Pacific and Atlantic stocks.

2 March 1998
Leadership

Daniel Johnson steps down from his position as leader of the Quebec Liberals. On 13 March, federal Conservative Leader Jean Charest announces that he will consider filling the vacant position.

6 March 1998
Senate

Three new Liberal senators are appointed to the Senate: British Columbia entrepreneur Ross Fitzpatrick, Newfoundland business woman Joan Cook, and former president of the Prince Edward Island Federation of Agriculture, Archibald Johnstone. The Senate is now composed of 52 Liberals, 45 Conservatives, and 4 Independents. Three vacancies remain.

6 March 1998
Sovereignty

Andre Jolie-Coeur, the lawyer representing the sovereignist's side in Ottawa's court reference on the legality of separation, files a document which argues that Canadians are not one people, but rather are a collection of four "peoples" — English Canadians, Quebecers, Acadians, and native peoples. With this established, he claims that each of these "peoples" has the right to self-determination. On 13 March the federal government submits a response to the Supreme Court citing evidence that there *is* a Canadian people and suggesting that Jolie-Coeur's argument defies logic.

6 March 1998
Labour

Newfoundland and Quebec sign a labour-mobility deal that will allow Newfoundland construction workers and contractors to work in Quebec. Before the agreement, Quebec's residency regulations prevented Newfoundlanders from working in Quebec, while Quebecers were able to work in Labrador.

10 March 1998
Aboriginal Peoples

After a ten-year legal battle, the Blueberry and Doig River bands of northeastern British Columbia receive $147 million from the federal government as compensation for the loss of mineral rights to part of their reserve.

10 March 1998
Aboriginal Peoples

At an Assembly of First Nations policy conference, chiefs vote to support a motion to accept Ottawa's apology and its establishment of a $350 million healing fund for Aboriginal people who suffered abuse at residential schools.

10 March 1998
Energy

After a 25-year impasse, Newfoundland and Quebec agree to preliminary negotiations for the development of a new hydroelectric project on the Churchill River system in Labrador. Native people protest the negotiations and say that they will not participate in discussions until they are compensated for the flooding of their land in 1971, when the first Churchill Falls project began.

12 March 1998 *Social Programs*	Social service ministers meet to report on how they will spend the extra money that comes out of a new national child benefit. In the recent budget, Ottawa announced that it would put an additional $1.7 billion, over the next three years, toward the benefit provided that the provinces announced matching programs to take children out of poverty and get parents off welfare. All the provinces, except Quebec, have announced such programs.
12 March 1998 *Environment*	Environment Minister Christine Stewart tables amendments to the *Canadian Environmental Protection Act*. Under the revised legislation, Aboriginal people will be included in a new committee that will advise Ottawa on how to manage toxins.
17 March 1998 *Unity*	A motion put forward by the Reform Party to allow Members of Parliament to place Canadian flags on their desks is defeated in a vote of 194 to 51. The vote follows a controversial "flag flap" that began in the House on 26 February when Bloc Québécois MP Suzanne Tremblay, who had complained that there were too many Canadian flags at the Winter Olympics, was unable to ask a question over the noise caused by Reform and Liberal MPs who were singing "O Canada" and waving flags. On 16 March Commons Speaker Gilbert Parent ruled that the Members were out of order when they silenced Trembly, explaining that it had been a question of free speech and not of patriotism.
19 March 1998 *Budgets*	Saskatchewan's NDP government releases its fifth consecutive balanced budget. Finance Minister Eric Cline also announces a 2-percent cut to provincial income taxes, bringing the provincial rate to 48 percent of the federal rate. Cline explains that with this new cut, families making $50,000 a year will save almost $600, while low income families will save even more. Cline also introduces $200 million in new spending, in areas such as health care, education, and programs for low-income children. $500 million will go toward cutting the province's $12.1 billion debt.
23 March 1998 *Senate*	Senator Andrew Thompson resigns his seat, one month after being suspended from the Senate.

23 March 1998 *Fisheries*	The House of Commons fisheries committee releases a report dealing with the collapse of the Atlantic cod fishery. The report lays blame on the federal government and foreign fishing, recommending that the Fisheries Department be decentralized and that foreign fishing be curbed. The report also calls for continued financial support for unemployed fishermen.
25 March 1998 *Premiers*	Nova Scotia's Liberal and New Democratic parties tie with 19 seats each in the provincial election. Liberal Premier Russell MacLellan retains governing status because his party was not defeated.
26 March 1998 *Leadership*	Jean Charest confirms that he will leave his position as leader of the federal Conservatives to seek the leadership of the Quebec Liberal Party.
27 March 1998 *Health*	Health Minister Allan Rock announces a $1.1 billion federal-provincial package to compensate those Canadians who contracted hepatitis C through tainted blood between 1 January 1986 and 1 July 1990. The announcement sparks outrage and notice of lawsuits from those victims who received the tainted blood before and after the set dates. Prime Minister Jean Chrétien criticizes the provinces for contributing only $300 million while the federal government is contributing $800 million.
27 March 1998 *Labour*	Federal and provincial ministers responsible for the labour market meet in Toronto to determine ways to tackle youth joblessness.
30 March 1998 *Health*	The Quebec government confirms its plans to establish its own blood system, thereby eliminating the possibility of a nation-wide system. Quebec Health Minister Jean Rochon says the new arms-length "Hema-Quebec" will be a non-profit entity with a budget of $125 million.
30 March 1998 *Education*	Prime Minister Jean Chrétien and Quebec Premier Lucien Bouchard agree to meet in order to find a compromise for problems arising surrounding the new Millenium Scholarship Foundation. Announced in the recent federal budget, the foundation was established to provide financial assistance to students across Canada. Emphasizing that

education is a provincial responsibility, Bouchard says Quebec should be able to decide where the money is spent.

31 March 1998
Budgets

Quebec Finance Minister Bernard Landry tables a budget that tackles the province's deficit, bringing it down from $2.2 billion to $1.1 billion. In order to accommodate the reduction, Landry announces cuts to education, health, social services, and municipalities. The budget is in keeping with the government's goal to be deficit-free by 1999-2000. Landry says the deficit cannot be eliminated sooner because the federal government, in its efforts to eliminate its own deficit, have made significant cuts to health care, education, and social assistance in the province. Beyond the deficit, the budget also focuses on job creation — planning to cut taxes for small and medium-sized businesses by $225 million in 2000-2001 and by $300 million in 2001-2002.

1 April 1998
Leadership

Conservative Leader Jean Charest says goodbye to the House of Commons as he prepares to leave his post to seek the Quebec Liberal leadership. Public opinion polls indicate that if a provincial election were held today, Quebecers would choose Charest and his Liberals over Premier Lucien Bouchard's Parti Québécois.

1 April 1998
Fisheries

Faced with a seventh season of the federal cod moratorium, union leaders representing Atlantic fishermen come to Parliament Hill to seek an aid package to replace the $1.9 billion Atlantic Groundfish Strategy that expires in August. Ottawa says it is looking into the matter.

2 April 1998
Aboriginal Peoples

Quebec Native Affairs Minister Guy Chevrette presents a new strategy for an improved relationship with Quebec's native peoples. Quebec's 11 bands are invited to establish self-governments that could include representation in the provincial legislature. The strategy also explores the possibility of giving taxation power to the bands and giving them the opportunity to share revenue from new projects from such things as forestry, mining, and hydro-electricity. The government also proposes a $125 million fund for community projects over the next five years. The strategy is part of Premier Lucien Bouchard's efforts to improve relations between the government and native communities in Quebec.

8 April 1998 *Sovereignty*	After Jean Charest predicts that Quebec will try and weasel its way out of another sovereignty referendum, Quebec Premier Lucien Bouchard says that a referendum *will* be held if his party is reelected in the next election.
8 April 1998 *Media*	Media baron Conrad Black announces plans to launch a new national newspaper.
15 April 1998 *Environment*	Alberta, Saskatchewan, and Quebec urge Ottawa to repeal its ban on the controversial gasoline additive MMT. The additive may pose environmental or health risks and may interfere with emission controls on automobiles.
20 April 1998 *Aboriginal Peoples*	The Indian Claims Commission recommends that Ottawa begin negotiations with the Athabasca Chipewyan First Nation of Northern Alberta. The band's reserve is located on what once was a flourishing delta that was home to muskrats and other fur-bearing animals. In 1967 a dam was built in the area which drained the delta of water, destroyed the flourishing ecosystem and thereby deprived the Cree band of their fur-trapping livelihood. The band seeks compensation for its losses.
22 April 1998 *Aboriginal Peoples*	The New Brunswick Court of Appeal rules against an earlier court decision that gave natives unrestricted rights to Crown trees and ownership of Crown lands. The ruling enables the New Brunswick government to order native loggers to stop their logging.
24 April 1998 *Environment*	Rather than taking immediate action to reduce the level of greenhouse-gas emissions in the country, Canada's environment and energy ministers agree to spend more time researching the economic impact of such a reduction.
27 April 1998 *Aboriginal Peoples*	British Columbia Premier Glen Clark announces the approval of a $250 million dam project in the West Kootenay area. Two days later, Okanagan First Nations chiefs send a letter to the premier saying such an announcement should not have been made without giving consideration to native concerns. The chiefs referred to a recent Supreme Court case in which it was ruled that native people who have not signed treaties for their land have the constitutional right to own that land and to use it as they wish. The chiefs threaten to ask for a court injunction to stop the project.

30 April 1998 *Leadership*	Jean Charest gives his first speech as leader of the Quebec Liberals. Charest attacks the governing Parti Québécois for making Quebec poorer in its pursuit of separatism. Charest says he wants to begin a new era in the province.
5 May 1998 *Budgets*	The Ontario government softens its image by focusing its budget on tax cuts and policies for helping children. Finance Minister Ernie Eves announces that the $5.2 billion 1998-99 deficit will be reduced by only $1 billion, but assures the legislature that future plans for a zero deficit are still in place. In terms of taxes, the budget includes the final phase of a 30-percent provincial income tax cut and the final step of the employer health tax exemption. Business education taxes are to be reduced by $510 million over the next eight years and the small-business tax rate halved. Support for children includes $140 million toward a new child-care supplement for middle and low-income families, an increase of $170 million over the next three years to the Children's Aid Societies, and $25 million in child-care subsidies to help single parents on welfare finish school. The budget also includes $120 million over four years toward marketing Ontario as a tourist destination.
6 May 1998 *Education*	Ontario's Education Minister Dave Johnson announces that the government is deregulating tuition in the province. Beginning in 1998-99, sharp increases in tuition will be allowed for all graduate programs and for professional programs for undergraduates such as business, law, and medicine. If a university is able to double its entry-level spaces by September 2000, then that institution will also be able to increase tuition for undergraduate courses such as engineering and computer science. Universities that choose to increase their fees must set aside 30 percent of that new revenue to assist low-income students. Despite this assistance, opposition parties and student groups accuse the government of limiting the accessibility of higher education.
7 May 1998 *History/Sovereignty*	Quebec Premier Lucien Bouchard attends the unveiling of a monument in Quebec City which commemorates the 1943-44 conferences between British Prime Minister

Winston Churchill and US President Franklin Roosevelt. Prime Minister Jean Chrétien expresses anger regarding the monument since it fails to recognize the role of former Prime Minister Mackenzie King in those conferences. Federalists protest King's exclusion.

9 May 1998
Unity

Prime Minister Jean Chrétien tells a Quebec news conference that the focus of his government is on jobs and the economy, rather than constitutional change.

12 May 1998
Leadership

Quebec Liberal Leader Daniel Johnson says farewell to Quebec's National Assembly. In March, Johnson announced that he was stepping down in order to make space for a new and more popular leader. Former federal Conservative leader, Jean Charest, was recently acclaimed to fill that leadership position.

14 May 1998
Leadership

New Brunswick Liberal leader, Camille Theriault, is sworn in as premier.

14 May 1998
Unity

British Columbia's NDP government introduces legislation that extends the original scope of the Calgary Declaration. While including the original seven principles, the extended proposal adds: an increase of provincial responsibility in areas important to that province; a federal equalization program for per-person funding of education, health, and social programs; and the establishment of national health standards. British Columbia, Ontario, and Nova Scotia are the only provinces that have not approved the original declaration.

14 May 1998
Sovereignty

In conformity with last fall's Supreme Court ruling, the Quebec government tables electoral amendments that will allow limited spending beyond the Yes and No committees for future referendums.

14 May 1998
Health

Health ministers fail to reach a consensus on new provisions for hepatitis C victims. Federal Health Minister Allan Rock is continuously under attack for Ottawa's compensation package that only assists those infected between 1986 and 1990. Meanwhile, on 4 May, Ontario Premier Mike Harris offered to extend compensation by $200 million in order to include all those infected with hepatitis C through tainted blood. On 6 May, Quebec followed suit, pledging $75 million more toward those victims outside Ottawa's time bracket. British Columbia says it will also consider an increase in aid, but not without national consensus.

14 May 1998
Aboriginal Peoples

The Saskatchewan Court of Appeal overturns an earlier court decision that would allow the province's 27,000 Metis the same hunting rights as the province's status Indians, who are currently exempt from many provincial restrictions. On 15 May, the Metis announce that they plan to ignore the ruling.

19 May 1998
Quebec

About 500 people attend a public meeting to protest Ottawa's appointment of a former Parti Québécois candidate as chief executive of Ottawa Hospital. David Levine, a Montreal anglophone, ran for the PQ almost 20 years ago in an effort, he says, to unite anglophones and francophones. On 20 May, Prime Minister Jean Chrétien expresses anger toward the PQ and the Bloc Québécois for using the incident to enrage Quebecers and bolster separatist sentiments.

21 May 1998
Immigration

British Columbia signs a five-year deal with Ottawa, giving the province more control over immigration. The deal will give BC increased control over programs to assist new Canadians and will also allow the province to nominate up to 200 immigrants and their families each year to match employment demands. The federal government will direct $45.8 million toward the deal.

26 May 1998
Unity

Ontario formalizes its support for the Calgary Declaration, leaving Nova Scotia as the only original signatory that has not yet passed a legislative resolution.

27 May 1998
Fisheries

As a result of improved stock off the south coast of Newfoundland, Federal Fisheries Minister David Anderson announces that quotas on cod in the region will be raised to 20,000 tonnes — doubling last year's limit. Newfoundland fisherman would like to see that quota raised to 30,000 tonnes.

28 May 1998 *Health*	Federal Health Minister Allan Rock announces a permanent, annual commitment of $42.2 million toward the fight against AIDS. Rock is criticized for guaranteeing funding for all HIV/AIDS victims, while providing compensation to only some victims of hepatitis C.
28 May 1998 *Budgets*	Nova Scotia Premier Russell MacLellan and New Brunswick Premier Camille Theriault call on federal Finance Minister Paul Martin to use surplus Employment Insurance premiums toward aid for Atlantic fish workers and tax cuts. The Quebec National Assembly calls for Ottawa to use the surplus toward support for young people and seasonal workers. Ontario Premier Mike Harris accuses the federal government of stealing from his province's workers and businesses. The surplus has reached $15.7 billion and is expected to rise to $19.9 by the end of the year.
4 June 1998 *Aboriginal Peoples*	A BC court rules that both the federal government and the United Church are legally liable for past sexual and physical abuse suffered by aboriginal students at a BC school in Port Alberni and orders that 30 former students be compensated. The ruling prompts the United Church of Canada and the Canadian Conference of Catholic Bishops to call on Ottawa to take a leadership role and to seek an out-of-court solution to compensate other aboriginal victims, rather than dealing with the 1,200 law suits on a case-by-case basis. Indian Affairs Minister Jane Stewart says that while the government is still dealing with the cases individually, Ottawa is looking for a "more human" route to compensation.
5 June 1998 *Unity*	Bloc Québécois MP Pierre Brien and Reform MP Rahim Jaffer meet in Edmonton to discuss their future visions of Canada. While the Bloc and the Reform Party seem like unlikely allies, both parties are interested in putting more power in the hands of the provinces. Jaffer discusses the Reform's New Canada Act, which advocates the rebalancing of federal and provincial powers, and Brien outlines his party's New Quebec-Canada Partnership.
9 June 1998 *Unity*	Nova Scotia is the last of the nine federalist governments to approve the Calgary Declaration on national unity.

11 June 1998 *Transportation*	A report released by the House of Commons transport committee suggests that the federal government should contribute up to $25 million for a new high-speed rail line to run between Quebec City and Toronto.
12 June 1998 *Senate*	Prime Minister Jean Chrétien appoints five new Senators: hockey superstar Frank Mahovlich, Nova Scotia activist Calvin Ruck, chancellor of Lakehead University Lois Wilson, Manitoba businessman Richard Kroft and an Ontario community organizer, Marian Maloney. Wilson will sit as an Independent and the others will sit as Liberals, bringing the standings in the Senate to: Liberals 55, Conservatives 43, and Independent 4. There are two vacancies remaining.
12 June 1998 *Unity*	Quebec Premier Lucien Bouchard announces that the Calgary Declaration is doomed, since not even Quebec Liberals are willing to defend the unity proposal. Bouchard held public hearings on the declaration even though his government has publicly ridiculed the proposal. New Liberal Leader Jean Charest refused to participate in the hearings, seeing them as a separatist trap. The declaration, which recognizes the "unique" character of Quebec while maintaining the equality of all provinces, has been rejected by Bouchard, who says that this is the least Quebec has ever been offered to stay in Canada.
15 June 1998 *Finance*	Provincial finance ministers come to Ottawa hoping to restore the $6 billion that has been cut from funding for health, postsecondary education, and welfare. While Prime Minister Jean Chrétien rejects their request, federal Finance Minister Paul Martin says he will consider the provinces' proposal.
18 June 1998 *Social Services*	In its effort to fight child poverty and to reduce Canada's number of welfare recipients, Ottawa launches a new national child benefit. Human Resources Minister Pierre Pettigrew explains that families making up to $25,921 a year will receive as much as $1,000 in extra child-tax credits. The federal government will start the program off with $850 million and promises to increase its contribution to $1.7 billion by the year 2000.

18 June 1998	Land that was taken from Aboriginal people and turned
Aboriginal Peoples	into a military base during World War II will be returned

to the Stoney Point natives of southwestern Ontario. Indian Affairs Minister Jane Stewart and Chief Elect Norman Shawnoo sign a $26.3 million agreement that returns the 900-hectare Camp Ipperwash to the band and provides money for community restoration, economic development, community healing, and environmental assessment.

18 June 1998
Aboriginal Peoples/
Taxes

The Supreme Court of Canada rules that New Brunswick has the right to charge its status Indians sales tax. In 1993, the province imposed the 11 percent sales tax on off-reserve purchases and was accused of violating the *Indian Act.*

19 June 1998
Fisheries

Federal Fisheries Minister David Anderson offers $1.1 billion in federal aid to assist Canada's coastal fisheries. Of that aid, $730 million will be directed to the East Coast, to carry the Atlantic Groundfish Strategy (TAGS) to its original expiry date of May 1999. TAGS ran short of funding after more people than expected applied for assistance. In addition to aiding the 20,000 TAGS recipients, the funding will also go toward licence buybacks, economic development, early retirement, job training, education, and moving expenses. On the West Coast, $400 million will go toward the establishment of a salmon fishery more attuned to conservation. Complaints come from both coasts that the government has not provided adequate funding.

22 June 1998
Economy

The Canadian dollar sinks to an all-time low on North American markets, falling to 67.77 cents US.

24 June 1998
Finances/Territories

Federal Finance Minister Paul Martin announces that the establishment of Nunavut, a new territory in the eastern half of what is now the Northwest territories, will cost Canada almost $100 million more each year. The new territory, which will come into existence next 1 April, will cover a land mass nearly twice the size of Ontario.

25 June 1998
Leadership

Former Prime Minister Joe Clark announces his candidacy in the leadership race for the federal Conservative party. There are now six men vying for the position of leader, including veteran Tory strategist Hugh Segal and former Manitoba Cabinet minister Brian Pallister.

26 June 1998
Quebec

Gilles Rocheleau, co-founder of the Bloc Québécois with Lucien Bouchard, dies of cancer at the age of 62.

26 June 1998
Environment

Heritage Minister Sheila Copps announces that Ottawa is freezing development in national parks for a year while a strategy to prevent encroachment of business and residential growth is established. She also announces that the federal government will have the final say on development plans in towns that exist within national parks.

Chronology: Index

History/Sovereignty 7 May 1998

Immigration 21 May 1998

Infrastructure 7 November 1997

Justice 5 December 1997, 15 January 1998

Labour 6 February 1998, 6 March 1998, 27 March 1998

Leadership 2 March 1998, 26 March 1998, 1 April 1998, 30 April 1998, 12 May 1998, 14 May 1998, 25 June 1998

Media 8 April 1998

National Unity 30 July 1997

Natural Resources 16 September 1997

Ontario 12 December 1997

Premiers 12 July 1997, 18 July 1997, 30 July 1997, 7 October 1997, 23 October 1997, 25 March 1998

Premiers' Conference 7-8 August 1997, 12 December 1997

Quebec 23 July 1997, 20 August 1997, 19 May 1998, 26 June 1998

Quebec/Premiers 25 August 1997

Senate 23 September 1997, 26 November 1997, 19 February 1998, 6 March 1998, 23 March 1998, 12 June 1998

Social Programs 12 March 1998

Social Services 12 September 1997, 18 June 1998

Sovereignty 14 July 1997, 17 September 1997, 29 September 1997, 6 October 1997, 9 October 1997, 30 November 1997, 11 December 1997, 18 December 1997, 7 January 1998, 15 February 1998, 6 March 1998, 8 April 1998, 14 May 1998

Sovereignty/Aboriginal Peoples 9 September 1997

Sovereignty/Unity 2 September 1997,

Supreme Court 24 November 1997, 8 January 1998

Taxes 14 February 1998

Throne Speech 23 September 1997

Transportation 11 June 1998

Unity 9 July 1997, 6 August 1997, 19 August 1997, 14 September 1997, 8 October 1997, 18 November 1997, 10 December 1997, 9 January 1998, 12 February 1998, 17 March 1998, 9 May 1998, 14 May 1998, 26 May 1998, 5 June 1998, 9 June 1998, 12 June 1998

Unity/BC 19 December 1998

Queen's Policy Studies
Recent Publications

The Queen's Policy Studies Series is dedicated to the exploration of major policy issues that confront governments in Canada and other western nations. McGill-Queen's University Press is the exclusive world representative and distributor of books in the series.

School of Policy Studies

The Communications Revolution at Work: The Social, Economic and Political Impacts of Technological Change, Robert Boyce (ed.), 1999   Paper ISBN 0-88911-805-1 Cloth 0-88911-807-8

Diplomatic Missions: The Ambassador in Canadian Foreign Policy, Robert Wolfe (ed.), 1998
Paper ISBN 0-88911-801-9 Cloth ISBN 0-88911-803-5

Issues in Defence Management, Douglas L. Bland (ed.), 1998
Paper ISBN 0-88911-809-4 Cloth ISBN 0-88911-811-6

Canada's National Defence, vol. 2, *Defence Organization,* Douglas L. Bland (ed.), 1998
Paper ISBN 0-88911-797-7 Cloth ISBN 0-88911-799-3

Canada's National Defence, vol. 1, *Defence Policy,* Douglas L. Bland (ed.), 1997
Paper ISBN 0-88911-792-6 Cloth ISBN 0-88911-790-X

Lone-Parent Incomes and Social-Policy Outcomes: Canada in International Perspective, Terrance Hunsley, 1997
Paper ISBN 0-88911-751-9 Cloth ISBN 0-88911-757-8

Institute of Intergovernmental Relations

Canada: The State of the Federation 1997, vol. 12, *Non-Constitutional Renewal,* Harvey Lazar (ed.), 1998
Paper ISBN 0-88911-765-9 Cloth ISBN 0-88911-767-5

Canadian Constitutional Dilemmas Revisited, Denis Magnusson (ed.), 1997
Paper ISBN 0-88911-593-1 Cloth ISBN 0-88911-595-8

Canada: The State of the Federation 1996, Patrick C. Fafard and Douglas M. Brown (eds.), 1997
Paper ISBN 0-88911-587-7 Cloth ISBN 0-88911-597-4

Comparing Federal Systems in the 1990s, Ronald Watts, 1997
Paper ISBN 0-88911-589-3 Cloth ISBN 0-88911-763-2

John Deutsch Institute for the Study of Economic Policy

Equalization: Its Contribution to Canada's Economic and Fiscal Progress, Robin W. Boadway and Paul A.R. Hobson (eds.), Policy Forum Series no. 36, 1998
Paper ISBN 0-88911-780-2 Cloth IBSN 0-88911-804-3

Fiscal Targets and Economic Growth, Thomas J. Courchene and Thomas A. Wilson (eds.), Roundtable Series no. 12, 1998   Paper ISBN 0-88911-778-0 Cloth ISBN 0-88911-776-4

The 1997 Federal Budget: Retrospect and Prospect, Thomas J. Courchene and Thomas A. Wilson (eds.), Policy Forum Series no. 35, 1997   Paper ISBN 0-88911-774-8 Cloth ISBN 0-88911-772-1

The Nation State in a Global/Information Era: Policy Challenges, Thomas J. Courchene (ed.), Bell Canada Papers no. 5, 1997   Paper ISBN 0-88911-770-5 Cloth ISBN 0-88911-766-7

Available from:
McGill-Queen's University Press
Tel: 1-800-387-0141 (ON and QC excluding Northwestern ON)
        1-800-387-0172 (all other provinces and Northwestern ON)

E-mail: customer.service@ccmallgw.gcnpub.com

The following publications are available from:

Institute of Intergovernmental Relations
Queen's University, Kingston, Ontario K7L 3N6

Tel: (613) 533-2080 / Fax: (613) 533-6868
email: iigr@qsilver.queensu.ca

Constitutional Patriation: The Lougheed-Lévesque Correspondence / Le rapatriement de la Constitution : La correspondance de Lougheed et Lévesque, with an Introduction by / avec une introduction de J. Peter Meekison   ISBN 0-88911-833-7

The Spending Power in Federal Systems: A Comparative Study, Ronald L. Watts, 1999
ISBN 0-88911-829-9
Étude comparative du pouvoir de dépenser dans d'autres régimes fédéraux, par Ronald L. Watts, 1999
ISBN 0-88911-831-0

Securing the Social Union: A Commentary on the Decentralized Approach, Steven A. Kennett, 1998
ISBN 0-88911-767-5

Comparaison des régimes fédéraux des années 1990, Ronald Watts, 1997
ISBN 0-88911-771-3

Assessing ACCESS: Towards a New Social Union, Proceedings of a symposium held at Queen's University, 31 October-1 November 1996, 1997
ISBN 0-88911-591-5

Equalization on the Basis of Need in Canada, Douglas M. Brown, 1996
ISBN 0-88911-585-0

The New Face of Canadian Nationalism, Roger Gibbins, 1995
ISBN 0-88911-577-X

Integration and Fragmentation: The Paradox of the Late Twentieth Century,
Guy Laforest and Douglas M. Brown (eds.), 1994
ISBN 0-88911-567-2

Working Paper Series

1. *The Meaning of Provincial Equality in Canadian Federalism* by Jennifer Smith, Dalhousie University
2. *Considerations on the Design of Federations: The South African Constitution in Comparative Context* by Richard Simeon, University of Toronto
3. *Federal Systems and Accommodation of Distinct Groups: A Comparative Survey of Institutional Arrangements* by Ronald L. Watts, Queen's University
4. *De Jacques Parizeau à Lucien Bouchard: une nouvelle vision? Oui mais ...* by Réjean Pelletier, Université Laval
5. *Canadian Federalism and International Environmental Policy Making: The Case of Climate Change* by Heather A. Smith, University of Northern British Columbia
6. *Through the Looking Glass: Federal Provincial Decision-Making for Health Policy* by Candace Redden, Dalhousie University
7. *Drift, Strategy and Happenstance: Towards Political Reconciliation in Canada?* Selected Proceedings of a Symposium held at Queen's University, May 28th and 29th, 1998, with contributions by Stéphane Dion, David R. Cameron, Richard Dicerni, Daniel Soberman and John Courtney, edited and with an introduction by Tom McIntosh